More praise for
Unrequited Infatuations

"What a wonderful, witty, incisive, moving, authentic, and beautifully written memoir. Stevie Van Zandt's *Unrequited Infatuations* is a heartfelt and soulful tour though Rock 'n' Roll history, politics, and pop culture from the vantage point of a rare talent and singular American life. I loved every page."

—HARLAN COBEN, bestselling author of *Win, The Boy from the Woods, Run Away,* and the Myron Bolitar series

"A glorious trip into the mind of a true Rock 'n' Roll Renaissance man. Stevie's autobiography digs beneath the surface of his music, evolving into something extraordinarily rich and complex. It's part Rock 'n' Roll history lesson, part political thriller, part revelatory dive into the brotherhood of a band. And so much more. What's most impressive is Stevie's self-deprecating honesty. He has the courage to write about his failures, alongside tales of his enormous success. The stories are also wildly entertaining, hilarious, and emotionally devastating. One of the best Rock 'n' Roll books ever written. It belongs on a shelf between Bob Dylan's *Chronicles* and Gerri Hershey's *Nowhere To Run.* A masterpiece."

—CHRIS COLUMBUS, director, producer, and screenwriter

"Steven and I grew up in the same town, two miles apart—unless you count the fact that creatively he was on another planet. Beneath the bandana is the beautiful mind of a polymath: singer, songwriter, actor, activist, arranger, thinker and creator. There is sex, there are drugs, and—thank the Lord—there is rock and roll. Names are named. Mistakes are made. Fights are (mostly) forgiven. And lightning strikes more than once. This is the beautifully told story of a great American life, and I dreaded the arrival of the final page."

—BRIAN WILLIAMS, journalist

"I was expecting a great music book with a bit more depth than most. What I got was the *Tao Te Ching* of Rock biographies! Only it's Lao Tzu with a fabulous sense of humor! This adventure is metaphysically amazing."

—MICHAEL DES BARRES, actor / writer / musician / DJ

"Steven Van Zandt is the ultimate Rock 'n' Roll soldier, an eyewitness to history who has made plenty of his own in the trenches and the studio. His stories of struggle and awakening, the mysteries of creation, and the ties that bind in every great band come at you like a blaze of killer 45s in a true voice of America: part Vegas, part Alan Freed, all New Jersey."

—DAVID FRICKE, journalist, SiriusXM, *Mojo, Rolling Stone*

"*Unrequited Infatuations* is as musical, soulful, funny, adventurous, inspiring, and real as the man who wrote it, the one and only Stevie Van Zandt."

—JON LANDAU, journalist, music producer, and manager

"A pleasure for music fans and one of the best entertainment memoirs in recent years.

—*Kirkus Reviews* (starred review)

Unrequited
Infatuations

Unrequited Infatuations

*Odyssey of a
Rock and Roll Consigliere
(A Cautionary Tale)*

Stevie Van Zandt
Edited by Ben Greenman

WHITE
RABBIT

First published in the United States of America by Hachette Books, an imprint of Perseus Books, LLC, a subsidiary of Hachette Book Group, Inc.

This edition published in Great Britain by White Rabbit, an imprint of The Orion Publishing Group Ltd
Carmelite House, 50 Victoria Embankment
London EC4Y 0DZ

An Hachette UK Company

10 9 8 7 6 5 4 3 2 1

A CIP catalogue record for this book is available from the British Library.

ISBN (Hardback) 978 1 4746 2213 4
ISBN (Export Trade Paperback) 978 1 4746 2214 1
ISBN (eBook) 978 1 4746 2216 5
ISBN (Audio) 978 1 4746 2217 2

'Killing Floor' written and performed by Chester Burnett, a.k.a. Howlin' Wolf. Copyright © BMG / ARC Music Group
A Streetcar Named Desire by Tennessee Williams, 1947. Copyright © Concord Theatricals / Samuel French, Ltd.
Lillyhammer written by Anne Bjørnstad / Eilif Skodvin / Steven van Zandt, 2012.

Printed in Great Britain by Clays Ltd, Elcograf, S.p.A

www.whiterabbitbooks.co.uk
www.orionbooks.co.uk

To Maureen,
my one requited infatuation

Contents

Overture

The distant music speeds up and slows down like vinyl on a warped turntable, holding, then yielding to the wind's caress, as the soft tinkle of breaking glass and tired car horns recede into the mysterious absence of light that becomes the exotic toxic wasteland beyond the city line, and the echoes of drunken revelry pass through their nightly metamorphosis, transformed on our soundtrack into the leaves softly rustling on the terrace, where on this particularly chilly December night in Greenwich Village our hero contemplates his fate.

It's a vagrant winter and you can't sell consciousness.

Nobody's buying it.

Hell, you can't even give it away!

Is what I'm hearing the icy wind blowing through the dead grey streets? Or are those echoes the sound of ridicule?

Once upon a time, consciousness was hard to come by, and nobody was buying it then either.

Information was rationed out by the clergy, witch doctors, power-drunk elders. People we foolishly trusted to do the understanding and interpret life for us.

Every hundred years or so, somebody would have a revelation and try to share it. They would usually be excommunicated, confined to asylums, or burned at the stake by our grateful society.

Who dug the Buddha when he was around? A bunch of poor homeless acolytes who hoped to someday actually understand what the hell the pleasantly plump man was talking about?

Who'd Jesus have? A dozen guys and an ex-hooker or two?

Socrates and Robert Johnson both got the same reward for their insights. A final toast from the Loving Cup.

No, my friend, you better come with something better to sell than truth.

Something we can use.

Like war, taxes, government, long tiring meaningless work, the phony scorecard of Wall Street, sexual frustration, suffering, false hope, disease, guns, drugs, gasoline, agribusiness, fear, booze, poison, hatred. Give us someone to blame. Fill the vacuum of our spiritual bankruptcy with religion.

We'll buy any and all of that. Speak to us condescendingly as children so we understand. There's a pandemic of stupidity, so no one will notice.

We will follow you anywhere.

Parents, teachers, priests, doctors, politicians, philosophers, poets, artists, gods, Lord Almighty, Holy Spirit, are your obligations so diminished?

Your offspring need suckling and you are busy doing what?

December's Children are orphans.

It's a vagrant winter and you can't sell consciousness.

Prologue

Silence.

He was under a blanket in the back of the car on the floor in the crazy spooky silence.

Nobody spoke. No radio. Just the lazy hum of the motor, and him alone with his thoughts. And ooh daddio, that was not his favorite thing.

His two coconspirators were sneaking him past the military blockade into the black township of Soweto. The "native unrest," as the government liked to call it, erupted every few years, but lately it had become more frequent, and now, constant.

Not coincidentally, the police had become less dependable. They had mixed feelings about beating their own family members and neighbors at demonstrations or turning their backs as people they knew ended up tortured and occasionally murdered in prison.

The government, no longer able to trust the police, had in an unprecedented move brought in the military. They were stationed at every checkpoint in and out of the massive ghetto. Not to protect the inhabitants, but to keep them contained for more convenient slaughter once constructive engagement gave way and the bloodshed levee broke. Tension was at an all-time high. It was no time to be the wrong color in the wrong place. Hence the under-the-blanket thing.

The seemingly endless township had no electricity, so a thick fog of fuel oil and coal smoke hung four feet off the ground, making the mystery and sense of imminent danger even more pronounced. It felt like a *Twilight Zone* ride at a Dostoevsky Disneyland. Or a *Star Trek* landing party where he was the expendable crew guy in the wrong uniform. In this case the wrong uniform was his white skin, dig?

Every country smelled different. In South Africa, the sweet scent of the jacaranda, cane, and banana trees was cut by an occasional breeze that carried traces of an acrid stench, a mix of burning rubber and human flesh that came from tires filled with gasoline, forced on perceived traitors, and lit as a means of execution.

They called it necklacing.

There was also, in the combination of the intoxicating beauty and smoldering hatred, the distinctive scent of revolution. And he loved every scary crazy exhilarating minute of it, baby.

A final showdown was coming and he had a ringside seat.

He was on his way to a very secret and very illegal meeting with the most violent sect of the South African Revolution, the Azanian People's Organization (AZAPO). The plan was to learn how they thought and hopefully gain their endorsement for the strategy he'd come up with to aid their liberation.

In 1984 South Africa, it was illegal for three black men to congregate in the same place at the same time. Illegal for anyone to suggest support for the cultural boycott, especially Blacks (as they were legally designated). And a capital crime to have a gun or to consort with anyone who did.

He was about to violate all of the above.

AZAPO were frontline soldiers, heroes to the struggling masses, terrorists in the eyes of the government.

What he hadn't planned on was that in one hour's time he'd not only be criticizing their strategy for revolution, but making the case for why they should let him live.

How the fuck did a half-a-hippie guitar player get here?

For seven glorious years, Bruce Springsteen and the E Street Band were Rock and Roll's Rat Pack, and he happily and naturally played the Dean Martin role.

If you were even thinking of throwing a party, you called him. That was the extent of his politics. He was the fun guy. The court jester. Always good for a laugh. Sex, booze, drugs, Rock and Roll, and . . . more sex. Yo bartender, another round for the house!

A whole lot had to go sideways to find him under that blanket.

And yet it was all perfectly logical that a Rock and Roller from New Jersey would be risking imprisonment and death. Logical to his new mind. New mind because he had become a different guy.

He'd worked night and day with the E Street Band, proudly contributing to making them the biggest and best in the world. Then, in a moment of clarity (or insanity, take your pick), he had left the band to discover who he was and how the world worked. It was now or never, he knew. Once you take that road to being rich, there ain't no going back. The rich had too much to lose. He chose to take the adventure instead of the money.

What a putz.

Early on in his crazy new journey, he'd made a surprising discovery. He'd found that with proper research he could analyze and find a solution to virtually any political problem, no matter how complicated. Of course, implementing the solution was another matter entirely, but all he was trying to do was collect research to write some songs. At least at first.

He had always known that he had the talent of improving things when it came to art. A song, an arrangement, a lyric, a production. You name it. For years, for others, he had made bad into good, good into great, and great into greater.

It wasn't all roses, by any means.

Even in art, this ability to fix and improve things was both a gift and a curse.

The gift part was obvious.

The curse was twofold. For starters, most people didn't want advice, no matter what they said. They wanted to think they could figure things out themselves. Sometimes they pretended to listen and then ignored the advice. It was also a tough way to make a living, in that it depended on others driving the wagon while he kept the wheels greased, occasionally leaping off to make repairs.

And then there was the biggest drag, which was that he had never been able to apply this beautiful logic to his own life. The frustrations of business constantly drew him away from the pleasures of Art. No matter how he fought it, the delusional devil down inside him was still waiting for that magical, mystical patron who should have shown up by now if they were coming at all.

When he found out that his ability extended beyond art, that it carried into the real world, it came as quite a shock. He considered himself half a moron who had barely managed to finish high school. Not to mention his mind's normal state, which, when not actively doing something, was a chaotic combination of frustration, impatience, self-hatred, or preoccupation with artistic and philosophical puzzles.

That's why artists became artists, wasn't it? To make order out of the chaos? To impose a rationale on the irrational? To answer the unanswerable questions? To create a structure that provided shelter from the contradictory tornados that constantly ravage the mind? Or was it all revenge? Best not go there, he thought. It risked emotional indulgence.

But this new insight, this awareness that he could focus his talent on the larger problems of the world, taught him that his destiny, at least for the foreseeable future, was to be a political Rock Artist.

And not in the way Jackson Browne, Bonnie Raitt, Graham Nash, and John Hall were political. They were heroes. On the front lines. His interest, at least at first, was journalism. Combining his art and journalism. The way Bob Dylan did as a Folk artist. He would be the first to make art about political problems all the time, with every individual song relating to a bigger theme on every album. Nobody had done that, not on a regular basis.

Why not?

Well, first of all, everybody else was too intelligent. It was a career-ending move, and they knew it. He didn't care. In the heat of self-discovery, a career was the last thing on his mind. This blind naivete would turn out to be a self-fulfilling prophecy.

He was interested only in the adventure of learning. His life had started over again, and he had become a seeker. He was in search of truth to absorb, of lies to expose. He was making up for everything he hadn't learned in school and maybe, just maybe, justifying his existence in the process.

When he had embarked on his solo career, he had outlined five albums that handled five different kinds of political problems.

But things had gotten more complicated when his creative passion and his practical research were combined and he was drawn into the real-world issues he was writing about.

South Africa was the best example.

The challenge of the remainder of his life was crystallizing on that back-seat floor.

The car slowed down for a moment, then sped back up. Had they been waved through the checkpoint? It was his second trip to South Africa trying to complete the research for his third solo album.

He should have felt fear under that blanket. But he didn't. All fear had left his being.

He realized it on the long flight from New York. He'd never liked flying. Always a bit squeamish about the turbulence. Suddenly it hit him. He was over it.

He was over it because he'd blown it. He'd worked his whole life to achieve the impossible dream of being a Rock and Roll star. And just as he'd finally, miraculously made it, he had walked away.

From the moment on the plane when he let go of his fear, suicide would be his constant companion and temptation. No longer fearing death, it turned out, was an asset. It let him go places and observe them without giving a fuck about his own safety.

He'd lost his band, his best friend, his career, his way of making a living. Everything. Why? Just to pursue some abstract idea of justifying his existence?

He still wasn't even sure about being a front man. He happened to be quite natural at it, but he just didn't need it. All great front men needed the spotlight. The adoration. The endorsement. The reassurance. The completion of something missing in their souls.

He needed some of those things, but not as much, and not in the traditional way. When he was a kid and fantasized about being in his favorite bands, he was never the front man. He was George in the Beatles, Keith in the Stones, Dave in the Kinks, Jeff in the Yardbirds, and Pete in the Who.

He liked to watch people, to sit at a sidewalk café and just be. All of that vanished when you were in front. You were crowded all the time. You couldn't observe if you were constantly being observed. It brought out his claustrophobia.

And yet here he was, in front, but also under a blanket in back. It was a strange state he'd gotten to. And yet surprisingly liberating. He had an unusual clarity. He felt like he'd finally discovered what he was born to do.

And so, like every mythological Greek hero in denial of the inevitable tragic results, he had set off on his quest. His odyssey. Relentlessly, calmly, and, yes, fearlessly, irrationally determined to fulfill it.

The car stopped.

They were . . . where? All the houses looked the same. Eight members of the executive council of AZAPO, machetes in their waistbands, waited inside to put him on trial.

He looked up from the mist, impenetrable, township shrouded in doom, into the crystal clear African sky. Is this where life began? Or was this where it all ended?

The eternal spirit of the world's original motherland was whispering in his ear.

Destiny awaits!

He smiled to his companions to calm their nerves. Shrugged with acceptance.

And walked in . . .

one

Epiphany

(1950s–1960s)

If you're gonna do something, do it right.

—WILLIAM VAN ZANDT SR., GIVING ADVICE TO HIS LAZY
OLDEST SON (THE UNWRITTEN BOOK)

My first epiphany came at the age of ten, in 1961, in my room at 263 Wilson Avenue, New Monmouth, Middletown, New Jersey, during my fifty-fifth consecutive time listening to "Pretty Little Angel Eyes" by Curtis Lee.

That's what we did in those days.

A song on the radio would stop your life and start it up again. Talk about the perfect relationship completing you? When you were a kid in the '60s, the right song completed you. It made your day.

Owning a great record wasn't optional. You had to have it. That meant convincing your mom to drive you into town and then, with great anticipation and reverence, entering the teenage church / temple / synagogue / sweat lodge known as the record store.

Mine was Jack's Record Shoppe in Red Bank, which had a Music Shoppe on the other side of the street. Getting in early with the British Invasion with that spelling.

It's where I'd buy my first guitar a few years later. Still there, incredibly.

The store was a beautifully constructed place of worship, as ornate and glorious as any European cathedral. I'd go through dozens of bins to find the record I'd heard on the radio, take it to the counter, and give the guy my hard-earned seventy-nine cents. Then, back at home, I'd listen to it over and over again until it became a physical part of me.

We were the second generation of Rock and Roll kids, which meant that we were only the second generation able to play records in the privacy of our own rooms. The 45 rpm single was invented by RCA in 1949 in retaliation for Columbia inventing the 33⅓ rpm LP the year before. Individual portable record players soon followed. Up until then, the record player was in the living room, in the same piece of furniture that held the TV and radio.

If it wasn't for that portable machine, Rock and Roll might never have happened.

A record player in the living room meant kids needed their parents' permission, or at least tolerance, to listen to what they wanted. Without the portable player, the first generation of Rock kids would have never gotten Little Richard, Bo Diddley, and Jerry Lee Lewis past their parents.

The older generation viewed those 1950s pioneers as an odd combination of novelty and threat. Humorous because of their onstage antics, flamboyant looks, and complete lack of talent (as parents defined it), but scary because there was an uncomfortable element of black culture connecting it all. What effect would that have on kids who already had too much time on their hands for their own good?

Rock could have been snuffed out right there!

But it went up to the kids' bedrooms. It isn't my imagination when I say that back in the '60s you didn't just hear records, you felt them. Sound waves entered your body. The needle, dragging through analog impulses miraculously etched into a piece of plastic, somehow had a deeper, more physical level of communication than modern digital music.

I happened to be in London for the twentieth anniversary of *Sgt. Pepper*, and EMI, my label at the time, invited a bunch of us to hear the original four-track analog tapes at Abbey Road. I have never heard anything quite like it before or since. I swear to you, I felt stoned for two days afterward. Drug-free.

There had been great strides breaking through to autistic children with music. They ended when the world went digital.

I remember reading that it took two hundred plays to wear a record out. The high frequencies would finally give up. Technology was no match for teenage passion and perseverance.

I passed that limit often. "Twist and Shout" by the Isley Brothers, "Sherry" by the Four Seasons, "Duke of Earl" by Gene Chandler. Had to buy them again.

So there I was, just getting started on "Pretty Little Angel Eyes," and even though I can't remember what I had for breakfast today, I vividly remember looking out my window, seeing a neighbor, Louie Baron, and experiencing a rush of exultation. The music had released my endorphins in a new and unexpected way.

I wanted to run down the stairs and embrace Louie and tell him he was my friend. And that friendship was everything. And that love and music would save the world. I could see a beautiful future clearly. It was there for all of humankind.

My first epiphany.

I didn't do it, of course. My bliss didn't make me completely stupid. Men didn't embrace other men in those days.

I was always a little slower than most kids, so my ecstasy didn't immediately trigger what should have been obvious curiosity. Who was making the music? How was it made? Could I make it myself? These thoughts wouldn't come for another couple of years. But music would soon replace my religious fervor.

Did I mention I was a very religious kid? I regularly went to Sunday School, accepted Jesus as my personal savior, got baptized at nine or ten. That's how Protestants did it, as opposed to Catholics, who baptize at birth. They don't take any chances.

I was extremely devout there for a couple of years.

Easter Sunrise Service was the test. You had to get up at 4 a.m. to make it to some mountaintop in Highlands by six. I don't remember my parents going to this, only the church elders and a few super extremist types. I liked the respect I got. I could see it in people's eyes. I went two years running, maybe three.

I've always wanted to be the guy who knows. The guy with the inside dope. I was willing to put the work in, to spend the time to find out. At the age of ten, I figured religion was where the answers were hidden.

In addition to that, I obviously had some genetic penchant for metaphysical zealotry. A need to be part of something larger. A sense of wanting to belong is built into human nature; the zealotry part is what separates the holy rollers, and holy rock and rollers, from regular, far more sane civilians.

Looking back, I also could have been trying to impress my new father. I was brought up kind of Catholic, and my mother changed teams when she remarried. Or at least she pretended to. She secretly kept eating fish on Fridays and prayed to Saint Anthony when something got lost.

When I was eight, the only father I would ever know, William Van Zandt, moved us from Boston, where I was born, to New Jersey so I could get on with fulfilling my destiny.

He was a funny kind of guy. Short, tough, quiet, stoic to the max. Ex-Marine, Goldwater Republican. He had a flattened, broken nose from boxing, either on the Marines team or maybe Golden Gloves. He had played trumpet as a kid, but I don't remember him ever playing it. Ironically, or whatever the right word is, trumpet should have been my instrument. But I never had the lungs for it. It's the most evocative instrument to me, especially for film scores. What's better than the opening of *The Godfather*? Or the Miles Davis score of *Elevator to the Gallows (Ascenseur pour l'échafaud)*?

The only records I remember my father listening to on the big living room phonograph were by Arthur Prysock. When he was in a particularly good mood, he would occasionally sing along. He had a good voice.

He spent every Tuesday night with the Society for the Preservation and Encouragement of Barber Shop Quartet Singing in America (SPEBSQSA), now wisely reduced to the Barbershop Harmony Society, or BHS. Thinking back now, I see how his singing with a Barbershop quartet, the Bayshore Four, could have stimulated my lifelong love of Doo-Wop and harmony in general. The Mills Brothers, sons of a member of a Barbershop quartet, and the Ink Spots are considered direct links to the roots of Doo-Wop.

I am deeply embarrassed to admit it, but I don't remember ever having one single conversation with him about his life. What he did as a kid. Who he liked. What his dreams were.

My mother never talked about my blood father. It must have been a bad situation, because people didn't get divorced much in those days. Especially Catholics. And double especially Catholics with kids. I never pictured my mother as particularly rebellious, but that was an extraordinarily rebellious act in those days. He died young is all I know. I should have asked her for more details, but I always felt it would have been disrespectful to my father.

She was a classic '30s/'40s woman. With the big exception of uncharacteristically leaving her husband, she accepted life as it was. No ambition. No opinions. No drama. Followed the rules. Great cook. Easy smile. Always in a good mood when I was young. Society didn't expect much and didn't allow much. Lived for her kids. And at that point, that meant me.

We moved in with her parents, Adelaide and Sam Lento, so I had two uncles and two aunts around to help bring me up. It takes a village . . . of goombahs!

When we split to Jersey, the family followed. Nana Lento said it was because of me, her first grandchild, which was a big deal in Italian families. Since four of her five children ended up living in Jersey, we gathered at her house every Sunday, a short walk from our church, for the classic Italian supper, a mix of lunch and dinner that ran from early afternoon until evening. Wives, husbands, kids—had to be fifteen, sometimes twenty of us.

My father's father was long gone, and all I know is he had turned down a job pitching for the New York Giants before they moved to San Francisco, because it didn't pay enough, and had come in second to Bobby Jones in a golf tournament in South Carolina.

We would visit Nana Van Zandt in Hackensack every month or so, and she was quite a character. She was from one of the Carolinas and looked exactly like Granny from *The Beverly Hillbillies*. So I grew up with grits. Real grits. Just butter, salt, and pepper, thank you, none of that horrible cheese people like to add.

One day I found a warped old acoustic guitar in her attic that my father said had belonged to his father.

My mother's father, Grampa Sam Lento, also played guitar, and he started teaching me the folk song of his village in Calabria in southern Italy.

Not songs. Song. Just one short repeating melody. Maybe he thought that was all I could handle.

Sam was an archetypal traditional Italian shoemaker, and I'd work summers in his shop in Keansburg. He'd have one of our two identical Pop stations, WABC or WMCA, playing loud in the shop. I can still smell the shoe polish and hear the hum of the machines accompanying "Baby, baby, where did our love go?"

Nobody wanted to talk about Sam's origins. All we knew was that he had left Calabria suddenly and ended up with a successful shoe business in the Italian section of Boston before moving down to Jersey.

I'd like to think he got out of the country with some stolen money from the 'Ndrangheta. It would have been totally out of character, but it's a nice fantasy.

Nana Lento, always the life of the party, was Napolitano. Picture Marty Scorsese's mother Catherine in *Goodfellas*. She was always good for a laugh, usually unintentional. Like the time my sister Kathi brought home a Jewish boyfriend for Thanksgiving and Nana sincerely asked if his people also celebrated the holiday. If there's any genetic showbiz in me it comes from her. She was always in a good mood with the rest of us, me especially, but she harassed my grandfather mercilessly. Maybe he'd disappointed her by not ending up successful and rich, the fate of most marriages. Or maybe it was what Nana mentioned to me fairly often, revenge for Sam's mother constantly mocking her accent. Whatever it was, she took it out on him. For forty years.

He just took it quietly. He was another stoic, Italian-style. More *omertà* than stoic, I guess. Old-school. He always had a smile behind his eyes that suggested he knew things he was never gonna talk about. Once again, I wish I'd had more conversations with him.

My blood keeps life interesting.

The Calabrése part is rock-solid. Simple. Not intelligent enough to do what's best for money or career or social standing if it means compromising ideals. No ambition whatsoever. He is satisfied with his position as the laborer. The loyal soldier. Work and family are everything. Just don't fuck with him. He never forgets an insult. It takes a lot to make him mad. But if you do, he will never stop until vengeance is his, no matter what it costs.

On the other side, the Napolitano exists for action. He thrives on wheeling and dealing, fixing and changing things. He has ambition but no patience. Learns on the job. Makes lots of friends. Achieves a foothold, then parlays. He's not as sneaky and conniving as the Sicilians can be, but he's a good actor when necessary.

It is a constant challenge to call on the appropriate balance of blood in the appropriate circumstance.

I had a lucky childhood. Played sports in the park three blocks from my house. I was too small but made up for it by being faster and more fearless than most.

All I really remember is that I couldn't wait to grow up. I hated being a kid. Nothing too traumatic, just hated it in general. Not enough control, I guess.

I wanted to be who I was gonna be and get on with it. I wanted to know what was going on and felt the world was full of secrets kept from us kids.

I did well enough in school. Life was simple and good. The country was as rich as it would ever be. The conversation at the dinner table was about when, not if, the country would go to a four-day workweek. And that was with mostly only one parent working in the middle-class suburbs.

I was completely oblivious to the nation's problems in the '50s and would continue to be when politics exploded in the '60s. The main contractor for our suburban development, who was black, had a son about my age. He became my first best friend. I didn't know black and white weren't supposed to mix, and my mother didn't say anything.

Our idea of fun in those days was riding our bikes behind the mosquito man's truck, its thick chemical toxic fog pouring out the back. I have no idea why I'm still alive. Maybe it was some kind of adolescent vaccine. Maybe the poison made my immune system bulletproof.

Most of the middle-class families had either a pool in the yard or a membership at the beach clubs, or they sent their kids to summer camp. I went to summer camp. It wasn't a sleepover camp. I am a relatively rabid environmentalist, but I was never that comfortable with nature.

A bus picked me up from home at six in the morning and returned me at six in the evening. It's where I learned to swim and learned practical crafts like weaving Indian bracelets and shooting a bow and arrow. My main memory is a jukebox in the outside eating area. I can still hear "Yakety Yak" by the Coasters echoing throughout the entire camp, probably the first Rock song I ever heard.

My only other memory is one of the other kids telling me that he lived behind a drive-in theater so he could watch movies from his room and would see naked women sometimes. I remember being quite impressed and envious at his remarkable good fortune.

I got so tan at camp that a local real estate agent asked my mother to keep me inside because she had lost several sales from people thinking I was black.

My mother told her to get lost. I overheard, so she had to try and explain it to me. "Some people don't like black people," she said.

"Why?" I said.

She didn't know.

I didn't get it then. And I don't get it now.

A few years later, must have been '63 or '64, my neighborhood friends Tom Boesch, Louie Baron, I think Louie's brother Robert, and Ernie Heath, from the only black family in the whole area, went with me to the Keansburg public pool one summer day. We had just gotten there and suddenly Tom says, "Come on, we're leaving." I was like, What happened? He said they wouldn't let Ernie in the pool. That freaked me out completely.

I do remember my father, who was a construction engineer inspector, coming home angry one day. There was the new thing called affirmative action that meant he had to fire a few white guys and hire some black guys at the construction firm. He was as pissed as I'd ever seen him.

Goldwater Republicans were different. They were more like today's Libertarians. The term "Conservative" in those days meant *Mind your own business.* There was no interest in what happened in the privacy of adults' bedrooms, for instance.

That would all change with Ronald Reagan, who was the first to invite religious extremists into the Republican Party and into the political process, technically a violation of the separation of Church and State.

Religious extremism is the reason half of America doesn't believe in equality for women or LGBTQ.

Real Conservatives would have legalized drugs, abortion, you name it, but they didn't believe in federally mandated civil rights. Or federally mandated anything. They believed in states' rights. That's about the only thing that remains in common between the new so-called Conservative Republicans and the true Conservative Republicans of my father's day. If states' rights could override federal laws, we'd still have slavery. So it was a mixed bag.

My father was a hunter, though he didn't go very often.

I went once but I couldn't do it. I don't understand killing defenseless animals and calling it sport. I even think fishing is sickening. Putting a hook in a creature's mouth and pulling it as it struggles to escape? Why is that OK? I am a natural-born vegan, but I hypocritically go off and on it.

Can you imagine me and my father in the same house? We were the Generation Gap.

My political ignorance extended all the way to President Kennedy's assassination, which happened on my thirteenth birthday. All it meant to me was wondering if my party would be canceled.

There was one more defining moment I'll mention before we leave the subject of my father. He was a tough, no-nonsense type of guy, and one day I made a wisecrack to my mother and out of instinct he smacked me hard right across the face.

We were all shocked there for a minute, each for our own reasons.

We were never quite the same after that.

My favorite TV show was *Zorro*. Did that influence my look with the bandana? Probably. I was drawn to heroes, not just Zorro but Tarzan, Conan, John Carter of Mars, Errol Flynn as Robin Hood and Captain Blood, James Cagney as Rocky Sullivan and Eddie Bartlett (heroes!), Paul Newman as Rocky Graziano and Billy the Kid, Marlon Brando as Johnny Strabler in *The Wild One* (my Uncle Sal got me a motorcycle jacket like Johnny's), and James Bond (the only time my father and I ever went to the drive-in together was to see *Dr. No*).

And then there were my more educational mentors: Moe, Larry, and Curly. Abbott and Costello. Maynard G. Krebs. The Bowery Boys. Kookie, Toody, and Muldoon. Soupy Sales. Sgt. Bilko. Sid Caesar. The Marx Brothers. Professor Kelp and Buddy Love. It's a wonder any of us survived.

When *West Side Story* came out in 1961, I went to see it in Red Bank at the Carlton Theater (now the Count Basie Theatre), five or six blocks from Jack's Record Shoppe.

The movie had a profound impact on me in two ways.

First there was the gang thing. It was so cool to us suburban fifth graders that we formed our own gangs and attacked each other with pens during recess. Whoever got written on the most lost.

For me, gangs weren't about conflict or competition. They spoke to my natural impulse to belong to something. I remember getting busted as the ringleader for that one.

It was also the first time I really absorbed Latino music.

I had had a taste of it from the *Zorro* score, Connie Francis's "Malagueña," Ritchie Valens's "La Bamba," Ray Barretto's "El Watusi," and the Champs' "Tequila," but the score of *West Side Story* is my favorite music of all time.

I loved the Sharks. There should be a football team called the Sharks. The New Jersey Sharks. Then we could have the Jets versus the Sharks!

I wanted to be Bernardo with his purple shirt. Pepe. Indio. I wanted to fuck Anita! The dance at the gym and the rooftop "America" scene blow my mind to this day.

Other movie music had a big impact on me too. I'm well aware of the influence of Ennio Morricone's work from the Sergio Leone Westerns ("Standing in the Line of Fire" on *Soulfire*), but every once in a while I'll write a riff and realize it comes from Miklós Rózsa's score for *Ben-Hur* or *King of Kings* or Jerry Goldsmith's score for *The Wind and the Lion*.

I wonder if Jimmy Page knows he got the riff for "Immigrant Song" from Richard Rodgers's "Bali Ha'i" in *South Pacific*?

Or here's a good one. Did you ever wonder where Morricone got the idea for that crazy opening riff in *The Good, the Bad, and the Ugly*? Check out the old Johnny Weissmuller Tarzan movies. But let's keep that to ourselves. What's the statute of limitations for Austro-Hungarian ape-to-ape jungle communication?

Johnny's estate might get ideas . . .

Contrary to popular scientific rumor, the Big Bang that gave birth to the universe did not happen ten million years ago. It happened on February 9, 1964.

To say that Ed Sullivan was an unlikely TV host would be an insult to the word "understatement." Picture Quasimodo attempting to be cute. But stoned. On mushrooms.

He had a Sunday-night variety show that the entire family watched. Same room, same time, on the home's only TV, black-and-white. I remember eventually getting a second TV for our rec room downstairs and the neighbors being awestruck by our wealth and decadence.

Ed made history on a regular basis, drawing something like sixty million viewers weekly. Every show that tried to compete with him failed, partly because other producers didn't realize that people were not only tuning in for the entertainment; they were tuning in to hear Ed mispronounce really famous people's names.

Still, he had a well-booked show, with acts for every age group and taste. The adults got Russian jugglers, Italian opera, Catskills comedians, and Broadway stars. Kids got puppets like Topo Gigio (an act Sullivan took part in), and Ed included something for the teenagers, usually the popular music of the day.

Much to his credit, he had welcomed black acts in the racist '50s, when it wasn't a regular thing.

Bo Diddley made an infamous appearance in 1955.

He had rehearsed "Sixteen Tons," a middle-of-the-road pop cover at soundcheck, but when the show went live he launched into his first single, "Bo Diddley." He got himself a hit single, a career, and a lifetime ban from the show.

A year later, Elvis Presley's first *Sullivan* appearance rocketed him and the new genre of Rock and Roll to the top of the charts. There would be no looking back.

Some would argue Elvis's appearance on *The Ed Sullivan Show* was really the Big Bang of Rock and Roll. But it wasn't mine.

As thrilling as Bo and Elvis might have been, America was not the least bit ready for that February night in 1964 when the act Ed had in mind for the teenagers turned out to be the Beatles.

It was my second epiphany.

The Beatles on *Ed Sullivan* had the cultural impact of a spaceship landing in Central Park. Except that we'd seen spaceships land before in movies like *The Day the Earth Stood Still.* There was no warning or precedent for the Beatles.

They were as alien as anything on that spaceship, completely unique, and in a way that could never happen again. You can only be *that* different once. Everything about them was special. Their hair, clothes, sound, attitude, intelligence, wit, and especially their accent.

But they were mostly different for one very big reason. There were four of them. They were a band.

This was new. Until then, the music business had been made up of individual pioneers like Little Richard, Chuck Berry, and Elvis Presley; Doo-Wop singing groups like the Cadillacs, the Dubs, the Channels, and the Jive Five; Soul groups like the Temptations, the Contours, and the Miracles; and instrumental combos like the Ventures, the Surfaris, and the Tornados. The Four Seasons and the Beach Boys were bands to some degree, playing live and recording with session guys, but they felt anchored to the past, the Beach Boys with their silly high school sweaters and the Four Seasons looking like your Italian uncles.

For me, the first true rock star was Ricky Nelson on *The Adventures of Ozzie and Harriet* when I was eight or nine. I'd look forward to him performing at the end of the episode and be disappointed when he didn't.

Before the Beatles, there had been only one true Rock and Roll band, the Crickets, who had inspired the Beatles to pick a bug for their name. The group released some records as the Crickets and some as Buddy Holly to get twice the radio airplay. And even though it was the same band all along, because of his shocking early death, it was Buddy who would be remembered. I was proud that in 2012 we finally got the Crickets and a bunch of other deserving sidemen into the Rock and Roll Hall of Fame.

The Beatles changed the world literally overnight. There were no bands in America on February 8, 1964. There was one in every garage on February 10.

What was the attraction of bands?

A band communicated something different from what an individual communicated. An individual was all about me, me, me. One personality. One spotlight. You fall in love with that guy or you don't.

Bands communicated Friendship. Family. The Gang. The Posse. The Team. The Squad. And ultimately, the Community. Each kid now had four or five choices about who to relate to. It was like the Three Musketeers (more heroes of mine), but better. All for one, and one for all!

My brother, Billy, was born seven years after me, four years before my sister. The gap was too large to let us share many experiences, and I regret I didn't find a way to spend more time with them.

The main thing I remember is arguing with my brother about which show to watch during dinner. He wanted *I Love Lucy* and I wanted *Star Trek.* Kind of ironic that his first movie when he went to Hollywood was playing an alien on the bridge of the *Enterprise* in *Star Trek: The Motion Picture,* and I ended up loving Latino music probably first introduced to me by Ricky Ricardo!

But my brother and I had one amazing moment. We slept in the same room. At night I snuck my transistor radio under the sheets. One night, on came "I Want to Hold Your Hand," the Beatles' first hit single in the United States. The American record company had turned down their first four singles, all of which were hits in England. Finally, the English parent company, EMI, urged on by Manager Brian Epstein and Producer George Martin, demanded Capitol Records release "I Want to Hold Your Hand."

I was listening. Billy was in the next bed listening also. When the chorus came, and the band hit those incredible high notes on the word "hand," we both burst into laughter. The Beatles communicated the one thing America needed after the assassination of JFK, the one thing that transcended the seven-year difference between me and my brother—unbridled joy. So among other things, I thank them for that moment.

For me, bands weren't just the week's teenage fashion trend or a new type of music or even some way to rebel against the paradise our parents had given us.

This was the beginning of life for me.

Suddenly everything started to make sense. Thank you, I thought. *This* is my species. *This* is my race. My ethnic group. My religion. My language. My creed. My purpose. *This* is *me*.

There was only one slight problem.

The Beatles were a little too good. A little too sophisticated. Yes, they were exciting, and just *liking* them felt like membership in a new tribe. But no matter how good my imagination was, I couldn't really imagine doing what they did.

They were perfect. Their hair was perfect. Their suits were perfect. Perfect harmony. They all sang lead!

This problem would be solved four months later, on June 3, 1964, when I had my third epiphany.

Dean Martin was guest-hosting *The Hollywood Palace*, a *Sullivan*-like variety show with rotating hosts on ABC, the night the Rolling Stones made their American television debut.

I witnessed my past meet my future.

In addition to being Italian American and a fan of Dino, both with Jerry Lewis and in his solo career, I would use his relationship with Frank Sinatra as my future role model in the E Street Band.

That night, Dino made fun of the Stones. Relentlessly. Callously. Obnoxiously as possible. He did it when he was introducing them and after they played a raw cover of Muddy Waters's "I Just Want to Make Love to You."

"They're going to leave right after the show for London," he said. "They're challenging the Beatles to a hair-pulling contest."

This pissed everybody off except me. Bring it up to Keith Richards to this day at your own peril!

Of course Dino made fun of them! He was supposed to! They were new! Young! Loud! Spitting in the face of tradition! Everything his generation despised.

Mick Jagger was a different kind of front man.

There was something about his casual attitude that contrasted with the Beatles' formality. And he didn't play an instrument.

Most white bands just stood there and played. Their guitars functioned as a wall between performer and audience. A front man with no guitar who moved and danced was a black thing. Jagger and Eddie Brigati from the Rascals were big exceptions to the white-guy rule.

Fronting liberated the performer to be the receiver of the energy as well as the transmitter. The Preacher, the Medicine Man, the Mambo, the Houngan, the Mystic, the One Possessed by the Spirit. More intimate. More sexual.

What changed me forever was probably the one thing that galled Dino the most.

Mick Jagger didn't smile.

How dare he display that ungrateful attitude as the Keepers of Traditional Showbiz generously granted him a national audience?

I suddenly understood. I didn't have to be perfect. Or even happy! Just look at them. It wasn't that they were ugly, but they were decidedly . . . simian. You couldn't have called the Beatles "traditional." They changed the world too much for that. But they were conventionally attractive. The Stones were more primitive. Even their clothes seem to be an afterthought. They were the first punk band.

The Beatles showed us a new world; the Rolling Stones invited us in.

It was the spark that would ignite a new way of thinking for me. A world without rules. Without limitations.

Where work isn't alienated from one's identity but *is* one's identity.

The concept of a job as unpleasant labor was instantly transformed. It was a "job" that could be satisfying, rewarding, and fun. Something that you would do for free. And you could get rich doing it? And get laid?

I was so in.

Goodbye school, grades, any thoughts of college, straight jobs, family unity, and American monoculture in general.

The Beatles/Stones exacta would change everything.

My religion had gone from Catholic to Baptist to Rock and Roll Pagan.

Society has never recovered.

And neither have I.

two

The Source

(1965–1967)

You're only as cool as who you steal from.

—THE UNWRITTEN BOOK

Here they come! Run for your lives!

It had started in the '50s, with Americans as economically super-secure Kings of the World. The horny wartime generation filled fresh suburbs with a new subspecies whose evolution stopped somewhere between adolescence and adulthood. They couldn't crank them out fast enough. It didn't take long for this phenomenon to be given a name. It was, as a Roger Corman poster might have read, *The Attack of the Teenagers!*

Represented by the shocking and revelatory ingratitude of Marlon Brando's *Wild One*, the disaffection of James Dean's *Rebel Without a Cause*, the cynical wisdom of the Beat Poets, and the unprecedented integration of the races in Elvis Presley's Rock and Roll, the teenager came fully formed for maximum adult aggravation.

Free, fresh, fearless, and too arrogant (or naive) to know (or care) that there were rules that had governed the previous thousand generations of young people, out they came. Not only with unprecedented discretionary money, but with unprecedented discretionary time to spend it.

The marketplace had to sprint to keep up.

Rock and Roll Records! Transistor Radios! Compact Mobile Phonographs! Cars! Clothes! Guitars! Bikinis! Hula-Hoops! Princess Phones! Pantyhose! Yo-Yos! Birth Control! Drive-In Movies! Malt Shops! Comic Books! Roller Skates!

The bounty was infinite.

But the freedom of the teen life was not. Those pioneering Rock and Roll fans made an impact, don't get me wrong. They set the cars-girls-beach-booze template. But they made a big mistake.

They grew up.

A few would keep their Doo-Wop 45s as a memory of their short but sweet liberation, but most became the society they were rebelling against.

We wouldn't be so easy.

By the time our generation came along, Rock and Roll wasn't a temporary social phenomenon anymore. It wasn't rebellion anymore, or even showbiz. It was a lifestyle.

Something new. And very troubling to the status quo. And guess what. We weren't going to grow up.

Ever.

My first band was the Mates.

Just in case the world didn't realize how influenced we were by the British Invasion.

It was me on vocals, along with Tom Boesch, my best friend growing up, who would turn me on to Bob Dylan, and two richer kids from the other side of the tracks, John Miller and Kerry Hauptli. Tom's father's job was silk-screening, so he created our Beatles-like bass drumhead, complete with a logo, which immediately elevated us above the other local bands.

It was the beginning of the methodology I would adopt for the rest of my life: dive in and learn on the job.

We did a residency at what would become the locally infamous Clearwater pool in Highlands and then faded away for reasons not remembered by me.

The first song I ever sang in public was Dylan's "Like a Rolling Stone." Here is a typical setlist in my handwriting that John kept:

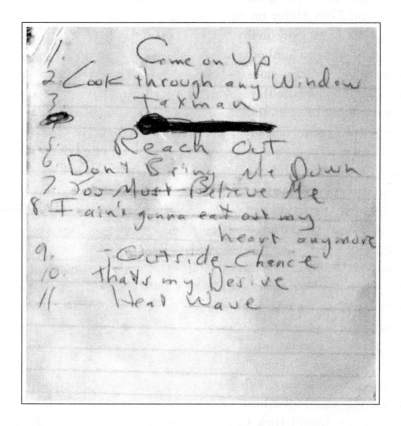

The next thing I remember is joining Buddy Norris's group the Shadows. Cool name. I didn't know it was stolen from England. I wonder if he did.

Around here it gets kind of hazy, but either Buddy invited me to the band rehearsal or John Miller, our former Mates bass player, did.

I met Buddy because he lived at the top of the biggest hill in Middletown, a few blocks from my house. My Aunt Angie, who spoiled her children and occasionally me, had bought me a brand-new thing called a skateboard. It was invented so that landlocked teenagers could enjoy the surf craze the Beach Boys had started. There was even a hit theme song, "Sidewalk Surfin'," by Jan and Dean. Jan Berry, after trying and failing to write a skateboarding anthem, had asked Brian Wilson and

Roger Christian to rewrite the Beach Boys' "Catch a Wave" with different lyrics, which they did.

In addition to lead guitarist Buddy, who greatly resembled Ricky Nelson, and John Miller on bass, the other guys were neighborhood kids, too: Bobby McEvily on drums and Chris Plunkett on rhythm guitar. I brought in Bruce Gumbert who, like every other accordion player— and there were many—had traded it in for a Farfisa or Continental compact organ after the Dave Clark Five did *The Ed Sullivan Show.*

For a couple of years there, Rock TV was spectacular. It started in the '50s when Soupy Sales had the first TV Rock show in Cincinnati. Then Alan Freed had a national show, *The Big Beat,* until Frankie Lymon jumped off the stage and danced with a white girl.

Rock shows exploded for our generation. There must have been ten of them on TV every week in 1965. We had *American Bandstand, Hullabaloo, Upbeat, Shivaree, Where the Action Is,* and *Hollywood a Go Go,* plus the shows hosted by DJs like Murray the K, Clay Cole, Jerry Blavat. Not to mention the variety shows with Pop segments: *Ed Sullivan, The Hollywood Palace, The Red Skelton Show, The Smothers Brothers Comedy Hour, The Dick Cavett Show,* Mike Douglas in the afternoon, Merv Griffin at night.

Impressive, no?

The Shadows made our TV debut, and finale, on *Disc-O-Teen* on Newark's Channel 47. Every local station had their own *American Bandstand* (band lip-synching, kids dancing), and ours was hosted by John Zacherle, a horror-movie host / Rock enthusiast nicknamed "The Cool Ghoul" by his friend Dick Clark. My future wife, Maureen Santoro, a Newark native, danced on the show all the time, so it's possible we overlapped.

We got on *Disc-O-Teen* because we won a local contest. It felt like a taste of the big time.

Rock was not only on radio and TV, but everywhere else. Our generation had more places for teenage Rock bands to play than ever before or since. We had beach clubs, high school dances, VFW halls, even teenage nightclubs like Le Teendezvous. Hullabaloo clubs, named after the TV show, were franchised around the country. The three in our area created a circuit, Middletown to the north, Freehold to the west, Asbury Park to the south, and the beach clubs to the east completed the square. Or more like a trapezoid, in this case.

As a result, the dozen or so bands in our area that got out of the garage were constantly running into each other. Nightlife in those days consisted of two things: playing with your band or going to see some other band.

What else mattered?

There were great local bands. The three biggest were the Mods, with the Lillie brothers, Phil Watson on guitar, and Ray Belicose on drums; the Clique, with the Talarico brothers and Jimmy Barr on guitar; and the Motifs, with Walter Cichon, who looked like a Native American Eric Burdon and would later die in Vietnam.

I had a friend, Mark Romanski, who was in a band with the unfortunate name of the Chlan. Mark was a motorcycle guy, and a spill we took has kept me off bikes to this day. One day in 1966, Mark said, "Let's go see the Beatles." We took the bus to Shea Stadium in Queens, which might as well have been Belgium.

The screaming must have been less noisy than at the previous year's show, because up in the second balcony we could hear the band fine. The very small speakers must have been pointing right at us. The band sounded just like the records, even without any stage monitors. They really were one of the greatest bands in history in every way. We found out later that the stadium wasn't sold out. The first indication Beatlemania was coming to an end. In three years they'd be gone.

Asbury Park was a stopover between New York and Philadelphia, and the biggest acts played Convention Hall: the Who, the Doors, Jefferson Airplane.

I saw the Stones there, with the Texas Blues guitarist Freddie King opening.

There was only one hotel in town, the Berkeley-Carteret, which could have been the location for *The Shining.* After the show, the other kids wanted to look for the Stones. I was not big on this idea. We wandered the endless hallways until we came to an open door. In the room was Freddie King.

My brave comrades urged me forward. Go, they said, get his autograph. I never got the whole autograph thing, but I figured, Let's get it over with. I knocked on the frame. "Excuse me, sir, but could we get your autograph?" He went over to the bed, picked up the pillow, and showed me a gigantic .45.

Never mind.

Never asked for another autograph, never again wanted to meet anybody I liked, and never played a Freddie King lick since.

It was during this period that I met Bruce Springsteen.

Battles of the Bands were regular events, happening every other month or so, so we may have met at one of those. I say that because we were two of the only bands that had Managers, and our Managers became friendly, so they must have met somewhere. But maybe that was later.

Anyway, I think we met at a Shadows gig at the Middletown Hullabaloo, formerly the Oaks, on the exact site of my old summer camp.

A bunch of scraggly, skinny guys with long hair came in, and I knew it had to be a band.

I went over to them during the break.

It was . . . what's the right word . . . inauspicious? Because there was nothing auspicious about us yet. I was fourteen or fifteen, he a year older.

I was wearing a top hat in those days and a huge tie I felt obligated to wear (our drummer's mother had made it), so he probably commented on my attire. Our band was good, so maybe the combination of sight and sound got his attention. I'm sure he invited me to see his band, the Castiles, wherever they were playing next. He didn't have a phone.

The Castiles were from lower-middle-class Freehold, out west, not a town you'd frequent if you could help it. It was one of the towns where the greasers lived. The real hoods. The soon-to-be-big-time gangsters.

It couldn't have been easy for Bruce and the other Castiles to be among the few long-haired freaks in town. Although they had the Motifs as local heroes.

In those days, if you met another guy who was in a band, you were friends. If you both had long hair, you were friends.

And if you both had long hair *and* were in a band, you were best friends.

That was it.

No thunder. No lightning.

Just two misfit kids who had found a common tribe.

It was the beginning of a lifelong brotherly love affair.

I would stay with the Shadows for only a short time. I had started playing guitar and wanted my own band. The minute I got moderately proficient, that's what I did. Within a few months, we had morphed into the Source. Buddy dropped out and John Miller went to college and was replaced by Joe Hagstrom (real name) on bass.

Before John left and changed his name back to his mother's pre-second-marriage name of Britton, he took me to the Red Bank House of Music, which had just gotten in their first Telecaster and was having trouble selling it. I played it and had to have it. The store gave me a good price, probably somewhere around a hundred bucks. I borrowed it from Nana Lento and became the first local Telecaster guy.

I found I had a talent for pulling songs apart and analyzing the pieces. This is where the craft of Arrangement, forever my favorite craft, begins.

Like the Mates and the Shadows, the Source started off playing songs from the top 40 Pop charts—it was the last time the charts were full of great Rock and Soul, not so strangely resembling a typical set of songs that would play in my Underground Garage radio format thirty-five years later. Paul Revere and the Raiders' "Just Like Me," Sam and Dave's "Hold On, I'm Coming," the Turtles' "She'd Rather Be with Me," the Temptations' "Ain't Too Proud to Beg," the Kinks' "Tired of Waiting."

What was different was that the Source was expanding the setlist to include tracks from the albums I had started buying that were being played on the new FM stations. But I didn't mind the AM hits.

They were the coolest songs anyway. That's why I refer to the '50s and '60s as a Renaissance period. When the greatest Art being made is also the most commercial, you're in a Renaissance.

It continues to be fascinating to me that with all the corruption and payola in those days, the best songs somehow made it through. You can't find half a dozen records that should have been hits but weren't! Amazing, really. Let's face it, just like Vegas—which we'll get to in a minute—the music business worked better when the Mafia ran it!

The Source rehearsed in the McEvilys' living room. Our backyards were diagonally across from each other.

Bands like the Source and the Castiles were different from other local groups because, like I said, we had Managers. Theirs was Tex: tall, gangly, cowboy hat, Colonel Tom Parker type. Ours was Bobby's mother,

Big Mama McEvily. The "Big" didn't refer to her size. It referred to her status as the undisputed boss. Picture Ethel Merman in *Gypsy*, only tougher. I wish I'd kept her.

I started going to Greenwich Village on the weekends. I didn't know the history of the place yet, the Beat Poets and the other famous writers

22...THE COURIER, October 5, 1967

If you are over 20 please turn the page

SMASH, SMOKE, TOTAL destruction will be the smash finale as The Source "Freak Out" Friday night at See 'N Surf. Everything will go -- guitars, amplifiers, drums -- promise Sourcers from left Chris Plunkett, Bruce Gumbert, Bob Mc Evilly, Steve Van Zandt and Joe Hagstrom.

Article about my band the Source announcing we would blow up our equipment after the show. The ad is about a different gig, a band battle that Bruce's band was also in when we were still the Shadows.

The Courier

Freak out before soul

SEA BRIGHT -- Freak out and soul mixed with some caged go go girls is on the menu at See 'N Surf this weekend.

Leading off Friday night will be The Source in a Freak Out show that goes from 8 p.m. to midnight at which witching hour the popular Middletown group will blow up their equipment with smoke and time bombs. At least that's what they say is going to happen.

Saturday night Go Go girls in cages will add that extra something to the Moment of Truth, featured along with the fabulous Broadways. Soul music is the

sound for Saturday with the Truth group direct from Asbury Park's Hullabaloo and the Broadways who have sung with the Four Tops and appeared several times with the Vick-ters.

The teen beach club snack bar and new Oceanside Surf Shop are open all day Saturday and Sunday and after school hours every weekday. Sundays bands rehearse and surfers surf.

AFS hosting student assembly

MIDDLETOWN -- The American Field Service Club of Mid-

and artists that had frequented those twelve square blocks. All I knew was that Bob Dylan had lived there and written "Positively 4th Street," which was enough for me.

The Cafe Wha? on MacDougal Street (still there) had music around the clock, new bands in the day, more established ones at night. I took the bus in by myself, watched bands, learned what I could, drank alcoholic Brandy Bastards, and made it home for the awkward dinner with the family, as I became more and more of a disappointment.

The bands I saw were a year or two ahead of anything in New Jersey. I was absorbing, and stealing, all I could.

It was a surprise when I started running into Bruce there, the equivalent of running into a Jersey neighbor while on vacation in Sardinia.

"What are you doing here?" I said.

"I come up to check things out."

"Yeah, me too."

Wow, I thought. This guy's as crazy as I am.

We started hanging out and taking the bus into the city together. Before we went, we would go to his room and play records.

It was always a little scary, because we had to pass the kitchen, where his father would often be smoking and staring off into space, occasionally sipping on something. Like my dad, he seemed always on the brink of exploding into violence to vent a lifetime of frustration intensified by having a son who was one of New Jersey's only freaks.

Bruce's father would turn out to be a real sweetheart, just like my own. But those early days were tough going. We were an embarrassment to them. Failures they took personally.

Bruce and I would play each other our favorite records, and he would also play me songs he had written.

I had written only one song. Big Mama had a friend, another Big Mama type, with a terrible Pop song she wanted us to record. If we did, she said, we could record one of our own for the B-side.

Big Mama suggested I write something, so I did. It was called "Traveling," a Rock song with a little Indian flavor, like what George Harrison was bringing to the Beatles. We recorded the terrible Pop song and put "Traveling" on the flip, but it was never released and all the test pressings have disappeared.

No great loss, believe me.

Bruce was taking writing much more seriously. He was already picturing himself as part of the business, even though we were in fucking New Jersey, where our chances of being discovered were only slightly higher than if we were in Tanganyika.

We both had the same crazy dream, but his was advanced dreaming. It was very encouraging.

As I mentioned, I discovered I had a gift for analyzing records and figuring out how they were put together. There turned out to be five crafts of Rock, and they weren't as easy as the Stones made them look.

First Craft: Learn Your Instrument. As a Rock musician, you either get a few lessons in person or you study video of where guys put their hands. Being a front man (singing without playing) is a little more complex. Singing is the easy part. Sing along with your favorite records. But every singer is also an actor. Every lyric is a script, and every song is a movie, performed for the audience. Good singers make it seem like they've experienced what they are singing about, as if it's true, whether it is or not. Some of the greatest singers of all time, like Frank Sinatra, Elvis Presley, Aretha Franklin, and Whitney Houston, never wrote much at all, if anything, but their songs seem autobiographical. While you don't have to take acting or dancing lessons to learn how to inhabit a song, it wouldn't hurt.

Second Craft: Arrangement. Make a list of your favorite songs and then find three or four other guys or girls who share the same vision. That will help you form your band. But now you have to dissect those songs. Your dissection should include an understanding of the lyrics, as Rock is basically a storytelling medium. But arrangement is about asking other questions. What are the chords? What are the instruments being used? What is each one doing, exactly? You will learn which instruments to include and how to configure the song: the verses, the chorus, the bridge, the solo. The rules are there to break. Some songs may start with a chorus, like the Beatles' "Help!" Some songs may not have a bridge, like the Kinks' "All Day and All of the Night." Some songs may not have a bridge or a solo, like the Rolling Stones' "Satisfaction." But understanding how songs are built is central to the craft of arrangement.

Third Craft: Performance. So you're feeling pretty good about your ability with your instrument (though you never stop getting better), your band has learned its favorite fifty songs, and you are ready to get out of the garage. Find a place to play. A venue. If you're over eighteen, it will most likely be a bar. If you're under, you will have to figure it out. Playing live is a whole different animal from rehearsal. It accomplishes three important things. You will learn what effect each song has on the audience, you will learn how to interact with an audience, and you will learn how to interact with your band.

Fourth Craft: Composition. You can now take what you've learned from arrangement and performance and start writing songs. There are really no rules here, but I would make one suggestion. Write with purpose. What do you want the song to do? To be? Do you want it to make people dance? Laugh? Cry? Think? Is your song a question? An answer? A confession? Who are you talking to? Yourself? It helps to have some direction when you're staring at an empty page or screen.

Fifth Craft: Recording. These days most people begin the recording process at home. We did too, usually with a cassette recorder in the middle of the room at rehearsal.

Some people record all on their own. That's both good and bad. There is a chance you'll learn quite a bit and maybe create something fantastic on your own. But most of the time, it takes an army to make a great record. Prince may be the only exception in history to this rule, and even he had help on *Purple Rain*. Everybody else benefits from collaboration. Input from an objective Producer is always helpful. And band members. And Arrangers. I don't care where a good idea comes from—I'll take a suggestion from the studio janitor if it makes the record better. You need help to realize your potential. You can do everything completely by yourself, but most likely you will achieve supreme, profound mediocrity. That's easy. These days everybody is doing that.

But what you want deep down in your soul is to do something great. We may not always achieve greatness, but we should always be reaching for it. Isn't that our best way to show our gratitude for life itself?

Bruce played me his favorite records—Tim Buckley's *Goodbye and Hello*, Van Morrison's *Astral Weeks*—and then an original or two, usually in that same Folk-type genre. Then we'd sneak out to Greenwich Village for more absorbing and more stealing.

My favorite band at the time was called the Source. I liked them so much I stole their name.

They were originally from DC but were living in the Village, where the action was. They would change their name to Kangaroo when they got signed.

John Hall, a future congressman I would help elect forty years later, was their genius bass player, and their guitar player was the amazing Teddy Spelios, the closest thing to Jeff Beck in our world. I still use the two-finger-picks-with-a-flat-pick style Teddy used when he played.

Aside from the mystery of his ridiculous talent, Teddy had the magic tone, a beautiful distorted sound. Bruce was a year or two ahead of me on guitar. I was catching up fast. But neither of us could figure out how Teddy got that tone.

We worked up the courage to ask him one day. He gave us a look to see if we were fucking with him, but he could see we were serious. "Just turn the amp all the way up," he said, predating Spinal Tap by seventeen years. It didn't work for us. Every time we tried it, the pickups would squeal bloody murder.

Then one day Bruce called. "I've got it!" he said. "I've got the tone!" I rushed over. He had found a weird guitar someone had thrown out that fed back the right way, sustaining a note rather than a horrible squeal. It was a major breakthrough.

He was having a tough time finding strings that were long enough because the guitar turned out to be a bass. But he played it for a while.

Bruce's role in the Castiles had grown in the short time I'd known him. A guy named George Theiss had started off as the lead singer, but he had issues occasionally and would refuse to sing, forcing Bruce to step up.

For all our overlap, Bruce and I had our own inclinations, which were reflected in our bands' repertoires. The Source played Rock-Pop like the Who's first album (still my favorite), the Youngbloods, Buffalo Springfield, the Byrds, the Hollies, the Kinks, the Stones, the Beatles.

The Castiles leaned moodier and darker. The Doors, Love, Them, the Yardbirds, the Animals. Between the two of us we had the new revolution covered. And those two complementary sensibilities would show up big-time thirteen years later on an album called *The River*.

Before John Miller, now Britton again, left for college, he came with me and Bruce to the Cafe Wha? one day to see Kangaroo. The guy who opened for them was a black guy doing wild things on his guitar with feedback—in a good way, like the Beatles had started doing and the Who were doing regularly. I didn't pay much attention to his group, Jimmy James and the Blue Flames, which seemed like an out-of-their-environment R&B group that had just dropped acid for the first time. The wild guitar player wouldn't change back to his birth name of Hendrix until he got to England. I was much more interested and anxiously awaiting the new Kangaroo lineup, having heard they had recently added a girl singer.

In between John Miller leaving and Joe Hagstrom coming into the Source, I mentioned to the guys that I would like Bruce to be in the band. He had mentioned having tough times in the Castiles every now and then. But the problem was the way we got to the gigs—our mothers took turns driving us. And since Bruce's mother didn't drive, he couldn't seriously be considered for the band.

There was one brief intrusion of reality into my tunnel vision. Like every other guy my age who didn't go to college, I got drafted.

Everybody had a different idea on how to get out of it. None of them appealed to me. I thought for a minute, Maybe I'll go. But who was I kidding? I couldn't take orders from anybody my whole life. When I got into the draft-board room, I decided to just deal with it.

My anxiety spilled out in a nervous monologue.

I said, "Listen, man. I don't really have the brains to bullshit you, you know? I mean I've heard of people successfully doing that, but I just can't get into it, man, so you've got to, you know, like, help me out here. I'm not that crazy about killing people, I'm being honest with you, as opposed to those guys in the other room, who, you know, can't wait. They are looking forward to killing people, and I've got to believe that's the cats you want. And the room is full of 'em. I, on the other hand, don't have that thing that just wants to kill people. So you're gonna have to explain this to me."

We were the last group and it had been a long day. The guy from the draft board squinted. "Whaddya mean, son?"

"I mean, explain it, sir. What's the story with Vietnam? Start there."

"Well," he says. "It's Communists, boy!"

"OK," I said. "So what's a Communist and why are we killing them? And all the way over there?"

"Well, a Commie is a . . . a . . . a dictator and uh, bad people, son. Bad people. And we're fighting him there so he don't come here."

Really?

"I'm sorry, sir, but I still don't get it. They're coming from Southeast Asia to take over New Jersey? For what? Our tomatoes? I just cannot buy that. They land on Bradley Beach, I'll be the first one there, but I ain't going halfway around the damn world to shoot people just because you say so. All due respect."

He stared at me for a long time. I figured, I'm going to jail. It wouldn't be the first time. The first time was when the local cops planted marijuana on me to try and get the only freak in town off the streets. Luckily, my parents believed me when it was discovered they had loaded the wrong brand of cigarettes. Soon after that I started smoking weed. I figured if I'm already being punished, I might as well do the crime.

Finally . . .

"OK, son."

"Check those boxes in the right-hand column," he said, "and I'd better see you on Bradley Beach when the time comes."

I said, "Yes, sir, you will, sir." And that was that.

Maybe he knew I was trouble. Or maybe I was the small fish that got thrown back into the pond.

I didn't have to hide in a college or run away to Canada. I was free to pursue my impossible dream.

But what were the odds of a kid from New Jersey becoming a Rock star? A million to one?

No. Worse.

three

Upstage

(1968–1970)

You don't want to piss off anybody from New Jersey. They're
already pissed off by being from New Jersey.

—THE UNWRITTEN BOOK

High school was a drag.

Who cared about the Peloponnesian War when John Lennon was
inventing feedback for the intro of "I Feel Fine"?

Just ring the damn bell and let me get to band practice.

Contrary to our most delicious fantasies, in New Jersey the girls chasing the Beatles in *A Hard Day's Night* would prefer the sports guys for
another five years.

We were at rehearsal one day at Joe Hagstrom's house when he came
running in with a music magazine. He opened it, pointed, and declared
with shock, "Look! Rod Stewart is white!"

"Get the fuck outta here!"

"It must be the way it's printed."

"The Equals all looked white too."

"I'm telling you," he said. "He's white."

The issue wouldn't be resolved until Stewart came onstage at the
Fillmore East.

The Fillmore East was a miraculous Rock oasis that Bill Graham had
opened in early 1968 as the East Coast sister to the Fillmore in San
Francisco. It was right in the middle of the Lower East Side, Second
Avenue and Sixth Street, and the rent must have been right because it

was a neighborhood of bikers, dealers, winos, homeless, junkies, and panhandlers.

Graham was a tough, controversial guy, a German Jew whose mother sent him to France to escape the Nazis. He ended up in San Francisco, where he helped invent the new Artform of Rock performance.

He called himself a Producer rather than a Promoter, and rightfully so.

His vision elevated the performance part of our Artform to its highest evolution, a level that, regarding three-act theater bills, has never been equaled.

The shows were a total immersive experience.

You entered a funky but chic chandeliered lobby leading to the main room, which held around twenty-five hundred of the first velvet seats we'd ever seen.

The Fillmore East usually had three acts per show, two shows a night on Fridays and Saturdays. The amazing Joshua Light Show, named for the Engineer and Lighting Designer who created it, Joshua White, was projected on the full-screen back wall. We had never seen anything like it. No one had. Between acts, Graham showed cartoons and newsreels.

The shows were curated by Graham's eclectic but exquisite taste and both reflected and influenced the open-minded hippie era of the late '60s.

Some typical Fillmore East bills:

March 8, 1968 (opening night):

Big Brother and the Holding Company
Tim Buckley
Albert King

April 27, 1968:

Traffic
Blue Cheer
Iron Butterfly

January 9, 1970:

Ike and Tina Turner
Mongo Santamaria
Fats Domino

Unbelievable, right? For five dollars or less!

Anyway, such was the state of Rock journalism circa 1967. We weren't even sure what color our Rock stars were!

At least until May 2, 1969. The Jeff Beck Group, Joe Cocker, and NRBQ. And I feel quite confident positively confirming it now. Rod Stewart is white.

⬦

As I entered my senior year of high school, I was blossoming into the full-blown hippie I would be for the next few years, or the rest of my life depending on how you're counting, and my father told me to cut my hair or get out.

So I moved in with my first girlfriend, Susan. Very straight. Very smart. Very cute. The star actress in school. It must have been her theatrical sensibility that attracted her to a freaky nascent underground underdog Rock and Roller. Her mother was a widow and an alcoholic, one of the few adults I could relate to even a little bit. I liked both of them a lot.

Being the school freak meant I was the last guy in high school to have sex. Or at least it felt like that, hanging with guys like Mark Romanski, who knew how to talk to girls, something I never did figure out. I heard he ended up in the CIA. That might be a rumor, but he *was* a clever Robert Culp type. I hope I'm not blowing his cover.

I finally had sex at a party with Susan after close calls with others. It was terrible. Couldn't get the rubber on. Couldn't get it off. Once I moved into her place, we got quite good at it. It was a little kinky be-cause we'd do it in her mother's bed while she was at work.

Then I got kicked out of school because I didn't live at home. Or was I kicked out of the house because I'd gotten kicked out of school? I felt bad for my mother, who was caught in the middle, so I went back home and—forgive me, David Crosby—cut my hair.

Oh, the humanity!

It was traumatic. I even saw sorrow in my mother's eyes. The only good that came out of it was that, since my hair was cut, I figured I might as well join the wrestling team to exact revenge on a kid who had a gang that had been bullying me. The whole thing was over in a day. I joined the team, selected him as an opponent, smashed his face on the floor, broke his nose, and started growing my hair back.

⬦

After I reluctantly and meaninglessly graduated from high school (the irony of my giving keynote addresses at education forums these days isn't lost on me), I hooked up with a working band from the Boston area. Gingerbread, I think the name was.

The experience only lasted about three months and was notable for only a few things. I met my second girlfriend, Vivienne, who was French and twenty-five and began my appreciation of older women. Every young boy and girl, of legal age of course, should begin their sex lives with older lovers. It should be treated as an apprenticeship just like anything else. It would be so much more enjoyable. Young kids having their first sex with each other is always pathetic. Mine certainly was. Older cultures used to do that for the boys. But probably not the girls, unfortunately. Society has always been deathly afraid of truly unleashing a woman's sexuality because they know it is infinitely more powerful than a man's.

The diner we ate in had a little jukebox attached to each table, and we played "Ramblin' Gamblin' Man" by the Bob Seger System and Donovan's "Hurdy Gurdy Man" every day.

The only other event of note from that experience was that my Grampa Lento's National acoustic guitar with the resonator was stolen by the other guitar player in the band. I couldn't prove it, but he had been drooling over it, and then one day it was missing.

I was very upset and told Nana Lento. All I had left was a guitar strap, and she asked for it. I'll never know for sure whether she did it or called her sister Zeze in Boston, but an Italian conjurer was approached and issued a *maloik* on whoever took Sam's guitar. (It's like a goombah hoo-doo thing. Every ethnic group has one.)

Cut to forty years later, an E Street Band show in Pittsburgh. On my way to the stage stands Joe Grushecky. "Hey," he said, "I know who has your grandfather's guitar."

"What?!? Don't you fucking leave!" I said as they pulled me onstage.

The story went something like this. Joe was at a funeral, and the widow came up to him and said, "I heard you know Stevie." Yeah, he said. "Well," she said. "I have his grandfather's guitar."

Turns out the *maloik* really worked. The scum that stole it died. Slow, I hope. Then the guy who got it from him died. Then the guy who got it from *him* died. At that point, the widow wisely concluded it was time to return the thing from whence it had come.

My name and address were on a card in the compartment, and the original thief never bothered to take it out. So I got the guitar back.

Gingerbread got boring. The gigs dried up. I moved back with my parents for a minute. And then one night I went to see Bruce play at Le Teendezvous in Shrewsbury, one of those teenage Jersey nightclubs. The Castiles had broken up by then, and he was with one of his new bands, Earth or maybe Child.

At the break, Bruce said, "You heard about this place Upstage?"

I hadn't.

"It's amazing. Down in Asbury. Open 8 p.m. to 5 a.m. All ages. Ask for Margaret."

All I knew about Asbury Park was Convention Hall, where we saw the big bands, and the Battle of the Bands on the roof of the Howard Johnson's where Tim McLoone's is now. We won.

Down I went to check out the Upstage Club.

At the door was Margaret, looking straight out of the '50s, probably in her forties, the owner Tom Potter's wife and the lead singer of Margaret and the Distractions.

"Bruce told me about you," she said. "If you're as good as he says, you'll get upstairs in no time. Now go in, but don't tell Tom I let you in for free."

The beginning of a beautiful friendship.

Upstage was above a Thom McAn shoe store. You climbed a tubular black staircase lit with colorful iridescence to get to the lower floor of the club. That was the café, reserved for auditions and Folk singers.

If you were designated as worthy, you moved up. That meant another long staircase up to the main room, maybe two or three hundred capacity, distinguished by, and locally infamous for, having the amps and PA system built into the black-lit psychedelic walls.

It was the place bands came to jam after the bars closed at 3 a.m., back when jamming was all the rage.

I vaguely remember having to build a band out of whoever was sitting around in the café that day for the audition. One of my first encounters would end up being one of my lifelong closest friends, a soft-spoken, southern-boy bass player named Garry Tallent. I introduced myself and said I was there to audition. He volunteered to play with me.

Big Bad Bobby Williams, the three-hundred-pound biker and drummer with the Distractions, a larger-than-life character in every way, volunteered to play the drums.

We did "Hi-Ho Silver Lining," "Shapes of Things," and maybe a Blues thing like "Rock Me Baby." All Jeff Beck, who was everything to me at the time (and pretty much still is). I'd be forever grateful to Jeff for introducing the world to Rod Stewart, who would be the reason I would become infatuated with Sam Cooke.

I graduated upstairs immediately. As I met more of the Upstage guys, I found out there was a scene in that part of Jersey that I knew nothing about. Bands like the Storytellers (featuring the impish Danny Federici on organ), Sonny and the Starfires (with the lanky and hyperintense Vini Lopez), the Bank Street Blues Band (with the cynical, peripatetic John Lyon), the Blazers, the Moment of Truth (also with Vini, and with Garry Tallent), Norman Seldin's Joyful Noyze, etc.

Sprinkled throughout, sometimes playing with one band, sometimes with another, were hot local guitar players like Billy Ryan, Ricky DeSarno, Sonny Kenn, Bill Chinook, and Paul Dickler.

In those years, the guitar players ruled because the guitar had become temporarily omnipotent. Hard to imagine now, but for a few years the guitar players were more important than the singers.

Rod Stewart worked for Jeff Beck. Robert Plant worked for Jimmy Page. No shit. Jimi Hendrix's group was called the Jimi Hendrix Experience for a reason, and not because he happened to be the singer. There would be one more example of this ten years later with Van Halen when Eddie gave the guitar its last evolution.

I became one of the kings of the jam, along with Bruce, Ricky, and Billy.

If you jammed all night at Upstage, you made five dollars. The few of us that led the jams got fifteen dollars for four or five hours onstage.

I only worked three nights a week, but I lived off that forty-five dollars a week for quite a while.

When Bruce wasn't commuting back and forth to Freehold, he was sleeping on the beach or in the surfboard shop of his second Manager,

Carl "Tinker" West. I had dropped by once or twice, maybe we rehearsed there with one band or another, but I thought the place was toxic. Literally. The chemicals used to make the boards smelled poisonous. So Bruce and I got an apartment together on Fourth or Fifth Avenue in Asbury Park.

One big loft room. Two mattresses on the floor. Not much else.

We were the original odd couple, as he immortalized in a speech he gave decades later when I was honored by Little Kids Rock.

Of course, when it came to who was Oscar and who was Felix, he lied. When there was no more room in the sink for the pile of dishes, we moved.

Along with Johnny Lyon, Albee Tellone, and Johnny Waasdorp, I got an apartment where Cookman met Kingsley. Johnny Lyon had worked in the post office and played harmonica. Albee was a Singer-Songwriter and guitarist. Waasdorp, who had started the Rogues and then replaced Phil Watson in the Mods, was a brilliant guitar player who switched to piano, gaining the moniker "Hotkeys" in the process. Bruce would stay there sometimes too.

We used the time together to really dig into the roots of Blues. As one of the bedrocks of Rock, Blues music was present in whatever we did. We were introduced to it through the Rolling Stones, but many of the lead guitar developments in Blues Rock came from the trio of guitarists who passed through the Yardbirds.

The first, Eric Clapton, defined modern lead guitar, both in the Yardbirds and in bands like John Mayall's Bluesbreakers and Cream. He influenced everybody who plays a solo to this day. Clapton's successor, Jeff Beck, founded the Jeff Beck Group, which introduced us to both Rod Stewart and Ronnie Wood (on bass at the time, brilliantly) and redefined the guitar player / lead singer relationship. And finally came Jimmy Page, who created the ultimate Hard Rock archetype, Led Zeppelin.

Right in the midst of that, Jimi Hendrix took it all to some new cosmic place. The only other guitar players of similar stature, representing Blues tradition rather than the progressive English style of playing, were Mike Bloomfield with the Paul Butterfield Blues Band and the lesser-known Danny Kalb with the Blues Project.

At Cookman and Kingsley, we traced the genre back from the white cover versions to the black originators.

We listened incessantly to Little Walter, Fred McDowell, Sonny Boy Williamson, Robert Johnson, Howlin' Wolf, Son House, Elmore James, and Muddy Waters. We also started playing cutthroat Risk and Monopoly in our plentiful spare time.

The early signs of a logical part of my brain I wasn't yet conscious of, and which would come in handy later, began to appear. I realized the way to win at Risk was to capture Australia first.

I had also figured out that the key to having a winning pro football team was the offensive line. They were the most important players. Not the quarterback, the running backs, or the wide receivers. Not any of what are still insultingly referred to as the "skill" players. It's the "unskilled" and probably lowest-paid offensive linemen that make the difference.

Our Monopoly obsession would continue onstage when we formed Dr. Zoom and the Sonic Boom a few months later.

One afternoon, a few of us dropped acid and went to see *Yellow Submarine* in New York.

Acid, of course, was lysergic acid diethylamide, or LSD (why not LAD?), and it was still a new thing in East Coast hippie culture. The drug, a strong hallucinogen, had been discovered by Albert Hofmann in 1938 in Switzerland, was used in experiments by the CIA on unsuspecting victims, and found its way to hippie gurus like Timothy Leary, Owsley Stanley, and Aldous Huxley.

I know it's probably hard to believe now, but my generation didn't do drugs to escape from reality. We were seeking enlightenment, the broader understanding of the universe that the Beatles were singing about in songs like "Love You To," "Tomorrow Never Knows," and "The Inner Light." And believe it or not, LSD wasn't illegal nationally until 1968.

Acid affected the mind in ways that gave the user a shortcut to understanding the basics of Eastern philosophy. Think of it as the hippie Google.

I only did three trips, but the second and third were redundant. The first one revealed to me the three truths that would link elementary school science to metaphysics and that remain the basis of my spiritual knowledge to this day:

Everything is alive (preons, the tiniest particles in the universe, are constantly in motion).

Everything is connected (for every action, there is a reaction).

Everything is forever (matter changes form but can never be destroyed).

Yellow Submarine was not only a Beatles cartoon but an incredible work of Art. Returning to childhood was an essential goal in the hippie philosophy as the seeker sought to release the ugliness of the spiritually bankrupt, materialistic adult society. We hippies were trying to get back our sense of wonder and enjoy the beauty of being alive.

As we watched and tripped, all the secrets of the universe were revealed to us. The inherent yin-yang conflict of positive and negative energy talked about by Joseph Campbell, which would be the basis of *Star Wars,* was there. And a lot more.

It took us a while to realize the movie had ended. As we finally got up to leave, we noticed Johnny Waasdorp was still staring at the screen, mouth open. His mind was completely gone.

We got him home, and over the course of the next few days he slowly returned to us, but in the form of a seven-year-old child. He never came back any further than that. We gradually lost touch with him, and some years later heard that he had killed himself. A sad loss of a great friend and enormous talent.

Stick with the Internet.

At a certain point in 1969 or so, Bruce called me and asked if he could switch to the Telecaster.

I know that sounds funny, but growing up when we did, your guitar was your identity. And I was the Telecaster guy. Bruce had his weird converted bass guitar for a while and then a Les Paul, which probably proved to be too damn heavy.

I said OK. I had been trying a Stratocaster out lately and liked it. And anyway, guitar playing was starting to feel kind of over. The Rock world was about to undergo a major transformation.

In 1969 the Beatles had already broken up, but we didn't know it yet. A world without them was going to be psychologically traumatic, and not just for me. They were our generation's leaders, teachers, and inspiration. I don't think the Stones ever quite recovered from having to try a little harder as the number two band in the world.

We were lucky to have had them as long as we did, keeping in mind we met them halfway through their career. They were together for twelve years and put out thirteen glorious albums in seven years of recording. Keeping a great band together that long isn't easy.

Cream did three and a half albums.

The Jeff Beck Group with Rod, Ronnie, Nicky, Mick, and then Tony did two.

Moby Grape did three.

Buffalo Springfield had broken up by the time their third record came out.

The Youngbloods did two, lost Jerry Corbitt, did one more.

The Byrds lost their main songwriter, Gene Clark, by their third album but still managed four more classics.

With a handful of exceptions, the great bands averaged between three and four albums.

Why? Because what made those classic bands classic was the amount of talent. The Temptations had five lead singers! With that much talent, it's hard to keep things together unless you have a Manager who understands that the band matters more than any individual. And that's rare.

Most Managers encourage the lead singer to go solo. More money for them both. And it's easier to control the situation. But the records are never the same. When the harmony voice joining Dave Mason is Stevie Winwood, it's better than when it's not. Traffic is one of the exceptions—they lost Mason after their second album, then did three more great ones.

Only the Rolling Stones, half of the Who, and two-fifths of the Yardbirds remain working from the original bands of the British Invasion. Lead singers abound, which is great, but it's not the same thing.

No matter how you sliced it, as the new decade began, the simultaneous evolution of sociopolitical consciousness and the nascent Artform of Rock was starting to come apart at the seams.

The optimism that began at the Human Be-In and the Monterey Pop Festival in 1967 got damaged at the Chicago riots in 1968, but made a comeback and peaked at Woodstock. It was now unraveling with Altamont, Manson's murders, and the Beatles' breakup.

As the election of Richard Nixon represented society's reluctance to change, and the failure of Rock to change it, the once-bright '60s limped to a politically disappointing dark end, and Rock and politics would go their separate ways for a while.

At the same time, the Renaissance of the '60s would end appropriately with a work of unparalleled genius that would complete the promise of *Sgt. Pepper*, sum up the entire Rock Era of the '50s and '60s, and reveal the pinnacle of the Artform of Rock:

The Who's masterpiece *Tommy*.

So how do we follow that?

four

Southside Johnny and the Kid

In this jungle we're slaves to politics,
And we call ourselves civilized,
If you ain't got the muscle,
Fear gonna run your life.

    —"FEAR," FROM *VOICE OF AMERICA*

Big Danny was having trouble concentrating.

Being a seven-foot-tall, flaming-red-haired, 380-pound real-life lep-rechaun may have come in handy when negotiating the tense situations encountered in the course of daily existence, but his intimidating girth could not help him now.

He had the option to build more houses on Boardwalk and Park Place, but Obie already had hotels on Marvin Gardens, Albee was building on St. Charles, and Eddie Larachi had swallowed up the railroads and Pennsylvania Avenue.

Big Danny checked again. He was low on funds. It was hard to think with 120 dB of Rock and Roll being blasted into the echoey old barn that was now the Asbury Park Hullabaloo Club. But that was part of the challenge of being a Monopoly Player onstage with Dr. Zoom and the Sonic Boom! This was his job, and he could handle it. He had to. It was the only gig in town.

The fragmentation of Rock wouldn't happen until the early '70s. In the '60s, there were a series of overlapping monocultural trends that happened like clockwork: the British Invasion in '64, Folk Rock in '65, Blues Rock in '66, the Psychedelic Summer of Love in '67, Country Rock in '68, Hard Rock in '69, and (mostly white) Southern-Gospel-Soul-Rock in '70.

Each major city had one main FM station that reinforced the shared artistic sensibility, so the whole country happily, fearlessly, explored the new artistic vistas right along with the Artists as the new Artform created them.

Some Renaissance artists would enter in the year the specific genre fit them—Jimi Hendrix in Psychedelic '67—and some would move from trend to trend, bringing their genius along with them.

Before the Beatles, Artists considered any hit a miracle, and they (and their record company) showed their gratitude by releasing a slightly rewritten version of the same hit as a follow-up single.

The Twist?

Let's Twist Again.

Perfect.

Simple as that.

But the first nine albums by the Beatles were a constantly changing story. They weren't thinking Art. They just did what came naturally. But by doing so they did something they don't get enough credit for—*they invented the concept of musical evolution.*

And in doing so, influenced everyone who followed, artists and audiences alike.

Each new Byrds album branched out into new genres. Every Who and Kinks release broadened the subjects Rock bands could write about. We waited for the next Stones single to vent our teenage frustration and to hear the new guitar tones. Bob Dylan would climb straight up reaching for his artistic persona through *Blonde on Blonde* before abandoning autobiography altogether and settling on his everyman troubadour persona for the rest of his life while continuing to surprise us to this very day.

The Beatles, incredibly, went from "Love Me Do" to "I Am the Walrus" in six short years, and we as an audience went with them, while we as artists/singers/musicians evolved on the backs of their amazing growth and those yearly genre trends, taking a little from this and a little from that as we built our own future identities.

In late 1969, Bruce started Steel Mill, a band that combined Blues Rock, Hard Rock, Southern Gospel Rock, and Roy Orbison's cinematic technique of going new places in a song without repeating where he'd been.

It was Bruce, Vini Lopez on drums, Vinnie Roslin from the Motifs on bass, and Danny Federici on the rare (because it was so gigantic and expensive) Hammond B-3 organ.

The closest thing to compare it to was a combination of early Rascals, Deep Purple, and Rhinoceros, with one voice instead of two.

When Steel Mill started to get popular on the East Coast, Bruce went west to audition for Bill Graham's new Fillmore record label. He didn't get signed, but on his way back he called me. "Vinnie's not working out," he said. "Would you mind switching to bass for awhile until we figure it out?"

My time with Gingerbread had ended and I had nothing better going on. "Sure," I said.

I got the new Dan Armstrong see-through bass and a huge Ampeg amp that I feel like I'm still paying off and jumped in. Our audience kept growing, especially in Jersey and Richmond, Virginia.

I'm not sure where the connection to Richmond came from. Maybe Tinker. But we were big down there. Richmond always felt like spring. Twenty degrees warmer than Jersey. Beautiful buildings and trees. Clean. The girls were lovely, less cynical, and, in those liberated times, very friendly. It was paradise. Bruce and I would drive down there in my '62 ragtop Austin Healey with the bug-eye headlights. No heat. No shocks. Five hours or so, but we didn't care.

Steel Mill was the first time we experienced the thrill of having what I call "live hits."

Bruce's songwriting was improving all the time, and if we got back to a town often enough, certain songs were so immediately accessible that they'd become favorites.

Steel Mill peaked on September 11, 1970, when we returned to the scene of my first experience onstage, the Clearwater Swim Club in Highlands.

There had to have been a thousand people there, maybe more, all having a great, mellow time. For no discernible reason, the Middletown police had bought riot gear, even though there was no crime in Middletown whatsoever, never mind riots.

The pool was set down in a valley, and all I remember was looking up and seeing what I'd seen in a dozen Westerns: we were completely surrounded by Indians up on the surrounding hills!

But these Indians were cops in military riot gear, and I had a Ghost Dance moment as they charged down the hill and brutally attacked the audience. They were beating everyone in sight with clubs and shields for the capital crime of having long hair and *possibly* smoking pot!

In the melee that followed, Danny saw two cops arresting someone and pushed the PA system down on them.

Now Danny was . . . well, picture an older Dennis the Menace, the kind of character who unscrewed the metal plate that held the elevator

Article about the "riot" at Clearwater Swim Club after a Steel Mill concert

The Courier

buttons as we left a hotel because he'd thought of a creative use for it on his B-3.

Anyway, some cops saw him push the PA, and the chase was on. He escaped and had to go on the lam for a while until things cooled off.

For once the neighborhood was on our side, acknowledging the psychotic police chief, Joe McCarthy, had gone too far.

Even though we were getting bigger and bigger, Bruce surprised the hell out of me and decided he didn't want to be the lead singer anymore. He found a guy named Robbin Thompson from a Richmond band called Mercy Flight.

Great guy. But what the fuck?

I guess Bruce was having existential doubts as to which identity would both work commercially and feel comfortable for the rest of his life. I'm still having those moments.

Predictably, that move totally confused Steel Mill's audience and killed whatever momentum we had. Next!

Whoever ran the Asbury Park Hullabaloo Club, also known as the Sunshine Inn (I seem to remember John Scher, who would become the main Jersey Promoter, being involved), got word to us that they could use a house band to open for the big acts coming through town.

We decided to put a band together that included everyone we knew, both guys and girls. Whoever didn't play an instrument could sweep up between songs. Or blow up balloons. Or play Monopoly or Risk onstage. That way, everyone could get some bread. We named the mobile commune Dr. Zoom and the Sonic Boom.

That's when Johnny got his nickname "Southside." He had started dressing like he did on his first album cover, with the hat and shades. Like the Blues Brothers five years later. Bruce started calling him Chicago Johnny. "No," I said, "the action's on the Southside, where the Checkerboard Lounge is, Pepper's, Theresa's, Florence's, the 708, Turner's." And so it was.

I remember opening for Black Sabbath and Humble Pie. I wish now I'd made a point of meeting Steve Marriott, just on the basis of "Itchycoo Park" alone, but I wasn't as big a fan of the Small Faces as I would become. We especially looked forward to the J. Geils Band, because

Geils had slicked-back hair on the band's first album cover, a cool rebellious throwback look. But he disappointed us profoundly by joining the modern world like five minutes before we played with them. Tragic. But Peter Wolf was one of the greatest front men we'd ever seen. Still is. I have a fond memory of opening for Big Brother and the Holding Company and of Bruce running for his life from Janis Joplin, who wanted to fuck him. She scared him to death.

Every month or two, the same group of guys more or less would turn into a different band.

We had the Sundance Blues Band, with Garry Tallent on bass, Big Bobby Williams on drums, Davie Sancious on keys, Bruce on second guitar, and me on lead vocals/guitar.

We had a soul group called Funky Dusty and the Soul Broom, with me leading.

We had a country thing for a minute called the Hired Hands with Albee Tellone up front, which is when I first picked up the mandolin and spent a few months trying to figure out the impossible pedal steel guitar.

We then decided to get into the final '60s genre: southern (mostly white) Soul.

Southern white Soul covered a lot of territory, from the marriage of Blues and Country by the Allman Brothers Band to the Band's creation of what would eventually be called Americana.

But it was Blues combined with Country and Gospel that got our attention: Delaney and Bonnie and Friends, then Taj Mahal (decidedly not white) with Native American Jesse Ed Davis (decidedly not white) on guitar, Ry Cooder, Bonnie Raitt. The ultimate example was Mad Dogs and Englishmen, with Joe Cocker up front and Leon Russell leading the band.

Cocker, the former plumber in the tie-dyed shirt, was a blue-eyed English Soul Man, channeling Ray Charles so intensely that his spastic body appeared to be completing some kind of invisible electric soul circuit.

And the band behind him included horns and chick singers. The Rolling Stones picked up on what was next and included horns and chick singers on their incredible *Exile on Main St.* album and tour.

We found our own chicks and horns. I think Bruce actually went to a local Gospel church to find the girls.

It was around that time that I convinced Bruce to start using his own name.

It was quite recently that he was still debating whether he wanted to be a lead singer at all. This time, I wasn't having it. "Look," I said. "You're gonna be the leader and lead singer and main writer. That ain't gonna change. It'll still be a band, but it's time for you to be recognized." That was me. Always looking out for my own self-interest.

What a putz.

It took a few weeks, but I would not back down. He knew if anybody criticized the idea, I had his back. He finally got over his embarrassment, and we became the Bruce Springsteen Band.

We continued to go down to Richmond regularly, still in my Austin Healey. The take was split nine or ten ways, but I don't remember even thinking about money in those days. Didn't need it. Never spent it. We were as free as we'd ever be in our whole lives. No responsibilities. Typical rent was $150.

Richmond was where the road to stardom would end for the Bruce Springsteen Band. Vini Lopez earned his new moniker, "Mad Dog," by punching our trumpet player in the mouth (where else?). Before the show.

It was the final straw. We'd tried everything. The ship was sailing and we couldn't get a ticket. We were twenty-one, twenty-two, on the verge of too old to be discovered.

Bruce went home to New Jersey to think. I stayed in Richmond, where Southside and I formed a devolutionary Country-Blues Folk duo, Southside Johnny and the Kid. We played Robert Johnson, Son House, Jimmy Reed, Fred McDowell, a cool arrangement of Elmore James's "Look on Yonder Wall." Davie Sancious sat in if there was a piano around, and Garry Tallent occasionally also. We were edging our way back toward being a band, when . . .

Rrrrrrrrrring.

"Stevie, it's Bruce. Come on back. I got signed!"

five

The Business

(1972)

A masterpiece is a thousand good guesses.

—THE UNWRITTEN BOOK

The band era had peaked and fragmented. Nobody was coming to New Jersey to sign us.

So Bruce wises up and gets signed as a Singer-Songwriter, what used to be called a Folk singer, by the legendary John Hammond, no less! The guy who tried to book Robert Johnson at Carnegie Hall for the *From Spirituals to Swing* concerts. He'd been a few weeks too late. Johnson had just been poisoned by a jealous husband or a pissed-off girlfriend. Hammond signed Benny Goodman and Billie Holiday. He integrated Jazz by encouraging Benny Goodman to use Count Basie and Lionel Hampton. He signed Aretha Franklin to Columbia Records for the first phase of her career and then Bob Dylan, known as Hammond's Folly when his first album didn't sell. The label wanted to drop him. "Over my dead body," Hammond said.

The tradition went back to the troubadours of antiquity and co-alesced in the Greenwich Village Folk clubs of the '60s where Dave Van Ronk, the Mayor of MacDougal Street, held court at places like the Bitter End, the Gaslight, the Night Owl, Gerde's Folk City, the Purple Onion, the Kettle of Fish, Café Figaro, the Village Gate, and Cafe Wha?

Those folkies followed the path of Woody Guthrie and included Pete Seeger, Fred Neil, Tom Paxton, Phil Ochs, Ramblin' Jack Elliott, Tim Hardin, Tim Rose, Tim Buckley, and Tiny Tim among others.

Then came Dylan, who revitalized and revolutionized Folk music before plugging in and becoming a Rock star. Donovan, Leonard Cohen, and Joni Mitchell had success in his wake, but it was the Beatles signing James Taylor to their new Apple label, which refurbished Folk as the new Singer-Songwriter genre.

Singer-Songwriters seemed to spring up every month in the early '70s: Kris Kristofferson, Jackson Browne, Gordon Lightfoot, Loudon Wainwright III, John Prine. Even Carole King, who had sung on her songwriting demos for more than a decade, was persuaded by Lou Adler to do an album. Which is still selling.

The one big difference between the traditional Folk singers and the new Singer-Songwriters was that the new acts all had hits.

In the '50s, hits were a risk for Folk credibility. The Kingston Trio's "Tom Dooley" was so big it disqualified them as cool. Peter, Paul, and Mary got away with "Puff, the Magic Dragon" because it was rumored to be about drugs and with "Blowin' in the Wind" because it was a protest song and put Dylan on the charts for the first time. That made them cool in perpetuity.

Folk music was never my thing, so I wasn't paying close attention. Bruce was. He figured that he needed a Trojan horse to get into that mysterious fortress called the Business. And so he reawakened his Singer-Songwriter persona.

It was an honest persona. I had witnessed his Folk side in his room in Freehold. It suited his loner aspect, while being in a band forced him to be social, which was healthy.

But at that stage of the game, a Folk singer was not who he needed to be. He had spent too many hours rockin' to stop now. And Pop hits were still a lifetime away. Now that he was signed, he immediately started assembling a band.

From Steel Mill, he took Danny on accordion and organ and Mad Dog, temporarily forgiven, on drums. He decided to use Davie Sancious and mentioned who he was thinking of for bass. "Oh, man," I said. "He ain't right." The best bass player in town was Garry Tallent. He had always been my bass player. I didn't want to lose him. But I also knew that it would be a small miracle if any of us found a way to break out of New Jersey. Bruce was going to have to be the horse we bet on. I suggested Garry.

"You sure?" Bruce said. I could tell that's what he'd wanted to hear all along.

I would also be going up to the session, of course.

Just to see what Fate had in mind.

As we educated ourselves in earnest in that Upstage period, Bruce and I became obsessed with the honking tenor sax solos that provided the break in the middle of virtually every hit record before the Beatles. Where had they all gone?

The unintended consequence of the British Invasion's dominance was that they put all their heroes out of work. The Drifters, Coasters, Doo-Wop, Little Richard—all the Pioneers—and all their sax players, King Curtis, Lee Allen, George Young, Red Prysock, Wild Bill Moore. Working their asses off one day, gone the next.

In our quest for our identity, we felt that if we could find that authentic sound, we could . . . we would . . . well, we didn't know what, but it would somehow be cool by being so uncool, dig? The saxophone would connect us to the already-starting-to-be-forgotten past. Tradition.

We found a wacky white guy, Coz, a '50s Sam Butera swing-type cat who could have come straight out of Louis Prima's band. Fantastic. He had the right sound but looked exactly like William Bendix. And white wasn't right. We kept looking.

Garry said he knew another guy who had played with Little Melvin and the Invaders. We piled into Garry's car. We couldn't all fit in mine, and Bruce didn't even have a license. We drove into the woods—to this day, I have no idea where. A club suddenly appeared. The place was jumping, and we could feel the bass pulsing as we approached the joint. The whole experience already felt surreal, assisted by the ganja that had been passed around in the car.

When we went in, it was like one of those movies where everything stops and everyone stares for a second before the party restarts. We were the only white faces, but I was too intoxicated by the thick, sexy hashish-and-perfume-scented atmosphere to be nervous. Chicks danced on the bar in a haze of smoke. And wait! There it was!

That sound!

Funny how those little mysterious details occupied us. Like the tone of a saxophone. We were seeking energy from wherever we could find it, and pure, cool sound was life-giving energy, whether from our guitars or a sax. The road was strewn with the broken bodies of those who had searched in vain for it. The few who found it were sanctified. With the sudden unprecedented infinite fragmentation, the zeitgeist was losing its equilibrium. We needed something traditional to ground us.

That sound!

Bruce looked at me with the same expression Cristoforo Colombo must have given his first mate when, after thirty-six death-defying days on the ocean, they spotted naked indigenous chicks sunbathing on Grand Bahama beach.

We met the sax player at the break. He was gigantic. He should have been intimidating but he wasn't. High as a kite wouldn't be an accurate description because kites don't fly as high as he was. We told him to drop in at what was to be a short-lived residency at the Student Prince on Kingsley some night, and that was about all the conversation any of us was capable of.

He was even bigger in the light. He even *looked* like King Curtis. He was just so authentic, we couldn't believe our luck. Afterward, I asked Bruce if he'd caught the guy's name.

"Clarence," he said. We laughed about that. I don't know why. Even his name was authentic. "Clarence Clemons," Bruce added.

So Bruce, who'd been signed as a solo guy, immediately pissed off John Hammond, everybody at Columbia, and his new Manager Mike Appel by telling them his thing was having a band! With a sax player! Named Clarence!

By the time I walked into the studio, the powers that be were in no mood for a second guitarist. Who needed the extra expense? And I was nervous enough as it was. I'd practiced a bottleneck part on "For You." I happen to be real good with a bottle—Duane Allman went out of his way to complement me when we played together—but the atmosphere was impossible. They gave me maybe two takes and said forget it.

That was it. I was out.

My best friend was on his way.

But he'd be making the journey without me.

By that point, I had been a bandleader for seven years. So being rejected from Bruce's new band shouldn't have been that big a deal. Even if I didn't want to front, I could just find a singer and start a new band, right?

I didn't.

I was a bit depressed that Bruce hadn't stood up for me. But it was more than that. I liked the idea of being the guy behind the guy. The Underboss. The Consigliere. I wanted to make Bruce the biggest star in the world, and I knew I had certain instincts that complemented the few he lacked.

Plus, it really did feel like the train had left the station. The Renaissance was over. Most of the '60s groups were being replaced by caricatures and hybrids. We were such fanatical purists that we didn't appreciate groups like Aerosmith, who were a combination of the Stones and the Yardbirds. Why take them seriously when we could go see the real Stones and Yardbirds? Who could have imagined that a decade later we'd be desperate for a band to have the good sense to combine those two bands?

There was financial stress as well. I had never paid off the big Sunn amp and the van I bought to carry it around. It was my first rancid taste of the horror of owing money, around $2000, as I recall.

Depression? Debt? Destiny? Whatever the reason, I quit.

My whole family, all my uncles, were in construction. My father called my Uncle Dick and got me a job.

The Calabrése laborer in my blood was ready to jump body and soul into my new life. Maybe I could fit into society after all? My religion of Rock was filled with ungrateful infidels! Who needed it?

I got a cool used Dodge Charger and listened to *Imus in the Morning* every day on my way to work for two years.

I started as a flagman, standing in the middle of the New Jersey Turnpike or Route 287 directing eighty-mile-an-hour morning traffic from four lanes down to two. Then I raked two-hundred-degree blacktop in ninety-degree heat. Carried bricks and bags of mortar. Reinforced bridge abutments. And worked my way up to the jackhammer, which permanently rattled what Rock and Roll had left of my brains.

On weekends I played flag football. One Sunday, reaching for a flag, I dislocated the ring finger on my right hand. Despite on-field surgery (it's still bent), I couldn't work the jackhammer.

So much for the straight life.

Now, let's see, what would be a good way to exercise my finger?

six

Vegas!

(1973)

We need to teach our students how to think, not what to think.

—THE UNWRITTEN BOOK

Shazam!

As if by wizardry!

A cloud of purple smoke and there I was . . .

. . . playing a Wurlitzer electric piano, exercising my inner Banana and my dislocated finger simultaneously.

Youngbloods. Never mind.

The band included some ex-Mods. Not the English kind, but the Rumson kind that was part of the Holy Trinity of Jersey groups, along with the Clique and the Motifs. Both the Mods and the Clique had asked me to join them a year or so before. That respect made me feel like I'd finally made my bones. Locally anyway. I don't know why I didn't join one of them.

As Fate would have it, and she usually does, the drummer in the bar band I joined for physical therapy happened to be the cousin of one of the Dovells. You know, "Bristol Stomp," "You Can't Sit Down," two of the greatest recordings ever made. They needed a backup band for the old-ies circuit, which was touring the country and would play the Flamingo Hotel in Las Vegas.

That's all I had to hear. Vegas, baby! My first Mecca!

Not only was I a Rat Pack fanatic and Mob aficionado, but I was a gambler. I had John Scarne's *Complete Guide to Gambling* near me at all times like a Bible. Scarne was the mathematics genius who figured out the odds of every casino game. He was banned by one casino after another for card counting (which is why blackjack now has a multideck shoe), until he finally wore them out and they hired him.

It was his math that would have encouraged Meyer Lansky to clean up the corruption when Batista made him gambling commissioner in Cuba in the '50s. Lansky realized the house didn't have to cheat to win. They just had to keep gamblers gambling.

So, let's see . . . socks, underwear, Scarne—I was ready. And I went on the road for the second time. Gingerbread. Remember? My grandfather's guitar?

The whole idea of "oldies" was at its peak in 1973. CBS-FM, the first station to create the format, '50s and early '60s music, had started in '72. *American Graffiti* would lead to *Happy Days.* But an ex-DJ, Richard Nader, was probably most responsible for what became the "Rock and Roll revival."

Nader started as a DJ, then worked at the Premier Talent Agency. Instead of embracing the British Invasion, he was pissed off that it was putting his favorite artists out of business. So he quit and started promoting oldies shows. A documentary about them, *Let the Good Times Roll,* came out in '73 and fueled the nostalgia obsession.

It was perfect timing for me.

I couldn't relate to anything going on in contemporary music at that time: Singer-Songwriters, Prog Rock, Heavy Metal, Glam. It was a good time for me to go back to school and complete my education.

I led a four-piece behind the Dovells that also performed as the opening act. Arnie Silver and Jerry Gross were original Dovells. Mark Stevens came soon after as comic relief. Arnie did the bass vocal parts and looked like James Dean. They were like big brothers to me. They old-schooled me in the ways of '60s-style romance. Like putting cologne on one's balls for the blow jobs between sets. It was a different time.

The Dovells wanted to open with a medley. Jerry had sketched it out, and I finished it off. It gave me a chance to actually play those classic records, which taught me more about them than hearing them a million times.

During that year, on the circuit, I met everybody that ever mattered. Little Richard, Bo Diddley, Gary US Bonds, the Shirelles, the Coasters, the Drifters. I was warned to stay away from Chuck Berry, but everyone else was friendly. The Drifters' guitar player, Abdul Samad, showed me some riffs and taught me about Arabic astrology. He did everybody's charts backstage. Lloyd Price, perhaps the most respected artist of them all—Little Richard had replaced *him* when he was drafted—taught me that if you wash the lubricant off the rubber you come slower. You know, life lessons.

I was having a great time, but the artists were all mostly miserable. They hated being called oldies acts. Many of them were in their prime, having regular hits when the Beatles arrived. Bam, over. Just like that. Tragically put out to pasture in their thirties and early forties by the British artists who loved them the most!

The atmosphere was invigorating. The spiritual power of the pioneers, stronger than they knew, scrubbed away any memory of my short construction career and replaced it with the new energy of a musical rebirth.

I figured since I was immersed in my own version of an adult education course, I might as well go all the way and see if I couldn't figure what was wrong with my songwriting.

I'd been writing for years and could never find my way to anything I was happy with. I decided to stop whatever I'd been doing and analyze it.

Where in the Rock world did songwriting begin?

I decided it began with Jerry Leiber and Mike Stoller. They had written countless classics. "Hound Dog" for Big Mama Thornton. "Jailhouse Rock" for Elvis. "Ruby Baby" for the early Drifters and then Dion. "Stand by Me" for Ben E. King. And most of the Coasters' hits.

I decided I would write a Leiber and Stoller song for Ben E. King and the Drifters.

First, I wanted to find a completely original chord change. Nothing crazy, just a new combination. I finally settled on G–D–E minor–C, otherwise known as 1–5–6–4. It must have been used somewhere, but I couldn't find it anywhere.

I wanted a universal theme, so I went with heartbreak. Your girl has walked out. Your once-happy sanctuary has become a cold, lonely place. "I Don't Want to Go Home."

Ben E. King came directly from the Sam Cooke school, so I wrote a Cooke melody, imagining the Drifters doing a call-and-response for the verse. I designed a split structure, verses and bridge like Frank Sinatra talking to the bartender in "One for My Baby," choruses a desperate delusional drunk talking to the girl in his head.

Man, I liked it. I felt like I had unlocked one of the secrets of the universe. I learned that day what I would teach forever in my songwriter master classes: when you get stuck writing for yourself, write a song for somebody else. But I didn't have the courage to give it to Ben E. King. He was friendly, but he was Ben E. Fucking King!

Between out-of-the-way hotels and clubs, we did arenas with the big Nader shows.

It was at a Madison Square Garden soundcheck that I heard Little Richard give what had to be one of the greatest performances of his life. And nobody saw it. It was the peak of his Jive years, when performances consisted of him performing a song or two and then jumping up on the piano, taking his shirt off, and waving it around, doing everything but singing.

For whatever reason, that afternoon, he felt like singing. He did an hour of Gospel, Country, Blues, Rolling Stones ("Jumpin' Jack Flash"!), songs he would never do in a show. He had the greatest voice I've ever heard, almost unrecognizable from his Rock records. It would encourage me to go back and discover his early Gospel records later, but that day it was quite a revelation.

I also caught a miraculous Bo Diddley performance that just for a moment took him back to his prime, although it took a weird-ass time machine to get him there. For most of the year, most shows, he was good but mostly going through the motions. Then, somewhere in the Carolinas, we were both hired for a high-society coming-out party for some rich sixteen-year-old girl. I'd never heard of a coming-out party, unless it was a gay dude celebrating self-liberation. But down south it signified some kind of adulthood. Like a redneck bar mitzvah, I guess.

I don't know if all coming-out parties were at nine o'clock in the morning, but this one was. And at that gig, I saw Bo lose twenty years and suddenly come to life. Surrounded by a hundred sixteen-year-old, very healthy southern girls exploding out of their Alice in Wonderland ball gowns into the hurricane of puberty, Bo gave one of the finest performances of his life. Every move, every lick, every trick made a reappearance, and he invented some new ones. After that, he went back to still great but legendary autopilot and stayed there for the final thirty-five years of his life.

On the road that year, the Dovells turned me on to Bruce Lee. I had never heard of him, but they took me to see *Enter the Dragon* just after he died. Wow. I was hooked. Whenever we were in a city with a Chinatown, I made sure to catch a kung fu movie.

I decided the actor most likely to replace him was a guy named Jackie Chan, who did all his own unbelievable stunts. He didn't make an English-speaking movie for a long time, and when he did he favored comedies, which disguised his true mastery. I had taken some karate but after that year I switched to kung fu, and even learned to fence and box because Bruce Lee recommended it and had included techniques from both in his Jeet Kune Do style. Didn't stick with any of it long enough to get really good, but it was fun.

Out on the circuit, I also got the news that I'd lost my grandfather Sam Lento, the man who taught me how to play guitar. It was my first big personal loss, and it hit me quite hard. I wondered then, and still wonder, why I hadn't asked him more about his life. Two deeply personal memories stand out: going with him to the Italian section of Boston, where the pushcarts still existed in 1955, and going with him to see *The Godfather* when it opened, where he leaned over to translate the Italian-language parts. I felt the pain of the news of his passing in my very soul. I still feel it. I could barely function for days.

Years later I would think back on moments like that and decide the brain must have a built-in limiter. And it works both ways.

I believe your mind cannot remember your most extreme emotions, one way or the other. That's why every time you walk onstage and hear that roar, it's like the first time.

If you truly remembered how bad every tragedy felt, you'd walk around crying all the time. And if you truly remembered how good sex was, you would get absolutely nothing done.

And then, suddenly, there it was . . . the House That Benny Built! (Don't call him Bugsy!)

The Flamingo, baby!

It was thrilling. I had read so much about it that I felt like I'd come home.

The Dovells stayed at the hotel gratis, while we were put up in some cheap motel off the Strip. Even so, I am glad I caught the last year the Mob ran Vegas.

First of all, there were vast tracts of land in between the casinos. Now you can walk the whole Strip rooftop to rooftop. Back then, the town was designed to make money strictly from gambling. Everything else existed to keep you there.

Rooms were around $20. There would be ridiculous all-you-can-eat buffets for like $3.95. With steak and lobster. The lounges and all the entertainment venues were five or six bucks. And Frank Sinatra might walk in spontaneously and entertain you for an hour.

Hookers were technically illegal in Clark County, but that was probably legislated to boost tips to the concierges, bellboys, doormen, parking lot guys, cabdrivers, and probably the janitors, all of whom had a few phone numbers for you.

The drummer bought me my first hooker. Man, was that fun! Why sex isn't legal everywhere I'll never understand. We should learn from the Netherlands and most civilizations through the centuries. Hookers are Angels of Mercy. Sex work is God's work. They are nurses for the socially retarded, therapists for the terminally shy, healers for the physically handicapped. They should be respected and protected from traffickers and pimps.

But Vegas wanted every penny gambled. Everything was a loss leader meant to keep you at that table for just one more hand, one more spin, one more roll of the dice. With no revenue from rooms, food, or entertainment and with the Mob probably skimming 25 percent off the top, everybody *still* got rich!

I couldn't wait to get to the tables to try out the Gambling Craft I had been studying under John Scarne.

I chose blackjack, although craps was the most fun. I played all seven hands. I was wiped out in about thirty minutes. Over two weeks, I continued practicing my gambling trade in all its forms, winning some, losing more. Cured my love of gambling forever.

Onstage, we opened for Frankie Valli one week, Fats Domino the next. I learned Fats was so in debt to the Mob he had to play Vegas every month, and one of the Four Seasons couldn't leave at all.

I was so visibly into the whole atmosphere I must have been glowing. The stage manager took a liking to me and offered a tour behind the scenes.

One afternoon, we went all the way up behind the top balcony. A pinspot picked out a tiny figure onstage, and as the soundcheck began I heard the last kind of music you would ever associate with the Flamingo or Las Vegas. I thought I was hallucinating. You know that weird feeling you get when you hear or see something but it's so out of context you're not sure it is what it is?

It was . . . Robert Johnson?

"You'd better come on, in my kitchen, because it's gonna be raining outdoors."

"Who's that?" I asked the stage manager.

"Dion," he said.

"'Runaround Sue' Dion?" I said.

"Yeah," he said.

I ran down and introduced myself. We hit it off right away. "Man," I said, "you ought to do something with that. First of all, you're great at it. But also, nobody would expect that from you." When I thought about it later, I realized it fit perfectly with what he'd always done. "Ruby Baby," "Drip Drop," "The Wanderer," all Blues.

Unlike some of the other pioneers, Dion refused to be put out to pasture. He never stopped recording, growing, exploring. The difference was he had deep roots he could rely on. That's one of the best things about Art. It speaks to you in a different way every time you visit.

Dion must have been watching the Dovells show from the wings, because afterward he asked if I could play the last couple of shows with him, including Dick Clark's New Year's Show at the Deauville Hotel in

Miami Beach, where the Beatles had played their second *Ed Sullivan Show* and where the Dovells got their name.

The Dovells wanted to manage me. They swore I was destined for greatness. I didn't see it. After a year on the road, the only destiny I was interested in was going home to New Jersey.

But I'd be going back in style!

I absolutely fell in love with Miami and the entire tropical lifestyle. I'll never really understand why I didn't move there permanently at that time.

Since I couldn't live in it, I decided to take it with me. I started wearing Hawaiian shirts and Frank Sinatra / Sam Snead hats and continued to do so when I got back to Jersey in snowy January. Bruce christened me "Miami Steve."

Later, when I became the slightly more serious Little Steven, I would bequeath the entire look to Jimmy Buffett, who I hear has done quite well with it.

seven

Asbury Park—Doubling Down!

(1974–1975)

I still remember, baby, those wild, desperate times,
Making love in crazy places, while the town around us died,
I played on broken stages, I watched the lonely cry,
You danced in iron cages, for the boys with hungry eyes,
All those wasted lives . . .

—"I'M COMING BACK," SOULFIRE

A light summer rain fell through the fog that rolled off the ocean. Southside Johnny and the Kid walked down Cookman Avenue, heading east from the neutral zone of Upstage toward the saloon-circuit part of town, where freaks, misfits, and outcasts, and the freedom they represented, had never been welcome.

It wouldn't be quite as dramatic as the walk Bruce and I would take eight years later through Checkpoint Charlie into East Berlin, but it had the similar tingle of trepidation that tickled your balls. You knew you were entering a world where you did not belong.

And trust me, the wall that kept us renegades separated from the bar bands protecting their turf on that saloon circuit was almost as real as the one in Deutschland.

Asbury Park was a crippled ghost town. Its once-proud Boardwalk managed to continue functioning at subsistence level on the weekends. The Ferris wheel, bumper cars, and Madame Marie Castello's Fortune

Telling staggered on. The smell of cotton candy, salt air, and stale popcorn somehow remained year-round.

Decades of neglect had run the place down, and then things had gotten worse. The town had always had an uncomfortable relationship between the races, black on the west side of the railroad tracks, white closer to the ocean. The riots that followed the assassination of Martin Luther King Jr. had further divided the town and killed it as a resort town forever.

Which added up to cheap rent for us.

I remember being the only guy in the classic gigantic movie theaters watching blaxploitation movies before they tore those beautiful palaces down. I was such a regular I became friends with the projectionist, who showed me how to thread the reels so he could take a break.

When I got home from the oldies circuit, it was January 2, 1974, and I was looking for some steady action. I had some ideas for a new band, but I needed a spark. It would come a few months later, when Bruce, Southside, and I went to see Sam and Dave at the Satellite Lounge.

It was a black club and mostly a black crowd, and Sam and Dave were ridiculously good. Seeing them in that small club, up close, playing "Soul Man," "Hold On, I'm Coming," "I Thank You," and the rest was truly revelatory. We went up afterward and said hello. They were nice, if a little curious about why these white Rock kids were so enthralled.

And that was that. Another epiphany. Johnny and I would become the Rock version of Sam and Dave, with double lead vocals and Rock guitar, integrated with horns. Not Jazz horns or Chicago horns or Blood, Sweat, & Tears horns. Something harder. Stax. Motown. Or what Allen Toussaint was doing in New Orleans. Simple but powerful.

We wanted to be the ultimate bar band. Our version of the Beatles at the Top Ten Club in Hamburg or the Cavern Club in Liverpool. The Stones at the Crawdaddy Club in Richmond. The Animals at the Club a' Gogo in Newcastle-upon-Tyne. The Dave Clark Five at the South Grove Youth Club in Tottenham. The Who at the Goldhawk Social Club in Shepherd's Bush. But with horns.

Even though the Renaissance was over, we thought the old rules still applied. We still thought, naively, that we needed an original identity to justify our existence. Well, now we had one.

Now we had to find a venue.

So Southside and I took that walk.

The Stone Pony, at 913 Ocean Avenue, was as run-down as the rest of town. By late 1974, the roof was half-caved-in from a recent hurricane, and the owners planned to squeeze out whatever they could from the remaining summer season and then shutter the place for good.

It was perfect.

For once the owners weren't in a position of strength. For once they couldn't demand that we wear suits and play what had become mostly mediocre top 40 Pop songs. In that half-caved-in roof I saw an opportunity. "Give us your worst night," I said. "We'll charge you nothing. Niente. Zip. We take the door, you keep the bar. But we play whatever we want." They agreed.

We couldn't have known that one move would alter New Jersey history forever.

Our band played an odd combination of Rock and Soul. A typical set included "Something About You" (by the Four Tops), "Hey Pocky A-Way" (the Meters), "I'm Not Talking" (the Yardbirds), and "Little by Little" (Junior Wells). Plus some Sam and Dave, of course.

We even introduced Reggae to the Jersey shore. *The Harder They Come* had come out. Its soundtrack was like Reggae's greatest hits, and some made it into our set: Jimmy Cliff's "The Harder They Come" and "Struggling Man," Toots and the Maytals' "Pressure Drop," the Slickers' "Johnny Too Bad," a few others.

Each night we played five sets, starting around ten and going until three in the morning. Forty-five on, fifteen off. We would also control the DJ's music before we started and in between sets to keep the vibe consistent.

The only band I knew of that had worked harder than we did before making it was the Beatles.

The first time I interviewed Ringo Starr for my *Underground Garage* show, he told me about his pre-Beatles gig with Rory Storm and the Hurricanes (is that a great name or what!), and how they alternated sets with the Beatles in Hamburg, six sets a night each, twelve hours a night, *seven nights a week—for months at a time!*

That's Fucking Work.

That's how you build stamina. That's how you learn how to perform. That's how you learn each song's effect on an audience. But it's more than that.

Listening to records, no matter how many times, is one thing. Physically playing them over and over is another. The songs get into your bloodstream and muscle memory.

That's one of the reasons the Beatles became such great writers. This was 1960 to 1962, and there just weren't that many songs to choose from. They knew everything that got released. All ninety-nine bands in Liverpool were playing the same songs, which is why they stretched into obscurities like "Devil in Her Heart" and B-sides like "Boys."

It's also why when John Lennon and Paul McCartney started writing, they looked beyond the four or five chords of the pioneers' songbook they had mastered so well. The incredibly inventive B-sections of verses and bridges of their earliest hit records, combined with their seemingly infinite wealth of great melodies, came from the intense repetition of those foundational songs, which transformed their influence from observance to DNA.

Our audience became the most sophisticated bar audience in the country because they got used to responding to songs they'd never heard before. We would always start the first set with a new song, which we would repeat in the final set.

When we threw in an original, we disguised it under a different name. We'd say that "I Don't Want to Go Home" was a B-side of a Drifters' single. Half the crowd had never even heard of the Drifters, so we got away with it.

Plus, the drinking age had recently been lowered to eighteen, so maybe the kids were just happy to be in a bar for the first time!

We made sure the songs were danceable because that was our job. If the audience danced, they drank. They didn't dance, you were out of work.

The job was harder than a decade before. Thanks to Bob Dylan's influence on Rock Artists' intellect and the ever-evolving imaginations of groups like the Beatles, the Byrds, and the Who, Rock audiences had stopped dancing and started listening.

But they still danced in the bars.

The first week we had about fifty people. The second week, a hundred. The third week, two hundred. The fourth, you couldn't get in.

They fixed the roof.

We went to a second night. Then a third. Then they expanded the place by adding an extension to the back wall.

By the end of the summer, we were pulling in a thousand people a night, three nights a week, at three dollars each. Relative to my overhead, I was as rich as I would ever be in my life.

Meanwhile, Bruce's first two albums had come and gone in a flash. He'd moved to Long Branch by then, but no sales meant he couldn't play the showcase venues that recording bands played, so he returned to Asbury to hang around with us.

He fit easily into what we were doing. The songs were mostly familiar to him, and he played along and sang whenever he felt like it.

As it turned out, it was a lot more fun to be out of the music business than in it.

Back on his first album, Bruce had blown everybody's minds by grabbing a postcard off the boardwalk and telling Columbia that that was his cover art. Greetings from Asbury Park? You gotta be kidding, they said. New Jersey was a punchline in an Abbott and Costello routine, not a place you brag about!

I figured if he had the balls to identify with Asbury Park, we should double down. I renamed the band Southside Johnny and the Asbury Jukes. Stolen from the greatest harp player that ever lived, Little Walter and His Jukes.

I didn't want to be the front man all the time, so I split the job with South. He wasn't that crazy about the idea, but he got used to it.

Bruce didn't get it at first. He was used to me fronting my own bands. And South was not an obvious choice. He was a crazy misanthropic manic-depressive who enjoyed being a grumpy, miserable, ne'er-do-well with no responsibilities—more W. C. Fields than W. C. Handy. But he surprised everybody by rising to the occasion.

Soon enough, it was clear that the Jukes had started a scene. The Pony was the hip place to be Tuesday, Thursday, and Sunday nights.

The walls were sweating just like they described in the early British Invasion days. Cocaine hadn't hit the suburbs yet, so it was mostly about booze, with an occasional joint in the parking lot.

I had stopped smoking ganja and hashish by then and had switched to Bacardi 151 rum to feed my Reggae habit. It was also better suited to my main preoccupation offstage, which was sex.

Girls were everywhere. Women's liberation was at its peak. Girls would ask *you* to have sex. I know. Impossible. But it happened. I was there. At one point I had seven regulars in the area and was meeting new ones from North Jersey on the weekends. In between sets. In the office. With the cologne.

My rent was $150 a month, and that was the extent of my expenses. Mattress on the floor. One fork. One plate. One knife, which I got rid of after I rolled over just in time to stop a New Orleans model from plunging it into my chest. Whatever I did, I am quite sure the punishment did not fit the crime.

I'm not sure exactly why, but I suppose I am obligated to explain the origin of my unusual habiliments. On top of the obvious standard hippie/gypsy/troubadour garb, there was an incident that married the bizarre to the bazaar.

One night I was driving a girlfriend home from the Pony, three in the morning, four lanes, when a guy coming the other way crossed over. I switched lanes as quickly as I could, but he drifted right with me. Head-on collision. Not too fast, but I smashed into the windshield, and though I didn't lose consciousness, I needed a few operations. After that, my hair never really grew in properly.

I asked Bruce what he thought. "You've been wearing these bandanas," he said. "Just make it a thing." I did.

We had been slowly working our original songs into the set, creating a unique identity, and felt we had earned the right to make a record. And it was now or never.

I asked Bruce what he thought about Columbia for the Jukes. He said to try Epic Records, which was a subsidiary. He had a guy in mind, Steve "Pops" Popovich, who used to be promotion at Columbia and then became vice president of A&R (that's artists and repertoire, the guys who sign bands) at Epic. Good guy, Bruce said.

Pops not only immediately signed the Jukes but would become one of our most important working partners and one of my best friends for the rest of his life.

He was a legendary character, the last of the Old School promotion guys. His constant companion was a huge cassette blaster, which he used as a lethal weapon. God help the radio program director he caught in a crowded restaurant at lunchtime. The guy would be quietly sipping his piña colada one minute and then bam! Pops would slam the blaster on the table, hit play, and his latest soon-to-be-hit would come roaring out into the cat's face. It was a beautiful thing to behold.

Pops started hanging around with us too. He was making the hour's ride from Freehold and fell in promotion-man love with the whole idea of making riot-ravaged Asbury hip. He even loved the little Italian joint we always ate in, Richie's, and wanted to franchise it.

The scene was picking up steam. Lines around the block every night, fighting to get in, and then seven hundred liberated maniacs dancing their asses off to Rock and Soul and Reggae they had never heard before.

I didn't realize it until years later, but we unwittingly redefined "bar band" forevermore to mean Soul-based Rock, usually with horns. That's not what it meant when we started. It was originally derogatory, an insult for bands that couldn't make it in the music business. It meant, among other things, that their song list was restricted to the top 40.

Rolling Stone used to have a feature where they would review one live show per issue on the back page. In 1976, for the first time, they wrote about an unsigned band, Southside Johnny and the Asbury Jukes at the Stone Pony, Tuesdays, Thursdays, and Sundays!

After that, "bar band" (and its British version, "pub rock") would be used to describe acts like Graham Parker and the Rumour, Elvis Costello and the Attractions, Nick Lowe, Dave Edmunds, Mink DeVille, Huey Lewis and the News. "Bar band" became a compliment for working-class bands who were proud of their traditional roots.

The audience became so used to hearing music they didn't yet know that for years after, national and even international bands with new albums would play the Pony first. They knew they'd have an audience who could react to new music in real time.

It would never be the Kaiserkeller or the Cavern, the Marquee, the Crawdaddy Club, or the Club a' Gogo.

But it was pretty damn cool for Jersey.

eight

The Boss of All Bosses

(1974–1975)

Greatness isn't born, it's developed. It's a decision
you make every hour or so.

—THE UNWRITTEN BOOK

"We're doing better than your wildest dreams," I said. "Three nights a
week, a thousand people a night. We need to make a change."

Stone Pony owners Butch and Jack were scary dudes. The smaller
one was six foot five, 280 pounds. They were picking up cases of beer
and tossing them to each other for storage like they were cereal boxes.

"What do you got in mind?" asked Jack.

"We want to go to three sets a night from five," I said. "And before
you answer, this isn't a negotiation. Agree or we'll go across the street
and take the crowds with us. Gabeesh?"

They stopped tossing for a moment and looked at me like I was lunch.
Long pause. They started tossing again. Slow smiles. Butch spoke. "OK."

And just like that, we made history a second time. Not only were
we the first bar band in New Jersey to play whatever we wanted, but
we were the first to break the ironclad five-sets-a-night rule. Our sets
became more like what signed bands would do at showcase clubs like
the Bottom Line in New York or the Roxy in LA.

I was good at doing business when I had to. The only problem was
that I hated it. I wasn't sure what my purpose was on this planet, but it
wasn't to become a fucking businessman. I knew I had to find the Jukes
a real Manager and Agent.

Good Managers are the hardest to come by, and in my opinion they are the most crucial factor in a band's success. The Mount Rushmore of Artists had a Mount Rushmore of Managers: Colonel Tom Parker, Brian Epstein, Andrew Loog Oldham, and Albert Grossman. Rock would be unthinkable without Elvis Presley, the Beatles, the Stones, and Bob Dylan, and yet everyone in the business laughed at, passed on, or ignored all of them at first. What's the main job of a Manager? Advocacy. If it wasn't for the advocacy, belief, and salesmanship of those four Managers, who knows how history would've been different?

Managers get paid, of course. Management takes 10, 15, even 20 percent of the gross. Agents get 10 percent. The whole concept of gross points is stupid and unfair, but that's the way the business mostly runs, and it's one reason Managers and Agents can do better than their Artists. The difference between Managers and Agents was and is that Managers, the better ones, usually have to invest in their Artists in the beginning, while Agents usually don't.

But without the right Manager, you are inevitably going to have a problem. Most critics would rank the Kinks third or fourth among British Invasion bands, after the Beatles and the Stones. So why were they never as big as the Who? Because their management was busy producing the Troggs when the Kinks toured America. The tour devolved into chaos. The band didn't get paid. They fought with each other onstage. Ray Davies traded punches with a union guy on *The Dick Clark Show*, which led to a ban from the United States for the most important four years of their prime, 1965 to 1969.

That's what happens when you don't have the right management.

As I set out to find the Jukes a real Manager and Agent, I was still acting as de facto Manager. I figured I needed something to make it more fun. An assistant! Just as a joke really. I drafted Obie Dziedzic, our number one fan, to be my first assistant. She turned out to be great, actually, a perfect buffer. She had that Big Mama McEvily quality of taking no shit from anybody. And like Big Mama, she was physically imposing enough to keep anybody in their right mind from fucking with her— and therefore me.

Bruce was recording what could have been his last record for Columbia. He was fighting for his life.

"Come check it out," he said. I made the trek up to 914 Sound Studios in scenic Blauvelt, New York, owned by the legendary Engineer and Producer Brooks Arthur. Not the happiest of memories, since that's where I got kicked out of the band. Bruce was there with Mike Appel, Mike's partner, and a new guy nobody introduced. It turned out to be another visitor, the writer Jon Landau.

They had been working on one song for weeks. Maybe months.

It sounded like it.

The song was like nothing Bruce had ever done before. This thing was *produced*, baby!

They were rightfully quite proud of it. Even Mike Appel was in a good mood.

There's the baritone sax fifths from "Loco-Motion"!

There's the Motown glockenspiel!

There's Phil Spector's doubling of everything!

There's Duane Eddy's baritone guitar riff! (He actually used a six-string bass.)

It was called "Born to Run," and it was a hurricane of sound. More aggressive and more Rock than Spector's wall because of the central guitar riff, which Spector never had.

And quite a complex arrangement, the most ambitious I'd ever heard Bruce do. It brought me back to Steel Mill, where he wrote almost stream-of-consciousness songs that moved unpredictably from part to part.

When we were kids, bands were measured by their ability to imitate hits. Bruce was never great at that. He heard things differently.

As he gained more experience, he came to understand basic theory, the so-called rules that so-called normal Arrangers live by. But it never limited his creativity.

The "Born to Run" bridge sections show how his imagination-gone-wild arranging style, which had been on full display since "Kitty's Back" an album earlier, was now working within basic rules, such as returning to the beginning key. That's what kept the middle section both exciting *and* coherent.

As impressed as I was, I thought the middle section was too complex for Pop. I kept that to myself. He didn't need the Pop charts at that time anyway.

I did comment on one thing, however.

Bruce walked me out of the control room, still glowing with pride. I was thrilled for him. A major breakthrough. And just in time.

"Man," I said. "That is something else!"

"It's been a lot of work, but it's been worth it." He nodded.

"That's such a new chord change for you, that minor chord in the riff. It's so Roy Orbison, which goes well with your new singing style."

He stopped walking. "What minor chord?"

"In the riff. It's great. Like something the Beatles would do."

"You're trippin'!" His smile was starting to slip. "There's no minor in the riff!"

"What do you mean? Of course there is!"

"Here," he said, throwing me a guitar, "play it!"

I played it.

"That's not what I'm doing," he said. He took another guitar and showed me.

"That's cool," I said. "But that ain't what's on the record!"

Without boring you nonmusicians too much, he had been bending the fifth note of the riff, the minor third of the 4 chord, up to the major third of the 4 chord, à la Duane Eddy. But the reverb was obliterating where he was bending the note *to,* so all you heard was where it was coming *from.*

They had been working on it so long that they thought they were hearing what Bruce intended. But it wasn't really there.

"Oh my God," he said, finally understanding. Into the control room he went with the bad news. If they hadn't already thrown me out of the band, they would have thrown me out again.

Either Mike Appel or one of the few believers left at Columbia sent "Born to Run" to Bruce-friendly DJs, including Richard Neer at WNEW in New York, Kid Leo at WMMS in Cleveland, Ed Sciaky at WMMR in Philly, Charles Laquidara at WBCN in Boston. They started playing the hell out of it. Leo ended his shift with it every Friday to send his audience into the weekend inspired. It saved Bruce's career, at least temporarily.

Mike then mortgaged his house to pay for the album. Even given the single's success, Columbia was still considering dropping Bruce. John Hammond had been moved aside, and Clive Davis had gotten bounced after some stupid scandal. The label was sending promotion men into radio stations to take Bruce's records *out* and put in records by their new kid, Billy Joel. No shit.

There were more complications within Bruce's camp. Appel was unsuccessfully pretending to tolerate Landau's presence, which Bruce was suddenly insisting on. And Jon, attempting to assert some control, had moved the sessions to the Record Plant in Manhattan.

One afternoon, Bruce and I were in his apartment in Long Branch. He was always broke, and I usually had a couple bucks in my pocket to give him. I would say loan, but that would falsely imply he paid it back.

"You've got a Manager and a record company now," I said. "That's big-time. Where's the money? What kind of deal do you have?"

He dug out a copy and showed it to me.

"Man," I said, "am I reading this right? It looks like Mike is taking 50 percent."

The only other fifty-fifty deal I had ever heard of was the one Elvis signed with Colonel Tom.

I got the impression that Bruce had never looked at it. I'm not even sure he had a lawyer when he signed it. I started asking more questions. And then he started asking questions.

It wasn't personal. I liked Mike when I first met him and I like him now. I just didn't like him when he was throwing me out of what was going to be the band back in 1972. And even then he was actually doing me a favor. All I missed was traveling around the country in a fucking station wagon.

The real problem with Mike, ultimately, wasn't just the issue of money. Mike came from the tough-guy camp. Lots of management guys in the '50s and '60s were either Mob related or just as tough as the Mob because that's who they were dealing with.

The business was full of them. Peter Grant and his hit man Richard Cole beat up Bill Graham's security guys. Don Arden hung competitors out windows. Mike Jeffery may have had Jimi Hendrix murdered and then got blown up in a plane.

Even Colonel Tom and Albert Grossman were in the tough-guy group. The colonel had possibly killed somebody in his native Netherlands. And who can forget that wonderful image of Grossman and Alan Lomax rolling around in the grass field of the Newport Folk Festival after Lomax declared the Paul Butterfield Blues Band didn't belong there?

But their time had come and gone. The modern Managers are more like David Geffen, Irving Azoff, and Jon Landau. Intellect over muscle. Persuasion over threat.

Plus, Bruce had discovered publishing and found out he didn't control his own songs. A lawsuit ensued, and things were gonna get worse before they got better.

I continued trying to get out of the Jukes business. I met Steve Leber and David Krebs, who managed Aerosmith and KISS and had invented the Rock T-shirt, for promotional purposes only at first, with no thought of selling them. I met Tommy Mottola, who had Hall and Oates and a few others. He had a little bit of that tough-guy thing I liked.

While I was mulling that decision over, I started meeting all the Agents.

Every single one of them started the conversation the same way. "So, you've probably already met with Frank, but here's what we can do . . ."

By the time the fourth guy said it, I was thinking, Whoever the fuck this Frank is, that's the guy I want.

Frank turned out to be Frank Barsalona, the third of the five important guys that would change my life, and another lifelong friend.

After brief semistardom in childhood as an urban yodeler (you heard me right), Frank became a very young Agent at General Artists Corporation (GAC) when Rock was merely a tiny department next to the janitor's closet. The real Agents were dedicated to the "real" showbiz of the time—movies, TV, and singers of Popular standards.

One day, early in 1964, GAC's Rock guy quit, and Frankie made one of the biggest moves of his life. He told the boss he'd like the job. The boss laughed at the kid's chutzpah but cared so little about the teenage market that he tossed him a booking book and said, "Go ahead, kid, knock yourself out."

The conventional wisdom at the time was that Rock and Roll was pretty much over. Elvis had been drafted. Chuck Berry was in jail. Buddy Holly, Ritchie Valens, and the Big Bopper had died. Dion became a junkie. Eddie Cochran was killed and Gene Vincent crippled in the same car accident. Bo Diddley went to Texas to become a US marshal. Little Richard saw Sputnik, considered it a sign from God, and became a preacher, and Jerry Lee Lewis was blackballed because people thought he had married his fifteen-year-old cousin (she was actually thirteen).

One of the first tests they threw at Frank was the difficult, perhaps impossible, job of booking a group from England. One of the agency's big relationships, Sid Bernstein, was all hot about these Brits. If it had been anybody else, they would have ignored him entirely. There had never been a successful *anything* out of England.

The bosses gave it to the kid, so he'd fail and go back to the mail room where he belonged.

Frank talked a Washington, DC, promoter into booking the English group, who happened to be the Beatles, and went down and witnessed the insanity that followed. He decided that not only was teenage Rock not over, it was just getting started.

He quit GAC a month later and started Premier Talent, the first agency dedicated to Rock, and single-handedly changed the world.

I've started to write a book about him a thousand times, and still hope to, but here is how Frank created the infrastructure of the Rock era, which flourished for thirty years:

- He introduced the game-changing concept that the first thing that matters is how good a band is live. Records and radio success will follow. This was a completely original thought.

- He divided the country into regions like Salvatore Maranzano did for the Mob.

- Like Charles Luciano did for the Mob after he whacked Maranzano, Frank stopped using the old Mustache Pete promoters, who hated Rock and were mostly thieves. He put in Young Turks like Don Law in Boston, Larry Magid in Philly, and Ron Delsener in New York, who owed their careers to him.

- He introduced the concept of *longevity* by telling the promoters they would lose money on a new band's first tour, break even or make a little on the second, and make money every tour after that. Sacrifice would be rewarded with loyalty.

The results were amazing. What had once been a novelty was suddenly a legitimate business. Well, maybe not fully legitimate, but a real business. With a future.

I started calling Frank the Godfather. *Capo di Tutti Capi.* Boss of All Bosses.

Frank immediately took on the Jukes. I had an ulterior motive. Bruce was at the William Morris Agency, and from what I could see they were not in Frank's league.

I wanted Bruce with the Godfather, the best with the best, and started making moves to make it happen.

Dion was doing an album with Phil Spector in Los Angeles, and he invited me to a session. Spector sessions were as legendary as the music that came out of them.

I wanted to bring Bruce, but I was a bit trepidatious, as the Cowardly Lion might say.

The press had been making a big deal about the Spector influence in "Born to Run," though in fact it was just one of a number of elements in the production. I wondered how Spector would react. Would he see it as a tribute? A rip-off? He didn't have the most stable reputation even then.

Still, a Phil Spector session at Gold Star with the Wrecking Crew! Engineered by Stan Ross or Larry Levine! Only Jack Nitzsche was missing.

I had to take the chance.

Dion walked us in and put us on the couch facing the studio. The board was behind us, which was a typical studio configuration in those days. That way, guests would be out of the way of the Producers and Engineers.

Spector comes in already talking a hundred miles an hour. He nodded in our direction and began a three-hour Don Rickles–style monologue that would have played well in Vegas.

They'd do a take every half hour or so, and the Engineer made slight adjustments, but the rest of the time Phil went around the room, musician to musician, making musical suggestions in the form of insults or just doing straight-out insults for the fun of it.

He started off with a gallon jug of *paisano* wine, which my grandfather used to drink, and it was gone by the end of the session.

And yes, he was waving his gun around threatening to kill Hal Blaine if he missed the fill going to the third verse again, occasionally screaming, "Don't embarrass me in front of Bruce Springsteen!"

I felt bad for Dion, who was stuck in the vocal booth trying to make a serious record while everybody else was laughing their asses off.

I wonder if anybody ever filmed Phil doing his act. It was shtick, do a take, shtick, do a take, shtick, until it seemed like the song was literally an afterthought. Then, with five minutes left, he'd get a perfect take. The whole thing was a Spector rope-a-dope!

Of course, a picture of us all together would have been nice.

But I never think of these things.

nine

I Don't Want to Go Home

(1975)

Art can provide insight, inspiration, motivation, even information, but at the very least it communicates you are not alone.

—THE UNWRITTEN BOOK

The '70s were the worst time in history to record.

Virtually every record sounded great in the '50s and '60s, and they would sound great again in the '80s and beyond. But in the '70s most recorded music sounded weird. Artificial. Claustrophobic.

The reason? Engineers had temporarily taken over. There's a reason most Engineers don't become great Producers and most Producers aren't great Engineers. They require two very different, complementary sensibilities.

Engineers have relationships with electrons and digits and knobs and meters, the science of sound, which is one-quarter of the record.

Producers deal with the songs, the arrangements, the performances, the living, breathing people. They rely on their own taste to shape emotional content. That's the other three-quarters of the record.

For a brief time in the '70s, the Engineers wrested control from the Producers and the Artists, resulting in total separation of instruments for the purpose of "complete control."

Lots of padding on the walls! Get those buzzes out of the drums! More rugs! Separation! Separation! Separation!

Everything that makes Real Music want to throw up.

Then, during the mix, the Engineers would reproduce room sound, resonance, buzzes, and hums to make the records more exciting! Really.

That was the state of the art when I found myself lying on the floor as horns were being overdubbed for Bruce's new song, "Tenth Avenue Freeze-Out."

It was only the fourth time I'd been in a recording studio.

The first time was when my teenage band the Source recorded my first song, "Traveling."

The second time was up at 914 Sound Studios, when I got kicked out of what was going to be the band.

The third time was also at 914, when Bruce played me "Born to Run."

So I was on the floor thinking, This is the big time? This is the music business we've worked our butts off to get in? This boring sound made worse by this terrible horn chart?

I remember Mike Appel looking like he regretted taking out that second mortgage to pay for this catastrophe.

Bruce did the last thing in the world the gang wanted him to do, which was to ask my opinion. "What do you think?"

"Fucking sucks," I said. There was no muffler between my brain and my mouth in those days. All I knew was my friend was trying to make a record and these guys were fucking it up.

Silence. A nervous chuckle or two. But Bruce knew it sucked, or he wouldn't have asked me. "So go fucking fix it then," he said, pretending to be mad so everybody knew who was boss.

So I did, pretending to be the loyal soldier doing his duty to make sure everybody knew he was boss.

This was in the earliest days of the nickname. I myself was a local boss, very respected, and at various points, more popular than he was. When the nickname started, it was just Bruce having fun, imitating Frank Sinatra. Nobody took it seriously until a respected boss like me joined up, which no one could believe, and started referring to him as *my* boss. That's when he became *the Boss.*

By then, I had been arranging the horns for the Jukes for a while. "Tenth Avenue" was a Stax-type song, but they were playing trumpet, tenor sax, and baritone sax, so I separated out the baritone, more of a Motown move (Stax typically didn't use a bari) and gave the trumpet and tenor some simple Memphis Horns–type riffs.

To explain what I wanted, I sang them the parts like I did every day in Jersey. I didn't know the guys were the biggest horn players in New York, the Brecker Brothers and Dave Sanborn. I don't think it would have mattered if I did. I believe they would have taken riff ideas from the maintenance guy just to get the session over with.

According to one of Dave Marsh's books, that was the moment Jon told Bruce that maybe I should join the band. Who knows? We're all making up half of this shit anyway.

On return visits, I managed to catch two of the coolest moments of the entire album. The amazing trumpet and stand-up bass on "Meeting Across the River," with Randy Brecker, again, and Richard Davis, who had played bass on *Astral Weeks*! Whoa. And the full sixteen-piece string section on "Jungleland," of which only about five seconds was used.

The Engineer for those sessions was a skinny, very Sicilian or Napolitano looking, very New York dude named Jimmy Iovine.

Jimmy . . . what can I say? He was a character like most of us, only a little more so. To call his life charmed was . . . well, let's just say that compared to him, Snow White couldn't pick a horse!

Remember *Welcome Back, Kotter*? Picture Arnold Horshack. That was Jimmy. One day, he was an assistant Engineer watching his boss Roy Cicala record John Lennon's *Rock 'n' Roll*, which Phil Spector was producing. Either Lennon or Spector got into an argument with Cicala, who walked. Lennon pointed to Jimmy: "You! Kid! Get in the chair." Jimmy faked his way through it, and suddenly he was the guy that recorded John Lennon. The King of the Parlay had begun his climb.

Jimmy wore Capezio ballet shoes, which no heterosexual from New Jersey had ever seen before, and he became Jimmy Shoes. The shoes were more than a nickname. They symbolized his whole being. He acted like a millionaire when he had absolutely nothing, and it became a self-fulfilling prophecy. He managed to drive a Mercedes and live on Central Park South on an assistant Engineer's income. I shit you not.

No furniture. I remember him, me, and Bruce going shopping for pillows to sit on. We were at the Navarro Hotel right down the block.

And he was sleeping with models, actresses, singers, DJs, while being broke like the rest of us.

I loved this guy. We bonded immediately.

He acquired an additional nickname soon enough, as people began to notice his extraordinary ability to change his personality, chameleon-like, to suit different situations. For a while he became Split-Screen Iovine. But that wasn't used as much as Shoes.

This was also the period where I tried to get Bruce to change the name of the band.

He had started calling it the E Street Band, which I didn't get. Not only did it have no real resonance or meaning, but it was named after the street where Davie Sancious's parents lived—a guy who was no longer in the band!

We had a softball team at the time. No idea how or why. We were pretty good. We'd regularly play and beat other bands like Crosby, Stills, and Nash, who had the disadvantage of not only running around the field but smoking it.

Our team was called the E Street Kings, which combined the name of the band with a line in "Backstreets." I tried to talk Bruce into changing the band name to follow the lyrics.

How much cooler would that have been?

Bruce Springsteen and the Duke Street Kings!

Fuhggedaboudit!

The E Street Band had like seven gigs lined up for when *Born to Run* came out. Bruce had decided to try fronting, singing without playing, so he asked me to play guitar for those shows. It didn't exactly make Southside or Popovich happy, but I told them I needed a break. I wasn't exactly sure what Ms. Destiny had in mind, so I was keeping my options open.

I had mixed feelings about where Bruce was going musically.

My issues started with the piano.

I was never a big keyboard fan, which was why I never got into the entire Progressive Rock genre, except for Procol Harum and the Left Banke, the two that invented it. Piano for me was Nicky Hopkins in the Rock world, Lowell "Banana" Levinger's electric Wurlitzer in the Country/Folk/Rock world of the Youngbloods, or Otis Spann and Lafayette Leake in Blues. A color instrument to complement the guitars. And sometimes not there at all.

Roy Bittan, the E Street pianist, was obviously overqualified for Rock and Roll. And still is! He had that Broadway-meets-popular-standards accompanist style of providing *all* the music, all the time. We had to literally tie one hand behind his back so he would fit into the less grandiose albums that came after *Born to Run*. He was simply too good.

What I didn't realize until later was that Bruce was not intending for us to be a traditional Rock band, making traditional Rock music. He didn't want the instruments playing the traditional roles all the time. He was imagining something else, something bigger. A marriage of Broadway storytelling, Gospel inspiration, and Rock dynamics. So Roy's style was essential.

We all had to adjust. Having both piano and organ indicated a Gospel influence, and like the other two most notable bands that used both piano and organ, the Band and Procol Harum, we were a hybrid from day one.

The church is where theater probably began in the first place. You've got to believe Scorsese's first infatuation with drama had to happen in the Catholic Church. The black Baptist Church is *all* theater.

I'm sure Bruce was absorbing some of the theatricality that had emerged in the Rock world. It had begun with Mick Jagger, who was transformed by his acting role in the film *Performance*, continued with David Bowie, became Glam and Disco, peaked with KISS, Alice Cooper, and George Clinton's Funkadelic, and ended up with Meat Loaf—an actor who modeled his style on a completely fictionalized idea of Bruce, to the point where he used Roy Bittan and Max Weinberg on his breakthrough album.

I didn't get it. Any of it. I was a street kid stuck in tradition, in Rock that was autobiographical and more straightforwardly authentic. It would take me a few years to understand how Art can illuminate life by illusion, abstract expressionism, distortion, surrealism, and exaggeration.

While I had been working a jackhammer on 287, my friend had never stopped searching and would keep reinventing himself until he found the mother lode. It was only an album away.

The *Born to Run* gigs included five days at the Bottom Line, on West Fourth between Mercer and Greene. It's gone now, like so many other of

Rock's sacred sites. It's a damn shame. Rock history should be preserved just like the George Washington Slept Here joints.

That's why I tried to save CBGBs, the historic club where Punk was born, when they came to me at the eleventh hour, even though I knew it was a lost cause. Wouldn't it have been amazing if a hundred years from now some teenage band could play on the stage where the Ramones and Richard Hell invented Punk?

Around that time, I went to the Bottom Line with Bruce to see the Dictators, who had just released their first album, *Go Girl Crazy*. We loved the hilarious brilliance of writer/singer Andy Shernoff (spelled Adny in those days) and the sheer lunacy of the group's MC, Handsome Dick Manitoba, who wore an old wrestling costume and did inexplicable, completely inappropriate intro raps. Humor hadn't existed in Rock since the Mothers' *Freak Out!* ten years earlier. What closed the deal for us was the backing vocalists on their cover of "California Sun."

> *And I'd Mouse,*
> *(And I'd Mouse),*
> *And I'd Robot,*
> *(And I'd Robot),*
> *And I'd Twist,*
> *(And I'd Twist)*
> *And I'd Shistanoobah)*
> *(And I'd . . . what?)*

Bruce had brought back Marlon Brando's leather-jacket look from the *Wild One*, which he'd wear on the cover of *Born to Run* and which the Ramones would soon adopt as a permanent tribute to teenage angst.

As we walked in to the Bottom Line, somebody yelled, "Hey, punk!"

I stopped and turned to Bruce. "I know you're in the business now, so you gotta act civilized, but you want me to go deal with this guy?"

He laughed. "No, it's a new thing. They mean it as a compliment."

He seemed OK with it, so I pretended I understood.

Our Bottom Line gigs were in August 1975, a week of doubleheaders that faced the stiffest of all possible headwinds at that time: the deadly accusation of hype.

Before joining Bruce's camp, Jon Landau had been the king of Rock journalists. After a 1974 show in Boston, he had written in the *Real Paper* that "he had seen rock and roll future and its name was Bruce Springsteen."

The world saw that lavish praise and showed up to put us down. In those days, authenticity still mattered. Hype was the enemy. But in this case, the hype was based on a misunderstanding.

Jon didn't say "rock and roll's future." He said "rock and roll future."

He did not mean that Bruce was, as the Dictators put it, *the next big thing!* He meant that Bruce was evolving Rock by using all the Artforms that came before him. The literature of Dashiell Hammett, Raymond Chandler, and James M. Cain. The films of John Ford, Elia Kazan, and Jacques Tourneur. The poetry of Rimbaud, Whitman, and Ginsberg. The explosive palette of Van Gogh and the formal invention of Picasso. Not to mention the audacity of Little Richard and Elvis Presley, the craft of the Beatles, the sex of the Stones, the social observation of the Kinks, the vision of Pete Townshend and the power of the Who, the blue-collar frustration of the Animals, the confessional lyrical genius of Bob Dylan, the spiritual elevation of Van Morrison, the musical ambition of the Byrds, the dark cinema of the Doors, and the historical breadth of the Band.

That's what Jon Landau meant, if you're asking me.

The pioneers of the '50s invented Rock. The Renaissance acts of the '60s elevated it to an Artform. Bruce was determined to create work that would not only distract, entertain, and transport but also educate, stimulate, and inspire. He wanted to provide irrefutable proof that life had meaning.

If an audience didn't leave a show feeling substantially better than when they arrived, we had failed. The E Street Band was delivering something that hadn't been delivered in its purest form since the Beatles.

Hope. Not hype.

Landau got there in that same article: "On a night when I needed to feel young, he made me feel like I was hearing music for the very first time."

Three hundred people? Four hundred? I don't know how many jammed into the Bottom Line twice a night for five straight days, or how many of them had come to scoff.

But a funny thing happened on the way to the hype. We lived up to it. We blew the audience's mind.

We had a big advantage. We'd been making our bones playing live for ten years by then, and we had done our residency as a dance band at a time when people had mostly stopped dancing. It took extra energy to get the crowd moving, and we carried that energy into the Bottom Line, and every show since.

One other thing happened at the Bottom Line. A big thing.

"Stevie, meet Maureen." It was Twig, aka Mark Greenberg, one of those friends who appeared out of nowhere and seemed like he had always been there. He was on our softball team. And since I don't know where Twig came from or why we even had a softball team, my memory tends to write the whole thing off as a *Twilight Zone* episode or a dream.

Except that I met Maureen.

Wow! Was she fine! Sexy. A New Jersey Brigitte Bardot. Always the prettiest girl in the room. Still is. Smart, too, as it turned out. I always found smart sexy and later found out there's a word for that, "sapio-sexual." And boy, was I a sap for her. All the way.

She had been a ballet dancer and a clothing designer, had gone to an Arts school in Newark and then the High School of Performing Arts in Manhattan. She had an encyclopedic knowledge of '60s music and literature and had studied acting with Herbert Berghof, Stella Adler, and Bill Hickey.

I'd never met anybody quite like her. Before or since.

I started pursuing her immediately. But she managed to fight me off for quite a while. Did I mention she was smart?

After we conquered New York, it looked like Bruce's career wasn't over after all. I figured I might as well stick around to see how the story ended.

The seven gigs I joined for turned into seventeen cities and nine-teen shows between New York and October: places like Atlanta, Austin, Chicago, Minneapolis, and Omaha. In Milwaukee, just before we went onstage, the theater had a bomb threat. The place was emptied and every seat checked. It took hours. The rumor was that some white supremacist group thought Bruce was Jewish.

In those early days, the record company threw after-parties in nearly every city. And in Europe, every country. Now if you see the record company once per tour, you're lucky. During the delay, they decided to have the party before the show.

We got plastered. I have never seen Bruce so drunk in public. On our way back to the theater, he decided to climb onto the roof of the car while we were going seventy miles an hour on the highway. I had to use all my strength to hold on to him to stop him.

Onstage, we reverted back to our drunken bar-band days, which were not that far behind us at that point, opening with Chuck Berry's "Little Queenie."

It was one of the best shows ever.

Next stop, Hollywood.

We were ready for our close-up.

ten

LA A-Go-Go

(1975–1976)

True bliss is a perfect drum fill.

—THE UNWRITTEN BOOK

The Roxy was the Bottom Line of LA, the showcase club for serious new contenders.

Rumors had Phil Spector and half of Hollywood in the crowd.

We opened with either "When You Walk in the Room" or "Needles and Pins"?

I know how hard this is to believe, but by 1975 just acknowledging the '60s existed was a revolutionary act. That's how fast music was progressing.

I glanced up midway through the first song and saw Warren Beatty, Jack Nicholson, Jackie DeShannon, David Geffen, and Cher. I didn't look up again.

We were something new for the jaded world of entertainment. We were characters, but the real thing. Journalists were having a hard time believing we weren't some company invention. We had an unusual amount of personality and played real good. A New Jersey bar band. Quite exotic.

Bruce's songs had become even more cinematic with "Born to Run," and the unique combination of elements in his art—a little Dylan, a little Orbison, some James Brown and Van Morrison—kept the cognoscenti off-balance. Onstage, we were a Rock and Roll Rat Pack with me in the Dino role and Clarence a Sammy on steroids.

We had the best light man in the world, Marc Brickman, a street character from Philly. I called him Mookie after we saw *Mean Streets*. Mookie's talent made the songs come alive. He heightened the drama. He made the audience pay attention. And all of it was done with a couple of friggin' Christmas bulbs and a flashlight.

The Roxy had been opened back in 1973 by Elmer Valentine and Lou Adler.

Elmer was a cop in Chicago who "retired" under murky circumstances in the early '60s and took a trip to France, where some friends took him to a new thing, a "discotheque" called Whisky a Go Go. It was a club where a DJ played records and people danced, an adult version of the '50s "record hop," where famous radio DJs appeared in high school gyms.

Elmer liked the idea so much that he came back, moved to LA, and opened his own Whisky a Go Go in the heart of the Sunset Strip. He immediately changed the concept to include live music and installed Johnny Rivers and his group as his house band. Everyone played there: the Byrds, Love, the Doors, Buffalo Springfield.

The Whisky started a nightlife empire. Elmer opened the Trip and, with Lou Adler and Mario Maglieri, the Rainbow Bar and Grill, and the Roxy, which replaced the Whisky as the showcase club for up-and-comers. Including us.

After our Roxy shows, I hung out with Elmer, who took a liking to me. He took me to the exclusive On the Rox club upstairs and threw a Hollywood party at his house in our honor, where he poured me my first hundred-dollar wine.

I didn't know wine could cost that much or taste that good.

He also loaned me one of his beautiful girlfriends for the night. I mean literally. The whole experience was surreal.

It was like walking through a movie. I felt like Peter Fonda in *The Trip*, minus the acid. Or like *Psych-Out* come to life. Jack Nicholson was standing right there!

The LA women were exactly what every Jersey boy dreamed about. Friendly, beautiful, openly sensual, casually sexual, surprisingly intelligent, totally in control of their own destiny, no games, no talking them into anything. They were just there to have a mutually enjoyable experience with you.

They actually made eye contact instead of avoiding it like the East Coast girls, who mostly still treated sexual pleasure as something reluctantly tolerated instead of sought after.

It was a little intimidating at first. You could see why societies down through the millennia had done everything they could to discourage women's true liberation. Unleashed female sexuality is an awesome force of nature. They fully expected to get their orgasms just like you did, so you had to bring it! Fortunately I had developed an early habit of making sure the girls came first, so I left them with nice thoughts about Italian kids from New Jersey. Richie Sambora would thank me later!

LA in the '70s was a rare magical paradise that made this mostly miserable life worth living. Elmer was conscious of that. He knew how to make your day. Loved him a lot.

As close as we were, I didn't find out his single most amazing achievement until I was doing research for my radio show thirty years later.

When he built the Whisky, he had no perfect spot for the DJ booth, so he built a see-through plexiglass cage and suspended it over the dance floor. On opening night, the female DJ didn't show, so Elmer drafted the cigarette girl, Patty Brockhurst, to spin the discs. *Mad Men* didn't make it up.

Patty was West Hollywood uninhibited. The fact that she had a miniskirt on in a glass cage didn't bother her at all. As she played the records, she danced to them, much to the salacious thrill of the boys below. The crowd loved it so much that Elmer built two more cages. One of the girls, Joanna Labean, created the costumes of fringed skirt and white boots. And that's how my lifelong friend Elmer Valentine invented the go-go girl!

Now that's a legacy! Fuck everything else.

My first trip to Cali included a memorable encounter with LA's finest, when I crossed the street and two patrol cars came screeching up. I was ordered against the wall by four cops with guns drawn—for jaywalking!

Playboy wanted to do a profile of me, and I brought Jimmy Iovine with me to the interview. The interviewer asked why Jimmy was there.

"He's one of my guys," I said. Anything went. We were hot. It was fun to be hot. No worries. No rules.

Marty Scorsese invited us to a special screening of *Mean Streets*, partly because of the line in Bruce's "Jungleland," "wounded, not even dead," which was how the movie ended.

He also showed us some dailies of the new film he was starting to work on, *New York, New York*. Jon Landau was friends with Jay Cocks, who would become a lifelong, important friend of mine, and Jay was friends with Marty. It had been Jay and his wife, Verna Bloom, who had introduced Marty to Bobby De Niro.

In those days Bruce always wanted me with him. I was like his little brother, and he knew I was always watching his back. It was always a complementary relationship. He was—he is—a year older, and very much a mentor when it came to the Art and the Business. But there were some things that I did better, like arranging songs, and I always had more street smarts. I was—I am—much more connected to the social world, because I had to work in it, where he was always a bit distant, focusing on creating his own world and living in it.

I drove back from the screening with Marty in his new Lamborghini, and we talked about Marty showing Francis Ford Coppola the Robert De Niro scenes from *Mean Streets*, which convinced Francis that De Niro would be his perfect Young Vito. It was the type of conversation with the type of guy I'd looked forward to my whole life. Things were finally starting to make sense.

One of my big regrets was not staying in touch with Marty. Even though our paths would cross every few years, we never really had a chance to become the close friends we should have been.

We were still in LA when Bruce made the cover of both *Time* and *Newsweek*. In the same week! I couldn't believe it. There was my friend, a local freak, misfit, and outcast like myself, on the covers of two of the country's biggest magazines. That had only happened for a president or two, maybe an astronaut and a few popes!

I remember the *Newsweek* reporter asking the oddest questions, trying to trip us up. She thought we were fabricated, out of central casting. She could not possibly have conceived of the amount of work we had put in, ten years by then, to be secure enough with our craft to appear casual and inevitable.

I bought out both magazines at the newsstand and handed them out to everybody around the Sunset Marquis pool. Bruce was embarrassed to death. He ran and hid in his room and had a nervous breakdown. After all the work he'd put in to make sure he controlled his own destiny, he felt it slipping away. How quickly Fate can deal new cards.

He'd end up climbing up to his billboard on Sunset Boulevard and painting a mustache on himself or something like that.

I loved the covers. While Bruce always had an inner confidence that he'd make it, I didn't. Validation like that was a big relief to me. And to my parents, who could no longer deny that we were onto something.

But then again, that's exactly why I don't like being out front. You gotta deal with shit like that!

Back in New York, Jimmy Iovine told me he had a key to the Record Plant. "We should sneak in after hours and do some demos for the Jukes," he said.

We went in with the band as they were. Kenny "Popeye" Pentifallo, Kevin Kavanaugh, Alan Berger, and Billy Rush. We had horn players coming and going, so I don't remember how or why we ended up getting a horn section from Philly on the actual record.

It was hard to get used to how bad the studio sounded. All I wanted to do was start with how a band sounds when you walk into a room. I thought the outboard equipment (equalizers, compressors) were making things sound phony, so I had Jimmy turn them all off. When I wasn't looking, Jimmy unscrewed all the bulbs and used the equipment anyway. It wasn't the outboard stuff, as it turned out. It was the fucking '70s. Everything sucked.

How different was radio back then? Steve Popovich sent the demos to Kid Leo, the biggest DJ on the biggest station in Cleveland, and the maniac broadcast them and told his audience that Bruce wasn't the only thing happening in Asbury Park. There was a scene.

So since we were already getting airplay, wouldn't it be nice if we actually had an album?

The deal took forever. Luckily, Southside and I were having a good summer at Monmouth Park Racetrack, where his old man (picture

Ernie Kovacs) was teaching us how to read the racing form. So whatever Jimmy couldn't steal, we paid for with our track winnings.

Producing a record is like directing a movie or executive-producing a TV show. You're in charge. And while producing has psychological, creative, and business aspects, there are logistical responsibilities hanging over everything. The physical record is really four parts—composition, arrangement, performance, and sound. You want the first two done before you get to the studio, especially back in those days, when the clock was running to the tune of $150–$200 an hour.

Southside turned out to have a very recordable voice, and Jimmy did a great job. He had a habit of getting up extremely early—that just seemed to be his natural clock—and that led to a habit of dozing off during our sessions, which might start at midnight. I'd wake him up to rewind the tape and then he'd check back out. The hours were no fun for him. I loved him all the more for doing it.

For free of course, by the way. Although I gave Jimmy the first percentage point he ever received. I made it a regular policy to give all my Engineers points after that. And like me, they're all still waiting to collect.

I Don't Want to Go Home took about three weeks mixed.

On that first album, I began my lifelong habit of proudly wearing my influences on my sleeve, bringing in '60s Artists as a way of showing my gratitude and reminding the industry and the audience that they were put out to pasture way too soon. We were hoping to expose them to a whole new generation.

Jimmy and I would go to Umberto in Little Italy after the sessions and strategize taking over the world. This was only a year or two after Joey Gallo got whacked there.

Jimmy says to me, You're a natural at this producing thing. You should do more. Like who? I say. I don't know, he says. Let me think about it.

He set up a meeting with Joey Heatherton. I had lunch with her and she looked unreal. I suggested to her Lorna Bennett's Reggae version of "Breakfast in Bed," originally done by Dusty Springfield. She loved it but it never happened. Very sorry about that.

Then one night Jimmy brought up Ronnie Spector, who was in some kind of early retirement. I suggested we try her on the Jukes album first to see how it worked out.

Then I was talking to Popovich about how much I love New Orleans, and I told him I just wrote a Lee Dorsey / Allen Toussaint song for the Jukes. "Let's get Lee Dorsey," he said. We dragged him out from under the car he was working on in New Orleans (a scene later re-created by Bruce, unknowingly, in one of his videos). On one of our trips, the E Street Band played Lee's Ya-Ya Lounge to help him out. He wouldn't join us onstage until he sold every bottle of beer he had.

Not only did Steve Popovich tolerate us putting our heroes on the records, he encouraged it! I realize now nobody else on earth would have done such a crazy, blatantly uncommercial thing. He did it because it was cool. And he knew what cool was. And didn't give a fuck what the rest of the industry thought. He was a miracle. The perfect guy at the perfect time.

Like most first albums, our material came straight from our Pony sets. We had R&B like Solomon Burke's "Got to Get You off My Mind," Buster Brown's "Fannie Mae" (stolen note for note by the Stones for "The Under Assistant West Coast Promotion Man"), Ray Charles's "I Choose to Sing the Blues," and an album track from Sam and Dave, "Broke Down Piece of Man." We added some comic Doo-Wop for Popeye, I wrote three songs, and Bruce wrote two.

Not a bad first production, considering I jumped in and learned on the job. It even won an award or two. Credit should go to Jimmy, who always knew more than he appeared to know. Like all southern Italians.

Looking back, I have only one thought.

Since we paid for the first Jukes record ourselves, how come we've never seen one dollar in royalties?

Anybody know a good lawyer?

eleven

This Time It's for Real

(1977)

Brewster: You're a very bad man, Walker, a very destructive man!
Why do you run around doing things like this?

—CARROLL O'CONNOR TO LEE MARVIN, *POINT BLANK* (1967)

The crowd had been building for months.

Building toward this night.

New Jersey in general and Asbury Park in particular hadn't had a lot to cheer about lately. A malaise had been suffocating the country since Nixon's reelection in '72. Not quite the Great Depression following the Roaring Twenties, but in some ways worse.

The death of the 1920s was the death of a hedonistic society that could not have gone on forever without violating the philosophy that life is supposed to suck, which I believe was spray-painted on the side of the *Mayflower*.

The death of the '60s was far more profound. It was the death of a dream of a better society, a new way of living and thinking. The hippies were going to finally implement the ideals of the Founding Fathers. We may not have had their intellect, but goddamn it, we had their spirit!

And then that dream disintegrated, with the assassination of one hero after another, the uprising of a frustrated black population (riots, they were called, but they were really a matter of a seventh of our population waiting for the Civil War to end—still are), and the systematic dismantling of activist groups working toward a more equitable society, from the American Indian Movement to the Young Lords to the Black Panthers.

And just for good measure, Nixon took the dollar off the gold standard, which would begin a fifty-years-and-counting decline in the purchasing power of our currency, directly leading to the permanent malaise we all now live with.

Jersey needed some good news.

And it came. A local hero, Bruce Springsteen, was signed. That hadn't happened since the Critters in 1965. Now a second act, Southside Johnny and the Asbury Jukes, had followed. One local celebrity was a surprise. Two were a scene!

Another local boy, a crazy renegade record executive from Freehold named Steve Popovich, who would have everything to do with the success of the Jukes, was going to broadcast the news of this new scene to the entire nation to celebrate the debut album.

A national broadcast out of Asbury Park? Impossible. But there it was.

The first thing the regulars at the front of the long line extending down the boardwalk toward the Empress Hotel noticed was the new faces.

New names too. Not just the Boss, but the King (Jon Landau), the Godfather (Frank Barsalona), the Duke (Dave Marsh), and one obvious gangster, Kid Leo (Kid Leo), who made the Fonz look like Mother Teresa.

Was this a Rock concert or a prizefight?

Ronnie Spector and Lee Dorsey, who were guests on the first Jukes album, were there, and we started the show with a bang.

As the national broadcast approached, Iovine suggested I write a new song for the occasion. It was strange request. Open the show with a song not on the album we're promoting? It didn't make sense, but I liked the idea. It was a good example of his instinctive genius, which would soon make him the big success he became.

What we couldn't have known at the time was that this innocent request would profoundly affect my songwriting for the rest of my life.

Up until "This Time It's for Real," I had been writing typical Soul-based Rock songs. But the unusual circumstance, a national broadcast introducing us to the world, called for a more autobiographical approach. My first.

It was a major turning point in my artistic life, the archetype of the style that would inform all my work in the '80s. I summoned up all my suppressed feelings about our circumstances. The hopelessness of being late for the party, the underdog status of New Jersey, the frustration of nobodies wanting to be contenders. It all came pouring out, a desperate reach for salvation, a last chance at the title.

I will always be grateful to Jimmy for inspiring me. The song was different. It stood out. It wasn't written with another group or artist in mind. It was written for the Jukes.

After the broadcast, the Jukes hit the road for a combination of clubs and festivals. I came and went, sometimes joining them onstage for a few songs. The first festival I ever played was in Cleveland. I was always claustrophobic and never liked crowds. I didn't know the protocols of festivals, where you're supposed to tolerate drunken cowardly pussies throwing shit at the stage. When a drunk threw a bottle at the stage, missing Johnny by an inch, I jumped into the audience and went after him. Lucky for me, security got to him before I did.

The Jukes were building a lifelong audience the old-school way, one gig at a time. We were getting better every day and were anxious to get back into the studio.

And then we were, this time in the hallowed halls of the old CBS studios on Fifty-Second Street, a huge soundstage where many classics had been cut. Dylan's "Like a Rolling Stone," Count Basie, early Sinatra. The room was so big we actually beat the claustrophobic '70s curse.

First albums are always easy. You're recording your live show, probably one you've been doing for years. Add a new song or two, and you've got it. Second albums are made up of new songs that haven't been road tested.

This proved challenging for the journeymen Jukes, whose lack of studio chops started to show.

Remember I said that the process of record production is basically four things: composition, arrangement, performance, and sound.

Drums are the core of the Sound part. They must sound great for everything else to sound great. The drums are also the key to the performance part of the equation. Since overdubbing became the norm in the late '60s, the essential factor in whether a take is a keeper or not is the drums. Everything else can be redone.

When Rock recording started, nobody had the patience or budget to do take after take, waiting for a drummer to play in time or remember the important drum fills. That's why there were so many session drummers, even for acts like the Beach Boys (Hal Blaine), the early Kinks (Bobby Graham), and the Four Seasons (Buddy Saltzman).

One of my trademarks in the early days as a Producer was to make every attempt to record the real band. This one was a challenge.

I had become obsessed with the African music of Babatunde Olatunji, Sonny Okosun, and Fela Kuti, so I took my eye (and ear) off the sacred snare drum sound I had gotten so right on the first album. My bright, crisp, perfect snare became just another African tom-tom.

It worked, though, and was part of the production experience (and experimentation) that would make the first three Jukes albums very different from one another.

If the song "This Time It's for Real" was a mission statement, the rest of the album went back to the mission. Writing Soul-based Rock long after it was fashionable.

The album continued to acknowledge and pay tribute to the Jukes' musical heroes. With Southside equally enthusiastic about the idea, and with the proud, fatherly approval of Steve Popovich and his boss Ron Alexenburg, we reunited the Drifters, the Coasters, and the Five Satins.

Popovich even found Richard Barrett to play on "First Night," my first Doo-Wop composition. Barrett had played piano on the very first Girl Group hit, the Chantels' "Maybe" (and, somehow, bass and drums also—on a two-track recording!). He had worked with Frankie Lymon and Little Anthony and cowritten "Some Other Guy" with Leiber and Stoller, the song the Beatles were playing in the only film clip I've ever seen of them at the Cavern Club.

On the first Jukes album I had written with specific artists and styles in mind, and I continued that idea on the second.

"Some Things Just Don't Change" was in the style of Holland-Dozier-Holland (or Smokey Robinson) writing for the Temptations. "She's Got

Me Where She Wants Me" was straight Curtis Mayfield and the Impressions. "First Night" drew on Doo-Wop in general, though it leaned on Jerry Butler's "For Your Precious Love."

My cowrites with Bruce, including "Love on the Wrong Side of Town" and "Little Girl So Fine," were among my favorites. The huge room gave us a nice fat sound. I found "Without Love" on a recent Aretha Franklin album and did one of my favorite string arrangements, with a sixteen-piece string section, on it. They sounded great.

The room sounded so good I didn't even double the horns.

While Bruce was tangled up in his management lawsuit, we couldn't go into the studio or tour. And Bruce was out of money.

He told us at rehearsal at his house in Holmdel, after which he went to make his usual two-hour phone call with Jon.

There was a general grumbling within the band. We were at subsistence level, getting maybe $150 or $200 bucks a week. Amazing when I think about it now. And some of the guys had been getting outside work, big session respect, and serious offers.

We voted on whether to break up.

When the first three guys voted to leave, I stopped the voting and made a speech. Not exactly Mark Antony, but I needed to buy some time. "Give me a week," I said.

I went to my go-to guys, Popovich and Barsalona.

Pops came back to me twenty-four hours later.

"I got it," he says. "Ronnie Spector and the E Street Band on my new label Cleveland International." I always laughed when he said the label name out loud. You can't be Cleveland *and* International, I'd tell him. "I'll pay double scale for a two-song double session. That'll hold you for a few weeks."

Beautiful.

Popovich even had the song. Billy Joel had written a tribute to Phil Spector and the Ronettes, "Say Goodbye to Hollywood." It hadn't been a huge hit. Billy was still a year or two from having everything he did be a success. But it was perfect for Ronnie.

The day before the session, Billy's wife and Manager stopped me in the CBS hallway. "Who gave you permission to do this? Of course you'll need Billy there. What time are you starting?" I hadn't met Billy yet. He turned out to be a really great guy, but I don't suffer bullies gladly, then or now. And I am big on gender equality.

"Billy won't be needed, thank you," I said and kept walking.

She left in a huff. Maybe a minute and a huff (sorry, Groucho).

An hour later Pops called. "What the fuck did you say?!?" She had called him to curse me out, and not just me but him, Johnny, Bruce, Walter Yetnikoff, Phil Spector, and probably Garibaldi, Fiorello La Guardia, and Pope John II while she was at it.

"Can she stop the record?" I asked.

"No," he said.

"Then fuck her and her uppity fucking spoiled brat Long Island fucking condescending attitude," I suggested.

Truth is, she wasn't wrong. I should have invited Billy to the session, at least to watch. Of course, after our hallway encounter, I couldn't give her the satisfaction. How poor Billy lived with that horror is beyond Buddhism.

And so it transpired that the original Magnificent Seven gathered to make a little history with one of our childhood fantasies and make about a month's salary, which would keep the E Street Band intact until I got to Frank Barsalona.

That was my third string arrangement. I was getting better and better.

Life has its moments.

I wrote the B-side, "Baby Please Don't Go," which Nancy Sinatra would do a great version of a couple decades later.

The session ended the talk of the E Street Band breaking up. I guess that's what was meant by me occasionally being "unintentionally destabilizing."

Right around that time, Ronnie and I had a brief affair. Early on, she wanted to go to Puerto Rico. On the day we arrived, outside by the pool, we ordered our first drinks of the vacation.

I did some research later and found out there are two kinds of alcoholics. The ones that just drink a lot are bad enough. But then there's the kind whose blood has a chemical reaction with just one drink. She was one of those. Terrible. Freaky to witness. Instant change of personality. It's Jekyll-and-Hyde time.

And did I mention we were in Puerto fucking Rico? Which I already despised because the taxi driver tried to hustle me for a couple hundred from the airport, and I'd caught the blackjack dealer dealing seconds and bottoms from a mechanic's grip (remember, I was a gambler), and now I had a girlfriend who couldn't stand up or speak coherently.

Scared the living piss out of me. It remains one of my top ten nightmares of all time.

We made it home, and I got her help and put her on tour with the Jukes. Johnny was on the wagon at the same time.

She ended up OK, and our involvement gave her some much-needed confidence that put her back onstage, where she's enjoyed an entire second career ever since.

To this day, however, whenever she sings "Say Goodbye to Hollywood" live, she introduces it as "the song Bruce Springsteen produced for me."

I'm the invisible man.

What are you gonna do?

twelve

The Punk Meets the Godfather

Focus on the Craft, the Art takes care of itself.

—THE UNWRITTEN BOOK

I had been chasing Maureen ever since our Bottom Line gigs in 1975. I finally caught her on New Year's Eve, 1977.

On our first date, I dragged her to the seen-its-best-days Capitol Theatre in Passaic, New Jersey, for a Jukes concert. Every girl's dream of a romantic New Year's! But I felt obligated since it was their first theater gig, a major rite of passage, and I was still their Manager.

After she visited my world, it was time for me to visit hers. What I couldn't have known is that she was about to expand my understanding and perspective of Art from sketch pad to CinemaScope.

Maureen took me to my first ballet at the Metropolitan Opera House.

After playing joints my whole life, I felt like I was walking into the Palace of the Gods. The red plush velvet seats—not ripped and worn and stained like the Fillmore's—the massive velvet curtain, the incredible chandelier that went up as the lights went down. And then . . .

Tchaikovsky!

What a divine discovery. My first real experience with classical music was ballet music at its most exhilarating. Melodic. Dynamic. Enlightening. Supreme. Delicious. A brand-new trip.

The latest epiphany.

The ballet was full-length, my preference ever since. I need a story to be fully immersed and satisfying, no matter how metaphorical or adolescent it might be. *Swan Lake. The Sleeping Beauty. The Nutcracker. Coppélia. La Bayadère.*

I fell in love with Maureen, and with ballet soon after. We caught the end of the last great era, Baryshnikov, Kirkland, and the most extraordinary human being ever to grace a stage, Rudolf Nureyev. I've never felt such charisma from a stage before. He just exuded Greatness.

Maureen's influence wouldn't stop with ballet. She would turn me on to Impressionist Art, too, and we would immediately fuse the two. We began writing "Impressions," set pieces that opened on tableaus of impressionist paintings. The dancers would come to life, perform a short scene, and end up back in the positions of the painting. Like too many of my ideas, I didn't have the machine in place to finance or sell it, which left me with no practical reason to finish it.

What ballet and impressionism shared was that they opened me up to a bigger artistic vista. After experiencing a few amazing ballet performances, being a Rock star could never regain first place in my imaginary goals.

I began to see myself less as a performer and more as a Producer. An Irving Thalberg of Rock, overseeing the big picture as well as the granular details, able to creatively realize something that would thrill, inspire, and enlighten audiences. My comfort zone remained on stages and in studios. It was where I started and where I could do what I knew best. But I was thinking big! Bigger! Biggest!

It would take me thirty-five years to even get close to my new daydreams. But let's not get ahead of ourselves.

Popovich had temporarily saved the E Street Band, but his fix wouldn't last forever. There was only one solution.

I went to the Godfather.

I told Frank that it was time to make the move. I'd seeded the garden, mentioning his name several times to Bruce, telling him Frank stories and about how well we were doing with the Jukes, so it wouldn't be coming out of the blue.

"Talk to Bruce," I told Frank, "or maybe Jon Landau. He's someone Bruce trusts. Or Peter Parcher, his lawyer. Whatever. But we need you right now."

"What can I expect?" Frank asked.

"We need some gigs until this legal problem is settled," I said. "I'm sure Bruce could use some lawyer money; we're broke. We can't record, so the main thing we need is your juice."

"What else?" said Frank, always thorough in those days.

"Well," I said, "I guess if you really want to provide a little extra comfort, you might want to consider grabbing Bruce's new guy at William Morris, Barry Bell. He replaced Sam McKeith, who signed Bruce, and Bruce seems comfortable with him."

Half the band was ready to rebel. The Promoters thought we were damaged goods. The record company was down to a few guys who were keeping the faith. The agency couldn't help. And even the press was moving on to the next potential big thing. We were going no-fucking-where if we stayed where we were.

"We need you to pull the strings of the Promoters until we can get a new record done. Bruce needs your sponsorship, gabeesh? He needs a rabbi. Your endorsement will stop the bleeding. And the entire industry will have to give us a second look, including his own record company."

"OK," Frank said.

I'm not even sure Frank had seen an E Street show. I had taken him to the Stone Pony, where he'd seen Bruce jam, so he'd gotten a glimpse of his charisma. Maybe that was enough. Otherwise he was taking my word, and whoever else's, that we were something special and going somewhere.

I think the amount was a hundred grand. A lot now, a fucking lot then. A lifesaver. And Frank generously brought over Barry Bell, who is still with us.

Next thing you know, we were back on the road. We saw lots of half-empty halls, but we were alive and doing what we did best. And by June '77, we were back in the studio to make the new album, *Darkness on the Edge of Town*.

And a dark experience it was.

There's a documentary, directed by Thom Zimny from Barry Rebo's footage, that more or less covers it, but suffice it to say it wasn't pretty.

The intense life-and-death struggle of *Born to Run*, reaching for greatness, continued unabated.

We all briefly became drug addicts on this one. Except Bruce. He was the only guy I knew who never did drugs. He had his own vice, which was mentally beating the shit out of himself.

I had a drug dealer friend who was making runs to South America. While coke is never completely uncut because of the chemical process of making it, what he brought me was as pure as it could be. At the time, conventional medical wisdom said cocaine wasn't addictive, but I noticed after a while that I couldn't get out of bed without reaching for the vial. I only used for a year before quitting—almost a year to the day, in fact. Still, it helped the band get through the album. Lots of bathroom visits.

As if Jon's new role as Manager wasn't complicated enough, his unique set of skills, knowledge of culture, and experience with psychoanalysis made his other new role equally invaluable as he redefined the role of the Record Producer.

Not that he wasn't musical. He was and is very musical. But the E Street Band largely produced themselves, and I would be taking more responsibility for the music and sound over the next few records.

His far more important role and unique value was in helping Bruce analyze and discover the bigger picture. The themes he would be talking about and his artistic identity.

Bruce even having artistic aspirations was already odd. Very few Rockers were thinking that way. Jackson Browne maybe, and . . . who else?

Even the Beatles didn't think about such things until they were liberated from having to reproduce their songs live, which resulted in *Revolver*. Then their imaginations were free to take them to wonderful new bizarre places as varied as "Eleanor Rigby" and "Tomorrow Never Knows."

In spite of his game-changing accomplishments, Bob Dylan didn't seem to have any artistic pretensions at all.

Was Bruce being influenced by the early writers like Landau and Paul Nelson and Greil Marcus, who were suddenly recognizing and celebrating this new Artform and treating it seriously as such?

Our third generation was the first to inherit Rock as an Artform. The first two generations were working strictly off instinct and traditional definitions of showbiz success. Evolving through some organic inclination.

And because we inherited it, we immediately took it for granted. There were very few thinking of what we do as Art back then, and that's true to this day.

But Bruce was. And Jon. Conversations we thought might've been self-indulgent turned out to be quite fruitful after all.

Jimmy Iovine was still engineering, but from his experience with *Born to Run*, he knew that he'd have tons of downtime during Jon and Bruce's endless conversations. Maybe more than before, since Jon had brought in a wonderful character named Charlie Plotkin to help with the mix. Charlie had some big hits with Orleans (fronted by John Hall) and would do a Dylan album and other things later.

Bruce, Jon, and Charlie had two things in common. They liked to take their time, and they loved to talk. This was a deadly combination for the rest of us. Jimmy, who had attention deficit disorder even worse than me, would have never made it through alive if he hadn't stayed busy. When Bruce, Jon, and Charlie left to talk, Jimmy would tell me to get him when they came back and run down to Studio 2, where he was producing Patti Smith.

I had met Patti once at a party. Jimmy brought her. I was eating an ice-cream cone, and she walked right up to me and knocked it out of my hand. "You shouldn't be eating that shit," she said. It was like talking to Anybodys from *West Side Story*! I would grow to like her by getting friendly with her guitar player Lenny Kaye, who was completely responsible for her being in the Rock world.

The songs on *Darkness* were among Bruce's best so far, and I was proud of my contribution, which was a significant part of the arranging of the songs, but overall the sound of the record was a disappointment to me. I've gotten used to it now, but at the time it sounded stifled, choked to death, and flat, as if it was recorded with close mics in a padded room. Which it was. Nothing close to how the band actually sounded. When the record was reissued in 2010, I begged Bruce to let me remix it. "Are you out of your fucking mind?" he said. "People have been listening to it this way for thirty-five years—we're gonna change it now?!?"

Somewhere during this period, Bruce opened a vein of creativity that had waited years to be spiked. Suddenly, it was as if every song he had heard in his entire life was channeled through him, was rearranged at a molecular level, and came spilling out in song after song. After having only a few outtakes for *Born to Run*, he suddenly was writing forty, fifty, sixty amazing songs per record, and just as quickly rejecting them.

No one had ever done this before.

You're making an album, you write ten good songs and you put it out.

There was no exception to that rule.

I didn't understand it at the time. Now, I realize he was reaching for something new. A theme for the album he couldn't articulate. He was on a roll, and he was going to see where it led.

He was so determined to find a new identity, he began to separate the songs by genre, Art lyrics over here, Pop lyrics over there. No one had ever made that distinction before, and I felt strongly (and wrongly, as it turned out) that it was a mistake.

Songs got discarded, including some of the best ones. There was an entire album of Pop Rock greatness that was shelved for decades, finally emerging on collections of unreleased material and deluxe reissues like *Tracks*, *The Promise*, and *The Ties That Bind*.

Every outtake a lost argument.

Looking back, it's obvious now that any song resembling a love song or a Pop song wouldn't have made any sense.

With one exception. Early on, we had worked on a song called "Because the Night." It was a different kind of love song, something special, something darker because of its minor key. We spent far more time on it than any other song, and I contributed considerably to the tricky arrangement. I thought it would be our breakthrough.

One day, when Bruce and Jon went to talk, Jimmy motioned to me. "I want you to hear something," he said. I followed him down the hallway and he put me in the Producer's chair. And on came my arrangement of "Because the Night," sung by Patti Smith. That's how I found out it wasn't going on our record. A week's worth of work!

I was happy for Jimmy. The minute I stopped wanting to kill him.

Bruce did what he had to do. And you have to respect the discipline required to throw away songs other artists would build their careers on.

But here's the thing. Bruce didn't just throw away great songs. He changed his entire persona. *Born to Run*, the culmination of his first three albums, not only yielded his signature song but established what should have been his lifetime identity.

The Jersey kid, the ragamuffin rebel underdog, crossing the river and conquering the big city, saving the girl on the back of his motorcycle and riding off to . . .

Well, it was all romantic fiction.

The only remotely autobiographical song, "Tenth Avenue Freeze-Out," immortalized his relationship with Clarence and fantasized conquering the Big City! Which hadn't happened yet.

Bruce had painstakingly constructed an identity over the previous three years . . . and then realized he couldn't live there.

Born to Run had been an album about hope in the midst of despair, about escaping a dead-end life. It was all there in the last line of "Thunder Road": "It's a town full of losers / And I'm pulling out of here to win."

On *Darkness*, Bruce realized that escape was impossible, that he had been running from himself.

He decided to stay and fight.

To confront reality. Yes, the average working life was a struggle, but instead of denying his connection to it, he would stand with the working class. He would speak for them. It might have been a town full of losers, but it wasn't their fault. The game was rigged against them. He was gonna even up the odds.

Darkness was about Bruce accepting that he was his father's son and winning one fight for him. It's a premise I would revisit with the Jukes on "All I Needed Was You," a song I wrote about Johnny and his father based on *Somebody Up There Likes Me*.

The entire setting would flip from *Born to Run* to *Darkness*. From urban / suburban to rural / small town.

Throwing away songs? Try throwing away an entire identity! Try throwing away success! Every entertainer dreams of an audience defining you and liking you. When it happens, you wrap your arms around that miracle, embrace it with all your might, and pray it lasts forever.

It takes some big balls to say, Thank you, folks, I know I asked you to fall in love in with this guy I introduced you to, but I'm still evolving. We're making a U-turn here, and I hope you follow.

I realize now the gestation was so difficult because in many ways, *Darkness on the Edge of Town* was Bruce's first true album.

The first three albums were development in public. Good as they were (and *Born to Run* was magnificent), the identity he found on *Darkness* remained the core of his being from then on.

That's what all those long conversations with Jon Landau were all about, I bet.

But could that same meaningful conversation take place with thousands of strangers? We were about to find out.

Darkness was the beginning of a new template. Say it with the record, sell it with the tour.

From that moment on, we would never again go onstage without the intention of *saying something*. Bruce made sure the shows engaged the entire spectrum of emotions, from confidence to confession, catharsis to comedy, and all of it entertaining. And the soundtrack to that epic movie included a big part of the history of Rock every night.

Those shows required a support system that began with the management of Jon Landau and Barbara Carr and the crew, including exceptional members like Marc Brickman and George Travis.

But the stage was the front line. That was where the battle was waged, where we won or lost, where our job was to inspire and motivate and convince the masses that Rock was more than entertainment.

And we did.

We felt for the first time, after a few false starts, we were in sight of actually becoming Rock stars, which gave the tour a new intensity. After years of being off the road, we were like seven lions released from captivity.

Before that, we were still very much in the bar-band tradition, and graduating to Rock star meant new responsibilities, including finding a signature look, Rock and fashion being married from the beginning.

I had recently seen a triple feature of Sergio Leone's classic spaghetti Westerns and thought, That's it! I had a full-length duster made. No one had ever used that look in a Rock show.

In Saint Paul, the Promoter told me that a young local musician who had just released his debut album was at the show. The name made an impression: Prince. He left before I had a chance to meet him, but you know he was taking notes on my coat!

Every night, Bruce balanced out the darkness of the record with his own exploding exuberance. We transformed "Prove It All Night" into a two-guitar, show-stopping rave-up, among other things. The shows were marathons of ferocity and determination, sometimes stretching past the four-hour mark.

Radio had abandoned us, the industry had forgotten us, and the press had moved on, but we were gonna make sure you remembered that live show for the rest of your life.

Cocaine may have helped keep me going at first, during those months when I had to fly home from the Darkness Tour to record the Jukes' third album, *Hearts of Stone*, but ultimately the drugs started to burn me out.

The third Jukes record continued my evolution of the Rock and Soul hybrid, especially in my writing. I managed seven tracks before I fried, but they were good ones. My influences were beginning to become more integrated, and my songs felt like something new. Even though I was still recording in the '70s and hated the studio I was told had a great room sound but didn't.

I followed the pattern I used on *This Time It's for Real* by opening with an autobiographical song, "Got to Be a Better Way Home." Funny how the story went from "Here we come, breaking all the rules, and we're gonna win anyway" to "Geezus Fuck, the music business really sucks!" over just one year on the road. Musically it was pure Otis Redding.

"I Played the Fool" was all Smokey.

"Take It Inside" borrowed a bit of the Animals but was mostly original, as was "Next to You," which drew on Sam and Dave and the Temptations.

"This Time Baby's Gone for Good" was . . . Gene Pitney meets the Shangri-Las with a variation on a Townshend lyric and a Beatles bridge?

"Trapped Again," a fave I would eventually use myself, was a nod to blaxploitation. Johnny had the title, Bruce picked up a guitar and sang the chorus spontaneously, I did the rest.

Finally, there was "Light Don't Shine."

The other autobiographical number, along with the opener.

That is one fucking depressing song.

My father's barbershop quartet: Joe Dellabadia, Vern James,
Jim Black, Dad. *Van Zandt family*

(Facing page):
My mother,
Mary Lento,
in 1945.
Van Zandt family

(Above):
Grandpa Lento and me
in Watertown, 1950.
Van Zandt family

RnR rebel from birth.
Van Zandt family

Sister Kathi, Dad, Ma, Nana Lento, Jake, me, Maureen, brother Billy. *Van Zandt family*

Southside Johnny and legendary R&B singer Lee Dorsey. *Renegade Nation*

Salute! E Street Kings, 1976. *Valerie Penska*

First fan Obie with her two faves. *Billy Smith*

Ronnie Spector with the three Asbury capos. *David Gahr*

E Street Band, New York, 1979. *Joel Bernstein*

The Dimmer Twins. *Renegade Nation*

"The Godfather"
Frank Barsalona.
Renegade Nation

Getting married by Little Richard, New Year's Eve 1982. With best man Bruce and maid of honor Michelle. *Jim Marchese*

Our wedding party. From front: Brother Billy, Jimmy Iovine, Bruce, Harry Sandler, LaBamba, me, Maureen, Sari Becker, Gary US Bonds, Jack Cocks, Michelle Priarone, Obie, Monti Ellison, Maria Santoro, Jean Beauvoir, Max Weinberg, sister-in-law Lynn Angelo, sister Kathi, Ben Newberry, sister-in-law Gail Napolitano, sister-in-law Lori Santoro, Garry Tallent. *Jim Marchese*

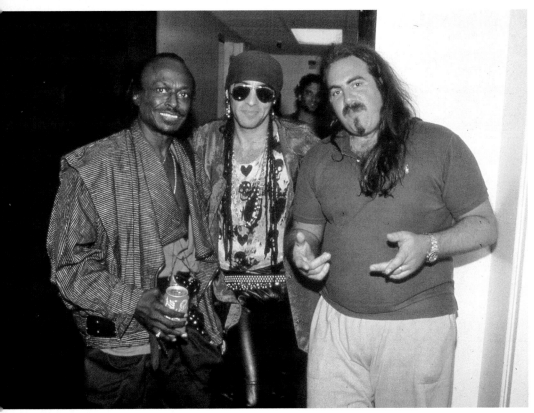

(Above): Big Youth, Lou Reed, Reuben Blades, John Oates, Danny Schecter, Jonathan Demme, and Hart Perry. ***David Seelig***

(Facing page, top): Honored in Atlanta by Coretta Scott King, Julian Bond, and Vernell Johnson. ***African Activist Archives***

(Facing page, bottom): Miles Davis and Arthur Baker. ***David Seelig***

(Above): With Bono and Jimmy Cliff.
Reuven Kopitchinski

(Left): At the '86 Grammys.
Ron Galella

(Facing page, top): With Abbie
Hoffman and Mark Graham,
National Convention of Student
Activists, 1988. *Debra Rothenberg*

(Facing page, bottom):
T. M. Stevens, '87. *Guido Harari*

With Gary Bonds, '84. *Mark Weiss*

My longtime assistant, Holly Cara Price. *Renegade Nation*

Sopranos premiere, 2000. *Scott Gries*

Nothing but fun working with David Chase on *Not Fade Away*.

Barry Wetcher—Paramount Vantage

Self-pity personified.

I was feeling abandoned by everybody. It could have been the drugs taking their toll, but there was more. Popovich had left to start his own label, Cleveland International Records. Lennie Petze, who had taken over, didn't have the faith. And the big boss, Ron Alexenburg, had his own problems, with his life being threatened by black activists who blamed him for the Jacksons leaving Motown for Epic.

I don't think I realized until that moment how important Steve Popovich had been as a supporter of our whole thing. Who else would have encouraged us to include '60s artists, a completely unfashionable thing to do?

The song reflected my first musical manifestation of unrequited infatuation. After wanting to be in the business my whole life, the business was not returning my love. I needed some commercial success to propel my dreams to the next level. But I kept getting stuck at first base.

Bruce gave me two final songs, "Talk to Me" and "Hearts of Stone," which I made the title track because it summed up the central emotion of the album. (My first thought for the album title was *Broken Hearts of Stone*, but Bruce thought it was too negative, so I left it more vague.)

The Jukes were ready to rerecord Bruce's songs, which we had cut with the E Street Band, but the budget was gone. Amazing how we went through $250,000 per album without a second thought in those days. We make fifty albums for that price at Wicked Cool Records these days. Literally fifty.

So I said fuck it and kept the E Street Band tracks for those two songs. We were one big family anyway, and since the Jukes were between drummers, Max was already playing drums on the album.

Thirty years later we would complete the circle when I gave the tapes to Bruce's Engineer, who took my horns off "Talk to Me" and put them back on his vocal version for *The Promise*.

Hearts of Stone ended up being our most acclaimed album. The Jukes were inches away from breaking through.

But there were obstacles.

The band got very little airplay because Rock radio, having discovered that profit could result from consistency, introduced into Paradise a virus called consultants. The first symptom of this virus was deciding that no bands with horns would be played on FM Rock stations.

Blood, Sweat, & Tears and Chicago didn't have to worry because they made their living in the Pop world, on AM radio. But the Jukes were Rock and Soul, which meant we needed FM radio, which meant we were fucked.

The good news was that even without airplay, we had gotten to the point where we were grossing a million dollars a year on the road. The Godfather was proud of that. I foolishly didn't take any commission as Manager, which I totally deserved, wanting Johnny and the band to make what they could.

But the lack of label support took its toll. After three increasingly acclaimed records, with one of the great live shows in the business, Epic dropped the Jukes to concentrate on Boston, the Jacksons, and "Play That Funky Music, White Boy!"

It was hard to blame them.

But I managed.

Still, *Hearts of Stone* had set the band up nicely for a new record deal, and it seemed like I might get back what I had put in.

At that point, Bruce wanted me with him in a hotel in New York while the *Darkness* drama unfolded, so I had no bills. Everything I made went into the Jukes, and when you added in the management commissions not taken, I was owed a couple hundred grand by then.

Since I hadn't been able to make up my mind on a Manager, I thought the safe thing for the band, and the safest way to get my money back, was to give the band to someone I could really trust, my personal lawyer. That way I could stay involved for management and production advice.

They made a nice new deal and took the money and ran.

I let it go but stayed pissed off for about fifteen years until the Better Days reunion in the '90s.

Which brings up the subject of the great train robberies of Rock. Here are three:

1. It remains one of the great sources of wonderment how Allen Klein ended up owning the first ten Rolling Stones albums. I asked Peter Parcher, who was involved, to explain it to me. He did, in great detail. I still don't get it.

2. The Animals got their first two singles from Bob Dylan's debut album. "Baby Let Me Take You Home" was derived from "Baby, Let Me Follow You Down" (a folk song credited to Eric Von Schmidt but actually written by Reverend Gary Davis, Blind Boy Fuller, or who knows who). And then there was "House of the Rising Sun," which was public domain, which means whoever adapted or arranged it got the publishing royalties. Because there wasn't room for all the band's signatures, only keyboard player Alan Price's name was on the record. When the song became a worldwide hit, Price took the cash and split!

3. Jack Ely, the lead singer of the Kingsmen, sang the classic version of "Louie Louie." Meanwhile, the mother of Lynn Easton, the drummer, registered the band's name. For herself. As the record hit, Easton declared himself the lead singer and Ely and guitar player Mike Mitchell quit. Easton is the only one anyone has ever seen perform it, and he didn't sing it.

Like Nick Tosches said, showbiz—the dirty business of dreams.

We closed out 1978 still on the road with *Darkness*, still fighting for our lives onstage.

We really became a band on that tour. Longevity, if you can survive it, brings unexpected rewards. That's why bands should stay together. It's not just talent, it's loyalty and, over time, history. Four of us originals left.

You can maybe find the talent. You can probably buy the loyalty. But you can't replace the history. And believe me, when it's a bad night—tough conditions, new audience, rainy and cold—or even a particularly good one, you don't want to look to your left and see a gun for hire.

You want to see me.

thirteen

Baptism

(1979–1980)

We essentially do three things. We learn, we teach, we practice
our craft. Any day we do all three of those things is a good day.
—THE UNWRITTEN BOOK

The first time I quit the E Street Band was in 1979, just as *The River*
sessions were beginning.

We were sitting on amplifiers in Studio A at the Power Station, Bruce
and me.

"Listen," I said. "I know your capacity to withstand suffering is
infinite. And the songs keep getting better and better. But I believe
in something called quality of life. For me the journey is as important as the destination. I can't do this thing again. You don't need me
around."

He thought for a minute and said, "Produce it with me."

Just like that. Maybe he had it in mind already.

"For real?" I said.

"For real," he said.

He knew I was a band guy, and it was time to make a band record.
For real. And that's what we did.

The River started the same way as *Darkness*, with the band working out
material at Bruce's house in Holmdel. He would come in every day with

ideas, sometimes just a chorus and a groove, sometimes a verse, rarely more than that.

One of my gifts is the ability to finish songs other people start. Give me thirty seconds and I can hear the whole thing. As satisfying and important as writing can be, my favorite craft is still Arranging.

I won't bore you too much, skip ahead if you want to, but I'll do a quick summary of the four aspects of Arranging.

The configuration of a song. This runs dangerously close to the grey area of composition. Do you repeat a verse? Double the chorus? Add a bridge? A solo? Where do you put them? Do you modulate to add the element of audio surprise?

Choosing which instruments to use. Does a song need an organ? Which kind? B-3? Farfisa? An acoustic guitar? Doubling the electrics? Congas? Tambourine?

What parts do individual rhythm instruments play on the basic track? What's the bass drum beat? The bass line? Should the piano play eighth notes in the chorus? How much distortion should the guitar have?

And the typical horn and string charts.

I loved it all. I sang or played the parts, since like most Rock musicians I don't read or write music.

I took the rough sketches and fed back a bunch of ideas, many of which Bruce used. At worst, my suggestions stimulated another round of ideas. Incredible as it seems, he maintained this pace for months at a time, bringing in three or four new ideas a day.

One day at rehearsal, he played a circular chord pattern in a medium groove. We all fell in. He told Danny to play the Four Seasons riff on the glockenspiel (from "Dawn") and started singing, "Everybody's got a hungry heart."

Then he got his daily Jon call. Everybody was tired, and the call usually meant the day was over. (They're probably still talking right now!) But there was something about the groove. "Let's keep it going," I said.

We got it cooking, and when Bruce came back he was a bit surprised that we were still there and still jamming on what he must have felt was just another chord change.

It was more than that. It was a hook, part of a chorus, and a title. Half the battle, at least. There was something about that phrase, "everybody's got a hungry heart," that felt like the perfect marriage of the personal and the universal. I wasn't going to let it get away. Bruce liked to finish some of the day's songs as homework. "Hey," I said. "Find a few more words for that baby."

◆

As we moved from rehearsal to studio, I stayed fixated on the sound of the record. I had finally figured out why virtually all the drums of the '50s and '60s sounded great and why they all sucked in the '70s.

It began with the way drums were tuned. The older drummers took lessons from jazz drummers, who knew how to tune their drums, but the craft was in the process of being lost.

Then came the way they were struck. Older drummers played with a lighter touch, left wrist up, which allowed the wrist to snap and thereby pop the loosely tuned snares and make them resonate. What most Rock drummers didn't understand was that the harder they hit the snare drum, the smaller it sounds.

Finally, it was the way they were miked. Older drummers were miked with an overhead mic, or one way in front with more distance, which allowed the sound to breathe, capturing the natural sound you hear when you walk into a room and hear a band playing.

John Bonham's drums were the only real exception to the bad-drum sound rule of the '70s because either he or Jimmy Page was smart enough to record his drums in a stairwell with plenty of room sound.

I had my eye on other factors too. The Engineer, for instance. I was looking for an Engineer who could get great sounds and do it quickly. Maureen was familiar with the studio scene from when she was going with Mitch Mitchell, the genius drummer of the Jimi Hendrix Experience, and had traveled from Woodstock to London and back with them. She remembered a guy named Bob Clearmountain, who had impressed her with his speed at a couple of sessions at Media Sound in midtown Manhattan, right across the street from where we lived at the time.

As Fate would have it, Max Weinberg mentioned he was going to the Power Station to do an Ian Hunter album, and the Engineer was going to be Clearmountain. I asked him to pay close attention to two things. Was he using room mics, and how fast did he get a drum sound? The torture of struggling and ultimately failing to get decent drums on *Darkness* was not an experience I intended to repeat.

Max came back with a favorable review, so I suggested to Bruce we use Clearmountain and the Power Station, where the bigger live room would give us a fighting chance to get a sound.

Bruce had switched managers by then. As I previously mentioned, Jon, with his vast knowledge of film, literature, and music, was helping Bruce refine his ideas during the game-changing *Darkness* sessions. They expanded my consciousness just from what I overheard!

Now Bruce had two trusted lieutenants. Jon took care of the record company, career planning, and big-picture conceptualizing, while I was free to focus on the music and the sound. My job, as I saw it, was to make sure every song was a joy to record.

So while they talked, I made the record.

Kidding.

But I had the studio and the Engineer I wanted. I made sure that every instrument sounded right and that everybody was playing the right thing, easy enough with the greatest band in the world. They literally produced themselves.

When the sessions for the new record started, it sounded great right away. This was gonna be fun! Bob was stupid fast, as advertised.

"Roulette" was recorded and mixed on the same day. I regularly got two mixes a day out of Bob when he used the manual, no automation, old analog Neve board. When things got automated later on that damn digital Solid State, everything slowed down. And never sounded as good again! (I'm exaggerating a little. Bob still gets good sounds with the digital crap. And he still does two mixes a day for me!)

The second thing we did was return to "Hungry Heart."

I felt this was our best shot at a hit single since Jimmy Iovine's genius theft of "Because the Night."

But it wasn't that simple. Remember, this was right in the middle of the Rock era, and a hit single had to be organic. If a song was seen as a conscious attempt to get a hit, it could hurt or even kill an artist's credibility. Once a song crossed over to AM, FM stopped playing it. And if you weren't careful, FM would stop playing you, period. Led Zeppelin became FM darlings partly by forbidding Atlantic to release any singles.

The dividing line had been *Sgt. Pepper*. The Beatles, the true kings of Pop/Rock, released no singles from their masterpiece. It made the irrefutable statement: We just single-handedly evolved the Artform we helped invent.

From 1967 through most of the '70s, the new lingua franca of Rock music would be the album. By the '80s, if it felt right, singles returned to the hip column.

"Hungry Heart" felt right. It had a universal sensibility, simplicity with substance. It was also a song that posed its own unique set of challenges.

For starters, it had an unusual structure, in that the verse and chorus were the same, which was very hard to make work if you weren't James Brown. Because of that, I suggested the modulation for the solo. A modulation is simply a key change implemented to surprise the ears. It's part of the fun of Arranging to jump to an odd key and then have to find your way back to where you started. Or not.

The rest of the song came together. For the Beach Boys–style harmonies in the chorus, I suggested we bring in the Turtles, aka Flo and Eddie, aka Mark Volman and Howard Kaylan. I had seen their show at the Bottom Line and loved it. The session made Mark and Howard relevant again. They'd thank me by later overcharging for a Jukes session and reneging on a deal for a benefit, but nobody's perfect.

Then there were the drums. Even tuned, struck, and miked correctly, there was still the challenge of the mix.

The mix is exactly what it sounds like. You take all your tracks of instruments and mix them down to two tracks. You balance the instruments, add equalization (makes the instrument brighter or fatter, etc.), compression, reverb, etc.

I could hear how close we were to the drum sound I wanted. But we weren't quite there. I kept telling Bob to turn up the room mics. He edged them up a millimeter at a time, the way good Engineers were taught. I'm sure he thought I was just the guitar player being a pain in the ass, and that no one had explained to him my new status as co-Producer.

I took Bruce out to the hallway. "Listen, man," I said. "We are close to the promised land, no pun intended. Nirvana is in sight. Bob won't take me seriously until you explain to him I am coproducing this fucking thing, but right now when you go back in push those drum-room mic motherfucking faders all the way up."

He did. And there it was. The sound I'd been looking for my whole recording life. The sound that would influence everybody in the '80s.

Ironically, incredibly, and much to my eternal aggravation, just a few months later some smart-ass invented sampling! After all my painstaking research and experimenting, all they had to do was push a fucking button for an instant magnificent snare. Usually, one of Clearmountain's!

There was one more thing bothering me. Bruce just didn't have a Pop voice.

On *Born to Run* and *Darkness*, he had been writing older than he was, thinking older than he was, and singing older. He made his voice big and dramatic and rough and lived in, which fit the songs perfectly. Remember the singer is always an actor acting out the script that is the song.

But to be a Pop hit, "Hungry Heart" required something else. Never mind that the subject, a guy abandoning his wife and kids, was not exactly ideal for a younger audience. I have always believed lyrics are icing on the cake, mostly ignored by everyone except critics and the most fanatical fans.

For a song to be a hit, it has to *sound* like a hit. Ideally it's a bright, uplifting sound that appeals to a Pop audience that will respond to the ear candy far more readily than the actual substance. So how could we make the record brighter in general?

And then it hit me. Speed the tape up! His big voice would become smaller. Thinner. Younger! Remember the Chipmunks? Same science, taller Artist. I stayed late with Neil Dorfsman, our Engineer.

The song was better faster! I sped it up a little more, and a little more. It took some getting used to, but it felt natural enough. If you'd never heard the original, you'd never notice the difference.

The next day I played it for everybody. They all laughed. When he saw I was serious, Bruce said I might be on to something, but it was too much. They slowed it back down, then sped it up one step at a time until it was a notch slower than my version.

When Charlie Plotkin mastered it months later, he sped it back up that last notch to my original speed and got the credit. It's OK. He's a good guy.

The River had a completely different atmosphere than the previous two albums. Bruce's identity had settled into the rural, stand-and-fight, speaking-from-the-working-class-perspective persona of *Darkness*. Which didn't mean he wasn't still in his write-and-record-a-million-songs-and-find-the-album-in-there-later mode. But at least this batch *sounded* great. So it was a much more pleasant atmosphere for our endless song arguments, which I usually lost. And *The River* was a double album, which meant more room for some fun songs along with the substance.

Bruce kept "Hungry Heart" but threw out classics like "Loose Ends," "Take 'Em as They Come," "Roulette," and "Restless Nights."

Who needs 'em?

I happen to like "Crush on You," but in place of "Where the Bands Are," or "Mary Lou," or "I Wanna Be with You"?

I don't know.

The other subject that was discussed enthusiastically was the treatment of slow songs. Bruce and Jon were together on this, the sparser the better. Bruce was always so concentrated on his writing on the page, with good reason and great results, that I'm not sure he ever fully understood the difference between a song and a record.

My attention deficit disorder couldn't take it. I was constantly trying to add production and arrangement ideas to songs like "Racing in the Streets" and "Wreck on the Highway," and he wanted stark and stoic because that's what the cinematic lyrics suggested.

But a record ain't a movie. It's a fine line how sparse you can make something, without the visual assistance, before you lose an audience. There's no right or wrong here—that's what makes the longest discussions—but according to my ADD, they'd occasionally go too far. Check out the two versions of "Racing in the Street" for a good example. But Bruce preferred erring on the side of desolation. And you have to respect the discipline of sacrificing the musicality of a song to make a point.

Whatever. If he's happy, I'm happy.

I am very proud of *The River*, which remains my favorite "official" album, but too many of the best songs ended up on the second disc of *Tracks*.

We did a couple of benefits in that period.

No Nukes at Madison Square Garden was promoted under the auspices of Musicians United for Safe Energy, or MUSE, which was founded by Jackson Browne, Bonnie Raitt, John Hall, and Graham Nash.

It's where Tom Petty, not known for his wild and crazy sense of humor, delivered his most memorable punch line. The organizers told him that the Garden was Bruce's home turf, so he shouldn't be bothered if he heard the crowd booing. They were just saying "Bruce."

"What the fuck's the difference?" Tom lovingly contributed to infamy.

That benefit was the first political thing I was ever part of. I understand it better now, but back then I didn't get it. What was preaching to the converted supposed to accomplish? How was a concert and audience full of hippies supposed to affect Ronald Reagan's decision-making process?

The best part of the event for me was meeting Jackson Browne, who would become an important major friend and affect my life greatly very soon.

The event would help me when I eventually established my own results-oriented political methodology, which was a better fit for my ADD.

A little later, in Los Angeles, we did a much-needed tribute for Vietnam vets. Bruce had become friendly with Bobby Muller, the president of the Vietnam Veterans of America Foundation, and I was glad he decided to do that one. A friend from my neighborhood, Rod Paladino, had been spit on when he came home from the war, so it was personal to me.

But mainly, we were looking toward to our new record's release. Landau had done his homework, learning the . . . complexities of the Pop world, and that homework ensured my first work as part of the official production team would get its shot.

"Hungry Heart" started up the charts. And as much as the modern Pop world would forever be a foreign planet, having that first hit was quite a thrill. Album sales went from a few hundred thousand to three million. That was around the average ratio of hit singles to the insane album sales at that time. Every hit single meant around three million album sales in the gold rush '80s. Our half-filled theaters turned into sold-out arenas.

When I met Bruce in '65, we were two teenage misfits who shared an impossible fantasy. And now, a decade and a half of hard work later, we'd made it. What a difference the right hit single at the right time made. Of course my gratitude only lasted until our second single bombed. "Fade Away" not being a hit was, as far as I was concerned, a crime against humanity.

We were on top of the world. Audience enthusiasm was unparalleled. And then a traumatic event diluted our bliss. On the first American leg of the tour, on the night we played the Spectrum in Philadelphia, we lost John Lennon.

I remember hearing the news and being surprised by how upset I was. The Beatles had stopped touring in the mid-'60s. They hadn't been a band for a decade. I had never followed their solo work very closely. But it felt like losing a brother or a father.

Brian Jones's death was important to me. Jimi Hendrix's, even more so. But my relationships with those artists had lasted three or four years. The Beatles had been my mentors for fifteen years. Plus, they had been first. They communicated such hope and joy. They saved my life. Lennon's murder hit me so hard that I expected we'd cancel. But Bruce gave me a wonderful speech about how people needed us more than ever in moments like this.

I remember opening with "Born to Run" and crying all the way through it. Once again, we were reminded by History to embrace those rare blissful moments with all your strength when you find them, because who knows what rough beast slouching toward Bethlehem is just around the corner waiting to be born.

fourteen

Checkpoint Charlie

(1980)

Checkpoint Charlie,
Brothers and sisters on the other side,
Livin' in the shadow of a wall so high,
Make me wanna cry, baby.

　　—"CHECKPOINT CHARLIE," FROM *VOICE OF AMERICA*

Dystopian.

Fifty steps took us from a technicolor *Hogan's Heroes* episode to a black-and-white, postapocalyptic sci-fi flick.

The farmers on the billboards all looked similarly creepy/George Romero, and after a while I started missing the vapid, consciousness-colorizing advertising that I usually despise.

Bruce and I had decided to go through Checkpoint Charlie to East Berlin. While the wall was still up.

I have lots of German friends, some of the sweetest people in the world, but Germans are one of those ethnic groups that can be really scary when they want to be.

And when the nasty fuck at the border takes your passport and says, "OK, you're on your own," it gives you a little shot of anxiety.

We walked in, and within a few blocks we were in the Twilight Zone. Very quiet. We looked at some shops. Not much on the shelves.

We might've gone into a bar and had a drink or something, but I don't remember striking up a conversation with anyone, all of whom reminded me of the Transylvanian townspeople who stop talking when the victims walk into the tavern.

We didn't stay long. The thought of people living in that atmosphere of acute paranoia was quite depressing.

I wrote a song for them.

Sometimes that's all a po' boy can do.

Frank Barsalona had insisted we go to Europe.

We had played just four shows in Europe after *Born to Run*, and none for *Darkness* because of our perilous financial situation. The River Tour went all over Europe—Germany, France, Belgium, England, Scotland, Spain, the Netherlands, Italy, Norway—you name it.

That tour began a love affair with European audiences that continues to this day. But at first, the culture shock was . . . shocking.

It was hard relating to the food, for starters. Not that we cared that much about food in those days, but the only hamburger in Europe was at the newly opened Hard Rock Cafe in London. The *only* burger in ten countries. I shit you not!

And no peanut butter!

And London is all about teatime, right? But ask for iced tea and they looked at you like you're an escaped mental patient and they're considering whether to report you to the authorities or not.

If I had the entrepreneurial gene, there were business opportunities everywhere. Of course, I didn't act on them. But looking back, I always had those kinds of ideas, those entrepreneurial compulsions, flying by in my head.

Thinking about it now, I think there are two reasons to be at least a little bit of a businessman. The first is a totally legit and in fact essential reason, and that is to protect your Art. This is serious. You have to force yourself to understand what the fuck your lawyers and accountants are talking about. If you get lucky, they might be smart and actually care, but you can't depend on that.

The second reason is a little scary.

It is getting into business because you are not confident enough that your own artistic talent will find an audience. I think this is my problem, which by the way has proven to be true.

Without that confidence, deep down you feel what your parents always said, which is that you need the dreaded *something to fall back on.*

I get shivers just writing those words, but it is funny how the older you get, the smarter your parents become.

In Germany, after we left the Twilight Zone and were back on the West Berlin side of the wall, a kid came up to me on the street. "Why are you putting missiles in my country?" he said.

What? Whatever you're smoking, give me some! The kid asked me again.

"Look, friend, come to the show tonight, on me. I'll show you it's a guitar in that case, not a fucking missile."

I walked on and that was that. Except it wasn't. I couldn't get what he said off of my mind. Why was it bugging me so much?

That's the government, not me, I said to myself. I've got nothing whatsoever to do with what my government does. Just because he's a naive foreigner and doesn't know any better, I shouldn't let that get to me. Just because he thinks I live in a democracy . . .

Holy Shit! It hit me.

He thinks I live in a democracy!

And that means—my mind was racing now—that he doesn't know the difference between a congressman and a musician, a Democrat and a Republican. To him, I'm an . . . American.

Whoa. Radical.

I was the least political guy I knew. I couldn't have cared less. I made it through the entire '60s without one single political thought in my head.

But the German kid sent me down a path, and I kept going. If America is putting missiles in Germany, through NATO or whatever, and America is a democracy, then I *am* putting missiles in his country!

A shiver went through my soul.

If I'm putting missiles in Germany, what else am "I" doing? I suddenly had a hunger to do something I had never done through twelve years of schooling. I felt the need to read a book!

When we got home, I went into my local bookstore, Coliseum Books, off Columbus Circle, and bought every book I could find on our foreign policy since World War II. Just my luck, the first one was by Noam Chomsky.

Game over, baby.

The second book was *Bitter Fruit*, by Stephen Schlesinger and Stephen Kinzer, about the CIA's overthrow of Jacobo Arbenz's government in Guatemala in 1954. Now the game was even more over. I felt like a member of the Nazi Party in 1939.

But there it was, America's ongoing nefarious and immoral activity, right in our own hemisphere.

There was a connection between big business, local slave labor, and military dictatorship? Paid for by American tax dollars? We weren't supporting democracy around the world? We were the bad guys?!?

Fuck me, I thought. No way. This is not what the Founders had in mind.

I proceeded to single-handedly keep Coliseum in business for the next ten years or so.

I started feeling the need to do more than just read.

I had to try and expose this hypocrisy. I had to at least let people know that Rock and Roll wasn't in on these decisions!

But how? I wasn't sure.

All I knew was that hearing foreign audiences singing every word of our songs was absolutely thrilling. The power of Rock to communicate was nothing short of revelatory.

Maybe the '60s did leave a legacy we could pick up on after all.

Checkpoint Charlie, the kid with the missiles, the ability of Rock music to carry messages—it was beginning to add up to something.

fifteen

Hemingway Appropriately

(1980–1982)

The way to do is to be.

—LAO TZU

"Come over," Bruce said. "I've been doing some demos for the new album."

Demos? This was new. We had always worked out the songs at rehearsal.

It was him and Mike Batlin, his first guitar roadie, acting as Engineer, with a four-track cassette tape machine!

The whole setup was bizarre.

He then proceeded to play me the wildest bunch of songs I'd ever heard.

They were stark and acoustic and reminded me of the first time I heard Son House or Charley Patton or Robert Johnson or Harry Smith's Folk recordings. I was completely transported to another time, another place.

Thunder Road. Not the song—the movie. I was suddenly with Robert Mitchum, barreling down the backwater dirt mountain roads of Tennessee and West Virginia, avoiding police roadblocks, or in Pretty Boy Floyd's Depression-era Ohio.

It was thrilling. The songs were so authentic that I didn't think about my friend sitting in front of me. But of course he was in them. They were all him, but a new him. Or maybe an old him that was emerging for the first time.

The difference was not just the writing but the acting. Every singer is an actor, whether they know it or not, and suddenly he had become a very good one. He wasn't narrating anymore. He embodied these songs and made them totally believable.

After listening, I was not my usual effusive and opinionated self. I was quiet.

This worried him.

"What?" he said.

I had to choose my words wisely. It felt like an important moment.

"Well, I only know one thing," I said. "And I know it with all my bones. This is an album. And not only that, it's a great album. I've never heard anything quite like it. It sounds like field recordings."

I named names. Harry Smith, Don Law, Alan Lomax.

He laughed. "What do you mean? These are the demos for . . ."

"Yeah, I get it," I said. "You thought these were demos. That's what makes this the most personal, intimate record you or anybody else will ever do. This has got to be released."

He was genuinely surprised. "Well, wow," he finally said. I could tell he knew he was going to have to listen to the songs much more intensely, in an entirely different context. No longer just as an exercise to entertain his friends, but as a potentially finished piece of work.

Everybody else in the band and organization thought I'd lost my mind. Judging from the last two albums, they figured a hundred more songs would follow before a record started to take shape.

We even attempted to cut at least a few of those "demos" with the band.

At the same time, Bruce started bringing in more songs. Or maybe Paul Schrader sent Bruce the script for a potential movie called *Born in the USA*, asking him to write the title song. In using the band to demo it, Bruce realized he had something special.

Those other songs, the ones that weren't the so-called demos, continued on in the spirit of the "live" sound we'd finally achieved on *The River*. It worked so well that we took it to an extreme. We did the album live. If a vocal didn't work, the whole band would play the whole song again. Crazy? Yes. Pointless? Not exactly. The more unrehearsed it was, the more primal it would be.

I worked on fourteen, fifteen, maybe sixteen songs over two weeks. No overdubs. For the mandolin solo on "Glory Days," I picked it up and played it into my vocal mic!

The more the band work came together, the more the so-called demos were taken seriously as a separate album. At least by Bruce— which meant everybody would be on board soon. So we had both the beginnings of our electric follow-up to *The River* and an acoustic album by the Appalachian moonshining Folk singer John Hammond thought he'd signed in the first place.

Hammond had retired from Columbia in 1975, so Bruce and Jon had to break the news to Walter Yetnikoff and Bruce Lundvall, the label heads at the time.

They played it smart. They said, We've got good news and bad news, and they put on a few of the full-band tracks to get them excited, maybe "Born in the USA" and "Glory Days."

I imagine the two executives lit up like Christmas trees, cash registers ringing in their heads.

I can hear Lundvall's mellifluous voice still echoing. "This is wonderful."

"Exactly the right record at the right time. Congratulations!" Yetnikoff (probably) barked.

Jon had to explain that the Rock record was only coming after the label put out this other record.

And then played them *Nebraska*.

I wish I could have seen their faces.

The heads of the biggest record company in the world, jobs always on the line, listening as their most important artist, accompanied by acoustic guitar on a lo-fi cassette recording, convincingly portrayed a serial killer on the frozen tundra of Oklahoma yodeling like a demon drunk on poisoned whiskey!

Ha-ha!

Take that, Beancounters of the Universe!

Anyway, Bruce and Jon pulled it off, and I'm proud that I encouraged the truly solo Folk part of Bruce, which I was probably the first to witness, back in his room in Freehold, to become a semiregular part of his work output—even if it was once again against my self-interest.

It's among the most uncompromising and uncommercial records any major Artist has ever released. It would keep his dignity forever protected and would ensure his credibility would remain forever bulletproof.

I had met Gary US Bonds on the oldies circuit back in '73. Though we never had a real conversation, I liked him a lot. Funny as hell.

Still, when Bruce decided to produce him just after *The River*, I didn't get it. Of all the phenomenal '50s and '60s cats, he had chosen the guy who sounded like he made party records in his garage?

At first, I was just playing as a member of his band. We did "This Little Girl" and "Dedication," and Jon shopped the single around. Everybody passed. That's when Bruce asked me to get involved.

I fixed a few things in the recording, but mostly I brought back Bob Clearmountain to mix it. Bob really got the song popping on that old analog equipment. Every riff from every instrument was perfectly clear. The handclaps were like gunshots, and that was probably ten of us at the most clapping. It would take forty guys with today's digital shit and still not sound as good.

I ended up taking the completed Bonds record to Gary Gersh, who had just joined Jim Mazza at a brand-new company called EMI America. Gary signed Gary and said he wanted more than a single. He wanted a full album. But Bruce was busy doing something, maybe mastering *Nebraska*, which took months. (I'm guessing an hour of work and two months of conversation!) So Bruce gave me the responsibility of doing the album. He'd drop in now and then to see how it was going.

Turns out, Bonds was one of the great Soul singers. There was no way to know it from his party records, but somehow Bruce knew.

Now that we had one of the great singers, I figured, Let's put him together with songs by the greatest songwriters.

There's an art to covering songs. The Beatles and the Stones both did covers through their first *five* albums. That alone should tell young bands how significant that stage of development is.

The Beatles mostly kept the original arrangements but still made the songs their own. How? They were the fucking Beatles, that's how.

The Stones occasionally sped things up, like on their Muddy Waters covers, but otherwise relied on their own strong identity.

The rest of us have to work a little harder. There are five ways an artist can make a cover song their own: change gender, genre, tempo, arrangement, and style.

You don't need all five. You only need one. But let's have a little fun. What are the greatest covers ever?

Joe Cocker's cover of the Beatles' "With a Little Help from My Friends" comes immediately to mind.

Same gender, pretty much same genre, but Joe (or Producer Denny Cordell) slowed it down, changed the arrangement with the organ intro, added Jimmy Page's guitar licks, girl singers, and a couple of classic B. J. Wilson drum fills Ringo would have been proud of. Then Joe sang the shit out of it, sounding like Ray Charles, while Ringo sounded like who we wanted him to sound like . . . Ringo.

Jimi Hendrix's version of Bob Dylan's "All Along the Watchtower" may be the greatest cover of all time. Same gender, different genre. Acoustic Singer-Songwriter Country/Rock changed to powerful electric Rock, slowed slightly, different emphasis on the chords, a few classic guitar solos in the arrangement, and a much more Soul Roots vocal style.

The most dramatic cover of all time would seem to be Trent Reznor's "Hurt," as performed by Johnny Cash. Surprisingly, it's not that different! The original catches Reznor in a rather mellow mood—meaning intensely suicidal, but quieter than usual. Rick Rubin took out the dissonance, changed the instrumentation slightly, lost the noise at the end, and let Cash's immediately identifiable vocal style redefine the context.

So what's the ultimate example of a cover, the one that satisfies all five criteria?

"You Keep Me Hangin' On" by Vanilla Fudge.

It checks *all* the boxes:

☑ Gender: From the Supremes to male Long Island hoods.

☑ Genre: From Soul to Psychedelic Heavy Rock.

☑ Tempo: Slower. A lot slower!

☑ Arrangement: From Funk Brothers precision to B-3 Rock organ, distorted Rock guitar, Rock drums, Rock every-damn-thing!

☑ Style: From foxy-but-tough woman wanting romantic closure to a desperate, tortured man experiencing a Shakespearean tragedy inside a Roger Corman horror movie.

For Gary, I picked songs by Lennon and McCartney ("It's Only Love"), Dylan ("From a Buick 6"), and Jackson Browne ("The Pretender"). I had a Stones song also ("Connection") but ran out of time.

I didn't change the arrangements much, knowing Gary's super soulful voice would turn the songs into his own.

Bruce found "Jole Blon" on a Moon Mullican record, a radical genre shift that Gary pulled off effortlessly, and gave him "Rendezvous," one of our countless outtakes.

He also suggested I contribute a song, and since we didn't have anything particularly personal, I wrote "Daddy's Come Home" for Gary in an attempt to capture the lifelong struggle of the traveling journeyman with a family at home.

Unbelievably, "This Little Girl" went Top Ten. Some things just hit with the public. We followed up immediately with a second record, *On the Line*, bringing in legendary Soul vocalists Ben E. King and Chuck Jackson.

I loved working with the '60s Artists so much that I told Bruce we should start a label and do nothing but that—and buy the Power Station to do it. We could have done it with Sony money, given them distribution. Game over! He was tempted, I could tell. But he couldn't stand the thought of being in a business of any kind. It's a shame. Can you imagine what great records we could have made? Not just with King and Jackson, but with Wilson Pickett, David Ruffin, Little Richard, and who knows who else?

There was no hit on the second album, in spite of containing all new, great Springsteen compositions and being one of my favorite productions.

Nobody heard it.

Ms. Destiny must have been lurking quietly during that first Bonds record, because Gary Gersh approached me to do a solo album.

I had never considered it.

"Let me think about it," I said, and went home to see if I could write some songs that felt like solo material. Nobody needed another side-man singing love songs. I thought about the kid in Germany and all the reading I'd been doing. Would that point me in the right direction?

I've always loved the idea of concept albums. There's something about the whole being greater than the sum of the parts that appeals to me. Bang for the artistic buck. It's part of my love of *big Art*. The bigger it is, the more significant the audience's experience, right? The songs might be great on their own—or the choreography or the lighting or the sets or the costumes—but they're all so much better if they are serving a story or a theme. Give the audience something to think about. Something to take home with them. That's why I was disappointed with *Love*, Cirque du Soleil's Beatles show. Why not make it a story? It's a great one. Begin with the London bombings and post–World War II depression in black-and-white and then blow it away with brilliant colorful fun led by Sgt. Pepper himself! Enhance it, symbolize it, fictionalize it, whatever, but tell an emotionally engaging story, or the show is nothing more than a momentary distraction.

There weren't that many true concept albums.

Frank Sinatra had invented the form with *In the Wee Small Hours*, *Come Fly with Me*, *Only the Lonely*, and others.

But it came to the Rock world with "A Quick One, While He's Away," a nine-minute montage of fragments strung together on the Who's second album at the suggestion of their Producer-Manager Kit Lambert, whose father was a classical composer. It grabbed me right away.

Pete Townshend would take things a step further, loosely connecting the songs with interstitial commercials on *The Who Sell Out* and then go all the way with *Tommy*.

Along the way the Kinks had *Village Green Preservation Society* and then *Arthur*, the Pretty Things had *SF Sorrow*, the Small Faces had *Ogden's Nut Gone Flake*. Some bands did it loosely, like the Stones with *Their Satanic Majesties Request* or Pink Floyd with *The Piper at the Gates of Dawn* (they'd do another loose one, *Dark Side of the Moon*, before tightening things up with *The Wall*).

All were interesting in their own way, but it was the concept that was abandoned after two songs that changed the world forever: *Sgt. Pepper's Lonely Hearts Club Band.*

It didn't matter that the Beatles were beginning to disintegrate or that there were mounting drug problems or that they were working strictly by instinct, by circumstance, or by accident—*Sgt. Pepper's* was the most important concept album of all time. Not the best or fully realized. That honor would forever go to *Tommy.* But the most *important.*

The sounds were fresh and unique, in complete contrast to the lyrics, which were nostalgic and sad, mostly about dysfunctional losers disappointed by life, and printed on the album sleeve for the first time. Why wasn't Columbia doing that on every Bob Dylan album, one has every right to ask?

It felt like the most extraordinary record made by the most extraordinary band, and it was the last time the world of culture was totally united by Popular music.

Don't believe all the revisionist bullshit you read now. Yes, *Revolver* had more innovations and was better song for song, but *Sgt. Pepper* changed the way our entire culture looked at Rock music.

I was there and I can tell you. You could walk down any street in the Western Freakin' World that first week of June 1967, and you would hear it playing.

For me, the walk was from MacDougal to St. Mark's in Greenwich Village, where I heard the record coming out of every head shop, clothing store, restaurant, and car that went by.

It elevated an entire generation's artistic consciousness and changed the world of Popular music from a singles-oriented, Wild West, fly-by-night hustle to a semilegitimate album-dependent business overnight.

We won't see that again anytime soon.

If I was going to have a solo career, I decided all my records would be concept records. I outlined five general themes that would help me investigate the world, put to use some of the books I had been reading, explore the relationships of power and control, and answer some important questions. Who has the power? Why? What does it mean? How much of the government is endorsed by the governed? Is Rousseau's social contract being honored? Who or what controls our destinies?

What is humanity's common ground? How much of a chance do we really have to change things?

The first solo album would look at how the government and various social forces affect the individual in society. It would also allow me to introduce myself as an Artist.

Then the next four albums would investigate how government affects and separates the human Family, how government manipulates various international States, the effect of that on Economy and how it needed to be transformed, and finally the political consequence of spiritual bankruptcy and the role of Religion. That would complete the circle, returning to the individual, but this time from the inside out.

Hopefully, I'd learn something about myself in the process. Who was I? What happened to those of us who grew up in the '60s? Was all that idealism just talk? I would mix in what little I knew about myself, what I believed, my responsibilities as both an American and a global citizen, my loves, my fears, etc.

These were big questions I had never even thought about. By fully embracing the Artist part of my identity, I could start to answer them.

Musically, for my first record, I decided to go back to the sound I had created with the Jukes: '60s R&B-based Rock with a five-piece horn section.

But I didn't continue in a linear fashion, which would have meant starting up where *Hearts of Stone* left off.

Instead I went for something rootsier. I thought the less produced the record was, the more open and honest, and the more direct my route would be to discovering my own identity.

Being a bit of an extremist back then, I recorded the whole album live in one day. I put the band in a semicircle, used the studio monitors hanging from the ceiling instead of headphones, and let it happen. Horns blowing into the drums, monitors blasting the whole mix back into all the microphones—I didn't care.

I used one of the greatest rhythm sections in the world, E Street's Garry Tallent and Max Weinberg. Dino Danelli from the Rascals and Jean Beauvoir from the Plasmatics came in near the end of the recording and became Disciples of Soul on the road. Bruce sang harmonies, though I couldn't credit him because Yetnikoff was on the warpath about something or other.

It worked pretty well, actually, thanks largely to my Engineer Bob Clearmountain, who probably thought I was nuts but was always game. We came back the next day and did the whole album again to see if we could get better takes. We may have used one or two takes from the second day.

I then spent a couple of weeks messing around, mostly to make sure I idiotically spent every penny of the record budget.

I put acoustic guitar on a couple of songs, did my double tribute to Ry Cooder as I added mandolin and slide on "Princess of Little Italy." Added the double guitar solo to "Angel Eyes." Resang the vocals where Bruce sang harmony live with Bruce because I wanted them spontaneous and loose and not Everly Brothers perfect.

If I had it to do over again, I would double some guitars and add some harmonies. Most of the album is one live rhythm guitar! But it holds up as an honest representation of where I was at the time.

There are two kinds of people in the world, my friend. Solo guys and band guys.

I'm a band guy, but in 1982 I was a band guy on the brink of a solo career. It's a paradox I learned to live with but never quite resolved.

The first time your name and picture are about to be put on an album cover, it makes you think. Being a person who'd rather be doing than thinking, I started to wonder what I'd gotten myself into.

It's a big job asking an audience to redefine you. In the world of showbiz you're lucky if an audience even finds you. If and when they do, they define you forever the way they first discovered you. And you're one in a million lucky it happened at all.

E Street fans knew me as Miami Steve, the always-in-a-good-mood party-guy sidekick. If I'd stayed in that role in my solo career, and written music to fit, I probably would have been very successful.

But that was one part of me, and that part had no time for Art. He was too busy fucking and drinking and fucking and drugging and fucking. He had to go.

It was time to introduce a guy the audience hadn't met yet. Well, unless they had been carefully reading the credits on the Jukes records.

This guy wasn't going to be as sure of himself as the other guy.

This guy would be taking a journey into the unknown, alone, to learn about how the world works, and finally learn about himself.

I knew I needed a new identity. But rather than use my own name, I decided to pick another nickname, for several reasons.

First, it suggests that no matter how serious you take the work, you're never going to be too self-righteous about yourself.

Second, it kept me connected to tradition, which I would need as I found my way through this adventure into the mystic.

And third, I believed in the fantasy aspect of show business. I have never related to the regular-guy look that John Fogerty started and Neil Young and Bruce adopted later. I'm not putting it down. It just never worked for me.

Maureen and I went to see the final Cream reunion. Apart from the fact that three-piece bands are by definition fraudulent since they don't record that way, they wore T-shirts and dungarees. For $350 a ticket, maybe you could put a fucking shirt on? If I go see Cream, I want to see the *Disraeli Gears* album cover, goddamn it!

What we do onstage is a complex, complete communication—songs, performance, clothes, lights, production. At its most effective, a great performance can not only transport an audience but transform it, taking them from tearful catharsis to blissful enlightenment. All in the same show. Nothing less. There is an essential element of Fantasy. Of Mystery. Of Masquerade. Theater!

And so I became Little Steven.

Little Anthony was one of my favorite Doo-Wop singers. "Tears on My Pillow" was the first record I ever bought and Little Anthony and the Imperials was the first live Rock show I ever saw. Toms River Roller Rink.

Little Walter was my favorite Blues guy and the greatest harmonica player ever.

And Little Richard was the embodiment and archetype of the philosophy of Rock and Roll freedom. My man. His flamboyant multisexual androgyny said you can be whoever you wanna be. He turned Rock into an Artform that not only tolerated reinvention but demanded it. He opened his mouth, and out came liberation.

As Little Steven, I would become the Political Guy, and release and embody my inner '60s gypsy forevermore.

Would the E Street audience have a problem with my new persona? Yes.

They never would show up.

One of the books I'd been reading was a collection of short fiction by Ernest Hemingway, *Men Without Women.* The stories were about bull-fighters and soldiers and boxers and the relationship between identity and profession. I felt that if Ernie had written it in the '60s or '70s, it would have included a chapter about a Rock band, so I used it for the title of my album.

It would be particularly appropriate since Hemingway had commit-ted suicide and I would be committing career suicide with this record. I'm not whining or being morbid, just saying one has to die in order to be reborn.

At the time, MTV had just started. Video budgets were rising every day. I figured that if we were going to spend a quarter of a million each on a few videos, we could make a real movie for the same money, couldn't we? One of my heroes, Roger Corman, did it all the time. Then we could carve the videos out of the film.

I called Jay Cocks and asked him what he thought. "Let's go see a friend," he said. We went to a hotel and took the elevator up, Jay knocked, and there stood John Cassavetes, wearing a tuxedo. Gena Rowlands flashed by in the background.

"I only got a minute," John said. "But the one-minute version of how to protect your work is this: get a script and make sure the Director sticks to it." Highly ironic advice from the king of improvisation! "That's why I direct all my own stuff. It's the easiest way to control it."

What a cool guy.

Why didn't I go back and spend more time with him?

Our script, by John Varnom, was more of a fluid outline describing our actual situation. It was a story about a band that didn't have the money to tour and decided to make a movie instead.

Because EMI didn't want to pay for the whole thing, we shot few scenes for potential investors. Our husband-and-wife Director-Producer team, Derek and Kate Burbidge, did an amazing job with no budget and a tiny guerrilla crew, and actually shot an impressionistic Indie Film, much more than the outline we intended.

We used crew members from E Street, Tony, Bubba G., and Tomasino; an actor friend, Sal Viscuso, who happened to be in town; and Maureen, who played my girlfriend Knuckles.

She was already all over the album—"Forever," "Save Me," "I've Been Waiting," the title track, and "Angel Eyes" with all the ballet imagery:

> *She dances in shadows, she bleeds in tears,*
> *She turns into animals, she disappears,*
> *Surrounded by mirrors while the spirits watch,*
> *They look now, baby, but they can't touch,*
> *The pain is intoxicating if the music is loud enough.*

We took our footage to Cannes, and the Disciples performed there, probably the first band to have done so, but the record company guy who was supposed to organize the investors' meetings didn't. It never got financed and never really got done.

Almost forty years later, when I watched the footage for the first time, I was surprised we'd done as much as we had. The movie feels like a street version of early French New Wave, or like Cassavetes himself. It requires a bit of filling in the blanks, but it kind of makes sense. "A triumph of style and character over exposition!" a fantasy review might've read.

Prince would do it the right way two years later, with *Purple Rain*.

The *Men Without Women* album came out on October 1, 1982.

Nebraska had come out the day before.

Technically, two band guys making solo records, but in very different ways. For me it was just another band with me out front; for him it was a legit solo project.

Anyway, it was a new adventure for both of us.

An exciting moment.

I was not the marrying kind.

How many guys have said that? Possibly all of us.

I loved the single life, answering to no one, no responsibilities, no guilt, no checking in, no schedule, no plans. Also, in the mid-'70s, I'd developed a temporary addiction to *ménages à trois*, which didn't lend itself to marriage except maybe in Persia or somewhere.

But then there was Maureen. I had pursued her since the infamous Bottom Line shows, but once I reached her I really reached her. Three, four, five times a day, for years!

I took her to Venice and proposed under the Bridge of Sighs. If I was going to get married, I might as well do it right. We set a date for December 31, 1982, five years to the day since we had first gone out.

Little Richard had left Rock and Roll to join the ministry, so we talked him into officiating. (Bruce Willis would steal the idea five years later with no credit—you're welcome, pal!)

Percy Sledge sang "When a Man Loves a Woman" as we came down the aisle at an old ballet studio on Manhattan's East Side, Harkness House. Little Milton performed, along with the band from *The God-father* movie. Unfortunately, Little Anthony was working a cruise ship and couldn't get out if it, and Little Walter was long gone; otherwise I would have had all the "Littles."

Bruce was my best man, and the wedding party included (on my side) Jay Cocks, Max Weinberg, Garry Tallent, Jimmy Iovine, Gary Bonds, Jean and Monti from the first version of the Disciples, my brother Billy, my roadie Ben, our tour manager Harry Sandler, and LaBamba from the Jukes. Maureen had her four sisters (Gail, Lori, Maria, and Lynn), her two best friends (Michelle and Sari), my sister Kathi, and my assistant Obie. Jay's wife, Verna, was there, and they brought Marty Scorsese, who kept our ongoing should-have-been-good-friends story line alive. The Chambers Brothers were there too. Maureen knew them from her New York days in the '60s.

I don't remember much else other than that our two hundred guests were augmented by another hundred or so crashing and stealing all the gifts. We had everything taken care of except security.

Fun, though, I'm told.

sixteen

Voice of America

(1982–1983)

I've been fighting my whole life for the privilege to work.

—"FOREVER," *MEN WITHOUT WOMEN*

Money and me, what can I say? We never got along too good.

The pattern of my life is investing everything I have in what I believe in. Emotionally. All my time. All my talent. All my energy. And, yeah, usually all my money. Because I hate asking other people for money, and, until recently, never had anybody to do the asking for me. And we'll see how long they last.

In 1982, I proceeded to spend what little money I had left after making the movie, taking an eleven-piece band around the world for a year.

Now, the Rock life isn't for everybody. You're basically packing your bags and unpacking them thirty years later. It's a lifestyle that requires dedication, perseverance, patience, ambition, and, most of all, having no desire or ability to do anything else.

People are always saying, Oh, how proud you must be! How righteous to have withstood the slings and arrows of outrageous fortune!

But no. I'm sorry.

I resist all accusations of nobility.

We were bums. Profoundly unsuited for any legitimate type of work. We did have honor for our outlaw profession. And a work ethic. I'll give us that.

So here's a few tips for keeping a band together.

As soon as you can afford it, get separate rooms. This is the one and only rule you cannot follow from the Beatles, who never had their own rooms. Don't ask.

Make sure everybody gets a moment in the spotlight.

Find out what each band member can do and find a way to use it.

If it's a real band with the same members all the time and one or two people are doing most of the writing, and you are successful, share a little bit of the publishing money. It won't kill you.

Try and keep girlfriends and wives—or if you are a Girl Group, boyfriends and husbands—off the road as much as possible. The band needs to bond, especially in the beginning. And the mates should be busy with their own lives anyway.

Keep a diary! How I wish I'd kept a diary. This book is only the 10 percent I still remember!

And I don't mean the fourteen-year-old-girl's Ooh-Joey-looked-at-me-in-math-class-today!-type stuff.

I mean make notes about the towns. Keep track of details about hotels and venues. Restaurants, local promoters, local friends, local journalists.

You'll be coming back to the same towns for the next thirty or forty years, with a little bit of luck. So keep notes, and you will thank me in the morning.

I guess I figured money was something that should be put to use and I could always make more. I don't know where that comes from. We weren't rich growing up. I had a paper route. I caddied, scraped boats in a marina, worked in a box factory, made a few bucks working at my grandfather's shoe repair store.

I didn't waste it either. I got into gambling for a while, but when I realized that in the long run, you couldn't win, I quit. I've always found people who worshipped money utterly repulsive. Still do. Which is why Wall Street doesn't like me very much. And why I can't relate to too many Managers or accountants.

Even before the tour, I had decided our whole Disciples of Soul thing was going to be a concept. I had full-length leather coats made with a variation of the Hells Angels logo on the back. I got permission from the head of the Angels in New York at the time, Chuck Zito, but the coats got us into trouble in Europe, and I had to have a few sit-downs.

I decided that we were going to be the ultimate Rock and Roll rebels—no drugs, no drinking—and that we'd get into amazing shape. To set a good example and prepare for the revolution to come.

This was before hotels had gyms. I had a personal trainer, Phil Dunphy, and we took his equipment out on the road, put it under the bus. When we got to a hotel Phil had the bellmen bring it to a room, which we would convert to a workout room.

Swear to God.

I'm not showing my age too much with all this, am I? I mean now that every Motel 6 has a five-thousand-square-foot gym?

Did I mention milkmen once came to people's houses every morning to personally bring you milk?

Doctors made house calls.

And a truck of the greatest junk food, the Entenmann's of its day—a Dugan's truck just flashed across my mind—would deliver daily ecstasy to your front door in the form of just-made cupcakes, Danishes, doughnuts. I'm not making this up. Let's face it, Americans have never had a chance healthwise.

In that first year, the Disciples did a couple of interesting gigs, like the US Festival, where we went on at 9 a.m.—Bo Diddley time—and the Reading Festival, where they threw bottles at us. We also opened for the Who and U2.

People didn't know what to make of us. Five horns, Rock guitar, a percussionist, multiracial. It was hard to categorize us, so we were better off playing our own gigs rather than trying to open for other bands.

Opening acts work in the Hard Rock world, or any genre where the opener is very similar to the headliner. If you're the least bit unique, you're better off building your own audience from scratch if you can find a way to pay for it. I'm still trying to figure that part out. But I'd rather play to five hundred of my own fans than fifty thousand of somebody else's. You sell more records with your own people, and they stay with you for life.

Plus, all I was interested in was talking about politics, which America didn't get at all and still hasn't. Well, maybe they're starting to get it now. So I started spending more and more time in Europe.

The turning point of my solo career may have come with the very first show.

It was October 16, 1982, on a live TV broadcast called *Rockpalast* in Germany, which went live to something like seventeen countries, was on all night, and was watched by everybody at a time when there were only three channels.

The creator, Peter Rüchel, who would become a lifelong friend, was such a big fan of *Men Without Women* that we headlined the show. Gianna Nannini, described to me as the Italian Patti Smith, opened, then Kid Creole and the Coconuts, then us.

We were a little concerned because we had just found out our record had come out in Germany that day.

We went on and the crowd went crazy. By the end of the show it was bedlam. Our local record company guy, a delightful wild man named Lothar Meinerzhagen (picture Werner Klemperer as Colonel Klink without the uniform), who was one of our true believers, called LA and begged them to support a European tour immediately. He told them the reaction was extraordinary, and the broadcast had gone out to all of Europe.

They turned it down. A life-changing moment. We could have broken all of Europe right then and there. If I'd had a Manager, it would have gotten done.

Kid Creole—who, with all due respect, put the audience to sleep—stayed, toured, broke Europe wide open, and never left.

Meanwhile, I was thinking a lot about that kid in Germany who'd gotten me hooked on politics in the first place. I wanted to find him. And beat the shit out of him.

The tour established the pattern of my entire performance life: having to win people over song by song, since very few songs I've written would ever become even remotely familiar.

The other pattern I would establish was starting to write the next album a few months into the tour. I was so excited about one new song that I took the band into a studio in Belgium on a day off and cut it.

"RocknRoll Rebel," which was going to be the title and lead track of my second album, referred to an incident from earlier that year when my friends and I got kicked out of Disneyland because of how I was dressed. My friends being Maureen, my assistant Obie, and Bruce.

It was my comic version of the Stones' "Street Fighting Man," and the main joke was that my rebellion was about dressing funny and *not* doing drugs. When I sang about being "straight" in the chorus, that's what it was about, not my heterosexuality, which isn't particularly rebellious.

Although, at one point in the early British Rock scene it *would* have been a rebellious act!

I did a radio essay on it, the substance of which was my sincere belief that the day the gay culture abandoned Rock and went to Disco was the day fashion left with them. Glam would be the gay culture's final endorsement of Rock. Before that, the industry was completely dominated by a culture so gay that the Stones' Manager Andrew Oldham told me he had to pretend to be gay just to have a seat at the table!

It began with the London Promoter and Manager Larry Parnes, who discovered talented and attractive young men, changed their names, seduced them (if possible), and tried to make them famous. His stable included Tommy Steele (originally Tommy Hicks), Marty Wilde (Reg Smith), Billy Fury (Ron Wycherley), Vince Eager (Roy Taylor), Dickie Pride (Richard Knellar), Lance Fortune (Chris Morris), Duffy Power, (Ray Howard), Johnny Gentle (John Askew), Terry Dene (Terence Williams), Nelson Keene (Malcolm Holland), and Georgie Fame (Clive Powell), among others.

Then there was the influential Pop and theater songwriter Lionel Bart. Not to mention virtually all of the early Rock Managers, including Brian Epstein (the Beatles), Kit Lambert (the Who), Robert Stigwood (Cream, the BeeGees), Simon Napier-Bell (Yardbirds, Marc Bolan), Billy Gaff (Rod Stewart), Ken Pitt (David Bowie), Barry Krost (Cat Stevens), John Reid (Elton John), among others.

The point being that I believe it was the gay influence that made fashion such an integral part of the Rock music scene, and I miss it.

Am I digressing enough?

After sitting with "RocknRoll Rebel" for a while, I reconsidered making it the title song, or even putting it on my second album. It was going to be the beginning of my completely political phase, and I felt it needed a harder edge musically than my typical Rock or Soul, so I decided to let the horns go. Plus the song had a lot of humor in it, and I felt I also had to let that side of me go for a while. Thirty-six years, to be exact. *RocknRoll Rebel* finally emerged as the title of my box set of early work in 2019.

Part of the rationalization and satisfaction of being a boss working for another boss was the ability to offer suggestions and advice.

I liked being the underboss in the E Street Band. The consigliere. It kept me out of the spotlight but allowed me to make a significant enough contribution to justify my own existence in my own mind. And there was a balance between me, Bruce, and Jon. We had artistic theory and artistic practice covered.

But somewhere in '83, it started to feel like Bruce had stopped listening. He had always been the most single-minded individual, with a natural extreme monogamy of focus in all things—in relationships, in songwriting, in guitar playing, in friends. Was that impulse now going to apply to his advisers?

At the time, I was hurt by the thought that maybe Jon resented my complete direct access to Bruce. I liked Jon a lot and thought he felt the same about me. If anything, I should have been the resentful one, but I wasn't. In the end, I don't think Jon had anything to do with the way things changed. There comes a time when people want to evolve without any baggage. To become something new and different without having to stay connected to the past. This was, I think, one of those moments.

Occasionally you need to be untethered.

Without all this retrospective wisdom, though, Bruce and I had our first fight, one of only three we would have in our lives.

I felt I had been giving him nothing but good advice and had dedicated my whole life and career to him without asking for a thing.

I felt I'd earned an official position in the decision-making process. He disagreed. So I quit.

Fifteen years.

We finally made it.

And I quit.

The night before payday.

It was fucking with Destiny big-time.

Or was it fulfilling it?

Briefly, let's leave emotion out of it and examine the balance sheet of this rather . . . incredible move.

On the positive side, I would write the music that would make up the bulk of my life's work. Had I stayed, in between tours I probably would have produced other Artists. Or continued writing for others. Or both. But I probably would never have written for myself.

I very possibly wouldn't have gotten into politics. Would Mandela have gotten out of jail? Would the South African government have fallen? Probably. But we took years off both of those things.

I got to be in *The Sopranos* and *Lilyhammer*. They probably never would have happened.

I would create two radio formats, a syndicated radio show, two channels of original content for Sirius (which has introduced over a thousand new bands that have nowhere else to go), a record company, and a music history curriculum. Would any of that exist?

It would change Bruce's personal life for the better; that's indisputable.

He would have been on the road for two years. Would he have had the time to hook up with Patti if she hadn't been on the road with him? Would their three wonderful kids exist if I hadn't left?

Patti Scialfa would find the love of her life, a mixed bag for her well-deserved career—a more visible shortcut but forever in his shadow (welcome to the club)—and most importantly, again, would those same three amazing kids exist if she hadn't joined the band to sing my vocal parts?

Nils Lofgren, hired to do my guitar parts, got a very rewarding second career, or third career if you count Crazy Horse, which he well deserved.

So some good things happened.

The negatives?

I lost my juice.

As Chadwick Boseman, playing James Brown, says in the excellent biopic *Get on Up* after he fires his band, "Five minutes ago you were the baddest band in the land; now you're nobody."

Let that be a lesson, kids. And believe me, I am nothing if not *the* cautionary tale.

Never, ever leave your power base.

Not until you have secured a new one.

I not only lost most of my friends and the respect of several different industries, I blew any chance of living a life without ever again having to worry about money.

Who knows what could have been created if I'd had the backing of the masters of the universe, who are nothing but thrilled to invest in the ideas of happy, successful Rock stars?

I might even have been financially secure enough to have kids of my own.

Next life.

Upon leaving the band, I became persona totally non grata. We didn't publicize any bad blood. Not one negative word from either of us. We just said that I had left to pursue my own career, but I was seen as a traitor by virtually everybody. People felt they had to choose sides. Guess whose side they chose?

I didn't think I had much in common with Trotsky, but we were both temporarily written out of history.

seventeen

The Killing Floor

(1983–1984)

I should have listened,
When my friend said come to Mexico with me,
I should have listened,
When my friend said come to Mexico with me,
I wouldn't be here now children,
Down on the killing floor.

   —HOWLIN' WOLF

Politics in Pop music began with an innocent enough couplet from Bob Dylan.

It was the first two lines of his fifth album, *Bringing It All Back Home*, and it would change the world forever.

The song, "Subterranean Homesick Blues," nodded to Jack Kerouac in its title and made liberal use of the symbolist poetry of Arthur Rimbaud and Allen Ginsberg. It was also the first time Dylan ever recorded with a band that anybody had heard. (He had played with a band a few years before on a B-side.)

He'd been to England and had seen the future of Rock and Roll, and at that stage of the game, its name was the Beatles.

That led him to accept an invitation from Jim Dickson to come see a group he was managing that would soon be called the Byrds. They were already being touted as the American Beatles, and Dylan didn't miss much. He was also aware that the most money he'd ever made was from the publishing royalty from Peter, Paul, and Mary's version of "Blowin' in the Wind."

The Byrds didn't like "Blowin' in the Wind" and didn't want to do it, so Dickson very cleverly invited Dylan to their rehearsal, forcing them to learn it to avoid being embarrassed. They played him their now-classic electric version of his "Mr. Tambourine Man." As the story goes, after Dylan heard the Bach-meets-Beatles version, he said, "Hey, man! You can dance to that!" And history was made.

It would be released five months after his acoustic version and would establish the Byrds as one of the most important bands of the Renaissance, single-handedly create the Folk Rock genre, and put America back on the charts after a year of British Invasion domination.

And by the way, it would be Dylan's only song to reach number one until "Murder Most Foul" fifty-five years later!

"Subterranean Homesick Blues" ushered in Dylan's electric future.

> *Johnny's in the basement mixing up the medicine,*
> *I'm on the pavement thinking about the government . . .*

I consider those the two most important sentences in the history of Rock.

The first line typified Dylan's unique way of having fun with the language, and no one since Allen Ginsberg has loved the English language as much as Bob. It's clever, secretive, metaphorical, streetwise, and hilarious, all at the same time.

What is Johnny doing in the basement?

Is he rolling a joint? Making a batch of grappa? Planning a revolution? Contemplating a paradox? Writing philosophy? Having sex? Denying he's an existentialist?

Bob leaves that up to you.

But the second line changed everything forever:

> *I'm on the pavement thinking*
> *about the government . . .*

What?

Thinking about *what*?

What the fuck does that mean?

All we thought about was sex.

All we knew was love songs.

That's all there was.

That line is the politics-meets-Pop shot heard round the world.

We were kids. We didn't know Folk music, or Country Blues, where ideas like this were commonplace.

Since when were we supposed to be thinking about the government?

Nobody ever thought about the government.

Not in my neighborhood.

Not in my family.

Not in my generation.

Not anybody in my parents' generation either.

So that was it. The Big Bang of political consciousness in Pop.

Bob Dylan had already taken Woody Guthrie's Folkie, Activist agenda to the highest-possible level on his second and third albums with songs like "Masters of War," "A Hard Rain's A-Gonna Fall," and "Only a Pawn in Their Game." But ideas like these were completely alien to Pop music.

So alien, in fact, that Dylan's words would combine with other ingredients—the Beatles' melodies, the Rolling Stones' sexuality, the Byrds' artistic breadth, the Beach Boys' blissful harmony, the Kinks' eccentricities, and the Who's operatic apotheosis—to create the new Artform of Rock beginning that summer of '65.

Over the years, other Rock songs with political consciousness popped up now and then.

Stephen Stills's "For What It's Worth" with Buffalo Springfield, Janis Ian's "Society's Child," Marty Balin and Paul Kantner's "Volunteers" with Jefferson Airplane, John Fogerty's "Fortunate Son" with Creedence Clearwater Revival, and the ultimate example, Neil Young's "Ohio" with Crosby, Stills, Nash, and Young.

In 1971 Marvin Gaye would make history by being the first mainstream major Soul Artist to do not just a song, but an entirely politically themed album, *What's Going On.*

Gil Scott-Heron could get away with it, and the Last Poets, but showbiz conventional wisdom declared politics and religion out of bounds for big stars.

Gaye had to fight Motown's founder and big daddy Berry Gordy all the way to the finish line. In the end, Gordy recognized that Gaye's passion for what his brother was going through in Vietnam and the daily uprisings in every Black neighborhood was not to be denied. Gordy surrendered with a speech that included "One of us will learn something from this." Gordy would be the one learning. The album was a huge hit.

Marvin would contribute to the writing of the record, his gift was his vocal genius. He belonged to that small club of singers that could completely make a song his own whether he wrote it or not. Only a few—Frank Sinatra, Tony Bennett, and Elvis Presley come to mind—share that gift.

His unique combination of Doo-Wop, Blues, Gospel, Soul, and Jazz was on full display in the title track, mostly written by Obie Benson from the Four Tops (they rejected it!) and Motown staff writer Al Cleveland, and continued to be impressive throughout the incredible album.

What would become his signature style of singing background with himself supposedly came from an engineer mistakenly playing back two different takes of a lead vocal at the same time. Marvin loved the accidental interplay and would use it to great effect on what would be his first (brilliant) Production.

In 1971, at the urging of Ravi Shankar, George Harrison organized the Concert for Bangladesh, which combined the consciousness of Dylan with the new political power of the Rock music generation revealed by Woodstock.

But these were one-offs. It wouldn't have made sense at that stage to practice politics full-time. And then came the 1980s.

We had gone from the Nixon era to the Reagan era, with only a brief, failed respite from the neofascism from Jimmy Carter. It seemed like the right time for an entirely political Rock artist.

In the wake of my first album, I put out a single, "Solidarity," to bring attention to the Polish trade union movement of Lech Wałesa, which was struggling to survive at the time. I kept the lyrics universal, referencing the movement only in the title and in a bit of the Polish national anthem I played in the guitar solo.

Horns were gone by then. I had decided to let the subject matter determine the music, which made for a more satisfying artistic marriage—every record would become the soundtrack to a different movie—but was not a good way to build an audience. As if I didn't have enough challenges already with my name change.

But I was possessed. I was on an obsessive unstoppable artistic adventure, no matter how irrational. There was an indescribable rush of adrenaline that came from feeling like I had found a purpose. A justification for my existence.

Surprise juiced the adrenaline considerably. This was not what I'd had in mind for my life. I wanted to be Diaghilev! Irving Thalberg! Orson Welles! Or at least Bob Fosse!

I wanted to Produce Big Things! I was on the path to doing just that. I had produced a massive hit record, and life is all about the parlay. I could have followed that success with producing other major acts or getting any project I could dream up financed for the rest of my life. Now, my significant contribution would be diminished to irrelevancy.

The adrenaline rush of feeling like I was doing the right thing, of having a purpose, fulfilling some sort of unclear but consequential destiny, had a big empty space to fill. And it did. It would get me through the '80s.

Voice of America, the second in my five-album arc, would be about how government affected the family and society in general.

The title track returned to the theme of an earlier song, "Lyin' in a Bed of Fire," but this time I was more aggressively pissed off, demanding action as opposed to merely observing the state of affairs. Talking to myself really, as much as anyone.

"Can you hear me? Wake up! Where's the voice of America?"

Jackson Browne would cover it, much to my elation.

"Justice" expressed my philosophy at the time, which has changed somewhat over the years. I now see a post-terrorism reason to have a worldwide military presence, which I didn't then. What hasn't changed is the need to give priority to the war at home, the lack of justice for our black, Latino, and Native populations.

The centerpiece of the record was "Checkpoint Charlie," about my trip behind the Iron Curtain. There was no better metaphor than the Berlin Wall to describe the way politics fucked with families, literally separating them.

"Solidarity" and "Out of the Darkness" were examples of the we-are-all-connected theme running through all my work, one Reggae, one Rock/Dance/Pop. With "Solidarity," I started embodying different characters' perspectives to make my points more dramatically, taking the every-singer-is-an-actor thing to its next level.

I sent "Solidarity" to Chris Blackwell, hoping he would release it on his Island Records label in Jamaica. Next time I heard from Chris, Black Uhuru had recorded it and had a hit!

"Los Desaparecidos (The Disappeared Ones)" was the story of our government supporting Latin American dictatorships that used their militaries to enforce slave labor for the multinational corporations. The military would "disappear" the troublemakers, meaning anyone trying to unionize or ask for fair wages or better working conditions.

My song was about a mother trying to explain to her young son why his father wouldn't be coming home. That boy would grow up to be the singer of "Bitter Fruit," a song on my next album. In addition to being one of my favorite songs, "Los Desaparecidos" was also one of my favorite records. Clearmountain's mixes were always great. That one was transcendent.

The album also included the most difficult song I've ever written, then or since.

I had a title, "I Am a Patriot," the subject of which was the disgust with political parties that George Washington expressed in his farewell address. I stared at that title for a year, knowing that my work in general would be criticizing our government, quite severely, and that I had to make it clear that it was coming from loyalty to our Founders' ideals and my belief that America was still a work in progress.

It was worth the effort. Jackson Browne, Eddie Vedder, and Kris Kristofferson, three writers I greatly admire, would cover it, much to my honored surprise.

A few months later Bruce called me. "Knowing you, if I didn't call you, we'd probably never speak again," he said. "Let's meet and get past this."

We reconciled.

I played *Voice of America* for him.

He was legitimately impressed.

"You've just been born," he said.

He had new music for me too. In the two years since I was gone, they had recorded a bunch of things and kept three new songs.

He played me one called "Dancing in the Dark" that was going on the record, and then "No Surrender," which he said would be an outtake for a B-side. (He never played me "Bobby Jean.")

"Man," I said. "You got it backwards! Throw that 'Dancing' thing in the trash and not only put 'No Surrender' on the record, but open with it! In fact, make it the damn title! *No Retreat, No Surrender!*"

To me, "Dancing in the Dark" had the potential to destroy his long-fought-for credibility. He had thrown out dozens of classic Rock songs because they very vaguely resembled rapidly-being-forgotten British Invasion songs, and now he was going to release what could easily be interpreted as a *Disco song* to blatantly try and get a hit?

A month or so later we had dinner. "This record is gonna be big," he said. I guess they knew; preorders from retail must have been huge.

"Good," I said. "You deserve it."

But I sensed a little trepidation. Not quite as bad as being on *Time* and *Newsweek* at the same time, but in that same Am I losing control? ballpark.

"I know you felt I'd stopped listening, but I'm listening now," he said. "What do I do with this?"

I thought about it. How could he separate himself from the pack once and for all?

"You have this identity of a working-class hero. With a big record, it's going to be a challenge to maintain that, even though I know that's where your heart is. I'll tell you what." It's funny how when you really need an idea, it comes. "You know how people do big events. Fundraisers. Shit like that? You know, once a year, once a tour?"

"Yeah."

"Well, what if you made every single show in every single city a fundraiser? Donate . . . I don't know . . . some percentage, something. Not once in a while. Every single show."

"Wow," he said. "That's radical. Gotta think about that one."

"Just like you always used to sign every autograph while we waited for hours on the fucking bus, this would connect you intimately to every town."

While he contemplated, I celebrated.

Waiter! More wine! I'm on a roll!

He would do the charity-in-every-city thing, but, luckily, I lost the "Dancing in the Dark" argument.

He not only put it on the album but released it as the first single! And not only released it as the first single, but filmed a stupid video! When I had been in the band, we'd had an understanding that we would *never* do a video. We had a reputation as the best live band around. If you wanted to see us, you'd have to come to the live show to see us!

But just to prove even the world's greatest consigliere can occasionally be wrong, that Rock Disco song and terrible video started the snowball that would roll to twenty million sales and pay my rent for quite a while.

And for the fans, like me, he put "No Surrender" on the record also.

Voice of America, the album of my birth, was suffocated in its crib by the Sony monster as it rolled out the marketing for Bruce's album, now called *Born in the USA*, which was released just four weeks later.

It never occurred to me that that would be his title. Or that the cover and marketing ads would have stars and stripes all over the place, just like my album.

The DJs' attitudes were, Why play an E Streeter when we can play the Boss! No thought at all that both records might have value.

The '80s caught the zenith of what had started as a teenage novelty distraction. We saw Rock record sales no one ever dreamed of and no one would ever see again.

One after the other. Ten, twelve, fifteen million. Michael Jackson, Madonna, Whitney Houston, Tina Turner, Prince, even Phil Collins— each averaging four or five hit singles per album, with each single bringing an additional three million more in album sales.

The era would last until Guns N' Roses's *Appetite for Destruction*, more or less, before slowing down, but it was a wild ride for those fortunate enough to be at the amusement park at the time.

I, once again, was not allowed in. My pirates were not in the Caribbean. They were busy attending the funeral of my very political, very invisible second album.

Still, we hit the road hard. We did *Rockpalast* again, and killed again.

That fall, with the presidential election looming, Ronald Reagan attempted to co-opt "Born in the USA" as a campaign song. Bruce stopped him, but Ronnie was probably responsible for another five, ten million in sales. Misinterpretation can be profitable.

I released another one-off political single with little room for misinterpretation called "Vote! (That Mutha Out)," backed by my only Rap composition so far, "After World War Three." I tried to find Melle Mel to do it, but we wouldn't meet until two years later, so I became Grandmaster Cobra Jones, and rapped it myself.

My research into America's role in the world's problems continued, but I had also started to feel that books weren't enough. I wanted to be there and see things firsthand. Feel them. Taste them. Absorb what was going on down in my bones.

I decided the third album, *Freedom—No Compromise* would use three examples to explore the theme of government's relationships with the people. The three would be Latin America, Native America, and South Africa.

First stop was Nicaragua with Jackson Browne, who had been everywhere years before I was even aware of these issues. Daryl Hannah came with us, and there were some congressmen down there at the same time.

Nicaragua was at a critical point. The Sandinistas, the rebel group that had overthrown the brutal dictator Anastasio Somoza, the US government's good buddy, had been legitimately elected to run the new government. In response, the Reagan administration's security apparatus and "off the book" friends had organized, funded, and trained the biggest group of terrorists ever assembled by a Western power, the Contras. There were about ten thousand of them at their peak. Literally the largest organized terror group until the Islamic State of Iraq and the Levant (ISIL) thirty years later.

The purpose of the Contras was to murder, terrorize, burn villages, and otherwise create as much havoc as possible against the people of Nicaragua.

It's important to keep this history in mind when you hear so many refer back to the universally revered, happy-go-lucky semisenile grandfatherly cowboy, Ronald Reagan.

Nicaragua had been the only country in the area since Cuba to free itself of the outrageous oppression in the region, and now our government was trying to illegally overthrow their internationally monitored elected government.

Regardless of what I thought about the Sandinistas, I decided I had to do everything possible to stop the terrorism against the Nicaraguan people by my government and try to head off the increasingly likely prospect of a military invasion, which would be justified under the pretense of preventing Nicaragua from supplying arms to rebels in El Salvador, who were trying to overthrow their own brutal military dictatorship.

So when Jackson mentioned he was going and invited me, I immediately said yes.

Reagan and his people were also trying to use Costa Rica as a staging area through bribery and threats as a southern front in this illegal war. This in spite of the fact that Costa Rica was the only country in Central or South America that was truly peaceful because they had completely disbanded their military years earlier.

On our trip, we met with various ministers and central committee members who took us around, showing us the improvements they were making and the plans they had.

I pissed off the agriculture minister immediately. He was explaining with great pride that the land was completely liberated, that people and entrepreneurs were free to do anything they wanted with it.

"Anything?" I said. "It is important that we are very clear about what is going on here."

"Yes," he said, "total freedom."

"So I can buy this land right now," I said, "and put a McDonald's up?"

"Well, not exactly, señor." He laughed and tried to change the subject.

I took him aside. "Look," I said. "I'm sure you have a good plan, and it's none of my business, but just be accurate with us. We're going to be reporting back to America, so it's important to be clear. When we say total freedom in America, we mean it literally. You don't. So let's not allow our cultural communication differences to turn us into bullshitters."

Now he was pissed. Discussion over.

Like most governments in the world, about half the Sandinista Directorate were OK and about half were incompetents, ideologues, or idiots. We were told we would meet the president, Daniel Ortega. "Fine," I said, but I really wanted to meet his wife. In politics, as in life, the wife is usually where the real policy action is.

We set up a meeting with Ortega's wife, Rosario Murillo, ostensibly to talk about culture. I asked Jackson if I could meet with her alone because I had an idea that was a little delicate that I wanted to try out. He agreed. I told her Jackson wasn't feeling well, which turned out to be true. Everybody got sick except me. Whenever I took a research trip I would fast to keep my mind clear. If the trip was too long to fast, I would eat as little as possible and never any meat.

I've heard that Rosario Murillo has become controversial in her later years, but back then she was great. Most of the government officials just wanted rubber-stamp approval from whatever mindless liberal happened to come through town, but she gave the impression she really wanted to know what I thought. And I happened to have a few things on my mind.

After a few drinks, I moved off the small talk and suddenly asked her if she loved her husband. She was taken a bit aback but said, Yes, señor, very much. "Well," I said, "you should spend as much time with him as possible, because he's a dead man walking. It's just a matter of time and time is running out."

She knew I wasn't kidding. The idea had probably crossed her mind more than once. She was a very smart woman married to a revolutionary. But she was expecting a pleasant conversation about the Arts, and the reality of what I was saying hit her hard.

She reached across the table, put her hands on mine, looked deeply into my eyes and asked, "What can we do?"

I suggested three things.

"The first thing may sound silly," I said, "but I sincerely believe there is only one way to save him, and to avoid an invasion by my country where a lot of innocent people will be killed. You have to get him out of those Castro fatigues and into a three-piece suit."

Her eyes widened.

" . . . and for him to make a speech at the UN where everyone will see how wonderfully normal and presidential he looks. Television is everything, and image counts more than you can possibly imagine. This is critical. The other two things are not as important, so if you only remember one thing, remember that."

She nodded. I had her full attention.

"OK," I said. "Here's something else." I had read an early draft of the new Nicaraguan constitution and noticed a big problem. There was something in it about the Sandinista Party being the official party of the country and their flag being the official flag. "The rest of the document looks great," I said, "but unless you separate party affiliation from national governance, you're doomed." Multiparty democracy, I explained, meant playing no favorites, regardless of how many war heroes or liberators a specific party had.

"There have been many discussions about this," she replied. I was guessing they hadn't gone well.

Finally, I asked her if she considered herself a Communist. If she had said yes, it wouldn't have thrown me. I'd studied the subject enough to know that there were many strains of communism, some malevolent (China), some benevolent (Italy), some a combination of malice, corruption, and stupidity (Russia).

"No," she said.

"Do any government officials?" She mentioned a few and explained that Fidel Castro was a big hero to the whole hemisphere because of his success in overthrowing Batista. The Nicaraguan Communists, she thought, would have their own party eventually, and they weren't ideologically extreme enough to be a real factor in her husband's plans.

"OK," I said. "It may be too politically complicated. You probably have to placate your extremists on both sides. But here's the third thing. Get a New York lawyer, and the next time the *New York Times* calls you a Communist country or Communist government, sue them!"

I explained to her that in the United States, the word meant something different than anywhere else in the world. "In our country," I explained, "it is a license to kill. Literally. We will send soldiers down here and they will kill your husband and no one will be accused of a crime. Do you understand?"

She nodded pensively, probably thinking she had no shot with the hard-liners on the second two points.

But the first point? Sure enough, soon after we left, there was Daniel Ortega, on TV, addressing the United Nations, looking like he'd just been to James Bond's tailor on Savile Row! I mean he was superfly, baby!

Did it work? Who knows? All I know is we never invaded. Eventually the arch criminal Ollie North got caught, the Contras were disbanded, and US-sponsored terrorism ended. The Sandinistas would go in and out of power, but I didn't care.

We got lucky. As long as innocent people weren't dying or being terrorized with US involvement, I figured our work was done and moved on.

After Nicaragua, Jackson helped set up trips to the Six Nations, Onondaga Reservation near Syracuse, New York, and the Pine Ridge Reservation in South Dakota, the site of Wounded Knee, where I got a crash course in Indian politics, culture, and religion.

The first thing that hit me was how much was going on, and how little attention it was getting from the general non-Indian public. There were (and still are) hundreds of land disputes, denial of access to sacred sites, the disappearing of native languages, grave robbing by museums, nothing less than a political prisoner named Leonard Peltier who remains in jail as I write this in spite of an outrageously unjust trial, and other issues resulting from the 370 treaties that have been broken by the US government.

Not to mention the efforts to store nuclear waste on Indian land, led by Hazel O'Leary, later picked by President Bill Clinton to be secretary of energy!

Many problems revolved around the Native American religion and its relationship to nature. The essence of Indian religion is that the Earth is sacred and all living and nonliving things are equally sacred, to be respected as separate but equal parts of an integrated universe.

Native Americans are the original environmentalists, and issues like pollution and mining have been major issues since gold was discovered in the Black Hills in 1874.

So first of all, why weren't Native Americans and environmentalists working together?

Those issues were intimately connected to the destruction of Native cultures through the "Americanization" of Indian people. Indian children were dragged to American schools, where their culture was literally beaten out of them. The most successfully Anglicized and co-opted were picked to run the US government-imposed "Indian" governments on the reservations, where these no-longer-Indians-except-in-bloodline would sign agreements allowing corporations to mine Indian land in direct violation of the most fundamental tenets of Indian religion.

Any ethnocide has two essential initial components: take the land and kill the language.

The divide-and-conquer strategy of the US government worked beyond the wars of the nineteenth century. In the late twentieth century, when I came on the scene, there was very little communication between the surviving 350 Indian Nations.

To address these issues, I started the Solidarity Foundation with my Native-blood friend Alex Ewen to serve as an information-gathering and networking service between the Indian Nations themselves, the Indian Nations and the non-Indian public, and the Indian Nations and environmental groups. One of our most important goals was to encourage economic development in harmony with the Earth.

This eventually led to the only disagreement I ever had with the Elder's Circle, the far more spiritual Native American version of the Mafia Commission. The issue of gambling had become a major internal struggle in Indian country. The elders of the National Treaty Council were against it for general reasons of morality, but I thought the potential for new revenue was too good to resist.

Maybe it was my New Jersey / Italian American / Rat Pack upbringing, but legal gambling on Indian land seemed to me the answer to all their problems. I figured it's a nonpolluting, enormous source of revenue, and it sure beat selling beads by the roadside to backpackers looking for a weekend commune with nature.

If it was handled properly, I thought it could turn things around for the whole culture. That meant owning and controlling it, using the money to build and maintain Indian-oriented schools and to cure the rampant poverty, unemployment, increasing drug problems, and devastated infrastructure.

I found myself uncharacteristically disagreeing with the Elders, so out of respect, Solidarity Foundation pretty much stayed away from the subject.

As usual, the Elders' instincts were more right than wrong. They were taken advantage of left and right until a kid from New Jersey named Jimmy Allen was brought in by the Seminole Tribe in Florida to help out a small casino of no great consequence that had recently licensed the Hard Rock name.

But more about that later.

eighteen

The Breathless Projectionist

(1984)

I feel like I'm in the world, but not of it.
—THE UNWRITTEN BOOK

I was in Los Angeles in 1983 and went to an Art theater on Melrose to see Jean-Luc Godard's *Breathless*.

Before the movie started, a song was playing. It was different somehow, oddly evocative. After the movie I knocked on the projectionist's door and asked him what it was. "Peter Gabriel," he said. "Biko." I had never heard of either one of them.

A little research revealed that Peter Gabriel had been in Genesis, a Prog Rock group, a genre I had never found my way into, and was now on his own as a solo artist. And Stephen Biko was a black anti-apartheid activist in South Africa who had been murdered in 1977 in prison.

I had already made a list of America's dubious and mostly hidden foreign entanglements since World War II. I added South Africa to the list.

I had a hard time researching the South African situation. The *New York Times* was saying there was reform going on, but it was unclear how much or what it was leading toward.

The history was easy enough.

The Apartheid Policy—the classification and separation of the races—was officially put in place in South Africa in 1948 when the National (white supremacist) Party took power, although the practice dated back as far as the 1800s. The white invaders—first Dutch (Afrikaners), then British and others—decided they were so outnumbered that they'd better figure out a way of controlling what became, basically, slave labor in the mines.

Their solution? They banned black Africans from "Church and State," meaning they couldn't vote, and made virtually all crossing of racial lines illegal.

This policy didn't sit so well with the rest of the world. Beginning in the late 1960s, the United Nations imposed a boycott to isolate South Africa. The National Party needed to figure out a way around the boycott. So they came up with a solution inspired by our Indian reservations.

They divided the unimportant parts of the country into tribal "homelands" (Bantustans), forcibly moved the black population into them by their tribal affiliation, and declared those areas independent countries. Never mind that South Africa was the least tribal of all the African countries, with the Zulu Nation the only exception. When the black Africans had been removed to these Bantustans, the Nationalists would declare South Africa a democracy and bring the blacks back in as foreign immigrant labor, with no political rights.

Evil brilliance, right?

They forcibly removed over three million black Africans. Knocked their houses down, put their belongings on trucks, and dropped them off in the wasteland of these Bantustans—many of which, by the way, were shaped like no country had ever been shaped. Fragmented, discontinuous, spatter patterns of land whose only purpose was to further divide and weaken the black population.

Much of the world supported the boycott, with three major exceptions: our president, Ronald Reagan, along with the British prime minister Margaret Thatcher and the German chancellor Helmut Kohl. They opposed any significant economic sanctions and isolation, instead favoring a policy they called "constructive engagement," which was little more than a bullshit way of maintaining the status quo in South Africa and pretending things were getting better.

So that was the central question. Was the boycott the right thing to do or not? In 1984, after Nicaragua, I went to South Africa for two weeks. My motive was nonadversarial, at least at first. I went with an open mind, hoping to find proof of the "reforms" the newspapers were talking about.

It was on that flight that it finally hit me. I had blown my life. All my aspirations big and small were finally coming to fruition with the success of the E Street Band, and I blew it. I never liked flying. Suddenly my fear of flying was gone. Completely. Just like that. In fact, my fear of everything was gone. I would express my feelings about suicide in the song "Guns, Drugs, and Gasoline" a few years later, but for now, I would continue down the road to see where it led and try and accomplish something before I ran into the inevitable unbreachable castle wall my once-upon-a-time career lived behind.

My record company at the time, EMI, was accommodating. They undoubtedly assumed that I was willing to violate the boycott and play there. They hooked me up with two guys, one white, one black, to guide me through the country and connect me with whoever I wanted to meet. Both of them were incredibly courageous and helpful, and they shall remain nameless to protect them from repercussions for the multiple crimes they committed on my behalf. Just by being there I was violating the boycott.

I traveled from Johannesburg to Cape Town and ended up in Pretoria. I met with everyone I could, from the labor unions to religious leaders and everybody in between. I met with Archbishop (then Bishop) Desmond Tutu and Cyril Ramaphosa (then head of the Miner's Union, now president of the country). While I was in Cape Town, my guides tried to arrange a meeting with Nelson Mandela, imprisoned on Robben Island, but the authorities wouldn't let me see him. And I couldn't get to the prime minister either.

We even managed a side trip to one of the so-called homelands, one they were promoting as a separate country called Bophuthatswana, and its main attraction, the gambling resort of Sun City.

My companions explained that Sun City had been built by Nationalist investors, principally a man named Sol Kerzner, in collaboration with the apartheid regime, and was an irresistible temptation to those willing to buy the elaborate con and score either a big payday or some inexpensive sex. There was no gambling in South Africa proper, but Bophuthatswana was an "independent country" with its own rules.

My new friends were surprised when I passed on the gambling and hookers and went up to my hotel room. I was absorbing lots of information, so I had to be constantly evaluating whether I had heard something merely interesting or something important. I had just heard something important.

Over the next days, I spoke to as many people on the street as I could, meaning as many as would talk to me. They were reluctant at first. The problem was that it was illegal to say that you were in favor of the boycott. If you did, you could go to jail, which in those days could be a death sentence.

Luckily, they'd never seen anyone like me. My Rock and Roll appearance helped loosen them up, and many of them ended up telling me that they did in fact support the boycott. I played devil's advocate, explaining that boycotts often hurt the very people they are trying to help. Most South Africans didn't care. They felt they were in prison. How much worse could things get? And most of the political parties were in favor of it. Mandela's African National Congress (ANC), the opposition Pan Africanist Congress (PAC), and even the young, militaristic Azanian People's Organization (AZAPO), which had been founded by Steve Biko.

I also spent a good amount of time with a wonderful righteous cat named Johnny Clegg, a local music star whose group, Juluka, fused Zulu styles like *maskanda* and *mbaqanga* with Western Folk and Rock. His feelings about the boycott were more mixed. He understood certain aspects of it, but he wanted his music to be heard worldwide.

If I wanted simple answers, I was in the wrong place. Views were mixed because the situation was more than complex—human rights, politics, and economics were wound around each other, choking off the air supply.

Just before that first trip ended, an incident provided the clarity I needed.

I was in Pretoria, riding in a taxi at dusk. A black man stepped off the curb and my taxi swerved—not to miss him but to hit him. "Fucking kaffir," the driver said. ("Kaffir" means "nigger" in the Afrikaans dialect.)

I was frozen in shock. "Uh, you can let me out here," I managed to mutter.

I walked and walked around the main part of town, absorbing what I'd just seen and what I had seen before that, trying to make sense of all the opinions I had heard. I ended up in a town square staring up at statues of South African military icons. I decided that this evil system couldn't be reformed. The government and its criminal apartheid policy had to be exterminated.

I looked up at the nearest statue. I'm taking you down, motherfucker!

I didn't know how yet.

But I meant it.

I studied my notes on the long flight home—in those days, it was eighteen hours, with connections in Lagos and Paris.

I was determined to keep my promise to the military icon in that Pretoria square. A picture was forming in my unusually clear head. It was obvious that the South African government should not have lasted as long as it had. And I didn't mean for moral reasons.

I was discovering a part of my brain I didn't know existed. The ability to analyze had shown itself in little ways as a kid. I figured out that the way to win at Risk was to capture Australia first. I figured out that the most important part of a football team isn't the quarterback or running back or wide receiver. It's the offensive line that makes all the difference. (And when are they going to stop being called the unskilled part of the team?) It showed up as I took apart songs to understand them better. But never analysis like this. On a global stage.

In spite of all the false bravado presented to a gullible world, a closer inspection revealed that the stability of the South African government was far more fragile than the world was being led to believe.

They couldn't trust their own cops anymore. They were employing the military to keep the increasing unrest down. Little old Cuba was kicking their asses in Angola. And their economy was hanging by a thread, entirely dependent on the kindness of three white supremacist world leaders.

They were surviving in part because the world was ignorant. Nobody knew the extent of the modern slavery that was going on down there. A little publicity and this whole thing would fold like the house of cards that it was.

I began formulating a plan.

My thought was to hot-wire the existing boycott structure. The United Nations had established the basic boycott, but it was moving along at a low hum, largely because the United States, the UK, and Germany were practicing constructive engagement.

The boycott was most effective when it was most visible. That had worked in sports. South Africa had been kept out of the Olympics for decades, which pissed them off profoundly. The grand slam, obviously, would be an enforced economic boycott. If banks cut the country off, it would put a knife in the heart of apartheid and maybe get Mandela out of jail.

And while I couldn't affect the banks directly, I was standing on the bridge that led from the sports boycott to the economic boycott: the broader cultural boycott.

The best course, I figured, was to expose the evil brilliance of the Bantustans: the way black South Africans were shipped off to these phony homelands, stripped of their citizenry, and converted into immigrant labor with no political rights. And the perfect symbol of this policy was the Sun City resort.

Because Sun City was a con!

It was one of the great cons of all time.

It wasn't in a different country. It was the clever way South Africa fooled everybody into thinking they were *not* violating the boycott by playing in Sun City. That's why all the entertainers were vastly overpaid to play it.

That would be my target.

We expose the con, we win.

And with respectful apologies to my man Gil Scott-Heron, this revolution *would* be televised.

I was only home for a little while when I decided I didn't feel I'd covered the subject completely enough to write what I needed. I had to go back. This time I wanted to meet the guys nobody wanted me to meet.

I knew I had to pitch my idea to all the opposition parties, Mandela's ANC, the PAC, AZAPO. After being engaged in research and meetings and politics for the previous three years or so, I'd started to get the hang of it. Just because individuals or groups were on the same side didn't necessarily mean they liked one another.

The conventional wisdom of conflict resolution was to get everybody in the same room and work out differences and negotiate. Not only was that method impossible in this case, with half the parties on the lam, but I didn't believe it would work.

I decided the better strategy was to present a plan and have them all endorse it separately. If everybody agreed with me, they'd be agreeing with each other without the ego conflicts and general infighting and drama that go on with virtually all pro-democracy, anti-fascist groups worldwide. That kind of petty backstabbing is why the bad guys usually win. I wanted to avoid that.

I managed to meet the PAC in New York. They endorsed the idea. That was a big one, one of the two main opposition parties. Once I got back to Johannesburg, I immediately flew to Zimbabwe to meet with the other one, Mandela's ANC.

It was a good thing I had lost my fear of flying, because that flight from Joburg to Harare was one I'll never forget. It was a twenty-seat propeller job, bad enough, but we somehow managed to fly inside a storm the entire time, which meant being hit constantly by monstrous African lightning.

I didn't think I was going to die.

I *knew* I was going to die.

When we somehow made it to blessed terra firma, I saw that the plane had black marks all over the fuselage where the lightning had struck. At that moment, I felt that Destiny had something in mind for me. There's no way that little piece-of-shit crop duster should have survived that flight.

In Harare I floated my Sun City idea to the ANC representative. I explained that publicity, not violence, was the only way to win the war. If nothing else, I would be publicizing their cause and supporting the ANC as the official voice of the opposition. Of course I had said the same thing to the PAC!

The ANC representative liked my plan, as had the representative of the PAC. After a few days of consultation, he gave me its blessing.

I now had an official mandate from the leading revolutionary groups in my back pocket. It would come in handy.

I asked both organizations to give me six months and to try and minimize the violence in the meantime. They said they'd see what they could do.

Back in Johannesburg, I told my (now trusted) companions about my meeting with the ANC. They were impressed. Then I made my request. "OK, boys," I said. "I've been trying to keep you away from the heavy stuff, but I need you to set up one more meeting. And you're going to have to break the law to do it."

"Are you kidding?" one said. "Half the meetings we've already arranged have been illegal. We're in all the way."

What I needed from them was a meeting with AZAPO.

AZAPO was among the most violent of the younger revolutionary groups. Meeting with them was risky, at the very least, and might be fatal.

Word went out, and a guy who knew a guy who knew a guy sent word back that a meeting could be arranged in Soweto. But getting into Soweto was easier said than done. Since violence was on the rise, the government had established a military blockade around the massive ghetto.

Clearly defining and separating neighborhoods was a strategy designed to anticipate the revolution and give the greatly outnumbered government an advantage to commit mass eradication once the revolution inevitably started.

We drove out to Soweto. My white companion and I were covered by a blanket on the floor of the back seat as our black conspirator drove through the blockade.

We stopped.

"We're here."

A ghost emerged from fog, dressed all in white. He motioned for us to follow. The machete in his waistband did not bode well.

My companions took a last glance my way. Their look seemed to say, Are you sure?

I took a moment to fully absorb the absurdity of the situation. Just a few minutes ago in my timeless mind I was sixteen, slowing down my record player to learn Eric Clapton's solo on "Steppin' Out." And now here I was . . . steppin' way the fuck out. I had the urge to laugh out loud. I suppressed it.

There are references to a biblical state of grace that suggest protection by some unseen force. I'm not religious, but I had that tingly feeling.

I smiled. I was sure.

We went in.

Inside, seven or eight guys were crowded into a single room. All of them were dressed in white. All were carrying machetes.

They immediately began berating me. What was I doing? I had violated the boycott simply by being there. As they spoke, they glowered and fondled their weapons, occasionally advancing toward me, threatening me, anything to intimidate me.

I wasn't having it. I was ready. I knew the only way out of this was to communicate supreme confidence. It was out-tough-guy them or die.

"Just fucking relax," I said. I explained that I was there to help, but that I had to see with my own eyes what was happening so I could report back to my people.

The spokesperson told me that they didn't need my help.

"Yes you do," I said. "Do you seriously think you're gonna win this war blowing up radio stations, assassinating rats, and necklacing traitors? The government loves it when you pick up a gun or a machete. They know they can win that fight. You want to commit suicide? Go ahead! But don't pretend you're some revolutionary heroes doing it!"

They were not enjoying this conversation.

"I know how to win this war without spilling a drop of blood," I said more confidently than I felt.

That got their attention.

"OK," the spokesperson said. "What?"

"We win this war on TV!"

They looked around at each other. Who had agreed to meet with this crazy fucker in the first place?

I made my case. It wasn't the easiest argument I've ever made, considering I was pitching a TV war to revolutionaries living in a black South Africa that had a rare nodding acquaintance with electricity!

I explained to them how focusing on Sun City would expose the homeland policy and let us use the cultural boycott to jump-start the economic boycott.

They went to the far side of the room. An intense conversation followed.

My compadres looked like they were mentally writing their wills.

My black companion was picking up some words here and there and whispering to me. The general consensus seemed to be they were being too soft on violators of the boycott. Especially white guys.

I interrupted. "What white guys?" I asked.

They were taken aback. How had I overheard, let alone understood?

They shouted at me. "First Paul Simon. Now you!" Paul Simon had been to South Africa just before me, doing research and recording for what would become *Graceland*. "We should be killing you both!"

"You're being ridiculous," I said. "You can't kill Paul Simon! He's too good a songwriter!" I had no idea of the problems Paul would soon cause me, but I'd like to think I still would have tried to talk them out of killing him.

They didn't laugh.

I played my ace.

"By the way," I said, "the ANC and the PAC have agreed to support me and endorsed my idea."

This sent them back into another intense conversation.

Bringing up the ANC and the PAC was a calculated risk. All the groups were opposed to one another in some way. There were competitive agendas to spare. But I also knew Mandela had a special place in their hearts. That was true of everyone, except Mangosuthu Gatsha Buthelezi, the leader of the Zulu, who wanted to *be* Mandela. Probably still does if he's alive. He would be one of the few leaders that would refuse to meet with me.

"OK," they finally said. "We have no fucking idea what you're talking about"—I'm paraphrasing—"but we'll give you a few months to see what you can do."

In other words, they might as well let me go since they'd never heard of me.

I wasn't important enough to kill.

I told them I would do my best. And I added my usual reminder: By the way, if at all convenient, please stop killing people and blowing shit up for a minute. It will help me help you.

They nodded tentatively.

It was one of my better acting jobs.

nineteen

Revolution

(1985)

The faces of the statues are tainted,
With an unclean righteousness,
But inside they're crumbling,
They know they ain't got much time left,
In Pretoria.

—"PRETORIA," FREEDOM—NO COMPROMISE

On the flight home, I began to feel the weight of my own promises.

Africa was a mess. Fifty countries devastated by colonization, ocean-to-ocean corruption, and endless tribal warfare. But because of the outrageous arrogance of apartheid, South Africa would always be the lightning rod for African injustice. Until that was fixed, the rest of Africa's problems would never be properly addressed.

I knew whatever I wrote about Sun City would be too important to just be another song on my next album. It needed more impact.

I had already decided not to include a song called "Hunger" about the Ethiopian government watching its people starve while they threw a multimillion-dollar anniversary party. Bob Geldof had that subject covered, even though he was selling it as a natural disaster. Which was smart. If you're looking for money, you score more with less controversy.

Up to that time, there had been three anti-apartheid anthems: Gil Scott-Heron's "Johannesburg" in 1975, Peter Gabriel's "Biko" in 1980, and the Specials' "Free Nelson Mandela" in 1984.

I would try and write the fourth.

The idea of a group song began to germinate, one that was more political than the other group anthems like "Do They Know It's Christmas," and "We Are the World." I would write more straightforwardly about the problem—I didn't believe in natural disasters—and include one artist from every genre to show unity.

I got home and started spreading the word. I needed help. Lots of it. I'd opened my mouth and now I had to deliver.

Somehow, a guy named Danny Schechter found his way into my life. Danny would make all the difference for this project. He was a TV Producer, newsman, and rabble-rouser of the first magnitude, infamous in Boston as "Danny Schechter the News Dissector." He had been politically active his whole life and involved with the South African issue for decades.

He would not only be the second Musketeer, the advocate and confidence booster I desperately needed, but the main reason we would reach the political intelligentsia and the world of news journalism. I've never been short of ideas, though paying for them can be a challenge. But the all-important marketing is always the most important hurdle, and without a Manager, my work rarely got any.

Danny and I went to a diner, and I laid out my plan to bring down the South African government. It was the first of a thousand conversations in a thousand diners.

He knew a woman named Jennifer Davis at the Africa Fund who was one of the leaders of the divestment movement. She was an extraordinarily intelligent and heroic South African woman who had gone into exile. She not only guided us politically but promised to help disburse whatever money we made, if we made any at all.

From moment one, I had decided to include Rappers in our group of vocalists. Danny enthusiastically agreed. Rappers were not yet in the mainstream—Run-DMC's "Walk This Way" was a year off—but it was already a rich genre of black artists finally telling it like it was. That wasn't easy, never had been. Even Marvin Gaye and Stevie Wonder had to fight for the right to express themselves politically back in the early '70s, and protorappers like Gil Scott-Heron and the Last Poets never broke into the mainstream.

Industry insiders questioned our decision. As with Rock and Roll forty years earlier, they thought this adolescent novelty would disappear as quickly as it had arrived.

I disagreed. By putting them on this record, we would bestow a credibility on them that we felt they deserved. And to accomplish that, we needed . . .

Our third Musketeer, Arthur Baker.

Arthur had produced Afrika Bambaataa's "Planet Rock"; he not only was a visionary combining early street rapping with European Kraftwerk-style Electronica but had also invented a new career creating dance remixes of Pop hits, including songs from *Born in the USA*. When Danny and I told him what we had in mind, Arthur offered us his studio, his Engineers, his musicians, and, most important, his phone book full of Rappers.

Wow. How cool was that!

Now all we needed was . . . oh yeah, the song!

I went to the apartment of my assistant Zoë Yanakis, where my little Akai twelve-track was set up and where I would write and record the Lost Boys album and *Born Again Savage* four years later, and did the demo for "Sun City."

Political music has a different purpose than the typical song. It's a sacrifice of poetry for prose. A sacrifice of Art for information. With a specific protest song like "Sun City," the challenge would be to explain the situation while still connecting with the listener emotionally.

Most message records were solemn and earnest. I wanted a different tone, a motivational call to arms. I'd been writing politically for three years by then, so the energy was right at my fingertips.

I wrote and recorded the demo quickly, in an hour or two. Then I ran down to Arthur's studio so we could build up the music.

Danny and Arthur listened. "These are just reference lyrics," I said.

"You're crazy," they said in unison. "This is the whole story."

I protested. I thought I could improve them a bit, but they were adamant—and right, by the way.

I made one more concession. Danny felt the subject was going to be a hard sell, so we needed controversy to spice things up. He wanted to mention the names of the Artists who had played Sun City as a way of getting attention.

We went as far as one version of the demo mentioning names before I changed my mind. I decided we needed to take the position that those who had played had been duped, that they had been offered huge money ($100,000 per week) and told they were playing in a separate country. We needed to present a united front. Arguments among musicians would only confuse the public.

I met with members of Queen and others and explained the situation. The bands wanted to know how to get off the UN boycott list, which was being taken very seriously by the European unions and interfering with tours. "Just tell me right now you won't go back, and I'll deal with that," I said. I got them all off the list including, with some mixed feelings, Paul Simon.

As we built our wish list of singers for the project, I looked for interesting artists from all genres, Rock and Soul, Punk and Funk, Salsa and Reggae, along with less-than-obvious international artists. Big stars were fine, but they weren't the priority.

My top four names were Peter Gabriel (who had alerted me to the issue), Gil Scott-Heron (who had been the first to bring it up in song), Melle Mel (my personal favorite of the Rappers), and Miles Davis (in my mind, I heard his iconic trumpet both at the beginning and in the middle of the song).

From there, I built out the list: Bonnie Raitt and Jackson Browne, George Clinton and Darlene Love. I couldn't leave out David Ruffin, my favorite living singer, and I kept my ear tuned to political engagement, which led me to Rubén Blades (a best-selling Salsa Artist who had started out as a law student) and Peter Garrett (an Australian activist who fronted Midnight Oil). I picked out a line for Bruce and saved it for him.

Danny and Arthur added names, and we started making calls.

One of my first was to an Artist I respected a great deal for his enormous talent, his incredible sense of humor, and his political vision. Including him, I thought, would illustrate the difference between our song and more-mainstream projects. As I dialed, I laughed to myself at the thought of him singing along with the chorus of "We Are the World."

Frank Zappa answered the phone.

"Hi," I said, introducing myself. "We're making a solidarity statement about what's going on in South Africa and . . ."

That was all I got out.

"Why would I want to participate in your meaningless bullshit record when all that's going to happen is that you are going to steal the publishing money?"

"No, no. It's . . ."

"I don't want to hear it."

"Frank, listen . . ."

"I've heard it all before!"

His arrogance and obnoxiousness were breathtaking.

I was tempted to remind him he was mixing me up with someone in show business who had something to lose, instead of a kid from Jersey who would happily beat the shit out of him if he ever dared to speak that way to my face.

I didn't even get to mention that I had started a separate publishing company and all royalties would go to the cause.

"Sorry for wasting your time," I said, and hung up.

And I had been such a fan.

My next two calls were to people from the Hard Rock world I knew fairly well. They both turned me down.

After that, I delegated the calls to a far more successful schmoozer, Arthur Baker.

Everybody he called agreed to participate.

Even so, we weren't as organized as Band Aid or USA for Africa. We never knew who was coming. Or when. Or what they would do when they got there.

Danny had had the foresight to bring in our fourth Musketeer, Hart Perry. Hart was tasked with filming the whole process, and he made himself available around the clock. If an artist happened to show up at two in the morning, we'd call Hart and he'd be there in ten minutes.

I look back in wonderment that we pulled it off at all. We didn't have the brains to reach out through publicists or Managers, who probably would have declined anyway. This was not a good career move for an artist.

We recorded a log drum as the click track, the basic rhythm, I threw on a quick rhythm guitar, added two keyboard horn riffs on a synthesizer, and we were ready for vocals.

We started with the Rappers.

Run-DMC came in, looking and sounding just like I hoped they would. When they did the opening line, "We're rockers and rappers united and strong . . . ," their Manager Russell Simmons leaned over to me. "You know, we're thinking about changing it."

"Changing what?"

"The term for what we do," he said. "Rapping."

"What?" I said. "Why? It's been an underground cult, but we're about to introduce it to the world!"

"Yeah," he said. "That's cool. But we feel like it's too limiting."

"What are you gonna change it to?"

"Hip-Hop," he said.

"Get the fuck outta here!" I said. "That is the stupidest fucking name I've ever heard! It'll never catch on!"

As the Rappers did their thing—Kurtis Blow, the Fat Boys, Duke Bootee, and Afrika Bambaataa—we realized we had all these great artists there just to say a few lines. It seemed like a waste. After we got what we needed, we told them to feel free to express their feelings about the subject any way they wanted.

Melle Mel went into the next room for fifteen minutes and came back with an incredible rap. We added news footage, Mandela's speeches, and sound effects, and Arthur turned it into a separate anti-apartheid montage. That was the beginning of the "Sun City" single growing into an album.

The whole thing was wild and spontaneous. The first twenty or thirty artists that came in sang the whole song, not just their line. We sorted it out later.

Peter Gabriel did a chant and layered it and layered it until it was a cool abstract expressionist piece. When we came back the next day, one of our Engineers, Tom Lord-Alge, and Arthur's drummer Keith LeBlanc had added drums to Peter's chant. I put on guitar and synth and Peter's electric violinist Shankar played on the track. Boom! Another song.

Gil Scott-Heron was on the lam at the time. I had to call a phone booth in Washington, DC, at 10 p.m. on Thursdays to talk to him. But when the time came, he showed up and did a great job.

I flew to London to record Ringo Starr and his son Zak, and got a guitar part from Pete Townshend.

And then he walked in.

By some miraculous stroke of luck, Miles Davis was using my old sound man, who was brave enough to bring up our project to him. He didn't do these types of things ever, but this was an important issue to him.

It was one of the thrills of my life when he walked in. Nobody intimidates me, but he came close. He sat next to me as I played him the song. About halfway through, he leaned over. "Hey," he said in that classic rasp, "you want me to play or what?"

I laughed. "Not really," I said. "I was hoping you'd take over as Producer so I can get some fucking sleep!"

That got a rare smile and loosened him up.

He played for maybe five minutes with the mute, which I asked for, and another few minutes without it.

I looked at Arthur, who looked at Danny, who looked at Hart, who looked back at me. This shit just got real. I had planned to use Miles for twenty seconds in the intro and fifteen seconds in the middle, but there was no way we were leaving five minutes of Miles Fucking Davis on the cutting room floor.

I called the Jazz Producer Michael Cuscuna and asked if he could get to the guys from Miles's Second Great Quintet—Herbie Hancock, Ron Carter, and Tony Williams. They all responded. Michael had found Stanley Jordan playing guitar in the subway and brought him in too. They improvised to what Miles had played, and it became a modal monochromatic impressionist masterpiece.

Bono was so inspired by the project that he wrote a new song, "Silver and Gold," which we recorded with Keith Richards, Ronnie Wood, and Stevie Jordan.

A few days afterward Bruce came in to do his line, then we went across the river and filmed the video for "Glory Days" at Maxwell's in Hoboken. Man, was he in a bad mood that day. I had to mug as exaggerated as I could just to make him laugh and loosen him up.

Meanwhile, we had gone from the original half-dozen or so artists I'd imagined to fifty, adding Lou Reed, Jimmy Cliff, Peter Wolf, Bobby Womack, Nona Hendryx, Joey Ramone, Pat Benatar, Hall & Oates, Ray Barretto, Big Youth, Kashif, and more. I wished we'd gotten the Last Poets, Taj Mahal, and Jerry Dammers, but if we didn't have their phone number we didn't pursue them.

And we weren't done.

Earlier in the year, I had gotten a call from Debbie Gold. Everyone knew Debbie. She was like everybody's confidante/intermediary, full of positive vibes. "Stevie. Bob Dylan wants you to produce him."

"Really? When?"

"Now. Get down to the Power Station."

Bob was playing with Sly and Robbie, the famous Reggae rhythm section, and Roy Bittan was there on piano. Bob pointed to a guitar and I joined in.

He had just started singing a ballad called "When the Night Comes Falling from the Sky."

We did a take and went into the control room to listen. I wasn't sure if I was producing or not; Bob hadn't said anything, but I lingered behind and made a quick dozen suggestions to the Engineer—add a mic under the snare, add 2 dB at fifteen hundred cycles on the guitar, put a compressor on the bass, shit like that.

After a second take, Bob turned to me. "What do you think?" he asked.

"Bobby," I said, "to tell you the truth I'm hearing this faster."

"Oh, yeah? Like what?" I showed him, and he joined in and sang along a bit. "I like it," he said, "but I like it slow too."

"How about this?" I said. "We can start slow with the first verse, then, after a drum fill, go to a faster tempo for the rest of the song."

That's what we did. He asked me for a solo, and I told him I was hearing more of a violin or horn melody line. We tried it and he liked it. "That gives me an idea for a cello line underneath," he said. He sang it and I added it to the solo.

His vocal performance was spectacular, his greatest at least since "Tangled Up in Blue" and arguably since *Blonde on Blonde*. I didn't get any credit for producing, which was fine with me. I was just honored to be there. But he didn't put this version on the record! Between him and

Bruce, I was starting to wonder . . . Is it me? Years later, it would appear on his first *Bootleg Series* box set.

We kept trying to get Bob for "Sun City." He had been responsible for the birth of consciousness in Popular music in the first place, and a record like this was unthinkable without him. Late in the game, he finally came aboard. Jackson Browne was able to record him on the West Coast. But with all those extra singers, we had run out of lines. Bob did the same line as Jackson, and we put his line in between lines to fit.

It was the mix of the century. Thirteen reels of tape times 24 tracks means 312 tracks, which had to be reduced to two. The single alone took weeks. Every Engineer in town worked on it. They'd pass out at the board, we'd carry them out, and bring in another one.

We used every studio in town at some point. Ten days into the mix at Electric Lady, the studio flooded, like it did every spring and fall. Nobody had mentioned to Jimi Hendrix that he was building the place over an underground stream. We lost the mix and had to start all over again, but somehow it got done.

Four freaks with no juice, no muscle, and no money had relied on street connections and a good idea to cobble together an artistically coherent album with as diverse a group of artists as had ever been assembled for a cause nobody had heard of yet.

And Jean-Luc Godard and a nameless projectionist will never know what they started.

twenty

Ain't Gonna Play Sun City!

(1986)

When will we finally invite our black population to join
the rest of us in America?
—THE UNWRITTEN BOOK

What if you spent a year planning a party and nobody showed?

I never had an attitude of superiority while doing research in South Africa, fully aware that America's own civil rights legislation had taken place only twenty years earlier.

And I knew that by pointing out the extreme racism of South Africa I would also be commenting on our own ongoing discrimination, which seemed to be going backward.

So irony of ironies—but not entirely surprising—we were deemed too black for white radio and too white for black radio.

Nobody would play the fucking record!

Not exactly what I had in mind by "Ain't gonna play Sun City!"

Fuck me.

I had gotten friendly with Bruce Lundvall while making E Street Band records at Columbia. Lundvall had moved to EMI Manhattan, signed me for my next record, *Freedom—No Compromise*, and was very enthusiastic about the issue of South Africa. We licensed "Sun City" to him for distribution at a higher than usual royalty—although, again, we weren't doing it for the money.

I knew Bob Geldof had gotten *all* the royalties for the Band Aid record, but I didn't have that kind of juice. I was happy *anybody* would distribute such a controversial project. But we made a good deal.

As I hadn't quite had the chance to explain to Frank Zappa, I had created a new publishing company, Amandla Music, for all the music on the album. The creative process was truly a collaboration, and none of us wanted the job of sorting out who had done what. It didn't matter anyway. None of us would have taken any money from this. The entirety of the record sales and publishing would go to Jennifer Davis and her Africa Fund.

We tried everything to get the record played. Calling stations. Calling in favors. Lundvall hired a few independent promotion men—all to no avail.

We even tried to get to Stevie Wonder's radio station. He was into the issue of South Africa and human rights in general. I took the record there personally, but they wouldn't play it.

There was only one shot left.

We needed a killer fucking video.

Hart Perry brought in Jonathan Demme, the perfect guy for the job and a soon-to-be-lifelong friend. He would eventually do a video for the E Street Band and win the Academy Award for *Philadelphia*, which also got Bruce an Oscar for the title track. We had a quick discussion with him and decided we wanted to capture the energy of an awakened anti-apartheid movement and the unrelenting passion of the record.

As for every aspect of the project, we didn't want it to be slick, though we didn't have to worry about that too much since we didn't have any money.

We decided we'd do the video guerrilla-style, like everything else. We'd shoot it right on the street, no permissions of course, and then have the individuals arrive at a location that represented our common cause and the stronger-together-than-apart symbolism that we hoped would spread throughout the country.

Jonathan was shooting *Something Wild* at the time, and we only had him for one day.

He shot the New York scenes while Hart flew to Los Angeles to get footage of Jackson Browne, Bob Dylan, George Clinton, and Bonnie Raitt.

Then we assembled as many singers as we could in Washington Square for the final scene. To edit the project, we somehow got the hottest video makers in the world at that time, Kevin Godley and Lol Creme. Peter Gabriel might have made the connection.

The conversation I had with them was similar to the one I had with Demme and everybody else: I wanted intense, unrelenting energy.

We gave them what Jonathan and Hart had shot, along with additional footage from another protest rally we had attended and some news footage—some of it stolen, but this was war!

Godley and Creme did an amazing job. In the intro, they used footage of police whipping protestors as a kind of visual percussion, synced to our snare accents, and also devised innovative ripped-from-the-headlines effects to transition from scene to scene. The result was fierce and violent and motivating, exactly what you want in a battle video. Like everyone else—all the Engineers, all the musicians, the crew—they worked for free.

At that moment, MTV was having its own war with the black community.

Since its launch in 1981, it had not played many black videos.

At first, it hadn't played any.

It had taken Walter Yetnikoff threatening to pull all Columbia and Epic product if it didn't play videos from Michael Jackson's *Thriller*. That had been in December 1983. Things had improved since then, but only slightly. Artists like David Bowie and Rick James criticized MTV for maintaining a color line, and the network responded by admitting that it was concerned about losing its midwestern audience.

I met with the entire executive team of MTV. "Listen," I said. "I hear you're having a public relations problem. I might have the solution right here in my pocket."

I laid out the situation in South Africa and our strategy. "You guys can not only go a long way in solving your problems with the black community," I said, "but you can be on the front end of a movement that is going to be sweeping the country. For once, instead of observing history, you'd be making it."

Of course, I was pretty much lying my ass off like usual. But it all turned out to be true.

I played them the video, and they loved it.

If you know "Sun City," it's because of MTV. Or BET, which also played the video frequently. But it's not from radio.

After the video started getting us more visibility, we started doing interviews and performances whenever possible to spread the word. We shut down the Sun City resort overnight, which meant that the cultural boycott finally had teeth—virtually no one broke it after our record and video came out. That was icing on the cake. But it wasn't the cake.

The cake, of course, was the economic boycott. Everything we had done from the beginning was to raise consciousness, knowing the day was coming when there would be important economic legislation that Reagan would not like. The clock was ticking on whether we would achieve critical awareness before Reagan vetoed the legislation. The goal was to establish such a powerful distaste for the injustice that even Saint Reagan's veto would be overturned. That showdown was imminent.

Senator Bill Bradley brought me to the Senate to explain the situation. It was my closest-ever encounter with our most revered lawmakers, and I must confess, it was a little frightening.

Very few senators had Bradley's intellect, and it was obvious most were hearing about the subject for the first time. How could I tell? By the way I had to point out where South Africa was on the map! And that's a country with two clues in its name!

While I waited for the world to change, I managed to sneak in a few side projects.

Southside and I did a benefit in New Jersey for fire victims in Passaic.

Gary Bonds wanted to do a third album, but all I had time for was a single, "Standing in the Line of Fire," which I cowrote with him and produced.

I produced two songs for my friend Stiv Bators and his great band, the Lords of the New Church. My pleasant memory of working with them was only slightly tainted by meeting their Manager, Miles Copeland. I've been very lucky in my life. After all these years in and around a showbiz full of creeps, I've only had to deal with a few. As temporarily as possible.

I didn't spend enough time with Miles for him to achieve official Royal Scumbaggery, but from the way he spoke to me in our first meeting I found him to be one of those arrogant, condescending slimeballs who make you want to take a shower after being in the same room with them.

My friend Brian Setzer needed a song, so we cowrote "Maria," a song about Mexican migrant workers in Texas.

We were honored by Mayor Bradley in LA and then by Coretta Scott King, Andrew Young, Julian Bond, and John Lewis in Atlanta.

Arthur Baker, who was working on music for Demme's *Something Wild*, came to me for a few songs, and I wrote "You Don't Have to Cry," about the gasoline riots in Jamaica at the time, for Jimmy Cliff and "Addiction" for David Ruffin and Eddie Kendricks.

When the United Nations decided to give "Sun City" an award, we sent a big delegation. Between the early Hip-Hop styles and the Rocker looks, we were the wildest bunch to ever enter the super-sanctimonious United Nations. I saw the secretary general, Javier Pérez de Cuéllar, walk in, take a look at us, hand the award to his deputy, and split!

Ha-ha. I thanked him in my speech anyway.

Somewhere in there, I made another run to the West Coast for Jimmy Iovine to write three songs for Lone Justice for their second album, *Shelter*, and got coproduction credit on the record.

Sol Kerzner, the main owner of Sun City, made the mistake of challenging me on *The Phil Donahue Show*, spewing the usual bullshit apartheid talking points.

I squashed him like the cockroach he was.

Peter Gabriel's latest obsession was something called the University for Peace in Costa Rica.

It was connected to the United Nations and run by an ex-ambassador of Costa Rica. As it was explained to me, it was a school to study conflict resolution; how to deal with the collateral damage of conflict, like refugees; and other international issues like that.

Costa Rica had been of particular interest to me ever since I discovered it was the only country in Latin America that wasn't constantly in conflict because they had the incredible wisdom and strength to disband their military.

I was a little dubious about the university, but Peter was way into it, and I was more than happy to help in any way I could. We pulled together a benefit for the University for Peace; Nona Hendryx, Lou Reed, Jackson Browne, and others participated. Hart Perry filmed it.

It was called Hurricane Irene and was held in Tokyo.

You'd have every right to ask, Why Tokyo?

Good fucking question.

All I really remember is that Irene was some kind of goddess of peace, hence the title of the show. Tokyo I can't help you with. To this day it's still the only time I've ever been there, so that was cool.

One memory from that show still makes me smile. I spent a good hour explaining the entire project to Lou Reed: the concert, the benefit, the peace goddess. He listened intently the whole time. "OK," he finally said. "I'm in. I just want to know one thing. Where the fuck is Costa Rica?"

At some point, Peter Gabriel and I combined our bands and performed at the United Nations to celebrate the International Day of Peace, September 21, which was connected to the university, and we were honored by the United Nations for the second time.

We did an anti-apartheid concert in Central Park with the usual suspects—Peter, Jackson, Bono—and new recruits like Bob Geldof, Yoko Ono, and Sean Lennon.

Geldof asked me to perform Bob Marley's "Redemption Song" with him at the upcoming Amnesty International Concert in New Jersey, which would be televised internationally.

After the show at Giants Stadium, I was backstage with Maureen when I looked across the room. "Holy shit!" I said. Maureen, used to me not being impressed by anybody, was impressed.

"Who is it?" she whispered.

"Muhammad fucking Ali!" I managed to get out.

"Why don't you go say hello?" she said. "He's probably friendly."

Are you kidding? I was too shy. And anyway I never liked meeting my heroes, in case they were assholes. A little while later, a well-dressed, cultured gentleman tapped me on the shoulder.

"Excuse me, sir," he said. "Mr. Van Zandt? Please pardon the interruption, Mr. Muhammad Ali would love to meet you, but he's too shy to come over!"

Right?

There he was. His handshake was gentle. His eyes twinkled mischievously. He bent down and whispered in my ear, sounding like Don Corleone. "You did good with South Africa," he said.

"You did good with George Foreman," I said.

He smiled.

So that was a good day.

The year ended big.

In Santa Monica, at a reception organized by Tom Hayden, Bishop Desmond Tutu gave us a special recognition for efforts on behalf of the anti-apartheid movement. I don't think he was an archbishop yet.

Hart Perry and I received the International Documentary Association Award for *The Making of Sun City*. A companion book written by Dave Marsh and a teaching guide went along with it.

And finally, Congressman Ron Dellums's Comprehensive Anti-Apartheid Act of 1986 was passed, by larger margins than we'd imagined.

As expected, Ronald Reagan vetoed it. Republican Richard Lugar stood up and declared that South Africa was tyranny and that all true Americans were against tyranny!

What became of that kind of Republican?

The Reagan veto was overturned.

The dominoes started to fall.

Both the UK's and Germany's pro-apartheid positions were now untenable.

The banks would soon cut off South Africa, just like we wrote it up.

In the world of international liberation politics, this was a rare complete victory.

It was time to get back to work.

twenty-one

Freedom—No Compromise

(1987–1989)

The Art is always greater than the Artist.

—THE UNWRITTEN BOOK

Freedom—No Compromise was not only my most ambitious album but also the first produced the way I would produce somebody else. The first produced by me the Producer, as opposed to me the Artist. That's why Artists should never produce themselves. The Artist takes over and you don't realize it until it's too late.

Prince is the only exception I can think of. A true genius. I crossed paths with him often in 1987, as we both spent most of that year touring Europe. "You stole my coat idea back in 1978, didn't you?" I said the first time I ran into him. He confessed with one of his sly smiles.

His album that year was *Sign O' the Times*. I took the fact that the gang in the title track was named the Disciples as a personal tribute. The tour behind that record was the best Rock show I've ever seen. I went three times, and it blew my mind every time.

The production was the highest evolution of the live, physical part of our Artform I have ever seen. It was Prince's vision, but his production designer, LeRoy Bennett, deserves much of the credit for pulling it off. It was Rock, it was Theater, it was Soul, it was Cinema, it was Jazz, it was Broadway. The stage metamorphized into different scenes and configurations right before your eyes, transforming itself into whatever emotional setting was appropriate for each song.

On top of that, the music never stopped, for three solid hours. Prince wrote various pieces, or covered Jazz, as interstitial transitions for those moments when the stage was shifting or the musicians were changing clothes. At one point, he even had a craps game break out, which made me laugh—it brought me back to Dr. Zoom and the Sonic Boom and our onstage Monopoly games.

They captured it pretty well on film, but it can't compare. When you're watching a movie, your mind is used to scene changes, different sets and lighting. Live, it's something else. That kind of legerdemain before your eyes is mind-boggling.

And the show was only the beginning of the night for him. He would do the show, then play into the early morning at a local club. At one of the after-show gigs in Munich, he called me up onstage to jam. Me and his dad! We did a Blues, "Stormy Monday" or something. All I remember is twiddling knobs and stepping on pedals, trying to find a tone before the song ended!

I begged him to take the show to the States, but he was in his pissed-off-at-the-record-company period and wouldn't do it.

The show brought me back to the ballet and the Met. There is nothing quite as thrilling as a live event, especially one I could imagine writing, directing, and producing. Music, dancing, acting, set design, lighting—I loved it all. It took me all those years to realize I didn't want to be Jeff Beck or Miles Davis or even Nureyev or Nijinsky.

I wanted to be Diaghilev!

Jerome Robbins!

Bob Fosse!

Fokine! Massine! Bakst!

Back on Planet Earth, I was still leading a band of my own, and a great one. My Rock-meets-Soul formula had evolved into Rock-meets-Funk. Pat Thrall, who had come from Hughes/Thrall and Pat Travers, was one of the great guitar players of all time. I had a bass player, T. M. Stevens, who could compete with Bootsy Collins and Larry Graham. Mark Alexander was a powerhouse on keyboards, and drummer

Leslie Ming had both the technique for the Funk and the power for four-on-the-floor straight-ahead Rock.

We also had an occasional appearance on the "Zobo," an oboe fed through a phaser and fuzz tone and played by my most excellent and versatile assistant, Zoë Yanakis. Zoë married Pat Thrall, and manages the recording studio at the Palms in Vegas, while Pat engineers and produces. Only time in my life two of my best friends married each other! Nice.

When I see concert footage from that time, it baffles me that we weren't huge. If I had a time machine . . . well, I'd do a lot of things, but one of them would be to go back to 1987, slow down my hundred-miles-an-hour-to-nowhere pace, and hire the first good Manager who came through the door.

We could feel success coming, especially in Europe, where we had built up lots of momentum since that first *Rockpalast.*

But we were still losing money on the road, so we had to reluctantly come home every now and then. Frank Barsalona had us open for the Who on our first tour, and in late 1987 we joined U2's Joshua Tree Tour on the East Coast of the United States. The normal hazards of being an opening act applied. Opening accomplished very little.

While I was home, I was asked to endorse Jesse Jackson's presidential campaign. An empty endorsement didn't interest me, but I said that if Jesse would meet with me to see how much our platforms had in common, I'd consider it. To my surprise, he said yes. We had a long conversation about our political ideas, which were very similar, and I ended up redoing "Vote! (That Mutha Out)" as "Vote Jesse In!" (It's in the 2019 *RocknRoll Rebel* box set.) I traveled with Jesse, spending time in black churches for the first time in my life, greatly adding to my education and to my understanding of the community. He ran a strong campaign, won eleven states—including Michigan—and was even the front-runner for a while, but he was beaten at the wire by Michael Dukakis.

Peter Gabriel, or maybe Jim Kerr from Simple Minds, called to tell me they were doing a Free Nelson Mandela Concert at Wembley Stadium, disguised as a seventieth birthday tribute to reach the maximum broadcast audience. Wise move, as it ended up being shown in sixty-seven countries to six hundred million people.

I was surprised an American network picked up on it at all. The consensus among the mainstream media was that Mandela was a terrorist and a Communist. And not just among the right wing. Famous liberal Paul Simon once cornered me at a party and asked how I could be supporting this Mandela character when he was obviously a Communist.

"Really, Paulie?" I said. "You sure?"

"Yes," he said. "My friend Henry Kissinger explained it all to me. Just follow the money!"

"Well, Paul, I know you and Henry are students of revolution, but I have news for the both of you. People fighting for freedom outnumbered by a better-supplied enemy don't really care where the money comes from. And by the way, your buddy Kissinger is not only an unindicted war criminal but was with the Dulles brothers in the early fifties overthrowing Mosaddegh in Iran and installing the shah. That's the direct cause of half of the *real* terrorism on the planet to this day. So when you see him, please tell your friend Henry to stick his Nobel Peace Prize up his fuckin' ass."

To be fair, Paul denies the conversation took place. But it did.

Wembley was a blast, except for one unfortunate moment. I happened to be in the office with the promoter, Jim Kerr, and Peter Gabriel when Whitney Houston's Manager came in. "We thought this was about celebrating a birthday, but we're hearing lots of politics from the stage. We don't want any part of it. We want the Free Nelson Mandela posters covered up or Whitney doesn't go on!" He stormed out.

We looked at each other in shock. I spoke first. "Throw that bitch the fuck off this show right now!"

"We can't," the promoter said. "We sold the show to the networks with her on it."

"Let 'em complain!" I said.

Jim, or maybe Peter, spoke up. "She was the only request from Mandela personally. They had a poster of her in prison and all the prisoners . . . fell in love with her."

We let her perform. It makes me nauseous seeing the documentaries since then proclaiming her as a proud activist who fought against apartheid her whole life.

The American network edited out everything I said onstage and trimmed whatever politics they could in general. Fox, of course. But the telecast was enormously successful and helped cement Mandela's status as a world leader and one of the good guys.

I continued to do favors for friends when I could. I wrote "While You Were Looking at Me," my contemporary companion piece to Sonny Bono's "Laugh at Me," and cowrote two other songs for *Not Fakin' It*, the solo debut of Michael Monroe. Michael, the former lead singer of Hanoi Rocks, was a star waiting to happen, but he was finding the solo path hard, especially without a Manager.

I would make my own solo path even harder with *Revolution* in 1989. Bruce Lundvall was leaving EMI to go to Blue Note. I knew his dream gig was to be a Jazz guy, so I was happy for him. One of the last of the great gentlemen of the music business. But, for me, the corporate curtain had started to fall. You can feed people in Africa, but when you start bringing governments down, people get nervous.

Lundvall had taken a lot of shit from EMI corporate for putting out *Sun City*. The powerful South African branch of EMI had tried to stop it, even calling the home office in London. Lundvall, to his credit and my undying gratitude, ignored them. That may have sped his departure from the label. Who knows? It sped up mine.

Luckily for me, one of the EMI Germany executives, Heinz Henn, was a fan. He had taken over BMG and not gotten the memo that I was bad news, so I went there.

At this point I really let my artistic vision dominate my common sense. I decided the deeper I got into international themes, the more universal the music needed to be. And I decided Rock wasn't the international common ground anymore, that the true world music was either Reggae or dance music.

I should have gone for Reggae, where my biggest successes had been. One song, "Leonard Peltier" was Reggae, but mostly I went deeper into the Funk. Double entendre intended.

I had already gone halfway to dance music on *Freedom—No Compromise*, where I used a drum machine for the first time and some bass synthesizers. It was Rock on top, dance on the bottom.

With *Revolution*, I went all the way. My initial concept was a sci-fi dystopia with music that was all samples, the vocals the only human element crying out from a cold robotic world.

The theme was the government's relationship to the economy and humankind's alienation, not just from its own labor, but from the Earth and all natural law itself.

The main subtheme would be the way the media was increasingly controlling and manipulating all of our lives.

Keyboard man Mark Alexander was the only link to the previous tour. I have no idea why I let the other guys go. They were fully capable of handling this new idea. But in came the very funky Warren McRae, who along with Mark helped with the production and played bass. For the tour we added the very cool Vini Miranda on guitar, and the great Perry Wilson on drums.

I had made the partial transformation to front man for the Freedom Tour and was completely there for *Revolution*. I still did a token solo or two but had basically lost all interest in playing guitar onstage.

The problem, of course, was asking the audience to redefine me yet one more time. It was weird enough that there was very little of what one would call pure Rock left in the set.

The accumulated momentum of the first three albums hit a wall. Nobody understood *Revolution*. And while audiences enjoyed the show, for the first time they were smaller than on the tour before. We soldiered around Europe, doing better in some places than others.

The tour ended in my best country at the time, Italy.

BMG had given me a new publicist, the brilliant Arianna D'Aloja, a classic Italian beauty from a bygone era. Her husband, Giovanni Tamberi, was and is the handsomest man on earth, straight out of Fellini's *La Dolce Vita*. They remain good friends of mine and Maureen's to this day.

On tour, I met my doppelgänger, Adriano Celentano, a legendary Italian singer and character who occasionally hosted a TV show when he felt like it. We had a good time together.

The final gig in Italy was a free show, a protest against the Chinese government for their actions in Tiananmen Square.

Claudio Trotta, the Promoter, asked for a favor. He had a cousin in Sardinia with a band. "Could they . . . ?"

"Yeah," I said. "Sure. Who cares? It's the last gig."

That was it, the entire bill. An unknown Sardinian garage band opening, and us.

It was a beautiful June night in Rome. The band, Arianna, Giovanni, and I walked up to the side of the stage and looked out at an ocean of audience.

It was startling.

"Do you believe this?" Arianna asked, stunned.

Nobody had ever seen so many people in one place before in Italy. It was a goombah Woodstock!

Giovanni testified wildly in Italian, enthusiastically seconding his wife's amazement. I somehow comprehended everything without understanding a single word.

Some estimated the crowd at a quarter of a million, but let's not get Trumpian here. It was a lot.

We went on not knowing what to expect. I had a fabulous audience in Italy, but had 90 percent of this crowd ever heard of me?

Everything came together that night. The new songs, the new show—which had been going over well in spite of being surprising—suddenly seemed to have been written for this event. The title track, "Revolution," was preaching to the converted. Songs like "Love and Forgiveness" and "Sexy" had the crowd dancing and chanting along by the time the second choruses hit.

As the show ended, I stood there drained, thinking . . . This is it.

Like the opening song of the album asked, "Where Do We Go from Here?"

I was experiencing an existential crisis in real time.

I knew I'd never be more popular than I was at that moment. But it was somehow not real. I could not generate revenue. Fuck, I couldn't even achieve my lifelong goal of breaking even!

The people in the crowd were having a great time, but they had nothing to do with my real life.

They were never going to buy my records.

They were never going to buy a ticket to a show.

I had become a symbol of political activism. So now what? Run for mayor of Rome? I had no interest in politics as a career whatsoever.

I soaked it in as long and as deeply as I could.

I had one more record to make to explore the final theme I had outlined seven years and so many lifetimes ago. I needed to fulfill my promise to myself.

But it was over.

And I knew it.

twenty-two

The Hero with a Thousand Faces

(1990)

I don't want realism. I want magic! Yes, yes, magic! I try to give that to people. I misrepresent things to them. I don't tell the truth, I tell what ought to be the truth. And if that's sinful, then let me be damned for it!

—MAUREEN VAN ZANDT AS BLANCHE DUBOIS,
IN A STREETCAR NAMED DESIRE

Rome finished off seven years of nonstop action, education, and evolution.

Every important band ends up with one important member missing. I was that guy. Shouldn't I have crashed in that plane in Zimbabwe? Wouldn't that have made more Rock and Roll sense?

I found myself at the outer reaches of the galaxy with my dilithium crystals depleted.

It was time for one of my meditative trips to a metaphorical desert to contemplate, reassess, reevaluate, and reenergize.

Only this time, the desert wouldn't be metaphorical.

I had arranged to meet in southern Algeria with the Polisario Front, the political representatives of the people of Western Sahara, the Sahrawi (sometimes Saharawi). They were camped in Tindouf, a semisafe distance from the war they were fighting against Morocco.

Yet one more war we were on the wrong side of. Namely, the battle for Western Sahara, which Morocco was—and probably still is—trying to steal.

The situation began with the end of the colonial era in the '70s, when Spain and France withdrew from northern Africa, specifically the Sahara Desert region bordering Morocco, Mauritania, and Algeria. Spain made a deal with Morocco and Mauritania regarding Western Sahara, but they forgot to include the people of Western Sahara in the negotiations.

The Sahrawi are a mix of Berber and Arab, and a bit of indigenous African, and had a history in the region. So began the war between Morocco and Polisario, which Mauritania quickly withdrew from. The United States and France—and, interestingly, Saudi Arabia—backed Morocco, which was dropping white phosphorus, similar to napalm, on the refugee camps. They sought to steal the indigenous people's land and keep the Sahrawi Arab Democratic Republic from the autonomy the International Court of Justice declared they were entitled to.

I wanted to bring attention to their situation, apologize for my country's position, and let them know that there were Americans who cared about right and wrong.

As always, there was a research component as well. My next album was partly about religion, and I wanted to get their views on spirituality. I'd heard they were moderate Muslims like my main interest in the Middle East, the Kurds, who have long deserved their own independent Kurdistan.

I flew to Paris, where friends I had made at *Libération*, the newspaper started by Jean-Paul Sartre, had agreed to accompany me and write about the trip.

We hoped to meet with Mohamed Abdelaziz, the secretary general of the Polisario Front and, again like the Kurds, a secular nationalist.

The first flight stopped in Algiers, and man, was it weird. The Muslim extremists were in an on-again, off-again war with the moderate government, and the vibe was tense.

First of all, there were no women in sight. Not even covered up. And not many cars driving around. Just a lot of guys: all in white, all with the same beards, fierce X-ray eyes, and scowling visages, all leaning against buildings, staring at us.

I realized we were the only entertainment they were going to get that day. Giving us dirty looks was their equivalent of going to a movie or having a drink in a bar or listening to a great record. They couldn't do any of those things.

So they just leaned and looked mean.

It was creepy as fuck. I couldn't wait to get out of there.

The next flight landed in Tindouf, and we were driven hours out into the desert by jeep.

The typical desert isn't like the one in *Lawrence of Arabia*. No golden waves of sand. It's hard and rocky. I couldn't discern any roads or signs of any kind. Nothing. Two or three hours later, a camp appeared out of nowhere. No idea how they found it.

They didn't want us going into the refugee camp itself, so we stayed a distance away on our own.

As we were led to our tent, my dedication to my craft was sorely tested. Not only am I as urban as it gets—Stevie don't camp—but the one thing in the desert that nobody warns you about is . . . the flies. I hate all forms of bugs, and desert flies are relentless. Where the fuck do they come from? Thankfully they took a break at night.

Our hosts served dinner. I followed my usual routine of fasting on a research trip. For three days, I only drank their tea, which was some powerful shit. I was simultaneously tripping and extremely focused.

We met with five or six guys every day. They were never quite sure they could trust us, so they never identified themselves. And with the turbans and beards and shades, I couldn't be sure if one of them was Abdelaziz or not.

They spoke English very well and occasionally spoke French to my companions. I was very well-read in those days, and they were impressed by how much I knew about religion, especially the more mystical esoteric stuff like Sufism, Kabbalah, monasticism, even Wicca and Yoga. That stuff was my specialty.

They agreed that the secular state, rather than an Islamic state, was what they wanted, which was as important to me then as it is now. I believe everyone who wants a country should have one, but my dedication to human rights will never allow me to endorse Sharia law, which is the problem with Hamas running half of Palestine right now. And the Boycott, Divestment, Sanctions (BDS) movement assholes aren't going to fix it. As I write this, there's Hamas on one side and Benjamin Netanyahu on the other, a perfect storm of neither one wanting the obviously correct two-state solution.

I tried to sleep, but my adrenaline was flowing nonstop, and the caffeine and whatever else was in that tea had me hallucinating.

I walked out into the desert night.

I concentrated and really listened.

Nothing.

I had never heard quiet like that. The silence seemed to elevate whatever North African drug was coursing through my veins.

The sky was ridiculous. An infinite array of galaxies on a vast canvas that only seemed real because of the moving meteors and vibrating constellations.

This must be how astronauts feel as they look out from the moon, I thought.

I had never felt so small, and at the same time so much a part of the universe.

I had read Joseph Campbell's work growing up, including *The Hero with a Thousand Faces*, which I'd penciled in as the title to my fifth album. The experience I was having was the bliss he was talking about.

It felt like the power of all those stars had nowhere to go and nothing to connect to—except me.

I walked until I couldn't see the camp anymore and took off my clothes.

I didn't want anything between me and eternity.

If there was any doubt before, there wasn't now. I was definitely tripping!

I lay down and looked up as my entire body experienced an electric tingling.

I felt like a lightning rod experiencing all of time at the same time.

I could feel the rumbling of the Earth's past and the iridescent buzz of the future.

It left me with an odd sensation. Something I wasn't used to feeling. It took me a while to recognize it. The feeling was . . . hope.

I hadn't felt it so clearly since my first epiphany back in Middletown thirty years earlier. Only now the Angels' Eyes were stars.

If the sky had opened up and invited me in, I would have gone. I had to force myself to return to the planet on which I felt I was mistakenly born.

It was what we would have referred to back in the psychedelic days as a good trip.

By the third day the obvious leader, Abdelaziz or not, was warming up a little. I told him I'd contact his rep at the United Nations and speak to a few congressmen about pulling our support and encouraging a cease-fire, at the very least.

I also suggested teaching the kids English in the camps, which would help them interact with the world community and would someday help their cause. I told him I'd arrange for books to be sent. He liked the idea and said he'd discuss it with the others.

By the third night of communing with the universe, I was clear about what I would do next. I knew my adventure was coming to an end, and I wanted closure. I wouldn't tour again. But I would go out big, creating a postapocalyptic, cinematic, down-and-dirty setting for my fifth, final, and most personal album. The political consequence of spiritual bankruptcy. And I'd throw in the connection between sexual bliss and spiritual enlightenment for a little yin and yang.

The best part? For the first time in many years I suddenly felt like playing guitar again.

I haven't begun to understand it all, but even a quick glance at the mystics of all the different religions—the shamans, the yogis, the saints, the sages, the Lotus Sutra Buddhists, the Kabbalists, the Sufis, the Taoist seers—suggests they have all had their own personal vision of the same immutable, eternal Truth.

One Truth, many names.

Early on in the process of learning about others to learn about myself, I found that religion was the key element in getting to the roots of a culture's identity. It helped me reexamine my own ever-evolving thoughts on the subject as well, which is worth doing every now and then.

When it came time for my fifth album, I knew I was in for the challenge of my artistic life. I had dug deeper and deeper, thought and tested myself, and eventually walked out into the desert and let the universe take me where it wanted to go.

My starting point for the album was recognizing that the essence of spirituality is a connection to something bigger than ourselves. It could be each other, society, the Earth, the metaphysical energy somewhere out there (as Captain Kirk likes to put it), or the ocean of all souls deep inside each of us. There resides the foundation of faith, optimism, brotherhood, society, law, ethics, and whatever else you want to add to the list.

For me, that connection was revealed in the 1960s, which marked the birth of consciousness. Our minds expanded on a mass scale like never before.

Civil rights for minorities, women's rights, gay rights; a politically active youth movement; the belief that questioning your government was a patriotic responsibility; environmental awareness; expansion of Eastern thinking; the end of colonialism; psychoactive substances; and of course, the Renaissance in all the Arts.

That consciousness was founded on a few basic spiritual principles.

The first was our fundamental understanding of our relationship to the Earth, and the vast gap between Western and Semitic religious belief, on one side, and American Indian, African, and Asian belief, on the other.

Genesis 1:28 says, "And God blessed them, and God said to them, 'Be fruitful and multiply, and fill the earth and subdue it; and have dominion.'"

What "God" meant by "subdue" and "have dominion" can (and should) be debated, but Western religion took it to suggest man's superiority over the Earth. Man the conqueror.

The other tradition—American Indians, Africans, Asians—did not believe that humans were superior to the Earth; rather, they believed that they were meant to live in harmony with it. This difference affected how we viewed our most essential relationship and contributed to a fundamental sense of alienation. That alienation was the first component of our spiritual bankruptcy. That was the theme explored more deeply on *Revolution*, but it would overlap with this one.

A second principle was our changing relationship to time. It seemed like there just simply wasn't enough of it anymore. This was true in the late '80s, and it's only gotten worse. Technology was supposed to give us more time, not less. But technology is being developed in ways that outpace the human mind. Information is great, but when we feel the need to know everything as quickly as possible, we can't connect with any of it. We scratch the surface, hold nothing, and move on. Which inevitably leads to the key malady of the twenty-first century, time deficit disorder.

Finally, I saw that we had demystified one of our greatest forces, our Art, and specifically our Rock music.

Art, like Religion, needs mystery. That is how we participate in it. But our society demystifying that mystery has the same effect as music Engineers separating the frequencies with pillows and rugs.

The advent of MTV was the beginning of the end of Rock's importance. The accessibility of videos diluted and in many cases eliminated the experience of seeing a live Rock band. It has also allowed Rock bands to exist without the essential prerequisite of being great live performers. The corporatization of Rock radio dealt another severely damaging, if not lethal, blow. As did consultants, whose only job was to homogenize and eliminate interesting, unique personality. As did lazy, ignorant, short-sighted record companies.

The result, of course, was the waning of the Rock era and the rise of a Pop era that was more vapid, meaningless, superficial, emotionless, soulless, unmemorable, and disposable than any previous era in the history of music.

Most importantly, now that Pop was big business, bottom-line corporate control took precedence over the Art.

Granted, I was a bit jaded, having lived through the Renaissance. But most Pop made after the '60s was wallpaper, a short-term distraction for kids. You could make the argument that Pop was always so. You'd be wrong, but you could make that argument. In the past, though, there was a balance between Rock and Pop. When that balance went away, Pop ruled unchallenged, and Rock became an endangered species in a world where music no longer engaged our senses or our intellect and where there were few artists we could invest in emotionally.

We don't have many Artforms. We can't afford to have one stolen from us, let alone one of the most powerful. Our spiritual nourishment depends upon it.

As I headed into the fifth album, that was my thinking.

I came home and went back to the Akai twelve-track in Zoë's apartment. She engineered (being versatile has always been a prerequisite for working for me!) as I wrote and demoed the album, which I called *Born Again Savage*.

My lifelong roadie Ben Newberry had been Zoë's boyfriend before Pat Thrall. We tried to keep it all in the family! He had gotten a '56 Les Paul for fifty dollars at a yard sale in the early '60s, and I used it on the whole album through a mini-Marshall amp. The guitar was probably worth $250,000 by 1989—and if you'd played it, you'd know why.

I decided to do the '60s Hard Rock record I always wanted to do as a kid. A little Who, a touch of Kinks, a dollop of Cream, a hint of Zep, a spritz of Hendrix, and a lot of Jeff Beck.

Not a keyboard in sight.

It took me a few weeks to write and record, to get the all-important nod of approval from Zoë, and then put it on the shelf, closure accomplished.

I was not into finding a way to tour or seeing if a record company was interested, so it would stay on the shelf for years. But the five albums I'd outlined when I started my artistic adventure of educating and discovering myself while figuring out how the world works were done.

Now what?

My career contemplation was interrupted happily by one of the most incredible events of my lifetime—one that, in spite of all my public bravado, I never thought I'd live to see.

Nelson Mandela was released from prison.

I watched awestruck as he walked out of Victor Verster prison, accompanied by his estranged but loyal wife Winnie. Geez, I thought, maybe Martin Luther King was right after all. Maybe with time the universe does bend toward justice.

The Afrikaners who ran South Africa were smart, and lucky, to keep him alive all those years. It wasn't the obvious move, since his existence gave the majority hope for an eventual overthrow of the government. But by keeping him alive, they avoided an inevitable bloodbath.

And now they were promising a real democratic election to follow!

I couldn't help but feel some pride.

We did it.

Fifty artists, dozens of studio Engineers and assistants, dozens of unpaid musicians, seven songs, one album, the European unions, the United Nations, journalists, college-age protestors, the Wembley Stadium show broadcast to millions, every company that divested, and on and on. Forty-five years of struggle had led to that exhilarating moment.

The South African government would have inevitably fallen. But we took years off their existence, saving who knows how many lives. Preventing how many more Sharpeville and Soweto massacres, how many more deaths in prison.

When we played Johannesburg years later, I met with the ANC and they thanked me again, explaining that it had been critically important that we had acted when we did, because as the government began to anticipate the possibility of Mandela's release, it began putting hallucinogens like LSD in his food to fry his brain. The ANC weren't sure how long he could have survived it.

Tears streamed down my face at my first sight of this new, grey-haired, distinguished Mandela. Looking very presidential already.

Good luck, my friend, I thought. You are walking into a fucking hurricane.

So now I had to at least pretend to plan the rest of my life, knowing full well that's not how my life had ever worked. Nobody was going to be interested in me producing the Hall of Fame show, or anything remotely as grandiose as my imagination, so I decided to go back to my smaller, more practical, first teenage dream.

I would be the guitar player in a band.

I'd write or cowrite and sing some backing vocals but mostly just play guitar. Start from scratch all over again.

And I knew how it would happen. I would write my second-ever Rock album, *Nobody Loves and Leaves Alive,* by a fictitious new group I planned to assemble called the Lost Boys. If *Born Again Savage* had been late-'60s Hard Rock, *Nobody Loves and Leaves Alive* was mid-'60s Rock, early Stones, Them, or (English) Birds. Guitar playing was fun again, so I used a whole different style on this one. No pedals, no distortion, very clean, some slide.

It was gonna be Steve Jordan on drums, a friend of mine named Jimmy on bass. I eventually relented and decided to have a keyboard, so I located my favorite Rock piano player, the legendary Nicky Hopkins. He was into it and told me to call back when we were further along. Tragically, he died a short time later.

Now all I needed was a singer!

I personally auditioned or heard the tapes of no less than four hundred singers. No one was quite right. One record company guy played me a song from a new record he wasn't sure was going to get a release. "What about him?"

"That's the right idea, but what about his group?"

"I don't know. There's trouble in the band, and half the company doesn't know what to do with it."

I asked if I could take it with me.

"Sure," he said. "It's in the out pile."

I called him the next day. "Listen to me. This is a good album, and it should come out."

"You don't want the guy?"

"I like him, but I'm not breaking up this band. They're good. I don't take good bands for granted and neither should you. And besides, I like the name—the Black Crowes."

Long story short, I never found a singer, and the Lost Boys went on the shelf next to *Born Again Savage*.

As the year ended, *Rolling Stone* named the Jukes' *Hearts of Stone* one of the best albums of the previous twenty years and *Sun City* one of the best albums of the decade. We were having a good year with the critics. But truthfully, I've always had good luck with the critics.

If only they had bigger families, I would have come closer to breaking even.

Once again, either Peter Gabriel or Jim Kerr called me to perform at Wembley. This time it would be a fundraiser for Mandela's ANC, with the man himself present!

Meeting him was a trip.

He had a vibe unlike anybody I've ever met before or since. He had an inner glow like I imagined the big religious icons had. I'm talking the Moses, Jesus, Buddha, Muhammad vibration.

That's how intense his quiet energy was.

This would be the beginning of a fundraising trip that would eventually take him to the United States. Five American cities had pledged $500,000 each to Mandela's ANC to help them compete in the first democratic election in South Africa's history, as if they needed it.

New York was one of them.

Bill Lynch, New York mayor David Dinkins's deputy mayor, organized a meeting to prepare for Mandela's arrival.

Suddenly every activist who ever lived laid claim to being intimately involved in the thinking, planning, and execution of the fall of apartheid. And suddenly, America's own racial animus reared its ugly head.

The meeting's mission was to organize as many events as necessary to net the $500,000 pledge.

Harry Belafonte, the legitimate godfather of activists, ran the show, and a lot of the other civil rights activists and community leaders assigned various people to various tasks.

Bill Graham, the most famous Promoter in America, offered to put together a major concert for the event. He was asked a bunch of stupid, insulting questions, read the room, and left. They were working hard to ignore the other three white people, Jennifer Davis, Danny Schechter, and me.

We were an embarrassment to them.

In their minds South Africa was a "black issue."

Only it wasn't. In fact, no racial issue is a "black issue." If there's racial conflict, by definition it involves more than one race, no? Which means the solution must as well.

In all fairness, there were a few in the room, like Harry, who had been vocal about South Africa. A few had protested. A few had signed petitions and cornered an occasional congressman. But there was no one in that room except me, Danny, and Jennifer who had actually *done* anything significant about it.

Still, every time we brought something up we were patronized, condescended to, or ignored.

Danny had to restrain me when somebody directed a disparaging remark toward Jennifer. She had been an anti-apartheid activist *in* South Africa until it became untenable and she went into exile in the States. Along with me, she was the only person who had actually been there.

She had more courage than the whole room combined.

So after a few hours of being insulted and watching the usual bullshit that goes down when a bunch of conflicting egos clash, watching defenses going up because they don't know what they're talking about, nobody really in charge, we gave up and left.

It was fine with me. Our job was done. We got the legislation passed and got the man out of jail. Now the South Africans could speak for themselves.

I didn't even go down for Mandela's inauguration. I was invited to travel on Air Force One or Two, whichever one went.

I didn't want any credit. I didn't do what we did because I'm some kind of nice guy. I'm not. I did it because the idea that my government supported apartheid was an embarrassment to me. And to our American ideals. And I figured we were never gonna get around to the vast number of other human rights violations on the African continent until South Africa was dealt with.

The meeting we walked out of was held a few months before Mandela came to New York.

Cut to the week before he arrived.

Rrrrrrrrrring.

"Yeah."

"Bill Lynch."

"What can I do for you, Bill?"

As if I didn't know.

"Can I buy you lunch?"

We met at the Empire Diner. This was the early '90s, when it was still good.

Bill spoke first. "Sorry about how the meeting went down," he said. "I had a lot of politics I had to contend with."

"I understand," I lied.

"We've got a problem."

"No shit? With that roomful of geniuses? I'm shocked!"

I liked Bill. I knew I was probably going to help him no matter what the problem was, but I was going to give him as much shit as I could in the meantime.

"So Mandela gets out of jail," Bill said, "and starts his fundraising trips. Some airport, he's going down the greeting line shaking hands, and one of the hands he shakes is Yasser Arafat's. Somebody snaps a picture. Makes the front page of the *Post*. My Jewish money, which we were depending on, vanishes the next day. We are fucked. We're going to be the only city that stiffs Mandela. And us with a black mayor no less!"

Oh, boo-hoo, I thought to myself.

But he was actually close to real tears.

"You got nothing?"

"Dick." I'm translating.

You gotta love the hybrid language we speak in New York. It's a combination of '50s Jazz Hipster, Italian American Mafia, Ebonics, Spanglish, and Yiddish, regardless of one's ethnic background.

"Oy vey!" I replied, Arafat reference intended.

That brought out a reluctant smile.

"Alright, let me think about it," I relented.

Bill was a tough guy. His eyes were pleading. I didn't like seeing him like this. I walked him out, and he delivered his parting shot. "It's next week."

"Oh good. You had me nervous there for a minute."

One way or the other, I connected up with Bobby De Niro, Spike Lee, and Eddie Murphy. Drew Nieporent, De Niro's partner in the Tribeca Grill, was also involved. I explained the situation.

They came in.

We sold dinner with Mandela at $2,500 a head times two hundred to get the $500,000 we needed.

Miraculously, because of those names on the invitation, we sold it out!

Smokin' Joe Frazier came to the dinner. My good friends Jay Cocks and Verna Bloom were there. Marty Scorsese brought Ray Liotta, who was starring in his new film.

Mandela was supposed to be there at 7 p.m.

At 7:15 my phone rang.

Uh-oh, I thought. Here it comes.

It was Mandela's guy. "Hello, my friend," he starts. "I hear it's sold out!"

"Yeah, baby." I'm thinking, *Don't fucking do this to me.* "The whole shebang cost us thirty-five grand. Everybody worked for free, Bobby and Drew took no profit." *Don't even think about it, you cocksucker.* "And I've got $500K in my hand waiting for you." *Go ahead, say it, motherfucker, say it!*

"That sounds great, comrade," he said. "That sounds great."

Enough bullshit small talk. Say it.

"So listen, Madiba has had a long day and he's very tired. So we're going to skip the dinner."

Man, why can't I be wrong every now and then?

"Just curious," I said. "Where are you right now?" As if I didn't know.

"We're at Harry Belafonte's apartment."

What a surprise. I knew somebody had been in Mandela's ear telling him not to worry about those fucking white liberals—you can step all over them.

"OK, baby," I said matter-of-factly. "No problem. I'll just give everybody their money back."

"What did you say?"

He suddenly wasn't so cool, calm, and collected.

"I said I'm giving everybody their money back. I sold this as dinner with Mandela. If he can't come, I understand. But everybody gets their money back."

"You can't do that! That's ANC money!"

I had had enough.

"Just watch me, motherfucker! This is *my* fucking money until Mandela comes down here and spends some time and shows these people some respect."

"Now wait a minute, comrade. Hold the phone."

Murmur murmur murmur.

"Alright. He's coming down. But he can't stay all night."

"He needs to shake some hands—at the very least the hands of my three partners, Bobby De Niro, Spike Lee, and Eddie Murphy, whose sponsorship made this a success. And he needs to make a speech and show some gratitude for this fucking money. And there had better be an attitude adjustment because, correct me if I'm wrong, but I don't remember owing you a fucking thing!"

And come he did.

In the only conversation I would ever have with him, Mandela asked me what he should say. I'd heard he had a good sense of humor, so I thought he was fucking with me. But he wasn't.

I told him to open with a joke.

No, I didn't. I told him we'd been using "Keep the pressure on" as our slogan to strengthen his negotiating position with the government so they'd keep their promise of a fair election. "Yes, that's good," he said. And he gave a nice speech.

And that, my children, is this week's lesson showing that no good deed goes unpunished.

The ANC got their money.

David Dinkins wasn't embarrassed.

New York City wasn't embarrassed.

Bill Lynch owes me a big favor.

Smokin' Joe Frazier made two cameo appearances on *The Simpsons*.

Goodfellas came out and became a big hit.

Mandela went home and was elected president.

All in all, an unusually happy ending.

Just wish I'd gotten a picture.

But guess who did?

The next morning, as Mandela's plane was taking off, I opened the papers to see his arm around a little guy with a big shit-eating grin.

I guess Paul Simon got over that whole scary dangerous Communist thing.

twenty-three

Seven Years in the Desert

(1991–1997)

There's a bad storm coming,
I believe it's coming our way,
The air is thick and cloudy,
The sky gets blacker every day,
The rebel children are waiting,
Their time is coming soon,
They face no future gamely,
They've got nothing left to lose . . .

— "SAINT FRANCIS," FROM *BORN AGAIN SAVAGE*

Only part of me came back from the desert. The rest of me remained there, forever wandering, searching for . . . what?

The '90s were a lost decade.

For the first time in my life, I had no clear mission.

I'd lost my way, and as usual I wouldn't find it; it would find me.

Mostly what I remember is walking my dog for seven years. Staying connected to little Jake was the one thing that kept me sane. Studying him, learning from his natural instinct to live in the moment. Giving him the best life I could while cursing a God I knew didn't exist for giving the greatest creatures on earth such horrifyingly short life spans.

Maureen helped by keeping me fantasizing about ballet and Broadway.

I'd blown my life twice at that point. First by leaving the E Street Band, and then by treating my solo career as a purely artistic endeavor.

It was an exhilarating ride while it lasted. I felt like I was finally doing what I was born to do, or at least was on the right road, embracing the life of an Artist and beginning to fulfill my destiny. But who was paying the bills? It was a bit unsettling at that stage of the game to still be looking for a steady job.

Spoiler Alert. I'm still looking.

The decade was spent walking my dog and doing occasional favors for friends. Cell phones didn't exist yet. Can you imagine such a thing? But I was easy to find.

Steve Weitzman, (in)famous for booking the legendary club Tramps, called and asked me to produce an album for a Nigerian artist named Majek Fashek.

The connection was Jimmy Iovine. I had smart friends. Some of the smartest in the business. Jimmy was one of them.

He had hooked up with Ted Field, who had an independent film company called Interscope and started a record division. No surprise, given his history of success—Patti Smith, Tom Petty, Stevie Nicks, Dire Straits, U2, etc.

He started off doing Rock records. They all bombed.

This told Jimmy one simple thing: if he couldn't break a Rock record, then Rock was over. Even though there would be another minute of commercial success in the form of Grunge, it was on the way out, and Jimmy knew it.

I clock the Rock era from "Like a Rolling Stone" in 1965 to Kurt Cobain's death. Thirty years of universal bliss. Cobain marked the last time an audience would invest in an artist emotionally to that degree. It was just too painful.

Iovine saw some action in the Salsa-meets-Disco world, but it wasn't his thing. It was too late to learn Spanish. He was from Brooklyn. He was still working on English.

He looked around. What was next?

Hip-Hop!

Uh, yeah, the name had caught on.

Jimmy signed Tupac.

Then, in the ballsiest move since Don Corleone's deal with Barzini, he decided to distribute Death Row Records. And somehow lived to tell about it.

There's street smarts, super–street smarts, and then there's Jimmy Iovine.

I had to shake my head in wonderment! This Italian kid from Red Hook, Brooklyn, which half the Mob called home and where a black man would never dare to walk down the block, became the king of Hip-Hop.

The same year he signed Tupac, he signed Majek Fashek. I ended up producing a great album for Fashek, *Spirit of Love*, an example of how deep Reggae had penetrated African consciousness.

Nobody heard it.

Gary Gersh called with another production job. An Austin, Texas, super-type group that included my friend Charlie Sexton. I was good at making individuals into bands, and Gary knew that.

Charlie was and is one of the great guitar players, but everybody kept trying to make him a Pop star, just because he looked like James Dean. And OK, he happened to drive a '49 Merc, but that was beside the point. He had never made the record he deserved, and I knew I could help him do that.

The band, named Arc Angels after their rehearsal space, was Charlie, another Austin guitar player and singer, Doyle Bramhall Jr., backed by Stevie Ray Vaughan's rhythm section, Double Trouble, Chris Layton on drums and Tommy Shannon on bass.

I thought the job would be nothing but fun.

It wasn't.

I get along with everybody. Because my life got off to a late start, I am constantly preoccupied with songs and scripts I haven't written, shows I haven't produced, hotels and clubs I haven't built, not to mention a detailed unrealized political agenda, so I don't have time for petty conflict. I never start fights, and never even engage in arguments if I can help it. I have to be nonconfrontational, because I'm too extreme. My Calabrése blood has infinite patience until it doesn't, and my Napolitano blood is always ready for a fight to the death over the slightest insult. It's all or nothing at all with me, which most of the time means nothing. I'm too busy to look for trouble. It has to find me.

For some bizarre reason, it found me during the Arc Angels in the form of Doyle Bramhall Jr. Every suggestion was an argument. He never liked anything I said. Didn't laugh or smile once.

Maybe he thought I'd favor Charlie. Maybe he wanted somebody else to produce. I don't know. He didn't want to talk about his problems, and frankly neither did I.

The adversarial zenith came midway through recording, when I suggested that a solo needed a more Bluesy, melodic approach rather than the jumble of psychedelic noise he was making. He sneered. "What do you know about the Blues?"

Ooh—once in a while I still see that face in my dreams.

I bit my tongue. Hard. I didn't bother to explain that by the time he was six years old I had learned, absorbed, and used onstage every guitar lick on every album by Muddy Waters, Little Walter, Sonny Boy Williamson II, Howlin' Wolf, Elmore James, Buddy Guy, Junior Wells, B.B. King, Albert King, T-Bone Walker, Jimmy Rogers, Jimmy Reed, Hubert Sumlin, Charley Patton, Robert Johnson, Son House, Fred McDowell, Lightnin' Hopkins, Slim Harpo, Blind Willie Johnson, Blind Lemon Jefferson, Reverend Gary Davis, John Lee Hooker, and Otis Rush—whom I discussed at length with Stevie Ray Vaughan when I picked him to open for me at *Rockpalast*. The only licks I hadn't played were Freddie King's, and that was because he'd pulled a gun on me when I was a kid.

I had to make a decision. I had promised Gary and Charlie a great record, but if I beat the shit out of this obnoxious motherfucker, it was going to significantly decrease the chances of success.

Anyway, I somehow managed to ignore him, pretend I was a peace-loving professional, and make a great album.

The Arc Angels broke up just after the record came out.

Nobody heard it.

A guy named Allen Kovac called to say that he had taken over as Meat Loaf's Manager when Meat had fallen out with Jim Steinman. Would I write and produce a song?

I'd met Meat Loaf when Steve Popovich defied the industry's conventional wisdom and worked relentlessly for a year to break him. He was a sweetheart of a guy. Happy to help.

I can write a song for whoever asks. No problem. It usually comes to me within a few minutes. If it's a script, the song comes as soon as I read it. If it's a film, as soon as I see it.

But a week went by . . . and nothing. I analyzed the problem.

Meat Loaf was very popular.

He was charming and talented.

But there was one thing he wasn't.

Meat Loaf was not an Artist.

So what was he? I asked myself.

An actor! I answered.

Aha, I thought! I'm not going to write him a song; I'll write him a show!

Of course, I didn't intend to make the Meat Loaf project my life's work, so rather than conceive of a show from scratch, I went in search of a classic that could be adapted.

Meat Loaf was big. Freaky. Kind of awkward in his own skin. He must have been made fun of his whole life. His nickname was Meat Loaf, for crissake!

So with whom in classic literature did he have the most in common?

Bada bing!

Quasimodo!

The Hunchback of Notre-Dame!

Freaky fucking book.

I don't know how it was a hit in 1831. Netflix must have had a slow month. But let me tell you, Victor Hugo definitely had issues. Here's the CliffsNotes version:

An evil fifteenth-century priest wants to fuck an innocent peasant girl who tries her best to avoid him. Meanwhile, a soulful hunchback dude falls in love with her, but she becomes infatuated with some shallow soldier type. The priest gets pissed, and ready for this, *he hangs her!* Like, by the neck until dead.

Hitchcock's *Psycho* and then some!

Maybe that's where he got the idea.

And how's this for a happy ending? The hunchback whacks the priest, finds the girl's dead body, lies down next to her, and starves to death so he can spend eternity with her.

Now is that a hit, or is that a hit?

I guess compared to cholera and bubonic plague, it must have qualified as comic relief.

On top of that bizarre plot, the book takes an endless digression, even worse than one of mine, discussing the cathedral in excruciating detail. Very weird, until you remember the book was actually titled *Notre-Dame de Paris 1482*.

The comings and goings of a bunch of fatally flawed humans will always be temporary, but Notre-Dame Cathedral is forever (or at least until some asshole sets it on fire six hundred years later!). Which makes it the first existential novel, doesn't it? Beats Dostoevsky by thirty years at least!

Anyway, I rewrote it with a happier ending—not a high bar—wrote half the songs, and demoed them with Mark Alexander playing everything and a Meat Loaf soundalike singing. I was quite proud of it. A whole new genre for me, and a step in the theatrical direction I wanted to go. I delivered my masterpiece and . . . silence.

After a few days, Allen and I met. "Meat doesn't want it."

"What?"

"He can't sing it."

"What is he talking about? I wrote it specifically for his voice, in his key, with melodies in his range."

"I'll tell you the truth," he said. "I think the demo guy intimidated him."

Intimidated him?

He was *imitating* him for fucks sake!

Allen shook his head.

No-go.

I thought fuck it, another six or seven songs and I've got a Broadway show. Several Producers loved it and were considering it when Disney put out its animated *Hunchback of Notre Dame*. The Producers assumed Broadway was the next stop, since Disney owned part of it, and ran for the hills.

Nobody heard it.

Kovac had another idea, a reunion record with Southside. Sure, baby. I got nothing but time.

I had seen the Jukes recently, and they had played a knockout new song Southside and Bobby Bandiera had written, "All Night Long."

So I knew I had one good song.

I love a challenge. *Hearts of Stone* had grown in popularity quite a bit in the fifteen years since we'd worked together. Could I beat it?

I wrote a comeback song called, imaginatively, "I'm Coming Back," even though Southside hadn't gone anywhere. It was probably more about me than him.

I wrote something that included Southside's father, who I always liked (Ernie Kovacs, I swear), called "All I Needed Was You." It was based on *Somebody Up There Likes Me*, Paul Newman as Rocky Graziano.

I got a nice melancholy song from Bruce, the kind I could never write myself, "All the Way Home," and to complete the Jersey reunion vibe, I even got Johnny Bongiovi involved, doing a duet on "I've Been Working Too Hard." It was his title so I tried to give him credit, but he wouldn't take it. Very honorable guy. Even when he stole my logo in his early success, he freely admitted stealing it from me. See, that's all we need. A little credit.

Finally, since these reunions weren't gonna happen very often, if ever again, I wanted a song that told our story, like John and Michelle Phillips's "Creeque Alley" did for the Mamas and the Papas. I caught a good one with "It's Been a Long Time."

The album turned out good.

We called it *Better Days*, a title Bruce would unconsciously steal for a song title about a year later.

That's OK. Careful as I've been, I must have stolen dozens of riffs, melodies, and ideas from him over the years. Plus, our songs had opposite messages. His was optimistic: "These are better days." Mine? "Better days are on the way / 'Cause you know and I know / it can't get much worse!"

I was wrong, by the way.

Allen Kovac's record label, Impact, went under, I don't know, five or ten minutes after the record was released.

Nobody heard it.

Aside from the work, which really is its own reward, one other good thing came out of the project. I found a new lifelong friend.

Lance Freed, the son of the legendary DJ Alan Freed, had become one of the last of the great music publishers. He ran Rondor for Herb Alpert and Jerry Moss, the *A* and *M* in A&M Records.

He heard the Jukes' album and called me. "Let's talk," he said.

We met at Elio's restaurant on the Upper East Side.

"This is some of the greatest songwriting I've heard in twenty years," he started off.

Oh, I'm gonna like this dinner.

For those of you wondering what the fuck publishing is, let me explain real quick.

Each time a song is sold or reproduced, it's worth nine cents, half of which goes to the writer and half of which goes to the publisher. The publisher also controls the composition, which in the old days meant literally publishing songs as sheet music. It was the publisher's job to get the music into all those player-piano scrolls and to get them to record companies and singers.

Since the '70s, most songwriters have had their own publishing companies and use publishers to administer songs—to find and collect the money worldwide; they keep a piece of whatever they find. They get a bigger piece if they place a song in a movie, TV show, or commercial. But that's rare.

Back to Elio's.

So there I was, walking my dog and doing favors, no real work in sight, and an hour later a complete stranger gives me a $500,000 advance to administer my music and saves my life.

God bless America.

One of the nice things about this world of showbiz is that no matter how low you go, you're always only one hit away. Or in this case, one heavy executive fan away. Your whole life changes just like that. So there's always an element of hope as we punch and punch and punch the wall, trying to make a crack to let the light in, to quote Leonard Cohen.

Or make a hole big enough to escape from. To quote me.

Bruce had decided to let the rest of the E Street Band go in the late '80s, and by 1992 or so he was putting a band together to tour his new records, *Lucky Town* and *Human Touch. Human Touch* had a song called "57 Channels (and Nothin' On)" that Bruce asked me to remix. I added some political content, which gave Reverend Al Sharpton a chance to brag that he had worked with both James Brown *and* Bruce Springsteen.

Bruce invited me to a rehearsal at A&M Studios.

This was his first post–E Street tour, and he was a little bit anxious.

The new band sounded good, and I told Bruce so. He had kept Roy Bittan, and I knew a few of the horn players and Shane Fontayne, who had been Lone Justice's guitarist. Seeing Shane there could only mean one thing—Maria McKee had gone solo.

That was a shame.

I knew Iovine was heading that way. Jimmy was just coming out of his affair with Stevie Nicks and saw Maria as a similar solo star. Usually he was way ahead of me, but this time I disagreed.

Nobody should ever take a band for granted. Bands are miracles. They're rarely perfect, but if a band has that magical chemistry, it should not be fucked with. If you need to do a solo record, do it between band records.

Chris Columbus—no, the other one—called and said he needed a song for *Home Alone 2: Lost in New York.* We agreed that it was the perfect opportunity to finally work with Darlene Love.

I had met her back in 1980, when we were in LA for the River Tour. I ran into Lou Adler, the great record and movie Producer who also co-owned the Roxy. "I've got something on tonight I know you'll like," he said.

"What's up?"

"How about the return of Darlene Love?"

Holy Shit! The greatest and most mysterious of all the Girl Group singers! And we happened to be there at this historic moment? Destiny.

Darlene had quite a history. Back in the early '60s, Phil Spector was in New York looking for songs. Jerry Leiber and Mike Stoller ran their labels, Red Bird Records and Spark Records, along with Trio Music publishing, in the Brill Building at 1619 Broadway, where they'd signed Ellie Greenwich and Jeff Barry. Up the street at 1650, an address often mistakenly included as part of the Brill Building, were Al Nevins and Don Kirshner, whose Aldon Music had the writing teams of Carole King and Gerry Goffin and Cynthia Weil and Barry Mann. (There's more detail about this in Al Kooper's great book, *Backstage Passes and Backstabbing Bastards.*)

As the story goes, Spector was in one building or the other going from room to room, looking for songs. At the time, that's what half the industry did. He saw Gene Pitney playing "He's a Rebel" for Vikki Carr, knew a hit when he heard one, got hold of the demo, and raced to get it out first.

Back then, music publishers were sleazy bastards who gave songs to multiple producers, telling each of them they had an exclusive. Carr's version was slated to come out on Liberty Records. Phil rushed to get his out on his own label, Philles Records (named for Phil and Lester Sill, a major mentor to Leiber and Stoller as well as Phil).

The Crystals, the first successful group on Philles ("There's No Other," "Uptown"), happened to be on the road, so he recorded "He's a Rebel" with a group called the Blossoms, featuring a young singer named Darlene Love—but he credited it to the Crystals.

Historic mistake. The only possible justification was that in those days, independent record companies had trouble collecting from distributors, and Phil felt it was risky to use a new artist's name so early in the new company's life.

Whatever the reason, it screwed up Darlene's life pretty good. She sang on a few more hits (with the Crystals, with Bob B. Soxx and the Blue Jeans, and under her own name) and enjoyed a storied backing-vocal career with the Blossoms, but by the '70s she was out of the business, working as a housekeeper. The greatest singer in the world cleaning toilets! (Check out the movie *20 Feet from Stardom* for a full version of her story.)

And then it was 1980, and Lou Adler was talking to me about her Roxy show. I couldn't wait to tell Bruce.

Not only was Darlene spectacular that night, but she sang "Hungry Heart." Ha!

Backstage, I told her that I thought she belonged in New York. LA was too trendy. People, especially women, became invisible after the age of twenty-one.

And damn if she didn't pack up and move to New York just like that!

I immediately got her a few gigs but could not interest a record company in signing her.

She ended up doing pretty well on her own. She got a couple of off-Broadway shows and then a couple *on* Broadway. Plus a steady movie gig playing Danny Glover's wife in the *Lethal Weapon* movie series.

Now, thanks to Chris Columbus, we were finally going to record together.

Only like fifteen years late.

But it was perfect. No worries about a label or radio airplay. All the song had to do was fit in the movie. And all I had to do was write it.

Chris screened the movie for me, and I wrote "All Alone on Christmas." It's one of the songs I'm most proud of.

Writing anything great is a challenge, obviously, but it is easier to write something original than it is to write a song that is genre specific.

I know that sounds backward. But trust me on this. If you write something original, you're mostly competing with yourself. If you write a Christmas song, you're competing with fucking "Jingle Bells"! With frickin' "Deck the Damn Halls." "Joy to the Motherjumpin' World!" Songs that are embedded in the world's consciousness.

Not to mention that Darlene Love was best known for singing what many regarded as the greatest Christmas rock song ever recorded, "Christmas (Baby Please Come Home)," first on Phil Spector's Christmas album in 1963 and then every holiday season on the David Letterman show.

Since the E Street Band was no longer with Bruce, I called whoever was around, figuring they'd not only be great but could use the work.

Chris wanted to direct the video, so I wrote a script. Clarence Clemons was Santa, with Macaulay Culkin on his knee. "What do you want for Christmas, little boy?" Santa would ask, and Macaulay would say, "All I want for Christmas is Darlene Love!"

Unfortunately, Macaulay's father was a nasty dude and nixed it.

But I finally fulfilled part of my promise to Darlene. It would be another twenty years until I delivered the rest.

Debbie Gold called me again, again about Bob Dylan. "He wants you to come to rehearsal and talk about producing his next record," she said.

"Are you sure this time, Debbie?"

"I was sure last time! I don't know why he didn't give you credit!"

I honestly didn't care. I was just bustin' her balls.

The rehearsal was in California, which meant I didn't know the musicians. West Coast guys were a different breed. Bob counted them in, and they started playing what was, to me, a very weird group of songs. "Light My Fire," by the Doors, "Somebody to Love" by Jefferson Airplane, "A Whiter Shade of Pale" by Procol Harum. It was like a bar-band setlist from 1967. Bob had been hanging out with the Grateful Dead, had recorded a live album with them. Maybe their influence had rubbed off.

When they took a break, Bob came over. "What do you think?"

"Let's take a walk," I said. "Bob," I said, "this might be my last conversation with you, but I've got to be honest. You cannot do this. Unless you're planning on playing somebody's bar mitzvah, you cannot do these songs. I know you're always seeking ways to have less celebrity, to be a normal guy. But you can't be this normal. You're too important."

"I'm just not writing right now," he said.

Every once in a while you find yourself in a situation where you have to do two weeks' worth of thinking in two minutes.

"How about this?" I said. "How about you go back to your roots? The Carter Family, the Seegers, Woody Guthrie, Lead Belly, whatever. It'll have real value. It's where you come from, and you'll be keeping that tradition alive."

He didn't react. It was a lot to consider. He moved his head around, maybe shaking it, maybe nodding, and said he'd think about it.

I left and never heard back from him, but Debbie said I must have got him thinking because he released two records of Blues and Folk standards, *Good As I Been to You* and *World Gone Wrong*. I felt good about that. And she got production credit! Ha-ha! I loved that!

Oddly enough, I had a very similar conversation with Bruce at around the same time. He wanted me to hear a new batch of his songs, so I went down to Rumson.

He played me a few things and said, "I'm not sure I have a single yet."

Whoa! That's a strange thing to say, I'm thinking. I've got to deal with this right now.

"Listen, man," I said, "I don't know what bizarre circumstances have led to you being on the hit single train, but you have to get off it as soon as you can."

"What do you mean?"

"You had some Pop hits, and they're nice when they happen, but you ain't no Pop star and you don't want to live in that world. If you don't have an album in mind, I suggest you go back to your solo acoustic *Nebraska* thing. Where you can own it. Instead of trying to compete with the latest fifteen-year-old refugee from the Mickey Mouse Club!"

He wrote *The Ghost of Tom Joad*. I felt good about that too. On the way out the door that day, I said, "You know, it doesn't seem right that we all seemed to disappear around the same time. Us, Bob Seger, Tom Petty, John Mellencamp, Jackson Browne, Dire Straits, all the '70s Classic Rockers. We asked the audience to make us part of their lives. An essential part. We asked them to fall in love with us. They did. And then we all disappeared. The next time you want to make a Rock record, you should put the band back together. There is nothing you can think of that the E Street Band can't do." That suggestion would take a little longer to land.

I had gotten friendly with Bob Guccione Jr., owner and editor of *Spin* magazine, who invited me to a small gathering. Midway through, I turned around and was suddenly face-to-face with Allen Ginsberg. I told him what an honor it was to meet him, and how he had influenced me, not only in my songwriting but also in my turn to Eastern religion.

Ginsberg stared at me for a minute and then said, "You've been to the mountaintop! What was it like?"

Michael Monroe and I finally pulled off an idea we'd been cooking up for years. We missed the classic Punk bands, so we assembled one with Sammy Jaffa from Hanoi Rocks, an amazing twenty-year-old guitarist named Jay Hening, and a really great drummer named Jimmy Clark.

Sammy came up with the name Demolition 23, from a William Burroughs short story, "The Lemon Kid." The album was the easiest one I've ever made. I wrote it all in two weeks—the words poured out of me so fast I had to consciously stop writing so Michael could get some writer credits—and recording and mixing took another two weeks.

Real Ramones / Sex Pistols–type stuff. Nothing but hits!

I took it around and was told Punk was dead. A year or two later Green Day and Offspring broke big, and Punk wasn't so dead.

Nobody heard it.

We did a residency at the Cat Club, hoping to start a scene. We had a different guest every week—Joey Ramone, Ian Hunter, Andy Shernoff, the occasional Monk or Bad Brain. Adam Clayton from U2 came down one night, and in the course of shooting the shit he asked me what I was doing. I told him I had two solo albums, half a Broadway show, and a Punk album on the shelf. "And I ain't writing anything else until some of this shit gets released!"

I described the most important project, *Born Again Savage.*

"I've got some time," he said. "Let's do it!" You don't see that kind of enthusiasm every day.

We had to fill out the band. Since it was a '60s-style Hard Rock album, how about Jason Bonham on drums? He'll get it!

We found him somehow, and he was into it.

The album, written in '89, recorded in '94, and released in '99, would never have seen the light of day if not for Adam Clayton, and I am forever grateful to him. You too, Jason! It's one of my favorites.

At around the same time, Jean Beauvoir, who had been in the Plasmatics and then the first version of the Disciples, put out a solo album. During Jean's time with me, he had filled the role that I had once filled for Bruce, the right-hand man, the consigliere. But he had ambition. What he wanted most was the thing I wanted least, to be a front man and a star. When he left after *Voice of America* in 1984, the fun kind of went out of it for me, and it was never quite the same again.

By the '90s, we'd gotten past it, and with his new solo album coming out, he wanted a favor. Would I ask Johnny Bongiovi if Crown of Thorns, Jean's band, could open for him in Europe? I talked to Johnny and Richie Sambora, who said Jean could have the gig, but only if I came out and did a few songs with them. They were getting worried about me turning into a hermit. It was touching, actually. So I agreed. One of the three songs I played, "Salvation," was from *Born Again Savage,* the album's only public performance until the rebirth of the Disciples in 2016, twenty years later.

While I was out with Bon Jovi, Chris Columbus called. He had a new movie, *Nine Months,* that needed a song.

I don't know what it is about Chris, but he brings the best out in me. As you travel through life, you meet very few people with blind faith in you. It makes you really want to deliver for them.

In that case, what he brought out of me was what might be my most important song. "This Is the Time of Your Life" is a Stonesy ballad about living completely in the moment, which is the core of my life's philosophy. I wrote it in Milan, in my hotel room, staring out the window at the great Duomo.

The song was supposed to play over the end credits. But when I saw the movie, there was a Van Morrison song there instead. Maybe Chris had gone out to multiple artists, and Van had turned in his song at the last minute?

Who knows. It was . . . awkward. I never asked.

Van's played, and *then* mine played.

I probably inspired a lot of cleanup crews.

Needless to say . . .

Nobody heard it.

Let's see . . . the '90s . . . the '90s . . .

We had a big victory with our Solidarity Foundation, unifying the Indians and the unions and pressuring the Quebec government to cancel the Grande-Baleine hydroelectric dam project.

I started a couple of books that I didn't get very far on. I had titles, though.

The American Identity: Who Are We? Who Do We Want to Be?

That one would have come in handy in 2020.

The Top Ten Coolest Events in Rock History.

And . . .

Frank Barsalona: Godfather of Rock and Roll

I videotaped everybody Frank knew and Frank himself. The tapes tragically disappeared, probably stolen by an insider, and I was so pissed off I couldn't continue. That one still needs to be written by somebody.

Bruce and I inducted Gary US Bonds into the Rhythm and Blues Hall of Fame. That was fun.

Did some liner notes for Dion.

And did some liner notes for Dino.

Dion released an amazing album in 2020, at the age of eighty!

And Dino. What can I say? Read Nick Tosches's book about him.

The first bio I ever read was Edmund Morris's first book about Teddy Roosevelt. Loved it. Teddy became a controversial hero. I wonder how that holds up.

Dave Marsh's book about Bruce, *Born to Run,* and his book about the Who were great also. As was Tim White's book on Bob Marley.

Bruce's *Born to Run* is an exception, but biographies are almost always better than autobiographies, aren't they?

So much for the '90s. Almost.

"Stevie," Zoë said to me on my way out of the office. "Somebody named David Chase on the phone."

twenty-four

A Night at the Opera

(1998)

In the world of show business—no news is always bad news.
—THE UNWRITTEN BOOK

The saga of *The Sopranos* began in Frank Barsalona's office one late summer day in 1997.

Frank wanted to discuss the annual meeting of the Rock and Roll Hall of Fame nominating committee. He was an important member and wanted my opinion on who he should be politicking for induction.

"How many years will go by before they put the Rascals in?" I said.

"They should be in," he said. "But so should Connie Francis!" He lit another More Red cigarette. "For fuck's sake, these guys forget how this whole thing started!"

"Frankie!" I said.

"OK, OK," he said. "I'll see what I can do."

A few years later, he put me on the nominating committee, but back then I needed him to argue my case—meaning the Rascals' case.

Do you believe in Destiny? I don't know if I do either, but let's pretend for a minute. Because if what happened isn't Destiny, I swear it's her stunt double.

Let's count the number of weird things that led from that moment in Frank's office to the *Sopranos* gig.

Frank gets the Rascals into the Hall of Fame by arguing their case at the nominating committee meaning. That's number one.

Then he told me that I should do their induction.

"No fucking way! They deserve better than me!"

He kept asking, and I kept turning him down. That's called ignoring Destiny's advances.

As the ceremony approached, Frank made one final appeal. "You have to do it," he said. "There's nobody else left."

"Alright," I said. "But goddamn it, it's a shame you couldn't find a real celebrity." That was number two.

I had been to a few inductions. They could be pretty grim, overly serious and overly long. I decided to do a little comedy to break the monotony. And because that year, for the first time, the ceremony would be televised—that's number three—I settled on a sight gag. I had one of my wardrobe girls make the same Little Lord Fauntleroy knickers and frilly shirt that the Rascals wore, and I hid the outfit under a long black coat like people were used to seeing me in so nobody would suspect anything.

At that point, the Rascals hadn't spoken to each other for twenty-five years or so. The conventional wisdom was that Eddie Brigati, one of the two lead singers, was the bad guy who had broken the group up, leading to a circular firing squad of lawsuits among him, Felix Cavaliere, and the other band members. I would eventually find out the real story, but that was still fifteen years away.

When I got to the hotel, I saw Dino Danelli, the original Rascals drummer and one of the first Disciples. He was packing his bag. "What's going on?" I said.

"I'm leaving," he said. During soundcheck, the band had started squabbling, and Dino had decided he had better things to do. "Listen," I said. "It took a lot to get you in. It's gonna make me and Frank look very bad if you guys don't perform. The show is in a few hours, and then you'll never have to see them again!"

He stayed. I delivered my speech, which was full of silly punch lines like "To sound that black you had to be Italian!"

The wardrobe reveal got a big laugh.

And who do you think was flipping around and caught the whole bit? David Chase, a television writer and Director looking for new faces for what he swore would be his last TV show. That was number four.

Chase told his people to call me. Georgianne Walken, a prominent casting Director (and wife of Christopher) told me later that she did a Hercule Poirot and tracked me down through the corporate papers of my Solidarity Foundation. That was number five.

Someone at Solidarity brought me a message. "They want you for a TV show," I was told, though I wasn't told which show, what exactly was wanted, or who "they" were.

"Tell them to send a script," I said, knowing it would be as terrible as the scripts I got every day.

At the time, a Native American man named Alex Ewen ran Solidarity for me. His main researcher was a Rhodes scholar named Jeff Wallich, who we called Doc, him being a doctor of probably several disciplines. Doc was one of those eccentric intellectuals, a bizarre and not-quite-socialized genius. At that point he had been in my office for five years, and I didn't remember him ever speaking a word. Maybe he had said hello once.

One afternoon I went to see a movie by myself to clear my head. As the lights went down, the phone rang.

"Steven?" It was a voice I didn't recognize.

"Who's this?"

"It's Doc."

Oh my God, I thought. The office must be on fire. I ran out to the lobby.

"What's the matter?"

"Well," he said. It was already our longest conversation. "I read the script" (number six).

"You what the what?"

"The script on your desk," he said.

I racked my brain. What the fuck?

"You know: *The Sopranos.*"

It clicked, vaguely. The new thing that someone had sent over. "Oh . . . OK?"

"It's great. You've got to consider this."

It was one of the strangest phone calls I had ever gotten. The office burning down would have made more sense. The guy had nothing to do with show business. He was an academic. Why he would even pick up the script was beyond me, let alone call me to offer career advice.

Because the call was so bizarre, I read the script. Doc was right. It was good (number seven)!

But I still wasn't sure why they wanted me. I assumed it was music supervision, or maybe writing original music.

That's when the call came from the man himself. David Chase turned out to be a fan, not only of my work with the E Street Band but also of my solo albums. He told me that he liked the fact that the E Street Band were not nameless, faceless sidemen. "You were the Rat Pack of Rock and Roll," he said. We talked a little more, and then he sprung a question. "So, do you want to be in this show?"

"In it?" I wasn't being slow. Everything else moving a little too fast.

"Yeah, in it. Like an actor in it."

Wow.

"Uh . . . wow." I had a pretty good imagination, but I'd never pictured being an actor. "That's really flattering, but no, not really."

"What do you mean no?"

"I mean I'm not an actor." Maybe I had been in a play or two in junior high, and there was the *Men Without Women* movie, but the closest I had come to real acting was reading for Marty Scorsese for his first attempt at *The Last Temptation of Christ.* Guess which part? A disciple.

"You are an actor," he said. "You just don't know it yet."

I had to think. Did I hear Destiny calling?

"Let's have lunch," I said (number eight).

We really hit it off. Chase was a huge music fan, had drummed in a band when he was young. And I knew some of his shows. I had never seen *Northern Exposure,* but I had watched a few episodes of *The Rockford Files* and I really liked *Kolchak: The Night Stalker.*

At lunch, we got around to talking about the script. I said that I liked it, and he said that he wanted me for the lead, Tony Soprano.

Wow. The lead.

I was interested in the whole Mob thing. I had grown up around it, the suburban side of it anyway. Like knowing where Vito Genovese's summer house was in Atlantic Highlands, bodies washing up on Sandy Hook, running into low-level gangsters running clubs on the Jersey Shore. I had seen every movie, read every book, and gotten a glimpse of the real thing in Vegas.

Other than the obvious jail-and-death part, I never really had a problem with Mob stuff. If the Beatles and the Stones hadn't come along when they did (and if it hadn't been for the end of *Angels with Dirty Faces* where Jimmy Cagney pretends he's gone chicken and begs as they put him in the electric chair), it probably would have been a viable career choice.

I always thought Italians who pretended to be insulted by the association were hypocrites. Like the assholes that banned all of us Sopranos from the Columbus Day Parade and the next year made Paul Sorvino the grand marshal!

The truth is that I never saw the downside of people thinking you're in the Mob. You can get palpable respect just from *playing* Mob guys!

Everybody thought Frank Barsalona was Mob. Of course, my referring to him as "the Godfather" helped perpetuate that fantasy. But it never hurt him.

My friend Tommy Mottola was always rumored to be Mob. That hurt his career all the way to him running Sony!

Morris Levy, the famous music publisher and label owner, wasn't Mob per se, but he definitely did business with them, and he did just fine for thirty or so years before he got busted. (Read Tommy James's excellent book *Me, the Mob, and the Music* for more about that subject.)

Chase and I talked like we had been friends for years, shooting the shit about music and the '60s. I didn't know enough about the acting world to be nervous. I felt very easy come, easy go.

"Not for nothin'," I said, somewhere between the first and second bottle of Brunello. "There is one thing in the script struck me as kind of strange. I grew up in an Italian family. I had a lot of Italian friends. But this mother character? I've never seen any kind of Italian mother like this. I mean, I don't think it's believable."

The mother in the script, Livia, was the most evil, passionless, manipulative character I had ever read, up there with the worst Shakespearean villains. It felt over the top.

"That's my mother," he said.

Stunned silence.

"Uh, what do you mean?"

"That's my mother."

"That's your mother??"

He nodded solemnly.

A million thoughts went through my head. First of which being, That's the end of this gig. My second thought was that if this guy hadn't gone into show business, he would've been a serial killer. Which is almost the same thing except there's less blood spilled in serial killing.

Not only did Chase not fire me even before he hired me, but as we were leaving he said he was more convinced than ever I could do it (number nine). Maureen, the real actor in the family, had studied with both Stella Adler and Herbert Berghof and had continued taking classes at HB for years. I read the scene with her, she gave me a few tips, and by the third time through, she thought I could handle it.

My friend Jay Cocks was the film critic at *Time* before he became the Rock critic, and his wife, Verna Bloom, was an acclaimed actress who had worked with Frank Sinatra and Clint Eastwood. I read with Jay and Verna, too, and they also were encouraging.

Frank Barsalona was careful, as always. He didn't trust any Artform he didn't control, and he knew he would not be there to protect me. "Do you think you can do it?"

"I don't know," I answered truthfully. "This first script is good, yeah, but what if the next one blows? What do I do then?"

He thought about that. "You tell them to fuck themselves and you split! What can they do? Make you act?"

Lance Freed was dead set against it. "You can't do this," he said. "You're an important Rock Artist. You are Mr. Credibility. You could throw away everything you've worked for your whole life!"

Peter Wolf tipped the scales. He had been one of my best friends for years. He left J. Geils at around the same time I left the E Street Band, and we both had Frank as a mentor. Plus, he had seen the film and TV business from the inside when he was involved with Faye Dunaway. We went to dinner and he thought about my plight.

"The thing about TV is, nobody remembers anything," he said. We were somewhere between our spaghetti and our second bottle of wine. "If it's a success, great! If not, no one will even know about it! Do you think anybody remembers Steve McQueen's TV show? Clint Eastwood? Jimmy Stewart? Lee Marvin? Warren Beatty was on *Dobie Gillis* for cris-sake! Definitely do it. Don't overthink it. If it bombs, it bombs. Nobody will care."

So now I had to figure out a philosophy of acting, a concept to make up for my lack of experience. I had heard all the accepted theories from Maureen—Stanislavski, Strasberg, Adler, Meisner, Hagen—frankly, they were beyond my intellect. So I had to make up my own.

I thought about it and decided that every human characteristic exists in everybody. From Gandhi to Hitler. From Wavy Gravy to Trump. The craft of acting (for me anyway) would be digging down and finding the appropriate characteristics of the character to be played. I then inhabit that part of me and bring it to life.

For me there would be one more necessity that lifelong actors may not need, and that was the physical transformation. I knew if I could look in the mirror and see the man, I could be the man.

I went to the gym and put on twenty-five pounds, eventually going to fifty. De Niro made the concept famous, but let me tell you, it worked for me. I said goodbye to the skinny Rocker, figuring I'd never need him again. I walked different, talked different. I didn't want anybody watching the show associating me with my previous profession.

I knew some guys who knew some guys, and I found out where John Gotti got his clothes made. He had just gone to jail, so the tailor suddenly had a lot of time on his hands.

The way I saw the character, he was a traditionalist, so I added a hairstyle that reflected his romantic reverence for the past.

I went down and read for Chase. He loved it. The part was mine. Almost. "We have to go to the West Coast and read for HBO," he said. "It's just a formality."

HBO's LA lobby was filled with other actors reading for various *Sopranos* parts. One guy, I recognized. Younger than me, a little heavy-set, balding. I had seen him in a couple of movies. *True Romance, Get Shorty*, not big parts but memorable ones. He stood out.

I quietly pointed him out to the casting girl, Sheila Jaffe, Georgianne Walken's partner at the time.

"Do you know who that is?" I said.

"No."

"Did you see *True Romance?*"

"Nope."

"Man! Nobody saw that movie! It's a supercool classic!"

"I'll rent it." Sheila was half a wiseguy herself.

"That's the guy who should play Tony Soprano."

Soon enough she would learn this journeyman character actor's name: Jimmy Gandolfini. But when I pointed him out she just looked at me like I had three heads.

And I did, in a sense. The acting world was very different than the music world, far more competitive. In Rock you go to a bar and say that you want to play. If they already have a band, you just go to the next bar. In the acting world, there are only so many parts, and way too many people want them. I'm quite sure no casting person had ever heard an actor say someone else should play the role they were reading for!

"Schmuck!" Sheila said. "You've got the friggin' part!"

"OK, OK, just saying . . ."

I read.

It was a mini–Roman Colosseum vibe, fifteen or twenty HBO people looking down from bleachers and me in the pit waiting for the lions to be released. I wasn't nervous going in, but the environment got me there pretty quick. Still, I got through it.

The next day, some of those bleacher people got back to David. "He's good," they said. "He can be in it. But no way are we giving the lead to a guy who's never acted before. This show is our biggest investment ever!"

The pilot had ended up at HBO because network after network had passed for one simple reason. David insisted on shooting in New Jersey rather than LA or New York. This simply was not done.

David called me to meet him somewhere, maybe the Polo Lounge at the Beverly Hills Hotel. "Sorry," he said. "They won't let me give you the lead. But you can have any other part you want."

"That's OK," I said. The whole thing was still completely surreal. I had spent the time since my Roman Colosseum experience running the opportunity by the people I trusted.

"Listen, David," I said. "I appreciate this opportunity, but I've been thinking about this, and I've got to tell you I've got mixed feelings about taking an actor's job. They train their whole lives. They take classes.

They dedicate their lives to this craft. I've seen my wife do it for years. So maybe it's better I say thank you and go back to where I belong."

He was unmoved. "I'm determined to have you in this," he said. "It just feels right to me. Your relationship to New Jersey is unimpeachable, and Jersey is going to play a major role in this thing. You don't want to take anybody's job? OK, I'll write you in a part. What do you want to do?"

Wow. You gotta love this guy, I'm thinking. He's nuts!

"Well . . . ," I said. Over the years, I had entertained fantasies about TV and the movies, though they ran more to writing and maybe directing. "I've got a treatment I had written about a character named Silvio Dante, an independent hit man, now semiretired, who owns a nightclub but still does diplomacy, conflict resolution, and an occasional special hit for the bosses."

My treatment was set in contemporary times, but both the character and his club lived in the past: big bands, Catskills-type Jewish comics, dancing girls, the whole schmear. All the Five Families had tables at Sil's place. The police commissioner and the mayor too. The intrigue began in the club. It was kind of like a Mob version of *Casablanca.*

David took my idea to HBO and then came back to me with good news, bad news. "They think the nightclub idea is too expensive. So we'll make it a strip club. You'll run it for the family, and you guys will use the back room as your social club / office."

Number ten.

And so, Bada Bing! A TV career was born.

The first meeting with the entire cast was at Silvercup Studios in Long Island City. It was a table read, where the cast goes through the entire script the day before shooting begins. It's a nice tradition because it's the only time the whole cast is together before splitting up into separate scenes.

I flashed on the first time I saw my brother Billy act. He was like, I don't know, twelve? A quiet, unassuming kid. You picture kid actors as the loud extroverted obnoxious type. He barely spoke. Out he comes, Alfred P. Doolittle in *My Fair Lady* singing "Get Me to the Church on Time" in a totally believable cockney accent! Completely blew my mind. I'm thinking, Man, I've got to act tomorrow. I hope I'm half as good as he was. So I'm half daydreaming, half following along, making sure I don't miss my lines, and midway through one of the early scenes, I looked up and directly across the table from me was Johnny Fucking Ola!

The guy who brought the orange from Hyman Roth to Michael Corleone as good luck in *The Godfather: Part II.*

Dominic Chianese. Now our Uncle Junior.

An electric current ran through my whole body.

The Godfather and *The Godfather: Part II* have a special, even sacred place for most of my generation. And for Italian Americans it was the *paisano Tao Te Ching.*

I was gonna be in a show with Johnny Ola! Suddenly the entire experience became real.

The strangest thing was that while I knew almost none of the other actors, they all knew me. I thought they might resent me invading their turf, but they were very respectful. Jimmy Gandolfini, who did get the lead role—luckily for all of us—was great with me right away, and everyone took their cues from him.

It took me a while to get used to the way TV worked.

For starters, you have to learn to accept that if the Director is happy, you're happy. And you have to take their word for it. You don't even see what you're doing. It was quite a shock artistically.

In the music business, you go in the studio, sing or play, go into the control room to listen to it, and do it again. You improve upon it or you don't. Each take has to be compared to the take before it, or the one after it, before you know if it's working. But you judge *yourself.*

Not in the acting world. Nobody wants actors looking at dailies. So I wouldn't see what I was doing for six months or so. I had to learn to live with that.

The other thing was that no one said anything to me. I was looking for a pat on the back, at least. I brought it up to Michael Imperioli. "Nobody's saying anything to me. That's bad, right?"

"No. That's good," he said. "That means you're not a problem."

HBO waited until the last possible moment to commit.

I had met Robert Wuhl, who had a comedy, called *Arli$$*, on HBO about a sports agent. He invited me to an event for his season premiere the night before HBO's deadline for picking us up.

I'm not much of a socializer, but I thought I would go and talk to the executives, see what I could find out.

The brass were all there: Jeff Bewkes, Chris Albrecht, Richard Plepler. All E Street Band fans. I asked them what was happening with *Sopranos.*

"We've been looking for a partner this entire year," said Jeff. He explained again that the show was a big expense, two or three times what they'd spent on any other show up to that time. "We've had no luck."

"Geez," I said. "We all really love this thing. It's a little eccentric, but it's great."

Eccentric was an understatement. Of course I wouldn't have said it out loud, but I didn't know how commercial it was. A Mob guy sees ducks in his pool, and when they fly away he has a nervous breakdown that lands him in a psychiatrist's office? That's the premise of a hit show?

I went on. "But wouldn't that be good for a network like yours? No offense, give it a little identity?" At the time, HBO had been around forever but remained an unrealized potential. A few original shows, some sports programming, and movies that were mostly R-rated to give people a reason to subscribe. They got no respect whatsoever.

Jeff nodded.

It was hard to read successful executives. That's how they got where they are.

"I'm not saying turn into an Art channel," I said, "but why don't you turn into an Art channel?"

A raised eyebrow.

"You know, Art and porno!"

I got a half grin out of him, and then moved on to Chris Albrecht. Same noncommittal answers. They really hadn't made up their minds.

The next day they pulled the trigger. Pun intended.

We were on HBO!

The network was still fighting David on the title. They thought the audience would assume the show was about the opera. David didn't know what to do, so we strategized in constant multihour conversations, which we've never stopped having.

"That's ridiculous!" I told him. "Tell those fools names become the content. What's the stupidest name of a band you've ever heard? The Beatles! What's the second dumbest? The E Street Band! But nobody thinks they're so dumb anymore now, do they?"

"Yeah, I'll use that," he laughed.

I was still playing golf at the time.

Frank Barsalona had gotten into it and bugged me like crazy to join the torture. My father was a golfer, and one Father's Day I decided to learn so we could spend some quality time together, which we'd never done. We managed to play for a year or two before Alzheimer's got him in 1998. The world's most evil, despicable disease.

I had fifty "The Sopranos Are Coming" shirts printed up, and I gave them out to everybody at a televised MTV charity golf tournament. I was politicking every way and everywhere I could.

HBO wisely gave up and accepted the name.

In some ways, doing a big TV show was the same as doing *Darkness on the Edge of Town*. Lots of downtime. I don't mind working. Waiting, I can't do. Whether I was in the scene or not, I spent my time learning and observing.

Everyone got along OK, but we were a little distant from each other at first. That was the acting world. It wasn't arrogance on anyone's part. There was a tone of humility set from the top down. Jimmy was a character actor, no diva. But I was used to working in a more congenial atmosphere. A cast wasn't a band.

I had written an entire backstory for Silvio, mostly for myself, but I shared it with the writers. Sil was the only character David Chase hadn't created from scratch, and even though I knew he would adjust as we went, I wanted them to have a place to start.

In the fictional bio, I wrote that Sil had grown up with Tony, that they had been best friends since they were kids. In my story, Tony was a year or two older and was always the big-picture guy, big ideas and big ambitions. Sil was a soldier, more street-smart, perfectly happy being underboss as well as consigliere and watching Tony's back. Chase would make Sil older of course, since I was, but keep the consigliere idea intact.

So after seven years in the wilderness, eighteen years after my last semisteady job in the E Street Band, thanks to the caprices of Destiny and only ten twists of Fate, I had finally, miraculously, found a new career. Something I could do for the rest of my life. I was determined to give it my undivided attention and effort.

Rrrrrrrrring.

"Stevie?"

"Yeah."

"Bruce."

"Hey, man."

"It's time to put the band back together."

twenty-five

Cross Road Blues

(1999–2001)

I went to the crossroads, fell down on my knees.
I went to the crossroads, fell down on my knees
Asked the Lord above, "Have mercy now,
    save Poor Bob if you please."

—ROBERT JOHNSON, "CROSS ROAD BLUES"

The reasons not to go back to E Street were obvious.

I had a chance at a whole new career as an actor.

That could lead to writing, which I was already doing on the side.

And that could lead to directing, which had always interested me.

And finally, to producing. The big picture. Overseeing all the details of a project. The ultimate goal.

Never mind that in my life plan, I kept getting to first base but couldn't make it to second. And never mind asking an audience to redefine me a third or fourth time. If I wasn't a performer, if what I did was behind the scenes—writing, directing, producing—I would only have to worry about how much an audience liked my work, not how much they liked me.

Another reason not to go back was that the dynamics of the organization had changed.

I'd given up my position as underboss and consigliere when I left. Bruce was now, more than ever, treated by the organization as a solo act. I would have no control or input whatsoever.

How would it feel being a real sideman for the first time? When I left back in the early '80s, Bruce hired Nils Lofgren to play my guitar parts and Patti Scialfa to sing my vocal parts.

So what would my role be in the reformed band, exactly?

The more I thought about it, the more I realized it would be the same as it always was. The role that couldn't be replaced. I would be the lifelong best friend. I was fine with that. In fact, I'd just been cast in the same role in *The Sopranos*.

The bio of Sil I had given the writers had helped them a little bit, but the character was still coming into focus as the show got started. Halfway through the first season, I realized I could use my relationship with Bruce as the emotional basis of Silvio's relationship with Tony, because I knew exactly what the job entailed.

Dreaming together, planning and strategizing, sharing the good times and the bad, suffering the undeserved wrath when bringing bad news that only you could bring because you were the only one who wasn't afraid of the Boss. They were all part of the job. Of both jobs.

Back in the late '80s, years after I had left the band, Bruce had me over to hear his follow-up to *Born in the USA*, *Tunnel of Love*, at his house in Rumson. I listened. *Tunnel* felt like a solo record, for starters. There were still great songs, but they were smaller in scope, with more personal lyrics. "And what's up with that first song, 'Ain't Got You'?" I asked. "I got this, I got that, and I got Rembrandts on the wall?!?"

"What?" he said. "That's how it is."

"I know you're trying to be funny," I said. "But it's only funny if it's *not* true! If it was a line from a Dave Van Ronk song, we'd all have a good laugh about it, right? Look, I'm sure it's more than a little weird to be rich and famous after almost forty years of being poor and struggling, and I know you're trying to come to grips with how that new reality fits with your working-class persona, but damn!"

"Well," he says, "in a certain way—an exaggerated way—I'm just being honest about my life."

"Honest?" I was getting kind of worked up. "About *your* life? I hate to tell you this, but nobody gives a fuck about *your* life! Your gift, your job, your genius is telling people about *their* lives! Helping them understand *their* mostly fucked-up existence! Letting them know that you understand what they're going through and that they are not alone."

"Oh, man," he said. "You're totally nuts! It's just a little humor!"

"People depend on your empathy!" I said. "It's what you do best. They don't want advice from Liberace or empathy from Nelson Fucking Rockefeller! You shouldn't be writing shit like this!"

He said I was crazy, overreacting like I did with everything, that no one else had complained about it. We yelled and screamed for a while and then he threw me out.

It was the second of our three fights.

We got over it.

I was right, of course. Like I always am when it came to giving advice to my friends. Because I care about them. A little too much, to be honest. Friendship is a sacred thing to me, and I can't be casual about it. I don't know where that comes from. But I realized early in life that if I'm going to have friends, the friendship has to be defined on their terms. Because nobody is as extreme as me. It's a flaw I can't fix.

So where was I? Oh, yeah. The cons and pros of going back to E Street.

There was the money.

Well, not really, because even though it was more than I made my first year of acting, they would soon even out.

Bruce has always kept us the cheapest concert ticket in the business while doing the most work. It's a Jersey work ethic thing. It was a typically unprecedented moral gesture from Bruce for the benefit of the working class.

But lately it was getting harder and harder to keep the tickets away from the scalpers.

It didn't matter anyway, because my allergy to money would never allow me to make a decision based on it.

No, it was all about the closure.

I shouldn't have left in the first place.

It didn't matter how justified it might have felt at the time, or what I had learned and accomplished since. It felt like I had fucked with Destiny, interrupted what was supposed to be, and abandoned my best friend when he needed me most.

I also felt the band's place in history needed to be secured. We were slowly vanishing from the mass consciousness. When magazines did their annual polls of best bands, or even best American bands, we had always been top five. But recently we had started to slip off the charts.

I wasn't big on competition. But all due respect, shouldn't we be ranked higher than the Spin Doctors?

One day, too, the band should be in the Rock and Roll Hall of Fame, and it would be best to be active if that day was ever to come.

There was a broader principle too. It had occurred to me somewhere along the way that we needed to preserve this endangered species called Rock. And not because it happened to be my main Artform of choice. Because there was something different about the Rock idiom's ability to communicate substance.

Folk music passes along stories and allegories. Blues talks about the conditions of life. Jazz operates through mostly wordless intellect. Soul is all about relationships. Rock has substance and the ability to communicate it worldwide. And that includes its greatest hybrid, Reggae. Bob Marley was the ultimate example. Got to be neck and neck with Muhammad Ali for most well-known human on the planet. Get Tim White's book on Marley. Incredible. I mentioned it once earlier, but I want you to remember it.

It's why I was so interested in Hip-Hop when it started. The early Rappers were carrying on the Rock tradition. Emotional information. Sometimes literal information. Inspiration. Motivation. Education. Melle Mel, Grandmaster Flash, Duke Bootee, Run-DMC, Ice-T, N.W.A., KRS-One, all the way to Public Enemy, Wu-Tang Clan, and Rage Against the Machine.

But Hip-Hop didn't turn out to be as consistent as I hoped it would be. Got a little too comfortable with the hedonism aspect, like Rock before it.

One more reason to go back to E Street?

Bruce.

I liked being with him. Always have. I still got a kick out of him as a performer. He still made me laugh. I still marveled at the fact that my shy best friend had become one of the world's greatest entertainers.

And if we could adapt to being back together, we'd not just get back what we had, but maybe even take it further.

Tony and Sil ride again!

David Chase made my decision a little easier by scheduling my scenes on days off the tour. It was an amazing thing to do and added to the infinite gratitude I already owed him for giving me a new craft.

Of course, my role became smaller if I toured. And I'd never get to write and direct *The Sopranos*.

But for the next seven years I found a way to be in a TV show and a touring Rock and Roll band at the same time.

Flew home and back every day off. Never missed a day on the set, never missed a gig.

Two Bosses, two worlds. One fictional, based on reality, and one real, reinforced by fiction.

A circumstance as improbable as it was unpredictable.

A reconciliation of brothers.

There was work left to do.

twenty-six

Gangster Days / Garage Nights

(2002–2004)

Get really good at one thing, and the whole world
will open up for you.

—THE UNWRITTEN BOOK

Lenny Kaye always had a good imagination.

Which is a big help when one is trying to survive growing up in New Jersey. One of the few subjects I know everything about.

He was in Rock bands like the Vandals by the mid-'60s and simultaneously creating sci-fi fanzines like *Obelisk*.

He was also a successful journalist for *Crawdaddy, Hit Parader,* and *Rolling Stone* while working at Village Oldies on Bleecker Street. That's where he met Patti Smith, which is why you know her name today.

I'm going to briefly digress with a huge mea culpa.

As a member of the nominating committee of the Rock and Roll Hall of Fame I've done OK. But not in 2007.

That was the year I was unable to convince the other committee members that the Patti Smith Group needed to go in, as opposed to Patti Smith solo, because, as history knows full well, there was no such thing as Patti Smith solo.

The reason she made the transition from poet to Rock star was Lenny Kaye, 100 percent.

Ask her!

My comrades remained irrationally unconvinced.

So him not being in the Rock Hall pisses me off every day. There's a growing list of self-disappointments, but it's high on that list.

Before Lenny met Patti, he curated a crazy compilation album for Elektra Records called *Nuggets*. It didn't make any commercial sense, so the label president, Jac Holzman, deserves credit for going along with it.

The album, which originally came out in 1972, was full of '60s artists of no consequence who immediately achieved immortality as ground zero influences on Garage Rock, Pub Rock, and Punk Rock.

Cut to 1998.

Mark "Twig" Greenberg would, from time to time, mention he'd been in a band.

You remember Twig? On our softball team, introduced me to Maureen, became one of my lifelong best friends.

So out came this glorious new Rhino Records edition of *Nuggets*, not just a reissue but a mind-blowing expansion magnificently curated by my friend Gary Stewart that added sixty tracks to Lenny's original double album.

And would you believe it? One of the new tracks was a track from Richard and the Young Lions, which turned out to be Twig's band from the '60s!

Holy Shit.

At the same time, a guy named Jon Weiss, who had been the lead singer of a band called the Vipers in the '80s, had been promoting a series of Garage Rock shows called Cavestomp! that both reassembled classic '60s bands and booked new bands who fit the genre.

He called Twig to reunite the Young Lions, and Twig invited me to the show. I had no idea what to expect. They hadn't played together in like thirty years.

When I got to the Westbeth Theatre on Bank Street, the joint was packed and the crowd was buzzing. Turns out Richard and the Young Lions had attained mythological Garage status, like the Sonics from Tacoma, the Moving Sidewalks from Houston, or Thee Midniters from East LA.

The lights dimmed, the crowd rose up, the walls began to sweat, and on they came, blasting into one of their three singles, "Open Up Your Door!"

Twig was on drums, Louie Vlahakes on guitar, Fred Randall on bass, and Rick Robinson on keyboards. In the center of the stage was a little old man straight out of *Lord of the Rings*, the legendary Richard Tepp, hunched over, mic clutched in his clawlike hands, looking like he was . . . not singing . . . more like summoning demons from hell, resembling not so much Richard the Lionheart as Shakespeare's Richard III. He eloquently croaked out the lyrics, the palpable drama enhanced by the audience's uncertainty of whether or not he would expire before the end of each song.

It was fucking glorious!

I fell in love instantly with the unlikeliest front man in history. He was Johnny Rotten as a three-hundred-year-old sorcerer! Amazing.

Jon Weiss had been struggling with Cavestomp!, so I became his partner to help keep the idea alive. He had been going from one venue to another like a floating craps game staying one step ahead of the cops. We needed a more stable location where our particular audience of freaks, misfits, and outcasts could find us.

I hooked Weiss up with Steve Weitzman, who booked Tramps and had a new venue I thought would be perfect, the Village Underground on Third Street.

Weiss would be at least partly responsible for bringing back the Zombies and the Music Machine, front men like Mark Lindsay from Paul Revere and the Raiders, and many others.

But we never quite jelled. No bad blood, no arguments. It was simply that the longer I knew him, the less I liked him. So after a year or so of monthly shows—and loaning him money he did not pay back—we parted company.

For the first time in a long while I started listening to the radio, and I was underwhelmed by what I heard.

Classic Rock was now a narrow subgenre that consisted of the same five hundred songs. They were great records, but even great records start to lose their luster when repeated that often. And nothing new was allowed into the format to update the repertoire. I mean *nothing*. If the same artist that was played every two hours released a new record, Classic Rock wouldn't play it.

And on top of all that, "oldies" stations were now playing songs from the '70s and '80s!

Uh-oh, I thought. "Oldies" was never meant to be a chronological term. It meant the music of the '50s and early '60s, the original pioneers through their progeny, the Naissance and Renaissance! Worse, sliding the category later and later in time began to erase the '60s themselves, the peak, the pinnacle, the summit of the Artform.

Rock radio disregarding the '50s and '60s because they were too old was the equivalent of a classical music format disregarding Bach, Beethoven, Mozart, and Tchaikovsky because *they* were too old.

The DJs had become as homogenized as the playlists. Their hands were tied. Out of the thousands of DJs playing Rock music in America, I knew of only two, Vin Scelsa in New York and Jim Ladd in LA, who kept playing whatever they wanted. They are both off the air as I write this, though Ladd is forever immortalized by Tom Petty's *The Last DJ.*

Personality vanished too. Most of the educated, experienced, passionate, and interesting voices went to talk and sports radio or were unceremoniously retired. The audience and ratings went with it, but nobody in the boardroom seems to have noted this "coincidence."

Rock radio had shaped my life, saved my life, inspired me, motivated me, given me a reason to live every day when I had nothing to relate to, nothing to do, nothing to hope for. First AM radio, with WABC and WMCA, then FM with WNEW, and oldies with WCBS-FM.

What the fuck happened? For a detailed account, I suggest Richard Neer's book *FM: The Rise and Fall of Rock Radio,* which remains the most accurate explanation of the tragic story.

I don't know why exactly, but I'm attracted to gaps and injustice and have a missionary conversion complex that refuses to tolerate the bland, the banal, and the boring. I have some bizarre flaw that wants the world to be perfect. And colorful. And interesting. And fun.

Suddenly I felt it was time to start a new radio format. Or two.

OK. So if I had the power to create any format I wanted, what would it be?

I knew I had to start with the center of my universe, the British Invasion, which had changed my life and affected virtually everyone else's.

That meant 1964–1967, roughly.

What it also meant was bands.

The British bands were more or less divided between Pop- and Rock-oriented bands, mostly from the north, and the Blues- and Soul-oriented bands, mostly out of London but stretching all the way to Birmingham and Newcastle.

The bands from the north were led by the Beatles and included the Searchers, the Hollies, Herman's Hermits, and Gerry and the Pacemakers from Liverpool and Manchester, along with the Dave Clark Five from Tottenham.

The Blues and R&B groups, mostly from the south, were led by the Rolling Stones and included the Kinks, the Yardbirds, the Animals, the Spencer Davis Group, the Moody Blues, the Who, and Manfred Mann.

I included a few solo artists and duos: Billy Fury, Dusty Springfield, Tom Jones, Petula Clark, Donovan, Billy J. Kramer (the "J." was suggested by John Lennon to toughen him up!), Georgie Fame, Peter and Gordon, and Chad and Jeremy.

And the more obscure but important bands that never invaded: the Pretty Things, the Creation, the Move, the Birds, the Eyes, the Action, and others.

That would be the basis of my format. Along with those core groups, I'd add everybody that influenced the British Invasion, and everybody the British Invasion influenced.

I combined all fifty years of the Rock era (it's now seventy!), and divided my favorite records into categories:

— Blues (Muddy Waters, Howlin' Wolf, Little Walter, etc.)

— Pioneers (Little Richard, Chuck Berry, Jerry Lee Lewis, etc.)

— Doo-Wop (Dubs, Chantels, Little Anthony and
the Imperials, etc.)

— R&B (Sam Cooke, Ray Charles, Jackie Wilson, etc.)

— Girl Groups (the Shirelles, the Crystals, the Shangri-Las, etc.)

— Surf and surf instrumentals (Beach Boys, Jan and Dean, the
Ventures, etc.)

— Soul (the Miracles, the Impressions, Sam and Dave, etc.)

— British Invasion (those already named, obviously, along with those from the second half of the '60s, including Them, Procol Harum, Traffic, etc.)

— Folk Rock (Bob Dylan, the Byrds, the Lovin' Spoonful, etc.)

— Country Rock (the Youngbloods, Buffalo Springfield, Moby Grape, etc.)

— Psychedelic (the Jimi Hendrix Experience, Jefferson Airplane, the Doors, etc.)

— Blues Rock (Cream, the Jeff Beck Group, Led Zeppelin, etc.)

— Southern Soul (Delaney and Bonnie, the Band, Leon Russell, etc.)

— *Nuggets* (the bands on the original compilation and the reissue, the Blues Magoos, Count Five, the Standells, etc.)

Beyond that, I gave each decade from the '70s its own category and added New Garage.

I then decided how often each category would appear in radio rotation. The Beatles and Stones every hour, Girl Groups every other hour, pioneers every third, and so on.

We might play some of the same bands as Classic Rock radio, but never the same songs. They'd play "Brown Sugar"; we'd play "Confessing the Blues." They'd play "Hey Jude"; we'd play "Doctor Robert." They'd play "Won't Get Fooled Again"; we'd play "The Good's Gone."

Voilà! A new format!

DJ Dan Neer, the brother of DJ Richard, learned how to engineer as I learned how to DJ. We worked hard on the pilot over a couple of months, and sent out 350 copies to every radio station.

It landed on their desks on September 11, 2001.

Yeah—*that* 9/11.

Maureen and I were living on Fifty-Seventh Street at the time. I woke up, put the TV on, and saw a plane sticking out of one of the World Trade Center towers. What the fuck? Had to be a pilot's heart attack, I figured. Or some really drunken asshole . . .

As I was saying to Maureen, "Baby, come here, you gotta see this. Some jerkoff . . ."

Boom! I saw the second plane hit the other.

I was stunned for a minute.

Like the time the white cab driver tried to hit the black guy in Pretoria.

You can't quite put together what your eyes have just told your brain.

Uh-oh. Two ain't no accident.

We were under motherfucking attack!

"Holy shit," Maureen said. "What do we do now? We are in the wrong town for World War III."

My mind was going a hundred miles an hour. No idea what to do. She was so right.

Hearing that a third plane got as far as the Pentagon was not at all encouraging. How many hundreds of billions on defense every year? And some fucking cave dweller drove a plane into the fucking Pentagon?

It understandably took a few weeks before things settled down and radio stations resumed reading their mail.

They all passed.

And I mean all: 350 stations.

I analyzed the situation. I knew I was onto something good musically, but we were obviously going about it all wrong. We were sending the show to the Program Directors, but they didn't run anything anymore. This was America. What's America all about?

Money.

I asked Richie Russo, a radio advertising sales guy and avid record collector (and I mean avid; he has one house for himself and another for his records), "How does this radio racket work?"

He told me they sold advertising by the week and sometimes by the month. I couldn't believe it, but it turned out to be true. Why not by the year?

I started talking to the General Managers. My basic rap was this: If I sell out my weekly two-hour show for a year, would you let your Program Director decide whether he wants it or not?

"Sure," they said.

"OK," I said. "Give me a list of your top ten sponsors." I started calling them, occasionally flying to meet them in person, and got on my first twenty stations, all sold out for a year.

At first, nobody thought that playing that range of music in one place could work, but we proved otherwise. It was just a matter of connecting the dots. And I knew which dots were connected. It's not something an outsider would ever understand, but there was, and still is, a method to the madness.

In the end, the *Underground Garage* show served three main purposes. It made the greatest Rock music in history accessible to future generations. It gave new Rock bands the only airplay they would ever get; we've introduced more than a thousand bands in the last twenty years. And it gave me a chance to say thank you to the greatest generation of Rock Artists. Not only do we play their best music, but if they kept making records (and many of them have—the Rolling Stones, Paul McCartney, Ringo Starr, Dion, the Zombies, the Beach Boys, plus slightly younger artists like Joan Jett and Cheap Trick), there was at least one place that would play it.

We brought in a friend of Dan Neer's, Mark Felsot, to be our in-house syndicator, and off we went.

We peaked at 130 affiliates in the United States alone, and although we're off that peak now, we make up for it by being in a hundred countries on the American Forces Network.

In our second year BBC Two offered me $20,000 per show before I got the chance to say they could have it for free! We shook hands, and I got on a plane. Tragically, by the time I landed, they'd changed their mind. They suddenly didn't want it at any price and never told me why. But we belong there. BBC Two covers the entire UK. We play more great British music than they ever will!

We had amazing ratings those first few years, with no promotion whatsoever.

I was touring with the E Street Band during the first years of the format, so wherever I was, I made a point of visiting my affiliates and going in to record stores and asking if there were any local bands making records. We were checking out everything.

Rock was at an all-time low when we started. We knew every Rock record that was being released worldwide. That's how few there were then.

It became a clear case of "If you build it, they will come." Each band that heard themselves on the radio for the first time was motivated to improve. Every next record was always better.

It had to be the same when Ronan O'Rahilly started Radio Caroline and changed history.

Ronan was born in Dublin in 1940. He was the grandson of Michael O'Rahilly, a leader of the Easter Rising in the fight for Irish independence in 1916—so he had rebel's blood.

He came to London in 1957 to study acting. By 1963, he was running a club called the Scene and managing Georgie Fame and Alexis Korner.

The BBC didn't play much Pop music at the time, so English fans had to try and dial in Radio Luxembourg; that was spotty at best, and the station's broadcast time was legally bought by the major record companies.

Out of frustration, Ronan bought a seven-hundred-ton Danish passenger ferry and anchored it in international waters, and Radio Caroline (named after President Kennedy's daughter) broadcast the British Invasion back to Britain.

England desperately needed it.

In America, we had great AM radio from the mid-'50s until 1967 and great FM radio after that. The British depended on getting records from seagoing servicemen or ordering them through the mail (like the very enterprising, very young Mick Jagger).

The historic significance of what Ronan did cannot be overstated.

His grateful Nation considered him such a threat for having a direct connection to teenagers that—the rumor went—the government seriously considered having him assassinated.

The rumor went on to say that it was his good taste that saved him. Half the Special Air Service listened to his station and refused to whack him!

A similar thing happened to Frank Sinatra: The Mob helped Joe Kennedy get JFK elected and the first thing Bobby Kennedy did was go after organized crime. Sinatra had been the intermediary in the deal, so the Mob debated whether to take him out to teach the Kennedys a lesson. But Sam Giancana and several others supposedly said they liked Sinatra's voice too much, so they let it go.

The bottom line is, Art saves lives!

After word of a possible hit leaked, the wrong kind of hit, Ronan became a paranoid recluse, relocating constantly for the rest of his life. After quite a search, I found him and actually got him out to see an

E Street show in the early 2000s. Only time I met him. Great guy. A hero who deserves a statue in Trafalgar Square. Though he might have been more comfortable in SoHo.

❖

Meanwhile, back on *The Sopranos*, Jimmy Gandolfini wasn't handling being a leading man very well. It just wasn't his natural inclination. He was a character actor, a great one, and that's what he liked doing.

He wasn't used to the long dialogues he had to do regularly with Lorraine Bracco, who played his psychiatrist.

In film, you might do two pages of script a day. In TV, you might do five or six or seven. And half or more of those were Jimmy! One paragraph is a lot to memorize. Try it.

We'd work from six in the morning to nine or ten at night, and then he'd have to go home and learn the next day's work.

Your brain is like a muscle, so it does adapt, but at first the work seemed impossible. So he quit every day. Sometimes disappear for a few days.

We'd take turns going out drinking with him. Sometimes it was me. Sometimes it was Michael Imperioli. Sometimes Stevie Schirripa once he came in, Bobby Funaro, a teamster or two.

Jimmy wanted out.

We'd have the same conversation at least once a month.

"Look," I'd say to him, "how many good movies you see last year?" He'd say, Like ten. "OK," I'd say, "if you're lucky, you're gonna get one of those, right?" Right. "You're not gonna get two, are you?" Probably not. "So you do that movie in between seasons. You don't lose a thing."

"Yeah," he'd say. "I guess." Then skip out for a few days anyway.

But he always came back.

I talked to David about it after the third or fourth time. "David," I said, "you have created like twelve interesting characters, every one of which could have their own spin-off series. Everyone would watch them. Can't you lighten up on Jimmy a little bit?"

Nope. David just fell in love with Jimmy. Could not get enough. And you really couldn't blame him. Jimmy was playing an exaggerated version of David himself, complete with mother issues. *The Sopranos* was the most effective therapy David could get!

During those first seasons, we were also watching Nancy March- and battle the horror of emphysema. The minute a scene ended, they slapped an oxygen mask on her. I'm sure that helped me and Tony Sirico quit smoking. I had smoked from my teens until 1977, and then from 1982 on, to the point where I was up to three packs a day. Quitting was hard. Without smoking, I had no energy. I couldn't concentrate. It used to be that you could give me a pot of coffee and a pack of cigarettes and I could write ten pages in a sitting. Suddenly, nothing. It panicked me for a while because I was writing a twenty-five-page script every week for my radio show. I literally could not write for weeks. Not a word. Slowly, my body worked it out.

But how hip were David Chase and HBO for hiring someone with emphysema? Just hiring someone older was unusual. My brother Billy was in TV the whole first half of his life (he's got a great book about it, *Get in the Car, Jane!*) , and he was a big fan of older actors, but the networks always gave him a hard time about hiring them.

And Sil got a new wife. Sort of. During the first season, we only saw his wife a few times. As Sil's character developed, David decided he was not only the consigliere but also a kind of ambassador to the outside world. So as the writers emphasized the "showbiz" connection in the family (after all, he was running a strip club!), they decided I needed more of a trophy-type wife, maybe a former showgirl.

When they decided to recast, either Georgianne or Sheila called Maureen and suggested she audition. Like I said, she's actually the actor in the family. I've seen her do serious drama: Tennessee Williams, Miller, Ibsen. She went down and read with a hundred other girls. That was one of the things about the show. They didn't do any favors. Edie Falco's mother auditioned to play her character Carmela's mother and didn't get the part. I never knew Maureen had auditioned until she got the part.

It was fun for her to revisit the old neighborhood—she grew up in Newark, right near where the show is set. Unfortunately, Maureen and I didn't get to be on-screen together much. There was one arc late in the show when Tony was in the hospital and Silvio was temporary boss, and we had a few nice scenes together. Otherwise, she was with the girls and I was at the Bing.

Over those first seasons, the cast warmed up to each other. We were mostly all from Jersey or New York. I was determined to do whatever I could do to turn the Sopranos into a Rock band.

Speaking of which, I happened to be in an actual Rock band at the time.

When the E Street Band was in Zurich, we spent a night off seeing a Bob Dylan show at the Hallenstadion. About halfway through, a guy came over to me and Nils and said Bob wanted us to play the encore.

I don't usually do it, but sitting in with someone onstage usually includes rehearsing something at soundcheck, but this was parachuting blindly into the chaos.

I walked on and said hi to my friend Charlie Sexton, who was just beginning his run with Bob's band. A roadie was desperately trying to hook up a guitar and amp for me. The audience was on their feet going nuts. Bob came over. "Hey," he said. "I saw you on TV!"

"Yeah, Bob. I'm doing some acting now."

"Oh, man. You were wearing a wig!"

"Yeah, well . . ." My mother had said something similar. She had watched an entire scene with me and rewound the take only because my voice sounded familiar. "You see, the character . . ."

The roadie was trying to adjust the guitar strap. I was half talking to Bob and half adjusting the tone to something in between a clean rhythm and a dirty lead in case he threw me a solo.

"Man, I wasn't sure it was you!"

Bob was so comfortable on the road that he might as well have been in his living room. That's how he arranged his band onstage. Very close to each other, like a club, even though he was playing a ten-thousand-seat arena.

"Well, that's the idea, Bob . . . uh . . ." The crowd was screaming louder. "How about I tell you all about it a little later?"

We played "Not Fade Away" and never did finish the conversation. Always memorable seeing Mr. Dylan.

One day a guy came to me from this new thing called XM Satellite Radio. My radio show had been on for a few years, kicking ass all over the country.

The XM guy said he wanted my show on this new satellite format. He wasn't offering much.

"First of all," I said, "to create my two-hour weekly show, I had to create an entire format. I have a whole channel ready to go."

"Whoa," he said. "Let's not get ahead of ourselves!"

As we talked, I realized that he thought he was in the hardware business—that the ultimate purpose of the company was selling radios!

"You don't understand what you've got here," I said. "You should be *giving* the radios away. The money is gonna be in the monthly content subscriptions. That's the business model of the future. HBO proved it!"

He looked at me like, Why do I even bother talking to these idiotic Artists?, and said he'd get back to me.

I wasn't holding my breath.

Chris Columbus recommended me to Joe Roth for music supervision on a movie called *Christmas with the Kranks*, and Joe became a good friend.

We staged a national *Underground Garage* Battle of the Bands, which aired on MTV.

Joe Strummer died, and Bruce and I played a tribute to him on the Grammy telecast with Dave Grohl and Elvis Costello.

Meanwhile, my friend Scott Greenstein got a gig at the rival satellite radio company, Sirius.

I met Scott sometime in the '90s; I would run into him from time to time at clubs and events. We became friendly. One night at a party, he asked if I could give him a little advice.

At that time, Scott was a lawyer at Viacom, and he wanted to make a move. He asked how he could make a connection to MTV.

"You don't want to be at MTV," I said. "They're on their way out of music. They're doing teenage reality programming, and it's gonna be a whole different scene. What other offers you got?"

He rattled off a bunch of companies.

"Wait," I said. "What was that last one again?"

"Miramax," he said.

"Well," I said. "Let me tell you something. Through learning the hard way, I've come to realize creating content is only half the story. Marketing is the other half. Except it's actually not two different things. It's two halves of the same thing."

I was a little bit of an expert in this area. I had been creating things my whole life that nobody knew about.

"I only know one thing about Miramax. Whenever they have a new movie out, I always know about it. That means whoever is calling the shots has real balls and knows what he's doing."

So Scott took the gig at Miramax with the infamous Weinstein brothers. After a few weeks, he came back for more advice. He had never been in a situation like this; one minute a lawyer was pushing papers around, the next he was in the social center of showbiz, celebrities, Agents, Managers, Publicists, all that. It was disorienting.

"You want to get things done?" I said. "Make contact with the Artists directly. Get close to the people who matter. The actors and Directors. Everybody else, the Managers, Agents, lawyers, accountants—they're all a pain in the ass. It's part of their job. What they do best is say *no*. *Fershtay?*"

I've given a lot of people a lot of good advice. Sometimes they take it, sometimes they don't. I have never seen a guy learn so fast in my whole freakin' life as Scott.

He went from a quiet shy lawyer nobody had ever heard of to the schmooze king of the world in like two years, and he ended up the number three guy at Miramax.

Let me say right here that neither Scott nor I ever witnessed anything having to do with Harvey Weinstein's horrifying sex life. When the news came out, we could not believe it was the same guy.

But other things began to worry me.

Scott had become close with the actors and Directors, like I suggested, and Harvey began to take advantage of Scott and use him as his hit man. Since Scott was friends with everybody, Harvey let *him* deliver the bad news.

Harvey was very good at knowing what was commercial, but he started to get heavy-handed, pissing off Directors and Producers by editing their pictures without their involvement.

I believe it came down to a Sean Penn project. Harvey was fucking with Sean. Scott had gotten friendly with Sean, as I was (my brother Billy had been in the movie *Taps* with him), and now Scott was caught between Sean and Harvey.

"Scott," I said. "That's it. I suggested you go there, now I'm telling you to get out. You've come a long way in a very short time, but you're gonna blow all your relationships if you stay there one minute longer. Your reputation has to be one where you are always on the side of the Artists and not the company. Get the fuck out."

Once again, Scott wisely listened. He got another gig at USA Films, won an Oscar or two, and eventually ended up as a consultant at Sirius.

XM, the first satellite radio company, was promoting the hell out of itself, something Sirius has never learned to do to this day.

"What can we do?" Scott said to me. "How do we compete?"

I looked at the existing content at both networks. "Everybody's treating this thing like it's regular terrestrial radio in the sky," I said. "It's a new medium. What would be hip is new-style content. Like mine for a start, which is ready to go."

"Obviously," he said. "But what else?"

I gave him a list of ideas, from a poetry channel that would feature the Beats and more (Langston Hughes, Kerouac, Maya Angelou, Ginsberg, Amiri Baraka, Ferlinghetti, the Dark Room Collective, Nikki Giovanni, etc.), to TV channels on the radio like CNN, to music channels devoted to individual artists.

"Why do that?" he said. I told him regular radio wasn't playing the greatest music ever made anymore. And since the Renaissance was over, there were only a finite number of truly great artists. They needed to be accessible at all times for future generations.

"You will be the museum where the Rembrandts, Renoirs, and Dalis hang," I said. "Where on radio can you hear Frank Sinatra? Elvis Presley? Nowhere. The Beatles? The Stones? On a regular basis? Only on my station. The best artists, from the Byrds to Led Zeppelin to Springsteen to U2 to Pearl Jam, should have their own stations."

No matter what was trendy, I said, people still wanted to hear the greatest music ever made.

"And by the way, I have a second format ready to go."

A quick digression (I should call this book *Unrequited Digressions*).

Ten years earlier, Lance Freed, my publisher, had sent me to Nashville to meet a wild dude named David Conrad who was running his Nashville office. I love characters, and he was one.

At the time, a new guy named Billy Ray Cyrus had a monster hit, "Achy Breaky Heart." The single was so big that the wiser executives felt he needed his next record to establish some credibility, or he'd be a flash in the pan. They asked me to write a song for him.

I didn't have the heart to tell them that if you don't start with credibility, it's a long slow climb up that mountain, but what the hell, I went. I had nothing better to do. Plus I was feeling grateful to Lance.

Billy was in the studio working on a new album. He turned out to be a really great guy. Probably as confused about what I was doing there as I was.

After the session, his band was packing up. "What's going on?" I said.

"We've got a gig tonight," he said.

"A gig? In the middle of recording?"

"Yeah. You don't do that in the Rock world?"

Fuck no.

We got to the arena. The crowd was coming in, and his band was setting up their own equipment.

In front of everybody.

I was appalled.

"Billy," I said. "What the fuck? You have a big hit. You're a big star. This is your *band*. They don't have to do that anymore, if they ever did!"

"Well," he said, "we have kind of an old-school Manager and he likes to save money, I guess."

After the show, the artist was obligated to go to a special fan area and sign autographs for an hour or two!

The Country world was sure different.

During that trip, I met Tony Brown, who had been Elvis Presley's piano player and was now a successful Producer running his own company. I was expressing my shock that Johnny Cash was no longer welcome at Country Radio.

"I can't get anything I do on the radio anymore!" he said. "George Jones, the Mavericks, Emmylou Harris."

"How do you establish a new format?" I asked him.

"Damned if I know," Tony laughed, "but if you ever figure it out, let me know. We sure could use it."

While I was there, I wrote Billy Ray a cool song that he didn't use. Somebody somewhere in Nashville has a hit sitting in a desk drawer waiting to happen.

And, by the way, Billy ended up doing just fine, and I'm very happy about his continued success. Nice when the good guys win.

So I started the format Tony was waiting for; I called it "Outlaw Country." It begins with the classics: Johnny Cash, Waylon Jennings, Willie Nelson, Kris Kristofferson, David Allan Coe, at the least. I added all three generations of Hank Williams; Alt-Country like Jason and the Scorchers, Uncle Tupelo, Drive-By Truckers; in-betweeners like Emmylou Harris, Delbert McClinton, Dwight Yoakam; newer Country like Sturgill Simpson, Kacey Musgraves, Jason Isbell, Margo Price, Hellbound Glory; and, finally, the Country side of Rock, the Byrds, Dylan, Buffalo Springfield, the Youngbloods, Moby Grape, the Flying Burrito Brothers, the Band, the Eagles, Jackson Browne, and Bruce.

How could the Band have no format? They had one now. But I didn't know what to do with it until almost a decade later, when I told Scott Greenstein that I had a second format ready to go.

"Don't you think we should get the first one going first?"

"Nope. This is too important to wait another minute."

For both formats, I wanted DJs who were either old-school or could tell stories firsthand.

My first call was to Wild Bill Kelly, whose completely insane format on WFMU was inspirational. He had worked there for like thirty years for free, so I felt good giving him his first paycheck.

I got my old friend Kid Leo out of the record-company business and back where he belonged, on the radio. He also became my Program Director until he moved to the Carolinas and Dennis Mortensen took over.

Andrew Loog Oldham had stolen the Rolling Stones from Giorgio Gomelsky and had publicized and produced their crucial first five years. I offered gigs to both Andrew *and* Giorgio, but only Andrew took it. Giorgio just wanted to talk. Andrew became my morning guy until he wasn't. Michael Des Barres, the Marquis MDB, enjoys that position now.

I tried to talk Jerry Blavat, one of the last of the legendary DJs, into it, telling him he would become a legend to a whole new generation, but he said he really couldn't relate to anything after 1959.

On the Country side, I knew I wouldn't be able to watch the channel as closely. A girl named Gloria who worked for me recommended Jeremy Tepper as Program Director. I got lucky; he got it right away and has done a great job ever since.

Again, I wanted characters, personalities who could deliver stories in first person, and I got them. Cowboy Jack Clement, Elizabeth Cook, Steve Earle, Shooter Jennings—and who the hell else would hire Mojo Nixon?

And so Underground Garage (Channel 21) and Outlaw Country (Channel 60) were born, and Sirius Satellite had its first two original formats.

By 2004, my syndicated *Underground Garage* format had really come together, and it became obvious to us that we should celebrate our uniqueness with an annual festival, broadcast on Sirius.

I entrusted the planning to Alex Ewen, who had started out as Director of my Solidarity Foundation and had pretty much taken over all my businesses.

We had quite an impressive lineup, I must say. A lot of reunions.

Iggy and the Stooges, the New York Dolls, Bo Diddley, the Strokes, Nancy Sinatra, Big Star (band), the Pretty Things, the Creation, the Electric Prunes, the Chocolate Watchband, the Chesterfield Kings, the Pete Best Band, Joan Jett, the Dictators, and twenty-five others.

We were snakebit right from the start.

First of all, we had two deaths before we started. A few months before our festival, the New York Dolls had reunited for a show in London curated by Morrissey. A few weeks after that, the band's bassist, Arthur Kane, came down with a flu and went to a doctor in LA. It wasn't a flu. It was leukemia. Two hours later he was dead.

Richard Tepp, lead singer of Richard and the Young Lions, also succumbed to leukemia, just days after we had finished recording the vocals for the band's first proper album.

But we soldiered on. I had a vision for the festival. There hadn't been a 3-D movie in a long time—and maybe never a concert film shot in 3-D—so I wanted to bring it back. Chris Columbus was going to shoot it, and we had a distribution deal under discussion. The day of the concert,

Chris received word that his young daughter had fallen off an exercise machine and injured herself. He rushed home to Chicago.

Even though Chris had positioned the cameras and designed the entire shoot, because he didn't actually physically shoot it, the deal fell through.

That same morning, Hurricane Danielle changed direction and headed straight toward New York.

Weathermen advised everyone to stay home.

Those brave enough to come to Randall's Island that day saw a miraculous and historic lineup of artists, along with equally historic technical difficulties.

I designed the show to resemble the old Alan Freed / Dick Clark multiact shows. We had a special rotating stage built so that one act could go right into the next. The stage broke after the third band, Davie Allan and the Arrows, so we went crazy with changeovers all day, but we got it in.

Even given the headaches and hurdles, there were so many highlights: Alex Chilton's Big Star, the reunited Creation, the rarely seen Pretty Things, Bo Diddley still rockin' thirty years after we'd done the debutante party, Nancy Sinatra with sixty go-go girls choreographed by Maureen, and Iggy running and leaping onto the huge 3-D camera.

We'll never see it because the amazing footage from the show, 3-D and video, was stolen or lost.

And the next morning, my main man Alex's last act as an employee was to inform me that he'd slightly miscalculated: I'd lost $3 million, and the union guys, who you really don't want to fuck with, were looking for me.

Making history can be an expensive hobby, but what a glorious disaster!

A few days later I went for a drive to clear my head.

I chose the Palisades, the most scenic of New York's outer arteries. After the first few miles I started to relax. The leaves were turning—autumn has always been my favorite season—and the quiet hum of the Cadillac's four hundred horses made for a smooth-as-silk magic carpet ride. It was as close to a perfect afternoon as I was likely to have for the next little while. The pretty girl sitting next to me was just a bonus. The only slight damper on the day was knowing that in just a few more miles I was going to have to kill her.

It was always depressing when a character was eliminated from *The Sopranos* because the cast had grown very close and you knew you would not be seeing that person again very often, if ever.

Drea de Matteo was very popular and her character, Adriana, was one of the show's more sympathetic, so it was a grim event indeed having to be the bastard who took her out. She had cooperated with the Feds and left us no choice.

It was the most difficult thing I've had to do as an actor.

Adriana came across as a tough broad on the screen, but when you put your hands on her in real life she was . . . a woman. Dragging her roughly out of the car made me physically sick. I despise bullies of all stripes. It's just in my DNA. And guys who assault women in any way are among the lowest of the low in my book.

Drea, a pro, told me not to hold back. "If this is gonna be my last scene," she said, "let's make it memorable!"

So I had to really concentrate and become that guy, get in that frame of mind. Completely eliminate my own thoughts and feelings. I just had to keep telling myself that Silvio was a traditionalist. There was no mercy for betrayal. Male or female, didn't matter. I had to rough her up for a couple of hours. Tough, tough day.

After it was done, we let ourselves collapse and lay down in the leaves, both of us mentally and physically exhausted.

"You just won your first Emmy," I said.

She sighed. "I certainly fucking hope so."

twenty-seven

A Wicked Cool Super Bowl

(2005–2009)

The old Kings and the Princes so recently dethroned,
Were prophets once upon a time, their words the law of the land,
They used to look so regal in their psychedelic colors,
There is no place for them now in the land of the bland . . .

—"FACE OF GOD," FROM *BORN AGAIN SAVAGE*

Scandinavia had become the Rock and Roll capital of the world.

The reason was subtitles. In much of Europe, TV and movies were dubbed. Scandinavian TV and movies were broadcast in their original language and subtitled, which meant Scandinavians grew up hearing and learning English. Since it was the universal language for both airline pilots and Rock and Roll bands, Scandinavians could make records that got played on the only Rock format that existed. Ours.

The Underground Garage channel played about twenty bands from the region, more than from the rest of Europe combined (minus the UK). We played the Cocktail Slippers from Norway, Hawaii Mud Bombers from Sweden, the Breakers from Denmark, and many more.

Scott Greenstein would even be knighted by the Swedish king for supporting Swedish music . . . played on our station.

Those bands and others urged me to start a record company because nobody had American distribution. We didn't foresee that the digital domain was literally around the corner and would make territories irrelevant.

We started Wicked Cool Records and signed a dozen bands just in time to catch the end of the record business and lose a bunch of money. At first, I mostly just picked the acts we signed and worked on the singles, but at some point I realized I had to be hands-on all the way to keep our quality consistent, and I started going through every demo, making suggestions on every song.

Two guys run my world. Dennis Mortensen took over from the legendary Kid Leo as Program Director of the SXM Underground Garage channel and has done an absolutely brilliant job making us better and better every single day. He runs the station with assistance from Olivia, Rebecca, and Casey. He also produces my weekly radio show and runs Wicked Cool Records with Louis Arzonico, who does everything else—websites, graphics, album covers, videos, archives, pictures, bios, speeches, scripts, three publishing companies, and the like. Devanshi does the books and Jeremy does whatever else is needed.

I don't possess the authoritarian gene, so the office staff come and go when they please and take days off when they want. I figure they are all adults and can get the job done without someone watching them.

I only offer one word of advice to them: anticipate. You anticipate, you win.

The one person missing is the one whose job it is to make money. So we don't. The entire operation runs at a deficit.

Wicked Cool follows the same philosophy as the Underground Garage radio format. No absolute rules, but each act, like each record, needs to have a connection to the Renaissance.

The original idea was to cross the generations, link older songwriters and Producers with young Artists. I loved it when Richard Gottehrer, who started out as a Brill Building songwriter and was in the Strangeloves, produced the Raveonettes, and when the Cocktail Slippers covered a Greenwich/Barry song.

We never realized my original vision for the company. Jeff Barry, Russ Titelman, Carole King, Barry Mann, Andrew Oldham, Cynthia Weil—all should have been producing records for us. Shel Talmy. All he did was the Kinks' first four albums and the first album of the Who, still my fave. We never did hook up a production for him. A shame.

But we have always encouraged the generations to work together in the name of connecting the dots. Old Wisdom with Young Energy.

◆

Speaking of wisdom, the wisest friend I had, Frank Barsalona, was showing early signs of the most tragic of all diseases, dementia. He had developed a strange obsession with fishing golf balls out of the water hazards between holes. "Go ahead," he'd say. "I'll catch up." He kept them, too, to the point where he had a garage full.

At first, it was funny. Then he started spending more and more time doing it, and it was less funny. By the time he stopped playing altogether and just fished, we were quite concerned. Justifiably so, unfortunately.

There's nothing worse than watching someone you've known all your life disintegrate before your very eyes. I discussed it with Frank's wife, June, and their daughter, Nicole, my goddaughter and assistant at the time, and decided we needed to move quickly to get Frank into the Rock and Roll Hall of Fame. We spoke to Jann Wenner and Jon Landau, who agreed.

A few years earlier, when Frank had been honored by the TJ Martell Foundation, June and Nicole had asked me to make a speech as Silvio Dante. They wanted a repeat performance of that for the Hall of Fame induction. I brought bodyguards Jimmy Gandolfini and Steve Schrippa to give Frank the royal treatment he deserved.

Frank just barely made it through his acceptance speech. I stood close by, quietly urging him on. It would be his last public appearance.

Once he stopped recognizing people, I stopped going to see him. I felt so bad for June and Nicole, but I loved him too much to watch him fade away. I'd watched it up close with my father and one time was too many.

Everybody in the music business, what's left of it, and everybody who got rich from it when it existed, owes a profound debt of gratitude to Frank Barsalona.

I had tried to extend his legacy. Our company covered a lot of ground: agency, management, record company, radio production, TV production, live events, publishing, publicity, marketing, and more. I hoped that Nicole would eventually run the company. I had trained her as best as I could, though she was pretrained, born with a booking book in her crib. She eventually got tired of the business carnage—everything we tried seemed to come up short of the finish line—and left to try management, which she's doing great at.

Renegade Nation, our parent company, was on a roll for a minute there, though we never solved our basic problem, which was not having someone whose job it was to actually make money.

We had a lot of so-called salesmen come and go, but I always wondered why they insisted on a salary if they were so good at selling. I paid them a 20 percent commission, and not one of them sold dick for what was, at the time, the biggest independent radio show in the world. I finally had to do what I liked least in the world: find us some sponsors to keep the radio show going and pay for the tours we wanted to do.

It's interesting what willpower can do. It's the tiniest part of who we are and the most important. Every once in a while I have to stop and think about how it powers us.

Who exactly are we, after all?

What are we?

We're four things.

We are our genetic makeup, our inclinations, talents, gifts. You can sing in tune or you can't.

We are our environment. You grow up in a loving environment or you don't.

We are our circumstances. You're born rich in Chicago or poverty-stricken in Uganda.

And we are our willpower.

Those first three factors are big, probably between 30 percent and a third each, which leaves us somewhere between 10 and 1 percent for willpower. The part we actually control.

We always think we're making decisions. I do not personally believe that. I think most of who we are is decided very early. Environment and circumstances can change as we grow up and that can affect us. But in the end, it's how we use that little bit of willpower that matters.

In the worst-case scenario, you could have genes, environment, and circumstances stacked against you, 99 to 1. But against all those odds you can still win.

Me and Jimmy. Miss him every day. *Kevin Mazur*

(Facing page):
Gabriella and Silvio.
HBO

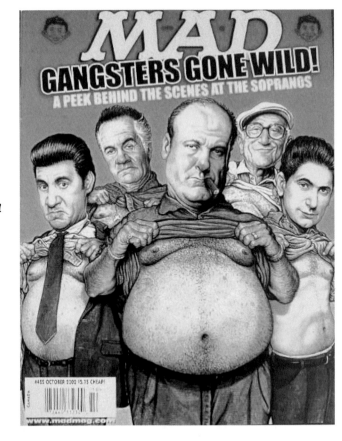

Top of the world, Ma!
Mad Magazine

Launch of the radio
show, 2002.
Renegade Nation

Steve Popovich, last of the great promo men. *Steve Popovich Jr.*

With Scott Greenstein, Keith Richards, Peter Wolf, and Benicio Del Toro, *Sopranos* premiere party, 2001. *Renegade Nation*

Richie Sambora killin' it on the Soulfire Tour. *Wicked Cool Records*

With Dion at the
TeachRock gala,
2019.
Renegade Nation

The Monday Night Football Band I assembled for Hank Williams Jr.:
Clarence Clemons, Bootsy Collins, Rick Nielsen, Charlie Daniels, Joe Perry,
Bernie Worrell, Questlove, Little Richard, Hank, and me. *Renegade Nation*

Jerry Lewis at the Friars Club in 2014. *Renegade Nation*

At the Emmys, 2006. *Steve Granitz*

With Tommy Karlsen Sandum, Ted Sarandos, Trond Fausa, and Fridtjov Saheim, *Lilyhammer* premiere, season two. **Laura Cavanaugh**

Michael Badalucco, Bruce, me, Tony Sirico, and Maureen in the final episode of *Lilyhammer*, my first directing job. **Netflix**

TeachRock seminar between the sound check and the show, Soulfire Teacher Solidarity Tour, Vancouver. *TeachRock*

With Catherine and Marc Brickman and Vinny Pastore at the *Once Upon a Dream* Broadway opening at Richard Rodgers Theater. *Bobby Bank*

Introducing Darlene Love. Renegade Studios, 2015. *Josh Goleman*

(Above): Lance Freed and his sister Sieglinde with David Porter at the Alan Freed memorial in Cleveland.
David C. Barnett

(Right): With the legendary Peter Rüchel in 2017.
Renegade Nation

Lowell "Banana" Levinger and Wavy Gravy—three Hippies forever!
Renegade Nation

Disciples of Soul. *Ryan Celli*

The family. *Renegade Nation*

Det. Danny Sprague, my founding partner Det. Kevin Schroeder, Officer Merit Riley, Det. Michael Paladino, Tony Sirico, Det. Brian Hunt, and honoree Jim Allen presenting checks to NYPD With Arms Wide Open and DEA Widows and Children Fund at Little Steven's Policeman's Ball, 2018. *Bobby Bank*

Me (as Wolfie) and Chris Columbus during the filming of *The Christmas Chronicles*. *Netflix*

Dr. Soulfire. *Bob Karp*

As Jerry Vale in *The Irishman*. *Netflix*

What can I say? *Kirsten Donovan*

I think about my friend, the late John Lewis, who I met during the Sun City years, when he was a newly elected congressman. John was born one of ten kids of sharecroppers in Nowheresville, Alabama, and ended up as the head of one of the Big Six groups that organized the history-making March on Washington in 1963. He helped pass the Voting Rights Act in 1965 and served in Congress for thirty years.

The voting rights legislation was gutted in 2013 by a Supreme Court that also tolerated gerrymandering and has been slowly losing its way for years. As I write this, a seventh practicing Catholic has been confirmed for the Supreme Court.

Our sacred separation of church and state has been slowly but surely disappearing ever since Reagan. Hopefully by the time you read this, there will be a new stacked court with six new justices who are all atheists or agnostics.

Why six? Because right now the religious extremists on the Court outnumber the others six to three. Assume one of the new justices fools you—there's always one—making it seven to three. We will need the other five to outnumber them eight to seven.

That will give us a shot at equality for women and for the LGBTQ community, not to mention democracy, all of which are rapidly disappearing. And speaking of the last of these, we will also hopefully have a new stronger voting rights act with John Lewis's name on it.

My moments of great willpower don't compare to John's, but I've gotten things done that I shouldn't have been able to. As long as it was for someone else. Or a good cause. And Renegade Nation had one. I took the energy I had previously invested in politics and redirected it toward the support, preservation, and creation of Rock and Soul. It was an endangered species, and something had to be done.

If you've been around long enough, it's easy to be cynical about this world we find ourselves living in. One quick happy story.

As I think I mentioned, as soon as we started Wicked Cool Records the entire record industry as we knew it basically ended. No more record sales. So we're thinking, How are we gonna survive?

We are going to have to survive by licensing our music to commercials and film. No sooner had we said that then one of my guys comes running in in a panic. I just made a deal for a commercial, he says, but the ad agency wants to own the publishing!

Ohhhh! You've got to be fucking kidding me. That's really the end. It's the last income we have left. This will spread like wildfire and kill what's left of the business. Who is the agency? Deutsch, he says. Find out who owns it or who runs it and get them on the phone.

Much to my pleasant surprise on the phone comes Donny Deutsch.

"Donny, I got to talk to you."

"Great," he says, "let me talk to my schedule girl . . ."

"No, Donny, I mean like right now."

"Right now?" he says. "Like now now?"

"Yeah, come on, I'll buy you a cup of coffee. Where are you?"

"I'm over here by the Four Seasons on Fifty-Seventh."

"I'll see you in the bar in ten minutes."

Never met the guy before, never spoke to him. He shows up, I explain the situation, and he fixes it. No argument. No demand for publishing. And life went on, damaged but survivable, thanks to him.

So every once in a while you find a guy like that.

They give you hope.

The Hard Rock Cafe was the first sponsor of the radio show, and, chief willing, still is as you read this.

The Hard Rock is owned by the Seminole Tribe of Florida, the rockingest Indians ever, and managed by one of my closest friends, Jimmy Allen.

The Seminoles had started Indian gambling in 1979 with high-stakes bingo, and within minutes everybody with an Indian great-grandmother opened a casino.

Where there's action, guess who follows? Right. Every Mob guy, wannabe Mob guy, hustler, and con man, many of whom successfully robbed every Native American tribe blind for decades.

Every tribe, that is, except the Seminoles, who had the wisdom to hire Jersey: Jimmy Allen, literally the Last Boy Scout.

At first, the Seminoles' only connection to the Hard Rock organization was that they had licensed the name for their casino in Hollywood, Florida.

Jimmy and I were having dinner one summer night at Morandi in the Village. As part of the license deal, he explained, they had international audit rights, which gave them a look at the books. "So I'm looking," he said, "and I see that our little casino is a big piece of their profits worldwide. I think I'm gonna try and buy the Hard Rock."

I almost choked on my artichoke.

"The whole fucking thing?"

"Yeah, why not?"

He talked to the chief of the Seminoles, who said let's rock! And bada bing, a billion bucks later, give or take, they owned it. Jimmy has probably tripled the value by now.

We held our first Halloween a-Go-Go show at the Hard Rock in Times Square, featuring Rocket from the Crypt, Gluecifer (a Norwegian Hard Rock band, no relation to the Russian hackers . . . I don't think), and Bobby "Boris" Pickett, with Maureen's dancers, the Garage Girls a Go-Go.

Then we got a sponsorship from Rolling Rock for a twenty-city tour. It was a great concept. We picked four Rock bands, one from each decade, fully paid for by sponsors like Rolling Rock and Dunkin' Donuts to keep ticket prices low. And not obscure bands either. We lined up acts like the New York Dolls, the Zombies, the Romantics, the Chesterfield Kings, and more. We boarded all the musicians onto a bus, wrapped it, and barnstormed the country.

We went back to the Hard Rock for New Year's Eve a-Go Go.

New Year's programming back then was totally boring, and I wanted to take over the holiday.

I had lunch with Hugh Hefner at the Playboy Mansion. "Check it out," I said. "New Year's Eve from here. Televised." I explained that our thing was a retro-'60s vibe, which he loved. "We bring in like five bands from different decades and use Playboy Bunnies as go-go girls. What do you think?"

"I'm in!" he said.

Next, I thought, it was on to the easy part, the TV sale. Keep in mind, there was maybe one pretty lame New Year's show at the time. Needless to say, we would have owned New Year's forever.

Nobody wanted it.

Nobody.

Sometimes I think, *I am so on the wrong fucking planet!*

I mean, look around.

Could life be any more fucking boring?

What the fuck happened to evolution?

What happened to fun?

Somebody had a connection at ESPN and heard they were up for something new, since New Year's happened to be a dead time on their station in those days.

I asked Johnny Pasquale, the manager of the Hard Rock Cafe in Times Square, if anybody had ever used the top of the marquee for a show. Nobody had.

The cafe was right under where the ball dropped. Being on that marquee is one of the coolest experiences you'll probably never have.

You are in it, baby. In the heart of the monster that is New Year's Eve, but also securely above it. Big screens in every direction, stages below, confetti raining down. A trip and a half.

So did I secure the marquee for future New Year's gigs forevermore? Of course not. Now Johnny rents it out for hundreds of thousands of dollars, and I can't get back in.

Our 2005 Rockin' *ESPN's New Year's Eve*, the world's best-kept secret due to zero promotion, managed to be third in the ratings that night. I cohosted with Stuart Scott. We just made things up as we went along.

We did a second Halloween show the next year, this time down at the Hard Rock in Hollywood, Florida. We called it Cheap Trick or Treat. Featuring guess who? It was also Roky Erickson's first gig out of Texas after coming back from the horrendous horror of being locked up—for five years for two joints—and after receiving shock treatments as if it was the snake-pit 1950s. He survived somehow and put on a great show.

Back in 2002, Congress, in its infinite wisdom, had passed the No Child Left Behind Act. They did this because American math and science scores had dropped to somewhere between those of farmers in Rwanda and baboons on the Yucatán Peninsula, but our legislators hadn't figured out that in order to prepare for these endless tests, the schools would start canceling all the Arts classes.

If anyone had checked, they would have found out that kids who take music class do better in math and science.

And somebody should also have explained that *testing isn't learning*. But for that to happen, somebody would have had to work for a living and . . . think. A concept rapidly disappearing in our disintegrating society.

The music teachers of America get to me somehow, probably through a lady named Susan McCue, who was working for Senate Majority Leader Harry Reid. Susan was and is my connection to Washington, DC.

The teachers told me that all the music classes were being cut. Could I go check it out and see if anything could be done about it?

Susan hooked me up with Ted Kennedy and Mitch McConnell. Separately, of course. And as I like to say, tragically, Ted Kennedy is no longer with us, and tragically, Mitch McConnell still is.

But both were very nice that day. I was probably the only meeting they had that wasn't about asking for money.

Teddy gave me a long rap about how all the way back to the Greeks, the Arts have always been included in education, and Arts classes being cut was an unintended consequence of improved science testing, but there wasn't a damn thing he could do about it anytime in the near future.

McConnell basically said the same thing, without the Greek rap of course.

I reported the bad news to the teachers. "But listen," I said. "I've got an idea. With our screwed-up priorities, the government is not going to put instruments in kids' hands for a while. We'll have to find another way to do that." We would eventually do that with Little Kids Rock. "How about we do a music history curriculum and sneak it into all the different grade levels? It can be cross-curricular, taught in music class, history class, English class, social studies. The best part is, it will work for all the students, not just musicians, and we can keep the Arts in the DNA of the education system."

They thought about it for a few days and then endorsed the idea.

My first step toward realizing the curriculum was to create another foundation, Rock and Roll Forever.

My second step was to assemble an impressive advisory board before I moved on to the third step, the extremely unpleasant task of raising money. I went to Bruce and Bono and Marty Scorsese, all of whom agreed to be on the board.

I'll always be grateful, because their participation meant that step three was less unpleasant than I feared. In fact, it was one of the two greatest meetings I've ever had. I met one of the loves of my life, Susie Buffett, who, in thirty minutes, on the strength of my idea (and, I'm sure, impressed by the board), gave me $2 million. And the Rock and Roll Forever foundation, whose main initiative would be the TeachRock. org music history curriculum, was born right there.

I quickly outlined two hundred basic lessons to get us started, hired Warren Zanes away from the Rock and Roll Hall of Fame as my first director, and started looking for teachers to write lesson plans. It would take ten years and a few directors to get the curriculum on the right track. It had to be bulletproof, since we'd only get one chance. We eventually got there.

Over that span, we kept promoting Rock any way we could. We made history by having an actual Garage Rock Chart in none other than *Billboard* frickin' magazine! And I wrote a column every week for eighty-three straight weeks before the editors regained their senses.

We did a very freaky residency at a bar called Hawaiian Tropic Zone in Times Square. It was the perfect setting for us. Fake palm trees, waitresses in grass skirts and bikinis, tropical drinks. Kitsch City! We ran horror films on the walls constantly, sometimes right on the bands while they were playing. It was fabulous.

Wackiest, wildest, campiest gig ever.

Only lasted six weeks; the owner got busted for sexually harassing the waitresses.

Bikinis, Garage Rock, and drinks with umbrellas.

A volatile combination.

June 10, 2007, was a day that shall live in infamy: the final broadcast of *The Sopranos*. Episode 86.

The cast had been making appearances at casinos, breaking records everywhere. We had become so big with the right kind of crowd, the whales and the wiseguys, that we were doing boxing numbers, Ali numbers, Tyson numbers, Mayweather numbers.

Jimmy Allen decided to throw a party at the Hard Rock in Florida. He invited five thousand of his closest friends and every international whale to watch the final episode with the entire cast.

It was one awesome event.

Jimmy constructed a tent with a giant screen on the property, about a fifteen-minute walk from the hotel. We assembled with security to walk out together. There had to be like five thousand people there, stacked twelve to fifteen deep on both sides, screaming and shouting and applauding the whole way. I leaned over toward Jimmy and Lorraine. "If you ever wondered what it feels like being a Rock star, this is it."

As I watched, I thought about the coming final scene of the episode, which was also the final scene of the series. Chase hadn't told the cast exactly how the show would end. The script just said that Tony played a song on the jukebox. We were all seeing it for the first time.

More specifically, I was thinking about the two-week wrestling match I'd had with David over what that last song should be.

I had four songs in mind, and made my best pitch for each.

My first suggestion, Bruce's "Loose Ends," might have been a little too on the nose, but it would have been cool. My other three were Procol Harum's "The Devil Came from Kansas" (coolest song ever), the Left Banke's "Pretty Ballerina" (would have worked beautifully as juxtaposition), and the Youngbloods' "Darkness, Darkness," which would have reinforced the ominous vibe.

After ten years and seven seasons of the most amazing music ever used on a TV show, David wanted to use fucking Journey!

Ohhhh! As we used to say.

Nothing wrong with Journey, of course. They made terrific records, had one of the best singers in Rock, and were huge.

But that was the problem. David had turned a lot of people onto much more obscure music through the eighty-six episodes, and the show had the reputation of having the coolest music on TV.

His final argument?

"Look," he said. "Tony is a Classic Rock guy. That's what he would have played."

End of discussion.

The day after the finale aired, I appeared on my Miami radio affiliate's big nationally syndicated morning show, where I heard a straight hour of complaints, consternation, and downright insults about the surprise ending.

People wanted to know what had happened, they'd thought their electricity went out, blah, blah, blah . . .

After an hour, I started fighting back. "OK, smart-asses," I said. "You don't like that ending, let's hear yours!"

Silence.

"Here, let me help you, did you want Tony to die?"

Grumble, grumble, well . . . no . . .

"Did you want Carmela to die?"

Uh . . . no.

"One of the kids maybe?"

No!

So maybe it wasn't such a bad ending after all?

By the time the radio show ended, the whole country had started to come around. David Chase had dodged the final bullet and regained his genius status.

Years later, *Vanity Fair* did a retrospective on the show and talked to actors and writers. Inevitably, the reporter got to the big question: "How did it really end? What happened?"

"OK," I said. "I've been asked this a thousand times, and I'm gonna settle it once and for all right now. You are going to get the scoop! This is the last time I will ever answer this, so sharpen your pencil."

The reporter got visibly excited.

"You wanna know what really happened?"

"Yes," he said.

"Alright. This is it. Are you ready?"

He was.

"The Director yelled cut and the actors went home."

Any excuse to go to Cannes, I'm there.

Nice is nice. Èze. Monte Carlo. Right into Portofino. Over to Barcelona. The entire Mediterranean coastline is one big groovy paradise, and I don't know why I don't live there.

All my life I've wanted to live on the beach. Came close in Miami many times. Lauderdale. But the hurricane thing—man, I don't know.

None of those problems in the Mediterranean.

I just wish I spoke the language. Italian. French. Spanish. Any of them.

I've tried. Maureen and I took Italian lessons for a while. The teacher was a crab. Very formal. Italian is all about informal expressions, and she was more by the book. If we'd actually learned what she taught us, the only people in Italy who would have understood us would have been about a dozen college professors in Milan.

I keep those fantasies alive in my mind, though. Living on the beach, and speaking at least one of those languages. I tell myself I've got to save something for my old age. So I'm saving that.

And the opera.

And breaking even.

And finding out who killed the chauffeur in *The Big Sleep*.

So in 2009, when I was invited to give a keynote address at the Cannes Lions International Festival of Creativity sponsored by the advertising world, I took it.

"The Future of Advertising" was the theme that year. Maybe that's the theme every year. I don't know.

A lot of people invite me to do speeches.

Once.

They rarely invite me back because my tendency is to tell them the truth with the hope of planting a seed or two that might result in a positive change.

In this case, this was the seed I planted. "Listen," I said,

You want to hear about the future of advertising? There is none.

Advertising is nothing but an aggravating pain-in-the-ass interruption that people feel they have to tolerate. The minute they find content without it, they will flock there.

HBO is the business model of the future. That's where it's at. The future is subscription. So you guys should focus on product placement and "Presented by"–type things like on Public Broadcasting channels. Limited-interruption-type programming. Other than that? Your future is sitcoms, reality programming, and Fox News.

They probably weren't thrilled to hear they were passé, but I got a big hand.

Once, like I said.

The E Street Band had been asked to play the Super Bowl for years, but in the old days, the audience was a mile away. Bruce wisely held out until they agreed to allow the audience to be right up against the stage the way we liked it.

That finally happened in Tampa, for Super Bowl XLIII.

I didn't care about the game. All I wanted to see was how the hell they assembled that stage so fast!

It was wild to witness. Like a hundred ants coming out of every possible gate with a piece of staging and zip, zip, zip, there it was.

The performance was timed like the Normandy Invasion, to the second. Thirteen minutes exactly is my recollection.

I wasn't at the meeting with the NFL and the production people, so I was a little surprised when Bruce came back with the setlist: "Tenth Avenue Freeze-Out," "Born to Run," and "Glory Days."

"Uh, not for nothing," I said, "but don't we have a new album coming out the week of the Super Bowl?"

"Yeah," he said.

"Well, call me crazy, but this Super Bowl thing seems like it could be a promotional opportunity!"

"We've got no time. Everybody decided on those three songs."

I thought about it for a minute.

"How about we leave out the second verse of every song? It'll buy us a minute or two, and we can throw in a bit of the title track, 'Working on a Dream.'"

And that's what we did.

We killed.

Bruce ended with a slide, a tribute to Pete Townshend. And if our cameraman hadn't caught him, we'd be looking for a new front man.

On the way out, Bruce looked into the camera and said, "I'm going to Disneyland!"

I thought to myself, Maybe they'll let you in this time.

And you know, to this day, no one has ever come up to me and said anything about those missing verses.

It could make you wonder why we work so hard on those lyrics.

Anyway, not a bad way to end a decade.

The E Street Band was back.

twenty-eight

Lilyhammer

(2010–2013)

Life requires constant vigilance against love of humanity turning
into profound frustration, resentment, and disgust. In other words,
let's face it, most people are assholes.

—GAUTAMA BUDDHA, THE FIFTH NOBLE TRUTH

American Idol was the kind of show the Rock world loved to put down at
every opportunity.

It was accused of being Phony! Fabricated! Superficial! Instant Stardom! A false picture of the realities of the business.

I only caught an episode or two, but Maureen liked it, and I figured
any show that introduced Smokey Robinson to a new generation was
OK by me, since at this point in our history, an era that future generations will look back on with pity, most of our world is phony, fabricated,
superficial, and full of instant stardom.

Jimmy Iovine was serving as head mentor, and he asked me to come
on as an assistant mentor. Not exactly my world, but I figured Maureen
would get a kick out of it, and it ended up being fish-out-of-water fun.
I enjoyed trying to find the common ground between traditional Rock
and the modern Pop world more than I thought I would.

I tried to share my experience as best as I could. Sometimes a brief
comment; when appropriate, a lengthier explanation that I thought
might prove useful if they ended up with a real career.

Mostly I focused on song choice. How to pick material that reflected their vocal style and sensibility. It wasn't easy for the singers, because after getting our advice, they had only twenty minutes or so to learn a song they had probably never heard before in their lives.

Can't remember whether it was me, Nigel Lythgoe, or Maureen who suggested it now, but I remember Joshua Ledet knocking me out with the Bee Gees' "To Love Somebody."

Maureen got friendly with quite a few of the singers on *Idol,* and David Cook surprised her with the gift of a puppy. It was a Cavalier King Charles Spaniel like our first dog Jake, this one named Edie.

I was not thrilled with this because half of me went with Jake when he left us, so I assured Cook that when Edie leaves, he would be leaving with her.

"Why didn't you drop off a couple of kids while you're at it?" I snarled. The first time he came to the E Street dressing room, I said, "Where's my gun?" just to scare the shit out of him.

Of course I love her more than life itself (I added Sedgwick to her name), but I'm not the only one who hopes she lives forever.

I also had a good year at the Hall of Fame.

Selection is a Darwinian process. No, that's not fair to Darwin—it's more ruthless than that. It's always a challenge, as each member of the nominating committee suggests two names, and then tries to talk the other twenty-five or so members into voting for our suggestions rather than their own!

Those first fifty names get winnowed down to fifteen or so, and that list goes out to the hundreds of members of the Hall of Fame plus I'm not sure who else, and they vote it down to five.

In 2011, I brought up the Hollies and, miraculously, got them in. I say "miraculously" because it's hard as hell. And it really pisses me off when honorees don't show up, because show up or not, I guarantee it will be the first sentence of their epitaph.

At the time, I was making a case for writers, based on the simple truth that our entire industry begins with the song. I had brought it up before and gotten nowhere, but this time I had extra passion in my argument, having recently lost my friend Ellie Greenwich. "Are we going to wait for them all to die?" finally got through.

A few writers were already in—Jerry Leiber and Mike Stoller, Carole King and Gerry Goffin, Willie Dixon, and the amazing Motown team of Holland-Dozier-Holland—but that year we managed to induct Jeff Barry and Ellie, Barry Mann and Cynthia Weil, Mort Shuman (his writing partner Doc Pomus was inexplicably in without him), Jesse Stone, and Otis Blackwell.

The committee tragically and arbitrarily cut off my list, leaving out Jerry Ragovoy, Luther Dixon, Dan Penn, Burt Bacharach and Hal David, Neil Sedaka and Howard Greenfield, and Bert Berns. We would get Bert in a year or two later.

I have a great deal of clarity when it comes to who deserves to be in, because, once again, I am quite sure that a Renaissance took place, and it was finite.

Everything important, essential, and truly original came from the '50s and '60s.

That doesn't mean nothing great came after. Lots did, and it should be recognized. But without the Naissance of the '50s and the Renaissance of the '60s, none of the rest would exist.

The further we get from those decades, the harder it is to justify the relevance of the pioneers when programming the Hall's televised induction ceremony. That is the frustration of trying to institutionalize historical significance, which ostensibly is our job, while simultaneously having to make a TV audience happy.

I once again suggested our meetings be broadcast live so the audience can witness the process and stop questioning the legitimacy of the decision-making.

I spend half my life defending the Hall of Fame and Jann Wenner, who everyone likes to blame for everything when he doesn't even attend the meetings!

The system is becoming more challenging, but it's still functioning. When it inevitably breaks down, I hope the executive committee has the wisdom to recognize the dysfunction and replace it with a new system that works as well or better.

It's an institution worth preserving, and I consider it an honor to be a part of it.

But if Junior Walker and the All Stars, Goldie and the Gingerbreads, Procol Harum, Big Mama Thornton, the J. Geils Band, Mamie Smith, Taj Mahal, Joe Cocker, the Runaways, Johnny Burnette and the Rock and Roll Trio, the Shangri-Las, Shel Talmy, and Mickie Most don't get in soon, I'm going to burn the fucking place down.

When Wicked Cool signed the Cocktail Slippers, a five-piece, all-female Rock band from Norway, I decided to produce the record with assistance from Jean Beauvoir, and I wrote two songs for it. We were told of a great mixer in Bergen, Yngve Leidulv Sætre, so we went to the west coast of Norway to mix it at his Duper Studios. Beautiful city, surrounded by mountains, like one of those snow globes.

During the mix, an assistant came in to the studio to tell me that there was a couple with a baby in the lobby wanting to say hello.

I courageously went down to the lobby, hoping it wasn't mine.

Kidding.

The couple was Eilif Skodvin and Anne Bjørnstad, and the baby, theirs, was nursing. Norwegians, conservative in every other way possible, like to do that in public.

They were TV writers, they said, and they had written a show for me.

Hey now! Talk about your pretty special celebrity-type flattery. You don't hear that one every day.

What's the pitch?

Eilif: A New York wiseguy goes into witness protection and chooses Lillehammer, Norway. Crime and comedy ensue.

Oh man!

"I just played a gangster for ten years," I sadly said.

"Well, think about it."

"OK, but I'm almost finished with the mix and will be going back to New York soon."

"We really want you to do this, and to be very involved. You would not only star, you would be one of the Executive Producers and writers."

"And of course do the music if you want to," Anne added.

The baby gurgled encouragement.

"The head of Rubicon, our production company will come to you if you want to continue the discussion."

"OK."

They left. Baby too.

I knew I couldn't do it.

It was partly a matter of taking on a similar role for my second acting job. What serious actor trying to maintain credibility would do that?

But it was mostly about the business.

It felt like my various projects were on a roll that could be close to the breakthrough I had been working toward for years. But they needed me to be there.

We had *Little Steven's Underground Garage* syndicated in over a hundred cities but had never achieved full sponsorship. The two 24/7 channels on Sirius required constant attention. We had the record company, which was trying to adjust to the advent of streaming. We had the management company, three publishing companies, the music history curriculum, live local shows, and national tours.

Plus, I had a really big idea for a website, a combination of a game and an educational tool that would have revolutionized both of those worlds. It was struggling to be born as a result of an ongoing war with the scumbag website creators, who kept robbing me blind.

Whenever I told them, "This is not what I wanted and not what you said you were going to do," they always referred me to some fine print in the contract. Hundreds of thousands of dollars later, I was no closer to my goal than when I started. And it was a billion-dollar idea that could've paid for everything. (Still is, by the way.)

So there was all that to consider. On top of that, everybody I knew tried to talk me out of it. My Agent, my friends, my own office.

"Now let me get this straight," they said in unison. "You're coming out of maybe the most important TV show in history, and you're going to do a local show in a country nobody can find on a map?"

What can I say? Whoever heard of somebody starring in a local TV show in a foreign country? It was going to be difficult to resist the adventure.

Once again, it felt like Destiny at work. And I'd fucked around with that lady enough as it was. I mean, come on! A Norwegian couple show up on the west coast of absolutely nowhere and say they've written a TV show for you? You gonna brush that off as just another day at the office?

The key was when they said I'd be one of the writers and Producers. I felt that that was enough protection to go for it.

Still, when the head of the production company, who shall remain nameless for reasons that will soon be obvious, came to my office in New York, I really did try to say no.

He walked in with a few guys and I thought for a minute a rugby match had broken out. He had a wild, working-class hooligan vibe, and though he turned out to be Swedish, he had mastered what I came to recognize as the Norwegian negotiating style, which involved pretending to be a dumb farmer as a way of concealing strategic thinking and a massive ego. I liked him.

He opened the conversation by pleading poverty, standard practice for all who have ever controlled the purse strings, but just as quickly he told me that it would be one of the most expensive shows in Norwegian history and the featured show on the country's biggest network. He also said I would have complete artistic control. Within reason.

No money, huh? Let me end this right now, I thought.

"OK then," I said. "I want 50 percent of the back end."

I said it as if it was my standard deal. You know—me, Spielberg, Hanks.

He didn't even blink an eye.

"OK."

Alarm bells should have gone off right then and there.

There were three or four of my people in the discussion, and I tried not to look directly in the eyes of any of them.

Uhhh . . . (think, man, think!) "And one more thing." (The kid's got balls, you've got to give him that.)

Blank stares. Scandinavians probably make great poker players.

"I've got all these businesses going on, as you can see."

They had gotten the tour earlier, seen it all, half the office full of employees, the other half taken up by a full-blown recording studio.

"So if I do this, I can only work every other week."

I figured that was that. Nobody's budget could handle that.

They spoke to each other in Norwegian.

"OK," he said.

Well, now I was fucked.

I had just scored the two most incredible deal points in TV negotiation history.

I was doing this show.

Eilif and Anne started coming to New York for brainstorming sessions.

I would find out later that even though Eilif and Anne had sold the show to me as a Norwegian *Sopranos*, Rubicon had sold the show to NRK—Norway's PBS or BBC—as a local family comedy. It would be the artistic challenge of my life to marry those two ideas and satisfy those two audiences.

Right from the start Eilif and Anne had big ambitions. They wanted a big international show, they said, but few in Norway thought the way they did. That's why they had taken the unprecedented step of casting a foreigner as a star. They asked me how could they make it work internationally?

As it happened, I knew exactly how to do that. "My friends," I said, "I watched it happen not once, but twice, in, of all places, New Jersey. Not dissimilar to your own residence. In fact, at one point in history, you could say New Jersey was the Norway of America!"

Without the money. Or the mountains. Or the snow. Or . . .

In any case here's what I knew, and what I told them.

As evidenced by the successful instincts of both Bruce Springsteen and David Chase, the way to be international was to be as local as possible. Counterintuitive, but true. Turns out, people are very curious. They want to know about things that they . . . don't know about.

So I wanted every detail about Norwegian life they could think of. Every eccentricity. Every cultural nuance. Everything they were embarrassed about or proud of. The more granular the local detail, the bigger the show would be.

"We can do that!" they said.

We got down to work.

From the start, there was a question of tone. The two of them were mainly comedy writers, brilliant ones as it turned out, but I didn't want to do that. I could not casually make fun of wiseguys and then make my living portraying them. Not if I wanted to keep living in New York.

It was going to have to be a dramedy, with serious moments in it too, and the humor would have to come from the characters and the circumstances. I didn't want anybody trying to be funny. It would be harder to write, but if we could pull it off it would give the show longevity.

There was also a question of language. How much English should we use? We had to make the Norwegian audience happy, but we also wanted the potential of an international audience.

We decided whoever I was speaking to would speak English in return, and we would see what else felt right as we went. We had to hope the audience would buy the idea that my character understood some Norwegian but didn't speak it. This is actually the case for many foreigners who live there because the language is a difficult one. Surely Gene Roddenberry borrowed Norwegian for the Klingon mother tongue. Take my fricative, please! Plus, Norwegians really do speak perfect English.

My character, who I named Frankie "the Fixer" Tagliano, would look very similar to Silvio Dante, but he needed to have a completely different personality for the show to work.

First of all, he needed to be a real boss. On *The Sopranos*, Silvio was the only character that *didn't* want to be the Boss, and he had to be conservative and careful to balance Tony Soprano's capricious impulsiveness. As a result, he was always on guard, not fully neurotic but always a little nervous.

Frankie was much more outgoing, brazen, and aggressive, with no fear whatsoever. In this way, he was more similar to Tony than Silvio, and his new environment, a practically crime-free Norway, only emboldened him.

There was also the matter of how he had ended up in Norway in the first place. In their version, he had fallen in love with Lillehammer because of the Olympics—beautiful scenery, beautiful girls—and chosen it as his new home. To fill out the backstory and make it feel authentic, I suggested we base the show loosely on the John Gotti scenario, which was still fresh in my mind at the time.

Gotti's *caporegime* (captain, his immediate boss) was Aniello Dellacroce, a street guy everybody respected who was expected to move up to Boss when Carlo Gambino died. Instead, Gambino surprised everybody by selecting a glorified accountant named Paul Castellano, thinking it would be good for the family business, which was investing in legit enterprises along with the usual criminal ones.

Long story short: Dellacroce died, and with no one left to stop him, Gotti whacked Castellano, got away with it (no one can kill a boss without permission from the Commission), and became the Boss himself.

We flipped that scenario. Frankie was considered such an implicit threat that the new Boss tried to have him assassinated.

This came as a shock. The whole neighborhood loved Frankie, and Frankie loved being loved. Whenever someone had a problem, Frankie would fix it. Need a parking ticket taken care of? Go see Frankie. Baseball tickets? Go see Frankie. Landlord raising your rent? Go see Frankie. In fact, he was so universally beloved that when the new boss tried to kill him, he ended up testifying against him, something Silvio could never have done.

And the whole thing freaked him out so much that he made his deal to go to Lillehammer instead of the usual Arizona or Utah or wherever Mob guys go where they can never find good Italian food again.

As we started to shoot, I learned that there were some significant cultural differences.

First of all, the budget was considerably smaller than I expected. They were do-it-yourself to the max. No sets. Every scene was on location, except the Flamingo Bar, which was the Quality Hotel's existing bar in Olavsgaard made over for the show. I wrote it into the script my first day as a way to get bands into the show, and as a defense against the audience going snow-blind.

The production would borrow people's houses to use as our base and give us a place to change. We'd be getting dressed, and the kids would come home from school. "Hi, Mom!" It was . . . different.

I was accustomed to changing in a trailer, which I had on every fifth location or so. During the brief negotiations with Rubicon, the trailer kept coming up, over and over again. I couldn't understand why. Turns out I had ended up with the only trailer in Norwegian TV history. They just don't go in for that American diva–type stuff.

The trailer ended up being a shit two-banger they had to bring in from Belgium and couldn't be used in half the locations. The other actors approached it like the *2001* obelisk. Of course, I told everyone to use it, not realizing it was something unique.

The government in Norway supports the Arts, as does pretty much every country except ours, and the actors were very flexible. They'd do our show during the day, shoot a movie at night, do a commercial on the weekend, and do theater, both Ibsen and children's, between seasons.

And they were all amazing. Great actors would take even the smallest parts, which I knew would give the show depth and longevity.

As brilliant as Eilif and Anne were at casting, they were equally good at knowing exactly how much self-deprecating humor a Norwegian audience could take, and how much cultural comedy international audiences needed.

Nobody knew a thing about Norway, which was perfect. Most Americans think it's a city in Sweden. You can't name one Norwegian product or celebrity to this day, can you? Didn't think so. A-ha doesn't count because they had to move to London to have a hit.

So we could be as surreal as we wanted to be. Ironically, the stuff the international audience thought we made up was actually normal Norwegian behavior. Like a driver's license taking months to get or fathers being forced to leave work and stay at home for a month with new babies.

We filmed about a quarter of the time in Lillehammer, which I fell in love with and whose name Eilif and Anne intentionally misspelled to be more incorrectly American.

It's a tiny town. The first thing that hit you was, How the fuck did they have an Olympics here? Everything important was just a few blocks from my hotel. Walk a block in either direction, and you'd find our two favorite bars: Nikkers, where we'd play table sand hockey and in the spring enjoy the back area that looked down on a pretty stream that leads to the Car Museum; and the Toppen Bar at the top of an old grain silo, which makes the best Stevie colada (piña colada with half a shot of Kahlúa) you'll ever have with snow on the ground.

Equally close was one of the city's half-dozen great restaurants, the Bryggerikjelleren (I told you—Klingon), whose exterior we used as the entrance of the Flamingo.

The Olympic ski jump is the only place that's a fifteen-minute drive away. Everything else is a short walk—even the pedestrian street that we would turn into a reindeer racetrack, complete with Keith Richards soundtrack, in one of my favorite episodes.

Filming in Lillehammer was a fundamental part of the show. It said so right in the title. But the producer, Anders Tangen, kept scheduling Oslo because it was cheaper. He kept running out of money by spending foolishly on the wrong things. He couldn't grasp the concept that fans of the show from all over the world would watch to see our Lillehammer locations.

I made it a point to film in the harshest winter months. Luckily, there were plenty. In an average winter, Lillehammer got between six and ten feet of snow. After a while, they had no place to put it, so they steamrollered it. The road just got imperceptibly higher as the winter went on.

It got so cold that the snow would freeze twice. When the moon was out I looked out my hotel window, the snow on the ground sparkling as far as I could see.

Absolutely magical.

One freezing February night—and I mean five below zero, Fahrenheit—I looked out the trailer window and saw about ten extras dancing around a spontaneously constructed fire.

"Is that some Norwegian actor–type ritual?" I asked the Director.

"Yes," he said. "It's called keeping warm!"

Such eccentricities were cute, but enough was enough. The next night, a tent was erected, with heat and an actual craft-service table with more than a pot of coffee and a bag of apples!

The contrast between our countries' filming process was made all the more dramatic to me when I flew home each week to work on David Chase's movie, where the craft service resembled your average 7-Eleven.

I learned everything I needed to know about Norway's TV culture. Namely, that they didn't have one. It was strictly a film culture transplanted to TV. What's the difference? I'm glad you asked. One big difference: in film, the Director is the boss. On TV, it's the writer.

I was usually the only writer on the set, because Eilif and Anne were off writing the next episode or casting. Too many times, I had to explain to the Director that the script wasn't an outline. If it said the scene ended when Frank sat down, the scene ended when Frank sat down. In the TV world, there's no time for philosophical discussions on the set. I welcomed all input, but not during shooting.

Another difference was that the actors were used to improvising.

I explained that since I came from the David Chase school of writing, every fucking word was sacred! So no improvising. If they had an idea, I wanted to hear it, but I didn't want to be surprised. "And by the way," I said, "if you're improvising in Norwegian, my character might understand you, but I don't!"

But after a while, I ended up enjoying the way their method of continuous creativity carried all the way to "Action!" We learned from each other and found a compromise. And being the only writer-Producer on the set—checking lighting, adjusting wardrobe, rewriting constantly—helped me a lot as an actor. I didn't have time to think. As soon as the camera rolled, I was just there, in the moment, no time for second-guessing.

About six weeks into filming, I started noticing a distinct dearth of grips and gaffers (yes—I am a little slow). And where were the production assistants? Why was the makeup man also the hair guy? And why was he carrying one of the cameras as we went from one location to another?

I called a meeting with everybody, including the elusive head of Rubicon. By the end of the discussion, I had come to the realization that something was rotten in the state of Norway and that we could not afford to shoot the show we had written.

I called my Agent and told him to book meetings with American networks. "I'll be in LA in two weeks," I said.

Why two weeks?

Because somehow, we had to make a trailer out of the first six weeks of shooting that would be impressive enough to get us an American deal. We didn't have one single completed episode.

It took four or five drafts. I knew what we needed to even have a chance: a little violence, a little sex appeal. We had been pretty much filming chronologically, which helped. In the end, Eilif and Anne and their editors did a great job, and off I went to Never-Never Land to try and score an American deal to save the show.

And my ass.

twenty-nine

Once upon a Dream

(2013–2014)

Warriors of the rainbow unite,
From the darkness of the wasteland,
Open up the inner light,
Oh, Great Spirit, your breath gives life,
I hear your voice in the wind,
I come before you as a child,
Seeking strength and wisdom . . .

—"BALANCE," FROM *REVOLUTION*

I called my Agent and told him to book an appointment with Chris Albrecht, who had moved from HBO to Starz.

I had learned a few things since I'd made my genius Spielberg-Hanks, 50-percent-of-the-back-end deal.

The naive Norwegian rugby farmer had hustled me. He was the con in Rubicon.

What he knew, and I didn't, was that the company would have given me 100 percent of the back end because Norway had never sold a show to anybody. Ever. There had never been a back end in Norwegian history.

I also found out that the "biggest budget in Norway" was somewhere around $750,000 per episode, equal to a decent reality show budget in the United States but nowhere close to the $3–4 million spent on the sixty-minute American dramas that were our competition.

I played Chris the trailer we'd cobbled together.

"I love it!" he said.

Wow.

"Chris, that's great. All I need is a million an episode and I can get it done."

"Brother, I'll give you two million an episode, but you have to wait until next year."

Oh man.

"Chris, you don't understand. We started production. I need the money now to finish."

"Fuck, I've got nothing left this year. All I can do is like half a million."

Fuck was right.

"I honestly don't think it can be done for that. I can get big bang for the buck over there, but not that big. Let me get back to you."

Chris had been my best shot. We knew each other. I could trust him. But I couldn't wait. We were already shooting.

And so I went to my second meeting of the day, with some unknown company called Netflix. I had read a single article about them. They were a Blockbuster-type movie-rental company about to start creating content, and they had just made their first deal with Kevin Spacey to star in a remake of a British political show.

There were only two names mentioned in the article: Reed Hastings, the tech genius who had perfected streaming (whatever that was), and the new content guy, Ted Sarandos.

A few weeks before, as Eilif and Anne struggled to finish the trailer, I'd made a phone call.

"Hello? You have reached Netflix."

"Hi. Stevie Van Zandt here. Ted Sarandos, please."

He got right on.

"Hey, man! This is Ted! Really good to talk to you!"

"Hi, Ted. I hear you're looking for stuff?"

"Yes, we're just getting started."

"I've got something."

"Great. Come on in."

That was it. The call that would lead to the greatest business meeting of my life.

My Agent and I walked across the street to Netflix.

The receptionist brought us in to Ted, who greeted me with the same enthusiasm he'd communicated on the phone. I wasn't used to liking

LA executives. They all seemed to be full of shit. Probably because most of them were. They were all smiles and compliments and never said no, but the deal never got done and you never found out why.

Ted was different. There was something unusually normal about him. Real confidence, not the phony LA kind. I liked him right away.

I explained that *Lilyhammer* was unique, to say the least. It was a bit of an experiment. My Agent's eyes were telling me to shut the fuck up, but I wanted Ted to know what he was buying.

I laid it all out. The ultimate fish-out-of-water premise, a gangster sent by witness protection to a country with no crime. The local color, dialogue in Norwegian with subtitles when I wasn't speaking. The unique tone of the show, both familiar and freaky at the same time.

"Sounds good!" Ted said.

Super cool. Nothing but positive vibes.

I showed him the trailer.

"I'm in," he said.

Man, I remember thinking, I'm having a heck of a day. I should leave here and go straight to the track.

I was still trying to talk Ted out of it. "You're starting a whole new company. Are you sure you don't want it dubbed or something?"

He shook his head. Norwegian was perfect, he said. They were planning on being the first truly international content network, and this would be their first international content.

Ted made his offer. "I'll give you a million an episode, and we'll do a two-year deal, eight episodes a year."

Holy Fuck! Maybe there was a God after all.

As far as I knew, this might have been the first two-year deal in TV history. They never did that, even with hits.

On the way out he put his arm around me. "Oh, one more thing. We're gonna be putting all the shows up at once."

That interrupted my groove for a minute.

"What do you mean?"

"You know how HBO has the whole season in the can before the first episode airs? Well, instead of broadcasting one week at a time, we'll put them all up at the same time."

I had to think about that one.

"Geez, Ted, are you sure that's the right move? I mean, you labor and suffer and someone can watch a year's worth of work all in one night? That seems a little weird."

"Oh yeah? You mean like working on a record album for a year and someone listens to it in an hour?"

Son of a bitch! He was right.

"You son of a bitch! You're right!"

And so, for the second time in TV history, I'd find myself at the medium's crossroads.

The Sopranos would change not only HBO but TV in general. For the first time in history, it would replace film as the go-to medium for creators of serious adult content.

And *Lilyhammer* would make Netflix the first truly international distributor and the preferred network for all future international content.

I didn't know that yet. All I knew for sure was that I had met the guy I'd be making TV with for the rest of my life, and I was not about to let him down.

When I returned to Norway to tell the head of Rubicon about Netflix, I was all smiles and expected the same in return. Amazing news, right?

Silence.

Hello? Did you hear what I just said? I saved the show. You know the budget you lied to me about? I just tripled it!

Rugby finally confessed. "There are a few other things you should know," he said.

What could possibly break my groove?

Turns out he was not your run-of-the-mill con man—he was a full-blown Scandinavian Zero Mostel.

Remember my incredible Spielberg-Hanks deal?

The one where I had 50 percent of the back end?

Well, I had 50 percent.

NRK had 50 percent.

The German distributor had 50 percent.

And probably a bunch of horny old ladies had 50 percent each.

How's that for a groove breaker?

Eilif, Anne, and I had lunch with the executives at NRK. Surely they'd see the brilliance of the deal?

Not exactly.

They explained that they rarely broadcast a series for more than one year. And on the rare occasion when they did renew a series, it only aired . . . wait for it . . . every *other* year.

I took my hands off the cutlery at that point. I was rapidly losing confidence in my ability to suppress the urge to slash someone's throat. I just couldn't decide if it would be one of theirs or my own.

We got our second season. Norwegian audiences were too enthusiastic to be denied. But of course, with that whimsical year off in between.

Every once in a while, Lady Destiny takes pity on me.

Ted at Netflix was cool about waiting, figuring that word of mouth would serve us well.

And Bruce decided to tour exactly when I would have been shooting the second season of *Lilyhammer*.

All I missed was a month in Australia. The first Australian trip for the reunited E Street Band had been a rare disaster. The power went out like three times during our opening gig. Not only did that show never get its momentum back, the entire tour never quite got on track.

For that second trip, Bruce took Tom Morello in my place, and that tour the band broke through.

Beautiful.

We lost Clarence Clemons in June 2011. He had been in bad shape for a while, but it was still a shock.

We'd lost Danny Federici in 2008. I still look over every once in a while and see him there. Who ever heard of somebody dying from skin cancer? It's still hard to believe.

Replacing original band members and keeping a band relatively the same is impossible. A band changes when members change. If it changes enough, you may have to even change the name of the band.

With Bruce's name up front we didn't have that problem. For us, continuing in a way that made sense was a profound challenge. Could we keep enough continuity to make a smooth transition and not disrupt the audience's expectations and experience?

In a way, the transition had already been happening. Clarence and I were always part of the show, the shtick, but I had been doing more of it lately because Clarence had to sit down for most of the show. The running-around-the stage vaudeville had shifted toward me and Bruce.

But Clarence's iconic solos were still central to many songs. Would an audience be reluctant to applaud someone new playing them? Would it feel like an insult to Clarence's memory?

The perfect solution dropped in our laps.

Clarence's nephew Jake.

Who, as it happened, could play the saxophone.

There would be no conflict about giving love to a blood relative.

The only problem was that Jake had established the beginnings of a career. He sang, played guitar, and wrote songs. The saxophone wasn't even his first instrument.

Bruce and I talked it over.

"Listen," I said. "We cannot have him stand in Clarence's spot. It's simply going to be too much for the kid. I know he has to play those solos, but let's go out with a horn section to camouflage him a little bit."

"Makes sense," Bruce said.

"And maybe he doesn't play every solo. Eddie Manion can play a few, to ease the pressure. Whoever solos can come out of the horn section and then go right back into it."

Rehearsals went well, but I could tell Bruce wasn't quite settled. After one of the rehearsals, he called me as I drove back to the city. "I don't know."

"What's the matter?" But I already knew.

"Jake."

"Talk to me."

"I think he wants to have his own career. I feel like I'm forcing him to do this. Like he's doing it out of obligation."

"Look, I'm sure he's nervous," I said. "Big shoes to fill. Literally. And he may not know it yet, but he's gonna love this. He's used to playing clubs. Just wait until he looks out at fifty thousand people screaming his name. He'll have an entirely new outlook on life."

Bruce wasn't sold. I could tell.

"Let me just suggest one thing," I said. "Two things."

"Go."

"You're always accusing me of being an extremist, but guess what? *You're* the extremist! OK, maybe we're both right, but we don't have to marry Jake forever. And Jake may not wanna marry us forever."

"I'm listening."

"Let's look at this as a transitional moment. Just this tour and then we see what happens. Maybe later we'll transform ourselves into some other thing, but right now he can keep the heart of the E Street Band intact. We are extremely lucky that he exists. I'm not sure what we would've done without him."

I could hear him thinking in the silence.

I went on. "The audience wants to grieve Clarence. We all do. But at the same time they'll see that his spirit is alive in Jake. That gives everybody something to celebrate instead of every night feeling like a funeral."

Plus, I told him I would talk to Jake and explain that he could pursue a solo career in between E Street tours. "I'm a little bit of an expert in this area. So we'll not only see how good and dedicated he is, but how smart. Because if he's smart, he's gonna embrace this opportunity with both arms."

More silence.

"OK," he finally said. "I hear you. I'll think about it."

He thought about it, and Jake was in. And man, did he rise to the occasion. He got better every single show.

Turned out to be a good kid.

Smart too.

I had another successful year at the Hall of Fame, where a cabal of us talked the rest of the voters into combining the Faces and Small Faces into a single candidate.

The Small Faces were the Faces' incredible predecessor, one of the five important British Invasion bands that never invaded. Combining the two was the only way to get Steve Marriott, the Small Faces' vocalist and one of the greatest white Soul singers ever, into the Hall—he was unlikely to get in with his other band, Humble Pie. I would try the same trick combining Free and Bad Company, who also had two common members, singer extraordinaire Paul Rodgers and the great drummer Simon Kirke, but that hasn't worked yet.

A few years earlier, Maureen had discovered an organization called Little Kids Rock that bought guitars for kids who couldn't afford them. It was started by a San Francisco teacher named Dave Wish. They wanted to honor me, but I'm generally not crazy about that kind of thing, and they honored Clarence instead. Maureen, who went to the ceremony, said it was nice but the organization needed help.

When Clarence left us, Little Kids Rock named their yearly honor after him. The first Clarence Clemons Award went to Lady Gaga, who told Maureen and me that she used to wait on us at Palma on Cornelia Street in the Village.

After Gaga, I told Dave Wish that I would accept the honor but that the show needed to be more elaborately produced. He didn't quite know what I had in mind, but I knew they could do better than the forty grand a year they were raising.

To make the show more interesting, we decided to have a bunch of artists do the honoree's songs. My year, performers included Bruce, Elvis Costello, Darlene Love, Tom Morello, Dion, and Jesse Malin. The next year, Joan Jett was honored by Cheap Trick, Billie Joe Armstrong, Gary Bonds, Kathleen Hanna and Ad-Rock. And Darlene Love's year brought out Elvis Costello, Brian Wilson, and Bill Medley.

We got them up to a million dollars net, and I moved on.

Meanwhile, David Chase, the man most responsible for making TV the go-to medium for the whole world of serious content, leaves TV and decides to make his first feature film. He decided on something small and personal. All due respect to my padrone, it felt like a Stevie move.

As a teenager, David had been a drummer in a band in New Jersey before he split to LA, went to film school, and got into TV. That was right around the time when the Beatles changed everything.

His movie, *Not Fade Away*, was largely autobiographical, exploring the tricky dynamics of being in a teenage band, and it was also about David meeting and falling in love with the girl who became his wife, Denise.

Midway through the writing, the script stalled, and he put it on a shelf. At around that time he asked me what I was working on, and I played him a new song called "The St. Valentine's Day Massacre" and later simplified to "St. Valentine's Day." As much as I love Bob Dylan's work, it was the only overtly Dylanesque song I'd ever written. I intended it for Nancy Sinatra, but for some unknown reason never got it to her and instead we cut it with one of my Wicked Cool bands, the Cocktail Slippers.

"Wait a minute," David said. "Play that again." He was always complimentary, but this was different. Turns out the timeline I'd used for the relationship in the song, Thanksgiving, Christmas, and New Year's, was the same one he had used for his movie. It brought the project back to life for him, and he finished the script.

I tried to talk him out if it.

I tried to reason with him, using the same arguments that people had used to try to talk me out of *Lilyhammer.*

"David, you just did the greatest TV show of all time. You can do anything you want right now. You can make Paulie Walnuts a Marvel Comics superhero and get a $200 million budget. Then you can make your small personal film. You'll have a built-in audience ready to go."

"I don't want to make *Big Pussy Versus the Martians*," he said. "I want to do what I want to do."

Fuck me.

I figured if I couldn't talk him out of it, I had to help him make it.

My job was to evolve the Twylight Zones, as the band would be called, through their various stages of development, leading to their one moment of glory, my St. Valentine's song.

The first question was, Do we find musicians who could act? Or actors who could sing and play? I leaned toward the former, David toward the latter. He needed great acting more than great musicianship. "Can you turn actors into a band in four months?" he asked.

"Maybe. But I've got to warn you. There is a certain DNA consideration at work here."

"What do you mean?"

"You can sing in tune or you can't. You can keep a beat or you can't. There are some things you cannot learn."

David found two actors, Jack Huston and John Magaro, who *could* sing, and we started giving them lessons right away. Pat DiNizio from the Smithereens came in to teach Jack guitar, and Andy White taught John drums. I needed an older drum teacher because I wanted Magaro to learn the old-school Jazz way of playing with his wrist up.

If Andy's name sounds familiar, it's because he had been hired by George Martin to play on the first Beatles' single "Love Me Do." It was a common practice then, since most band member drummers weren't consistent enough and there was a very limited amount of time to get it right.

Max Weinberg had found Andy working in a North Jersey music store some years earlier. Lord knows how he recognized him, but Max works in mysterious ways. We found and hired Andy.

He was in his early eighties at the time and took the bus in every day from Caldwell, New Jersey. Sweet, sweet guy.

Max, Garry Tallent, Bobby Bandiera, and I recorded the music for the soundtrack, and I sang guide vocals for the actors.

By the time we shot the movie, the Twylight Zones had become a real band. I had fantasies of them playing film festivals after movie screenings.

The festivals that never happened.

Lilyhammer was the most popular show in Norwegian history, drawing one million viewers out of a national population of five million. It was the prime minister's favorite show. He would tweet to be left alone for an hour because "I am watching *Lilyhammer*!"

The tightrope act had worked. We had satisfied the NRK audience that wanted comedy and the Netflix audience that wanted more. We had made Norwegian viewers feel like the show was theirs while drumming up international appetite for Norwegian content for the first time.

In the wake of that success, I had to call Harvey Weinstein.

Miramax had gotten worldwide distribution, outside the United States, for *Not Fade Away*.

I had suggested to David that he release the movie in Europe first. It was more a European art-house film than a blockbuster, more *400 Blows* than *Transformers 5*. Rock and Roll still had some cultural capital in Europe. And though *The Sopranos* was big everywhere, as an auteur

David was more appreciated over there. No Jerry Lewis jokes, please; I agree with the French!

Break *Not Fade Away* in Europe, I figured, and maybe, just maybe, we'd have a shot at home.

So while David was discussing the domestic release with Paramount, I called Harvey. "Listen," I said, "I've got a really big show on in Norway right now. Let's do David's premiere there. Red carpet and the whole schmear! The entire cast of my show will come, we'll fly over a few Sopranos for fun, plus the prime minister is a fan. I know half his cabinet. I bet they'll all come too."

"Yeah, yeah, yeah," Harvey said. "Good idea. Let's make it happen."

It never happened.

The movie went straight to eight-track in the States. Another beautiful piece of work blowing in the wind. This time it wasn't mine, but I felt very bad for David. He and the film deserved better.

Nobody saw it.

The entire three seasons and four years I was in Norway, I loved everything about the country, the people, and the mystery of both. I wanted to leave something meaningful behind. I felt there was enormous untapped potential, and my natural instinct as a Producer was to realize the potential of everyone and everything I saw.

Norway is a very complicated place, and many of the complexities are buried deep.

You could vacation there for the rest of your life and never catch a hint of what is actually going on in the hearts and minds of Norwegians. The longer you are there, the less you know.

The complexity starts with wealth and how it's used.

Norway is one of the richest countries in the world, a well-kept secret. Up until 1972 or so, it was a nation of simple, mostly happy farmers. Well, happy might be a stretch. Content maybe. There's a reason Ibsen's plays aren't a laugh a minute.

Then one day, up from the ground came a-bubblin' crude. Oil, that is. From the sea, actually, but then you can't do the *Beverly Hillbillies* theme sing-along. And if Flatt and Scruggs ain't the ultimate name for a Bluegrass duo, I don't know what is!

So somebody struck oil, and what did they do? They tried to give it to Sweden, of course. Who promptly turned it down. Probably a relative of the schmuck who decided not to quarantine.

So, against their better nature, Norway became crazy rich.

I'm only half kidding about their nature. Norwegians are not all that comfortable being rich. Hard as it may be for Americans to understand, it is simply not a materialist society. No flashy cars, no designer clothes. Even at the homes of the richest Norwegians, no expensive paintings, no Louis XIV chairs, no kooky $50,000 lamps.

As rich as they are—and it's Saudi rich, I shit you not—they don't spend it. On anything. Individually or as a country.

There are potholes in the streets. The trains break down every month or two. Costs are high, taxes are high. With trillions in the bank. Or whatever the next thing after trillions is.

On the other hand, they guarantee free health care and education, from womb to tomb. No homelessness. No poverty. No crime (until Frankie Tagliano showed up!). Really scary socialism!

And don't fall for the we're-just-dumb-farmers routine, like I did. They're in the European Union, but they're not. They use it for trade, but they keep their own currency, which helped them avoid all the recession problems everybody else had a few years back.

Endlessly fascinating place. I miss it. If we could restart *Lilyhammer*, I'd go back in a minute.

One of the secret keys to the deeply mysterious Norwegian sensibility is a philosophy called *Janteloven*.

I won't do a whole big discussion about it—that's why God created Google—but among other things, it suggests that a society is healthiest when everyone is equal.

Radical! I know.

Extremist *Janteloven* acolytes look down on any Norwegians who think or act as if they are superior to anyone else.

Ambition ain't cool.

They make a huge exception, however, for sports stars. As long as they win, they can enjoy as much celebrity as they want.

And foreigners get a pass, luckily. So everybody loved me! And I loved them right back. Not in spite of, but because of all their eccentricities. Many of which we put in the show.

I got friendly with the cultural minister at the time, Trond Giske—and still am—introduced by either Stine Cocktail Slipper or Cecilie Launderette, both members of Wicked Cool bands.

Giske wanted to encourage the Arts and interaction with the rest of the world. I would make speeches occasionally, with his support, trying to explain the difference between equality and equal opportunity, which is one of our proudest American ideals we've never lived up to.

I always spent part of my speeches trying to encourage investment in a new industry—namely, entertainment. The existing industries—fishing, shipping, oil—all centered on the coastline. The interior didn't have a whole lot going on. Wood, maybe. Lots of trees.

When that industry wanes, what can be done? Art can be done. Culture can be done. A town like Notodden in Telemark is a good example. When its industry dried up, it started a Blues festival that has since become legendary in the Blues world.

The same could happen with TV and film. There's room for half a dozen production companies spread out in the countryside.

It only takes one hit show, or one group of talented craftspeople, to make a production company a success.

I had a joke in my speeches: "You'd better hurry and get something going before you run out of oil." Later I changed it to "You'd better start a new industry before oil is banned worldwide, which is in sight. Me and Greta Thunberg hope."

The message wasn't received in a simple way. Norway isn't simple. There were people who thought more or less the way I did and wanted to encourage everybody to realize their potential.

But most Norwegians were just fine being isolated. They had no interest in interacting with the rest of the world. They don't like tourists. They don't need TV. Just give them a cabin in the woods and snow to ski on.

I managed one victory in my battle to promote the film and TV industries.

I became friendly with Jo Nesbo, an amazing author of Norwegian noir / crime fiction. To understand how popular Jo is, you'd have to visit the Oslo Airport, where his books take up the space of an average New Jersey suburban house.

As I was trying, mostly in vain, to bring the TV and film industry to Norway, Jo decided to sell the movie rights to his latest book after years of resisting.

I seized the moment and met with both the prime minister and then cultural minister (by then, the one after Trond). "Jo Nesbo has just agreed to a film deal," I said.

"We heard." They were being polite.

"Every scene of his book takes place in Norway. But if you don't create a film incentive right now, the film will be made in the Czech Republic, or even worse, Iceland!" I continued in my best Cagney. "I sure wouldn't be in your shoes on Election Day if that happens," I said, half joking. Not.

There are complex film incentives having to do with tax breaks, but there's a simple version too. Say a movie company comes to town and spends money. They can rent equipment and production facilities if they're available, but there are expenses even without that: hotels, restaurants, electricians and carpenters, location scouts, extras, etc. The company keeps receipts, and the town gives back part of the expenses, maybe 20 percent, maybe 25. The town cannot lose, because without the movie the money would not have been spent at all.

In this case, Norway was the town. And they did implement the incentive for Nesbo, though I don't know if they kept it. A fleeting triumph.

I started doing master classes for the university in Oslo and the film school in Lillehammer, specializing in subjects that were rapidly becoming irrelevant, crafts like songwriting, arranging, producing. If I do it again, I'll add blacksmithing, Viking navigation, and the care and feeding of dragons.

I tried to organize the first international TV festival, not just a marketplace and showcase but workshops and, overall, a more produced and entertaining convention than what I witnessed at MIPCOM in Cannes, where me and Kiefer Sutherland were the only actors.

But it was hard to get investors interested. I've never been good with them. I explain what I'm doing and answer questions, and then it's up to them. But many investors want to be chased. They want their asses kissed. I guess you're supposed to call back and ask, That discussion we had the other day, any thoughts? Or some schmoozy bullshit like that. I just can't do it.

I also encouraged adding a TV class at the film school in Lillehammer. I explained again that except for a few dozen Oscar contenders and documentaries, the film world would soon be all comic books and video games.

They looked at me like I was nuts.

One of the things I'd been working on during my trips back to New York was reuniting the Rascals in a meaningful way.

Barbara Carr and Dave Marsh held a yearly fundraiser for the Kristen Ann Carr Fund to support sarcoma research. It was named for their daughter, who had died in 1993. The event is a massive meet and greet at the Tribeca Grill, and it usually consisted of just a dinner and a few speeches.

But Kristen Ann had been a real firecracker, full of energy, and the year the fundraiser honored me and Maureen, we thought the night should reflect her energy somehow.

Way back in 1980, Gary Bonds's Manager John Apostol had brought me in to try and get the Rascals back together. It was basically impossible; but I gave it a try every five years or so. The Kristen Ann Carr fundraiser was another try.

"What the hell?" Maureen said. "They won't reunite for their own good; maybe they'll reunite for someone else's good."

And sure enough, that's what happened. That night was the first time they'd done a full set in thirty years, having barely survived the three songs at the Hall of Fame.

For years, every Promoter had told me that the Rascals were the Holy Grail of reunions! Now that I'd done it, no one was interested. It was too late, they all said. The group had been away too long.

There was one place where it wasn't too late. *Jersey Boys* was a big hit on Broadway, and the Four Seasons were a generation *before* the Rascals.

I came up with an idea that I would end up calling *The Rascals: Once upon a Dream.*

I would film the band members telling their stories.

Meanwhile, I would produce the band's live show like no one had ever heard them.

Then they would play in a theater, and between songs the stage would go dark and their interviews would appear on a massive screen behind them. We would film some staged segments as well.

It would be a hybrid, but it could work.

I called Marc Brickman, who had been Bruce's first light man back in the day and had gone on to do lighting for everyone from Pink Floyd to Paul McCartney and even to light the Empire State Building.

Marc had just done the interior light design for the Capitol Theatre in Port Chester, New York. Peter Shapiro, who had refurbished the place after having great success with Brooklyn Bowl, turned out to be one of the world's truly classic characters. Like from another dimension. When we described our project, he took maybe five seconds to think and said, "Debut it here."

With a venue secured, I started writing the show. I needed to sequence the songs to tell a story, to rotate through different perspectives, to build and release tension.

We taped the band for the interview sections, and Marc designed visuals to transport the audience back to the '60s during the songs.

I wanted to start with a film clip of a little girl. I had a helluva time casting her until one day, at the office, I glanced down in the elevator and saw the cutest thing I'd ever seen on her way to ballet class. She turned out to be the daughter of Graydon Carter and Anna Scott, and they graciously allowed her to be cast.

The show would be my masterpiece. It gave the audience a much more satisfying evening than just guys standing there playing their hits. Marc and I started thinking of all the groups we could do next.

The opening night at Peter's theater will always be one of the most thrilling moments of my life.

Because Brickman's technology took up the entire back row, the soundboard was in the middle of the audience.

The lights went down.

I snuck down the aisle and took my place.

I gave the sound man a smile of confidence I didn't feel and tried to remember how to breathe.

There was an intro to my script narrated by Vinny Pastore, then music, then more narration, then Graydon's daughter, and then it happened . . .

The entire audience laughed. At something I wrote!

An electric current shot from my fingertips to my balls to my toes and back.

Marc ran down the aisle in a crouch with an ecstatic look I've never seen on anybody's face before or since.

"This is gonna work!" he whispered loudly.

He was right. The interviews were amazing in large format, more intimate than onstage banter could possibly be. The songs sounded better than ever. I suddenly understood the whole theater thing. The Writer thing. The Producer thing. The Director thing. All at once. It was my Diaghilev moment.

It took me a few songs to stop crying.

This was what I'm on this planet to do.

I'd finally found it.

thirty

The Golden Nymphs

(2014–2015)

Awop bop aloobop awop bam boom!
—LITTLE RICHARD

SC. 1-01 INT. FLAMINGO BAR,
FRANK'S OFFICE—DAY
ON BLACK.

> SNOW REMOVAL GUY (O.S.)
>
> I believe in Norway. I've always said it's the best
> country in the world ...

(A man in his fifties, THE SNOW REMOVAL GUY, appears. We open
with a close-up of his face, then slowly zoom out.)

> SNOW REMOVAL GUY (CONT'D)
>
> ... But with all the idiots we let in, I'm not
> so sure anymore. Those damn politicians opened a
> refugee camp next to my house. That was two months
> ago and I haven't slept since.

(We pull back and see that the Snow Removal Guy's wearing
overalls. Next to him sits a German shepherd. The dog has a
funnel on its head. We begin to glimpse the silhouette of
FRANK TAGLIANO.)

SNOW REMOVAL GUY (CONT'D)

The other afternoon, I went to tell them a thing
or two. I brought the dog—I was polite and all,
but they refused to turn down the music. Carita's
sensitive, so she started barking. That's when one
of them smacked her with a belt.

(He fights back his tears.)

SNOW REMOVAL GUY (CONT'D)

Broke her jaw. Carita has always loved bones, but
now she can't eat anything but soup. I told the
police, but they do nothing.

(He starts to cry. From behind we see Frank signal with his
hand for someone to give the man a Kleenex. He blows his nose
and regains control.)

SNOW REMOVAL GUY (CONT'D)

People tell me there is only one person who can
help in situations like these: Johnny Henriksen.

FRANK

Why did you go to the police? Why didn't you come
to me first?

SNOW REMOVAL GUY

I didn't want to get in trouble ...

FRANK

I understand. You grew up in the old Norway.
Paradise. Everybody made a good living. Everybody
was taken care of. Well, that's gone. It's a new
world, my friend.

SNOW REMOVAL GUY

I know, but all this happened before ... before ...

FRANK

Before what?

SNOW REMOVAL GUY

Before I understood what kind of man you are.

SC. 1-02 INT FLAMINGO BAR,
FRANK'S OFFICE—DAY

(Frank smiles with satisfaction and rises. We see the room; others are present. Arne, Torgeir, and Jan get up as well. The Snow Removal Guy follows Frank, and Frank lays his arm over his shoulder.)

FRANK

Good. Someday, and that day may never come, I may call upon you to shovel some snow. Until that day, accept this as a gift on the weekend my kids are baptized. We'll look into your problem.

SNOW REMOVAL GUY

Thank you, thank you.

FRANK

And please: I understand Norwegian.

SNOW REMOVAL GUY

          (in Norwegian)
Of course.
          (to the dog)
Happy now eh, Carita? The man is so nice to us!

FRANK

Now if you don't mind, I'd like to go to my kids'
prechristening party.

(The Snow Removal Guy is escorted out by Jan.)

FRANK (CONT'D)

(straightening his tie in the mirror)
What a putz.

Just before season 2, Eilif and Anne were rattling off ideas they had gathered in the off-season. "Wait, wait," I said. "What was that last one?"

"Torgeir wrecks a gangster's Ferrari?"

"No, before that."

"We replicate the opening of *The Godfather*?"

I could see the whole scene immediately. "Eilif! This is fucking genius! This is not only gonna be great; it's a device we can use all the time!"

In that season 2 opening, Baard Owe played the Snow Removal Guy, the Bonasera the Undertaker role, and did a great job, except he was speaking English with absolutely no accent.

I was already pissed. I had told the Director, the Director of Photography, and the Production Designer to study *The Godfather* because I wanted everything to match exactly. But when I walked in, the lighting was all wrong and the furniture was in the wrong place.

I had to stop production and completely redo it. I got the distinct impression the Norwegians never quite grasped the significance of *The Godfather*'s place in cinema history, let alone in Italian American history.

And then there was the English. I said to the Director, "I need to hear the actor's Norwegian accent."

"He has no accent," the Director proudly told me. "He speaks English perfectly!"

"Yeah, man, I'm grokkin' that, that's really cool." I was starting to lose it. "But check it out. We're in Norway, doing a Norwegian parody of *The Godfather*, so he needs to have a Norwegian accent or it's not funny, dig? If he ain't gonna sound as Norwegian as he, in fact, is, I could have fucking filmed this in fucking Staten Island and slept in my own fucking bed tonight, gabeesh?"

He got it. And I love it.

During the second season of *Lilyhammer*, the completely opposite expectations of the audiences of NRK and Netflix started to take their toll.

Specifically, they started to take their toll on the relationship between me and Eilif and Anne. I was told from the beginning that we would be doing a Norwegian version of *The Sopranos*, more or less. We needed the "cultural differences," but we also needed sex, violence, nudity, and language that would be expected on any subscription network.

I had an enormous obligation to Ted, who was trusting me to deliver a great show for a subscription audience. That meant adult subjects, adult depth, adult characters, and yeah, adult language, sex, and violence.

Eilif and Anne must have been getting pressure from the network because suddenly, everything I wrote was an argument. And even if I understood fighting for every act of violence—Norway was less tolerant of violence than the States—fighting for every sex scene or nude shot started to wear me out.

I had to remind them that Netflix was paying two-thirds of the budget and that the expression "tits and ass" did not refer to women breastfeeding or showing a baby's ass during a diaper change!

It was a crazy combination of contradictory goals and working methods, and sometimes it felt like me against a whole country, but in the end we somehow created a completely original hybrid dramedy and managed to satisfy both Norwegian and American viewers. Plus the international audience, which eventually included 130 countries.

And most important to me, I delivered what I promised to Ted Sarandos, who had staked his company's new content creation on me with blind faith, without notes or second-guessing.

We'd accomplished more in a few years than the entire Norwegian film and TV industry had in the previous fifty in regards to introducing the country's enormously talented artists to the world.

I wasn't exactly expecting dual citizenship or my own cabin in the woods, but not one of the big brass at NRK ever thanked us, visited the set, or seemed to know we existed. We never received one dollar from a very generous government that funded anybody and everybody that even called themselves an Artist.

The creeping tension among the creative team lifted when our second season was nominated by the International TV Awards in Monte Carlo in two Comedy categories, Best Show and Best Leading Man. The competition for the awards, the Golden Nymph Awards, included the whole planet. Just being nominated was amazing.

Would you believe it? Our little local show, underfunded and underpublicized, won both awards? We beat everybody in the world. Shows with three times the budget and big celebrity stars and massive publicity.

The only bummer was that no one was there from Netflix to enjoy it with.

Ted deserved to be there. He had gambled on us and won big. The ballsiest TV executive in history should have taken a bow. I had justified his faith. I wanted to celebrate with him.

In spite of our amazing victory, NRK was not planning on a third season. Remember, they hadn't even wanted the second one.

Luckily for us, NRK got a new boss, Thor Eriksen, who arrived just in time. He was a friend of Trond Giske, the former cultural minister, who set up a dinner the night before Thor was starting his new job. Jo Nesbo joined the three of us. Thor turned out to be a real fan and gave us a very, very rare Norwegian third season.

Ted was into it.

Netflix was going to start expanding worldwide, and I suggested what Ted had undoubtedly already thought of: since they already had a local show in Norway, they should make Norway the first country they expanded to. It was a template they could use everywhere. They literally owned the concept of international cross-fertilization at that point. They'd invented it with *Lilyhammer*, and it was a great strategy.

Start a local show when you start broadcasting in a new country, and then share all your international content. Just make sure you have a worldwide license, which is where HBO and many international franchisers fucked up. They may have had a presence in many countries, but they gave up control to the local territories. Big mistake.

By Netflix's third show, *Orange Is the New Black*, they had surpassed twenty years of HBO's subscribers in three short years.

That third season continued to broaden the show's creative horizons. It opened in Rio, which gave us new sights to see and new music to play.

We were taking our reputation as the first international show seriously. There was simply no country or ethnic group we wouldn't hesitate to corrupt!

While *Lilyhammer* was beating the odds in Norway, my Rascals show was fighting a losing battle back home. The investors never showed up. *Once upon a Dream*, despite being an artistic triumph, had become my usual financial nightmare.

It was the same story as always. I have never been able to raise money for my own projects. I can do it for others, but not myself. I spend every penny I have while I wait for lawyers or investors or sponsors or donors or patrons, because if I don't do that I would never create anything.

And I need to work constantly. I simply cannot function at the normal speed of this planet. The minute I stop moving, I start dying. That's the pattern of my life, and hard as I try, it never changes. I do what I have to do and then try to get it paid for after the fact.

I don't like it. I don't like it one bit. I do not like living this way. I don't have some martyr complex. I come to win.

I always wonder what would have happened to *Once upon a Dream* with a Manager. Maybe they could have gotten me money up front. Then again, I know from experience that nobody has any imagination. No matter how well you describe something, how passionately, how specifically, investors won't be convinced until they have seen it themselves.

Still, as we moved the show to Toronto and then to the rest of the United States, it worked better than we could have dreamed.

The show actually transcended the Rascals themselves. Our real achievement was transporting the audience back to the '60s for two hours.

We spoke to audience members after the show, and they all had the same questions.

What happened?

What happened to joy?

What happened to hope?

Back in the '60s those questions were asked, and answered, every day. In spite of the turmoil of chaos and protest marches and urban unrest and the Vietnam War and assassinations, we felt every tomorrow would be better than yesterday.

Optimism, man. Anybody remember that? The evolution of consciousness, the combination of joy and hope, the thrill of unlimited possibilities. That's what we had experienced in the '60s, and what we brought back with the show.

We had big plans beyond the Rascals. There were so many bands that conveyed the spirit of their time and that had endless stories to tell. Marc and I figured we'd be doing the Eagles next. Then the Who. The Temptations. A Kinks reunion (after the Rascals, nothing would be difficult).

There was no end in sight, and our new template could change the entire future of the Rock and Soul business for the remaining Renaissance Artists.

But then, unbelievably, as Marc took the show on the road, the poisonous relationships in the Rascals, the band dynamics that we had analyzed and filmed and laid out for the world to see, surfaced again.

Three out of four band members started acting like they had just been thawed from four decades of suspended animation, and they resumed being the assholes they always were.

One of the lead singers, Felix Cavaliere, who I'd thought was a friend, had seemingly decided the money he was making—more money than he'd ever made in his life—wasn't enough. He got two of the other guys, Dino Danelli (who had been in the Disciples for two years) and Gene Cornish (whose rent I'd paid for more than a year to keep him from literal homelessness), to go along with him.

The fact that this very costly show was losing money didn't seem to matter to them. The fact that I had written, directed, and produced, at my own expense, a Broadway show that let them showcase their greatness—a greatness that the world had long since forgotten—and restore their place in history also didn't seem to matter to them.

The fact that it was the best they'd ever sounded, even going back to their prime, didn't seem to matter to them.

Apparently what mattered to them was their egomania. I think what was particularly galling to Cavaliere was the fact that each member of the group was getting a separate standing ovation. I don't think he could stand that. To me it seemed like he felt, with absolutely no rational basis, that he'd always been a one-man show.

As it turned out, he was just using the entire two years of the show's run to raise his feeble solo fee. It went $5,000 per gig to $25,000 per gig, and he returned happily to what was, to my mind, a pathetic version of the music he was playing when I'd found him on the oldies' white chit-lins circuit three years earlier.

For forty years, the conventional wisdom had been that the breakup had been caused by Eddie Brigati, the second lead singer, and his decision to capriciously quit the band. As it turns out, Brigati was the only one with any sense of honor, and he had originally split to preserve the integrity and dignity of the group, even after his publishing was stolen and his royalties had diminished to nothing.

Not only was the show the best creative work I've ever done, but I felt an additional sense of accomplishment at bringing Eddie Brigati, one of the most beautiful, soulful cats who has ever lived, back from cultural exile. His voice, confidence, and reputation were restored, and his corrected important place in history was secured forevermore.

A few years later, Maureen and I designed a cabaret act for Eddie—I supplied the Rock and Roll songs; she made a list of the best show tunes—and we played that at the Cutting Room in New York. We were proud of that show, and especially proud of Eddie, who really stretched to make that radical transition.

Along with the second death of the Rascals, actual death started to become a regular part of my life.

In the spring of 2012, my mother passed away after suffering horribly for months with complications from diabetes. She hadn't had any quality of life for years. The kindest, simplest woman I knew, she had lived a life of preliberation, old-school obligation. No fun since she was a kid, when, as the oldest of the five children of an Italian family, she became the de facto responsible mother.

I wish that I'd had more conversations with her. My father too. I was just too self-centered. Felt under siege my whole life. Always behind, always running to catch up, never quite getting there. Why couldn't I relax long enough to talk to my own parents?

My mother's passing was bookended by other deaths. We lost Steve Popovich, my early champion, in the summer of 2011, and Frank Barsalona, my mentor and one of my best friends, succumbed to his dementia in November 2012. And then, in June 2013 we lost Jimmy Gandolfini. David Chase called me in Spain with the news.

Jimmy's death was a huge loss to the industry, but I felt it personally. We had been looking to open a restaurant/bar together. We had been talking about the fact that there were no places like the old Columbus, Paulie Herman's joint, where people in the business, actors, musicians, and writers, could hang out together.

I had also talked to him about filming a scene for *Lilyhammer*. It was going to be a dream sequence where Frankie wanders through a blizzard and comes upon a cabin in the middle of nowhere. He knocks. The door opens, and there's Jimmy, Edie Falco, Jamie-Lynn Sigler, and Robert Iler. And Jimmy says, "Sil! You too!"

David Chase had even agreed to direct it.

I began to develop a method to cope with all these deaths.

Denial.

We spend most of our lives breaking down our defenses and trying to confront the truth. When you're young, denial is the enemy of quality of life. But as you get older, it becomes your friend. I have no real sense of time. I go long periods without seeing my friends, and when I do see them, we pick up our conversation where we left off. It's like the five or ten years apart never happened.

So when I lose a friend now, I try to avoid the funeral, unless the family really needs me there. Because in my mind, I keep all my friends alive. I tell myself it's just that our schedules aren't crossing at the moment.

Eventually . . . they will.

One other way to keep people alive is to respect their memory and history or to support institutions that do. The Rock and Roll Hall of Fame, for all its flaws, remained important for that reason.

The Hall mostly gets its mission right. Over the years, I had campaigned for the inclusion of Managers, starting with the Mount Rushmore of Managers: Colonel Tom Parker, Albert Grossman, Brian Epstein, and Andrew Loog Oldham. We got Epstein and Oldham inducted in 2014.

Colonel Tom and Albert Grossman were deemed too controversial. It's a shame. Just as the Art is always better than the Artist, the Manager's historical impact is always more important than the Manager.

There was one ugly moment when the Hall decided it didn't want Alan Freed's ashes anymore, despite the fact that Freed was the reason the Hall was in Cleveland in the first place. Instead of the situation being handled calmly and with dignity, it was dealt with in an unnecessarily disrespectful way.

I didn't learn about the situation until it was too late. Lance Freed was distraught. He is the gentlest, kindest soul I have ever met, completely unaccustomed to adversarial situations.

"Let's turn this into a positive thing," I said. Years earlier, Maureen had read about Rudolf Nureyev's grave. The next time we were in Paris, we went to the Russian Cemetery and found it. It was amazing. A stone mosaic that looks exactly like one of Nureyev's Persian, tapestry-woven kilim rugs. You would swear it was a blanket until you touched it.

I told Lance about it and suggested having the same artist, if we could find him, create a gigantic jukebox as the gravestone for his father.

Lance loved the idea. He started looking for real estate while I looked for the sculptor.

I found out the Nureyev grave had been created by Ezio Frigerio, the former set designer from the Paris Opera. And, incredibly, we found him! He was a hundred years old, but he was into it.

I connected him with Lance, but the cost of commissioning and shipping something that large turned out to be prohibitive, so Lance decided to have somebody in Cleveland do it.

But it turned out great.

That same year, the E Street Band finally made it into the Hall of Fame. We were inducted by Bruce, who had been in as a solo artist since

1999, and in his speech he admitted that I was right when I'd said the band should have gone into the Hall before he went in as a solo artist.

That had been the third of our major fights.

It was a stunning admission. I give him a lot of credit for admitting he was wrong. Especially in such a public fashion.

I had been promising Darlene Love that I would produce an album for her since I met her in Los Angeles in 1980.

Maureen and I would go see her perform at least once a year.

We were sitting in the audience at the old B. B. King Blues Club and Grill on Forty-Second Street in Times Square when Darlene did a Gospel number, "Marvelous" by Walter Hawkins, and as usual, wiped out the entire audience, including me.

This time I just snapped.

"People have got to hear her do this song," I said to Maureen.

"Well, why don't you do something about it?" she said. "You've been waiting for the right time to work with her. But there's never gonna be a right time."

After the show I talked to Darlene backstage. "What are you doing tomorrow?"

"Nothing."

"We're going in the studio."

"What are we doing?"

"We're doing 'Marvelous.' The rest we'll figure out as we go."

The next day I started calling every great songwriter I knew. "I'm doing Darlene Love's debut album. Write her a song!"

Elvis Costello sent me four songs in forty-eight hours, which was very encouraging. The legendary Cynthia Weil and Barry Mann wrote Darlene a great song. Bruce gave me two.

I got a cool song from Joan Jett. One from Michael Des Barres. And Linda Perry wrote a great one.

I had a good opener in mind. A song from my second solo album called "Among the Believers." Never got much attention, but I knew it would resonate with Darlene's faith.

Jimmy Webb sent his song in, and it was great but not quite "Mac-Arthur Park," so I made up an instrumental middle section that made it more epic, which is what we needed.

Darlene had always resented Phil Spector taking "River Deep, Mountain High" away from her and giving it to Tina Turner because they were fighting at the time. She wanted to do it. I was like, uh, Darlene, you know that's known as Spector's greatest record, right?

"I don't care," she said. "We can beat him, Stevie!"

Fuck me.

Now I'm not big on remakes to begin with. As we discussed, a cover has to be either spectacularly different, or simply spectacular, and I wasn't so sure we could be either one.

I solved it with a *West Side Story* intro and by bringing out every riff you remembered and a few more. And then, oh yeah, there was the greatest singer in the world with fifty years of pissed off ready to explode.

As the story goes, Phil quit the business when his greatest record wasn't a hit. Ironically, if he had let Darlene sing it, it would have been. Darlene's Gospel voice can handle the upper registers and smooth those notes out, where Tina's Bluesy R&B voice breaks up in a way that scares little young teenage girls to death. And that was and is the Pop audience.

I later played it for Jeff Barry. He gave me a look I'll never forget.

"I can't believe you had the balls. But goddamn if you didn't pull it off!"

The last thing I did is what I always do when I produce an album. I wait until the end and see what else is needed. This one felt like it could use one more Gospel song. I stayed up late listening to the Soul Stirrers and woke up with "Jesus Is the Rock That Keeps Me Rolling." Dave Clark happened to be in town just after we recorded it and flipped over that one. He said it was the greatest song I had ever written and would be the one that would "ironically live on forever in every church long after your atheist ass is gone!"

I made an amazing deal with Rob Stringer at Sony. I'll forever be thankful that he had so much belief in what he was hearing that he agreed to put out a seventy-three-year-old woman's debut album.

Once we signed with Sony, I figured that was it. The album, *Introducing Darlene Love*, would not only be nominated for Album of the Year but would win going away. I was quite sure no other album could touch it. And since everyone had seen *20 Feet from Stardom*, the Oscar-winning documentary about background singers that featured Darlene, this album would complete the story. A perfect, beautiful, happy ending to an extraordinary career.

We weren't even nominated.

Nobody heard it.

With around three episodes left to shoot in our third season, I got the call from Ted.

The business had gotten too complicated to continue. Was there anything I could do? No, he said, nothing we could do.

Netflix had come a long way since my first promo tour where I promised to bring the stock price back from 47 to 100! I even did CNBC and explained to Maria Bartiromo what Netflix was, because I knew all the stock market freaks watched her. They're creating content, I explained. Why? she asked.

Knowing the show was ending gave me a chance to write in a bit of closure.

In the third-season finale, the show that would be our last, Tony Sirico returned as my older brother Antonio the Priest. Maureen returned as Frank's ex. And Bruce made his acting debut as Frank's middle brother Giuseppe, a mortician and part-time hit man.

For most of the run of the show, Eilif and Anne were only comfortable with me doing first drafts of the last show of each season. They were afraid I was going to hijack things into triple-X pornography. For the third season, not only did I write the first draft, but after seven seasons of *Sopranos* and three seasons of *Lilyhammer*, I finally got to direct.

I had always thought directing TV was the job of a traffic cop. Very limited creativity as opposed to film because the show had to look the same every week. But there was more creativity than I expected, and I enjoyed it more than I thought I would. With the big picture taken care of by the writing, I enjoyed getting into the granular details, the nuances of the actors' performances, timing, expressions, tone, and texture, all the more challenging since they were mostly speaking in Norwegian! And I was able to include more Lillehammer locations, which we should have been doing all along if the producer hadn't been an asshole.

I finally got back to the *Godfather* for inspiration, using Fredo's execution as a model for Fridtjov's. Next time you watch it, note that I did not show Fridtjov actually being shot. You just hear it. Just in case we got another year through some miracle, there was no way I was gonna lose one of our best actors.

As we were packing up in Norway and heading for New York for the final few scenes, which would include Bruce's scenes, the Producer, Anders Tangen, turned to me. "By the way," he said, "we're out of money. If you want to shoot the New York scenes, you're going to have to pay for it."

I had caught Anders overspending on various things over the previous two years, building unnecessarily elaborate temporary sets and overpaying for locations, and ratted him out regularly to the heads of the production company to no avail. This was his revenge, I suppose.

"I hope you are joking."

"No, we're broke."

I called my Agent. He may have been completely incompetent until then, but I was sure he would rise to the occasion and finally use the muscle of his major agency to put Anders in his place!

"What do you want me to do about it?" he said.

Those were his actual words.

As if I could make that up.

"Sorry for bothering you."

I hung up.

He was so fucking fired.

I paid the $180,000 to film the New York scenes, because without them the show would've made no fucking sense. Plus, nobody involved seemed to have the intelligence level to recognize that after years of being pursued by every major Director and Producer, Bruce Springsteen, arguably the biggest star in the world, was giving us his acting debut.

Unfortunately, his appearance would barely be noticed, never mind publicized, because by the time the episode was broadcast, the show had been canceled.

For those New York scenes, I needed someone to play Pasquale, the son of the Mob boss Uncle Sal. Maureen suggested a young actor she'd directed in a play, Nicky Cordero, and I proudly got him his Screen Actors Guild card. Nick would go on to star on Broadway in *Rock of Ages*, *Waitress*, *Bullets Over Broadway*, and *A Bronx Tale*, and he would be our most personal loss to the COVID pandemic, murdered by a scumbag ex-president and a political party that doesn't believe in science.

The last piece of the finale was the music. I used a Procol Harum song, not "The Devil Came from Kansas," which I'd suggested for the *Sopranos* finale, but the melancholy "A Salty Dog," which summed up my feelings of leaving both Norway and Netflix, two relationships that would mean so much to my life and that still feel as though they have been only temporarily interrupted.

And I ended the series with another *Sopranos* suggestion, Bruce's "Loose Ends," which also gave the episode its title.

I don't know what lies ahead, but don't forget about me, Norway. We're not done yet.

Ironically and incredibly, that third season of *Lilyhammer* won the Golden Nymph for the second year in a row for both Best Comedy Series and Outstanding Actor in a Comedy Series. That had never happened in the thirty years of the award's existence.

This time, I felt it necessary to apologize to Sir Ian McKellen for beating him. His performance in *Amadeus* remains my most memorable Broadway experience among the rest of his extraordinary life's work.

All the other shows congratulated us. Producers offered me guest spots on everything. But the one group I wanted to see was missing again. Where was Netflix?

Even if they didn't want to continue because of the vast business complications and unscrupulous nature of the partners of the show, I still wish the man who made it all possible would have been there to take a bow.

What balls to gamble on a first show with one American actor and subtitles.

Not only would the meeting with Ted Sarandos forever be my best business meeting of all time (the meeting with Susie Buffett wasn't business), but he was one of the few truly courageous, visionary leaders in a cowardly, myopic business.

He deserves every bit of Netflix's success.

It hurt me to my soul that he wasn't there.

thirty-one

Ambassador to the Court
of Ronald McDonald

(2016–2017)

Write, Act, Paint, Play, Perform, Work, Think, Speak, Live with
Purpose. Or hide under the bed until checkout time.
—THE UNWRITTEN BOOK

Thanksgiving of 2015 Bruce announced there would be no E Street
Band tour in 2016.

We were onstage in January.

As any Tour Manager doing arena tours or bigger knows, that is a
physical, mental, and spiritual impossibility.

For George Travis, our Tour Manager, the impossible took only six
weeks in this case. That's six *fucking* weeks, if you're keeping score.

Find fifty or sixty crew members that aren't booked. Find venues that
aren't already booked. Contact the band and the rest of the touring
party and inform them that whatever they thought they were doing,
they are not doing. Hotels. Planes. Trucks. Buses. Flights. Customs. Staging. Sound. Lights. Screens.

In six weeks. Try it.

George started as a truck driver. Depending on how long the drive
was to the next show, drivers would often work during the show as rig-
gers and spotlight operators.

George was a rigger. They're the crazy mamajamas that climb up high to secure hanging points for lights and sound and screens. Real high. With no net.

He worked his way up, or down in this case, to being the flashlight guy as the band walked on the stage. Might not seem like much, but it put him in contact with humans—well, the band anyway—for the first time, which was a risky move for his immediate superior, in this case Marc Brickman, our light man and production head.

Suppose George said the wrong thing to the wrong guy at the wrong time? Suppose the Boss didn't like his face? Or the shirt he was wearing? A bad flashlight guy could fuck up an entire show! "I like him," I told Marc. "I think he's destined for bigger things."

"Ain't we all," he mumbled with his typical sincere cynicism.

George eventually became Tour Manager, one of the very best.

The River Revisited was my second favorite tour ever, after the original River Tour, because that album has my favorite material. It's also got Bruce's best singing. He is one of the greatest white Soul singers of all time, but since that's not his favorite part of his identity, he only becomes that guy every once in a while. Much to my eternal aggravation, he takes that gift totally for granted.

On this tour he was that guy every night, which was awesome to behold. As a Student Prince advertisement from 1971 said, he was "That Sensational Soul Man."

Featuring the "Hoochi-koochi Guitar Player Steve VanZadt"! And "Pro-Football in Color"!

Bruce managed to ruin my personal fun a little bit by deciding not to do the full *River* album in Europe.

"Why?" I asked, disappointed that some of our greatest audiences wouldn't be seeing one of our greatest shows.

Too many slow songs for stadiums, was the answer.

Now Bruce has to sing the songs, so if he doesn't feel like singing that many slow songs, that's that. But the implication that the audience wouldn't like it was simply incorrect.

I was in in LA having dinner with the very cool *Game of Thrones* guys David Benioff and D. B. Weiss sometime in 2015. They asked if I wanted to go with them to see the Rolling Stones, who happened to be doing the entire *Sticky Fingers* album. "I don't know," I said. "Let me think about it." *As if!* It was phenomenal, and afterward I told Charlie Watts, "This will be the greatest tour you've done since Exile in '72!"

"No it won't," he said in his famous deadpan delivery. "What you just saw was the only time we're doing the whole album. Mick says it's too many slow songs for stadiums. Maybe you can talk to him."

No thanks.

The thing was, I'd spent the entire '80s in Europe, seeing dozens of shows, and half of the biggest Rock acts did nothing *but* slow songs. The Eurovision Song Contest, the single biggest event in Europe, is nothing but slow songs.

Yes, *Sticky Fingers* has a lot of slow songs. But look at what they are! "I Got the Blues," "Sister Morphine," "Moonlight Mile," "You Gotta Move." Not to mention "Wild Horses."

And yes, *The River* has lots of slow songs, but they are "Independence Day," "I Wanna Marry You," "The River," "Point Blank," "Fade Away," "Drive All Night," and . . . well, maybe they had a point.

Anyway, if those two front guys feel the same way about something . . .

I felt really bad the River Revisited Tour had to skip one of my favorite parts of America, North Carolina. For some reason the audiences in the Carolinas are among the most enthusiastic audiences for us in the country. I think they saw our brand of northern bar band as something slightly exotic. It was almost like playing Europe.

But North Carolina had just passed their ridiculous bathroom bill, the first of the Orwellian-titled religious freedom bills. The legislation that had nothing to do with religious freedom and everything to do with imposing extremist religious ideas on a rapidly disappearing Separation of Church and State society.

As soon as they passed the bill, we decided we had to show solidarity with the LGBTQ community and so couldn't play the state. We helped lead a boycott of artists, athletes, and professional organizations to make the point that the North Carolina political leadership was living in the past and needed to be voted out. The boycott worked, to some degree—they adjusted the law without quite fixing it—but within a few months it became impossible to stay away from states that were imposing fanatical anti-LGBTQ legislation. There were just too many.

When the River Tour hit London, Maureen came over. It was her favorite town in her favorite country. She could live there permanently, and I've been promising her at least an apartment there for years, but I keep blowing it. The festival was one apartment. The Rascals show was another. Maybe we'll get there eventually, but between me and you—come here a little closer; I have to whisper—I like visiting and living in hotels better.

We had tea with Bill and Suzanne Wyman, and they invited us to his eightieth birthday party. They are the original odd couple, Bill quietly bemused by much of the modern world and Suzanne as wild and kinetic as can be.

A couple nights later I went to see the soul singer Madeline Bell at Ronnie Scott's Jazz Club with Leo Green, one of our Promoters from Live Nation. "When you coming back to London?" Leo asked.

"We come every year for Maureen's birthday in November and sometimes stay through Christmas, but Bill Wyman just invited us to his birthday party in October."

His eyes lit up. "That's the same week as my Blues Festival. Why don't you throw a band together and headline one of the nights?"

Wow . . . I had to think about that one.

I hadn't fronted a band since the '80s, but doing the Darlene Love album and the *Lilyhammer* score had given me a whole new set of musician friends.

There are two kinds of musicians in the world, band guys and session guys. Band guys are the ones you grow up with and start out playing with, and if you're lucky, you hit on some magical chemical combination.

Session guys are professionals. They play in time, and they play in tune.

The members of the Rolling Stones (and almost every other important band you can name) could not find work as session musicians if their lives depended on it. You're more likely to be overqualified for Rock than underqualified.

What bands have is personality. And chemistry. Alchemy. Every great band is a matter of individual eccentricities blending in different ways with unpredictable, inconsistent, occasionally glorious results.

Session guys generally don't have strong musical personalities. They are trained to take on the personality of the Artist they're working with. That's what makes them valuable. A session guy may be (and often is) the craziest mofo you'd ever want to meet in real life. But at a session he's going to adapt.

In recent years, I had started meeting more of a third type, a hybrid of the first two—session guys that perform live.

There was some precedent. When Rock and Soul began, the revue-type shows used session guys because there were multiple acts, and the band had to read the charts, be great, fast, and consistent. There was no performance requirement per se. They were in the background and just played.

All the big shows had them. The Alan Freed shows, Murray the K shows, Dick Clark shows, the Motown Motortown Revue. Even Soupy Sales emceed a revue show. Those revues needed bands, and they couldn't use the labels' house bands. There were exceptions. Booker T. & the M.G.'s did Stax tours, since they played on most of the records. And that had to be some Funk Brothers on the twelve-year-old Stevie Wonder's live and incredible "Fingertips." But if the house band was on the road, who was left to make the damn records?

Beyond Rock, the Popular standards artists who toured—Frank Sinatra, Tony Bennett, Jerry Vale, or in-betweeners like Tom Jones, Shirley Bassey, and Engelbert Humperdinck—brought along a Music Director, and maybe a drummer, and then hired most of the musicians in each city as they went.

The drummer was often there for shtick as much as for sticks.

It was left to solo artists who lived in the Pop world but had Rock roots or unusual complexity to begin taking true session guys on the road. Artists like Paul Simon, Sting, Linda Ronstadt (half of her band was session guys; the other half turned into the Eagles!). Or even Jeff Beck these days, who requires supreme musical excellence to keep up with him.

I took that path. I had drafted Marc Ribler to be Darlene's Musical Director and brought in higher-level musicians to mix with a few of her old band and excellent singers, Ula Hedwig, Milton Vann, and Baritone Williams. When Leo Green asked me to throw together a band, I decided what the hell. This crazy gig might be fun.

I could do some Paul Butterfield things with the horns, which nobody hears anymore. I could do some of Mike Bloomfield's Electric Flag stuff, which nobody's ever heard live. I could do regular Blues like Little Walter and Howlin' Wolf, and maybe even some blaxploitation for a jazzier change of pace.

Suddenly, I was actually looking forward to this thing!

I called Darlene. "Baby, I've got to borrow Marc back for a minute. I'm actually gonna do a gig!"

"Of course!" She was the coolest.

And it was only one gig. I thought.

Marc put an excellent band together: Richie Mercurio on drums, Jack Daley on bass, and Andy Burton on keys. I added Eddie Manion and Stan Harrison, who went all the way back to the Jukes, on horns.

At rehearsal, along with the Blues and covers, I threw in some of my own songs, which I hadn't sung or even thought about since the '80s.

As I started to sing them, the strangest thing happened. I couldn't make it through a song without beginning to cry. I had to stop for a minute and figure out why. I realized it had been so long since I'd sung them that there was no distance between the emotions that created the songs and the process of performing them. I was literally living the words as I sang them. Feeling the melody and the chord changes with no buffer.

I had heard Maureen talk about the acting theory of "sense memory" from her classes in the old days, but it suddenly occurred to me that that theory may be built on a faulty assumption.

Sense memory theory suggested that when actors needed to cry in a scene, they should think back to an incident in their life that made them cry and use it. But what I found out was if you're really in the moment, you *can't* use it. You can't act. You can't speak. You can't sing. Your throat tightens up. You need a little distance.

When I told Bruce about it, he had a deeper explanation, the result of his forty years of therapy, which was that I was feeling a combination of guilt and despair at having abandoned my children (my songs) for decades.

He probably had a point. He always does.

Either way, it took me a couple of weeks to be able to get through the songs.

I got one of the great phone calls of all time in 2016.

"Stevie?"

"Yeah."

"Chita Rivera."

Wow!

"I'm doing my debut at Carnegie Hall and I want you to perform with me."

"Me?!?"

"Yes, please, darling—you'll make my show so cool!"

Ha-ha! As if her show could be any cooler. Me and Maureen have been catching her show for years and it just gets better and better.

She is the best part of show business personified, and not a bad résumé either—*West Side Story, Bye Bye Birdie, Chicago, Sweet Charity, Pippin, The Rink, Kiss of the Spider Woman,* and more.

We sang a duet on James Taylor's "Secret O' Life." I think that's about as nervous as I've ever been onstage. But it worked out great.

At around the same time, my friend Kenny Schulman, who had been involved with the New York Ronald McDonald House for years, asked for my support.

There are many reasons I'm quite sure there is no such thing as an anthropomorphic white guy with a beard up in the sky looking down personally on all eight billion of us, especially football players that score a touchdown, but the main one is kids with cancer.

"It's God's will," say the religious extremists that make up way too much of our country.

Really?

I feel sick whenever I see them. They wear bandanas when they get chemo, so many years ago I thought it would be nice if wearing the bandana wasn't an embarrassment but a badge of coolness.

So we created very colorful "Little Steven's Magic Bandanas" and told the kids that wearing one made them Rock stars.

I called John Varvatos, who called Tommy Hilfiger, and they also designed bandanas, which was supercool. Every celebrity and clothing designer could and probably would design a bandana if approached. It really makes the kids feel better psychologically.

Kenny loved the idea, and so did the executives at the Ronald McDonald House, and they made me the first Ambassador of Ronald McDonald House in New York to promote the whole thing.

Made it, Ma! Top of the world!

Maybe they'll make it a national campaign eventually.

If it makes these kids feel 1 percent better, it's worth it. All it takes is our will. Not that of God, who is busy making sure Rappers win Grammys.

Leo's Blues Festival gig was at a joint called the Indigo at the O2, part of the O2 Arena complex, which has the coolest configuration of a theater I've ever seen. Nice big stage, big dance floor, but then it has a huge, steeply raked balcony much closer to the stage than any I've ever seen. It made a 2,500-capacity theater feel very intimate.

Our best friends in London, Karl and Anita Sydow, brought Dave Clark, who emceed the evening for us, and the response from the eight hundred or so punters was fabulous.

Doing my own music after all those years was quite emotional for me, and I'll never forget that evening.

Richie Sambora was playing next door at the arena, so I joined him onstage and he joined me. He's one of my best friends, and I don't get a chance to see him often enough.

We went to watch Jeff Beck, who was also playing and was his usual amazing self. It was interesting to see Jimmy Page, not so bad himself, in as much awe as we were.

Backstage, I asked Jeff if he knew how annoying it was that he never missed, no matter how crazy a lick he was going for.

"That's what *you* think," he said. "I've just learned to cover it up well!" He was lying, I'm sure, to keep me from jumping off London Bridge.

As Richie and I were leaving, Leo stopped us. "Come say hi to Van Morrison," he said.

I'd never met him, but I'd heard . . . things. And I never like to take chances meeting my heroes.

"Thanks, Leo," I said, "but no thanks. I've heard he can be a bit . . . well, shy. And so am I."

"You don't understand," Leo said. "He asked for you. He wants to meet you." Richie and I went into his dressing room. Van was in a great mood. A sweetheart really. He talked about getting off the road and going back to his roots. Just grabbing a residency at some local pub and living the rest of his life that way.

After a few minutes our mutual shyness started to take over.

There happened to be a vacuum cleaner sitting there.

"Van," I said, "I don't know any better way to show my gratitude for all the pleasure your music has brought me through the years, so I'm just gonna clean up a bit for you." I started vacuuming his room.

His Tour Manager said it was the most he had seen Van laugh in ten years.

Bill Wyman's eightieth birthday party was filled with Rock celebs: Robert Plant, Bob Geldof, and Mark Knopfler, among others. Mark and I talked about our mutual friend Lance Freed, who had administered Mark's publishing along with mine for years. Lance had left Rondor to venture off on his own.

"Have you heard anything yet?" Mark asked me, as anxious as all of Lance's friends were to be back with him. Quite a compliment, considering that Dire Straits had been among the biggest bands in the history of European Rock. Mark hadn't needed a publisher for forty years. But like the rest of us, he was perfectly willing to give up an administration fee just to hang out with Lance. That's how cool Lance is.

After the party, it was time to get back to E Street, where the River (or at least River-ish) Tour would resume in Australia in January.

But the gig felt so good and the band was so amazing that I couldn't shake the experience. Something significant had taken place. "Hey," I told Marc Ribler, "I've got a month or two off. Why don't we make an album just for the hell of it? No heavy lifting. We can record a bunch of the songs I've written for others through the years." The rehearsal alone had already sounded like an album.

He was down. The band was into it. I talked to Bruce to see what he thought. He said it was a great idea. And that's what we did.

Every album I've ever done has a theme and a concept. In this case, the title said it all: *Soulfire*. A summation of the songs written for others that combined the raw power of Rock with the emotional depth of Soul, in the process creating something uncategorizable and uniquely uncommercial!

I mostly picked songs that still had emotional resonance for me. There were two that Southside had recorded, "I'm Coming Back" from the '90s, which obviously made sense, and "I Don't Want to Go Home," Johnny's signature song, which I rearranged back to the way I'd originally pictured it for Ben E. King and the Drifters. I did an Ennio Morricone arrangement for "Standing in the Line of Fire" from the third Gary US Bonds album, and finally my own version of "St. Valentine's Day" from both the Cocktail Slippers and David Chase's Twylight Zones. I still hope to do it with Nancy Sinatra, who I wrote it for.

I also did some new writing, finally finishing what had been going to be the first song on my first album forty years earlier, "The City Weeps Tonight." My idea back then was to introduce myself as a new artist by going chronologically through the history of Rock and Soul genres, beginning with Doo-Wop. But then I decided to go political.

The other new song on *Soulfire* was "I Saw the Light," a song I'd written for Richie Sambora and his partner at the time, Orianthi. I had talked with Richie casually about producing them. I thought they were a great couple, and I wanted to make them the Delaney and Bonnie of Hard Rock. I could see it, hear it, clear as day.

Richie was in New York with his daughter, who was going to NYU, and he was supposed to come over a dozen times to hear the song and discuss the album. He never made it.

By the time Richie and I reconnected, they were doing an album with Bob Rock and had like thirty songs. I figured they didn't need me or my song, put it on the shelf, and found it again just before I made *Soulfire*.

I always wonder what would have happened if Richie had come over that day and we'd grabbed Orianthi and gone into my studio four blocks away and cut that song.

I'd never recorded a cover on a solo album, but I happened to be listening to an Etta James record and heard "Blues Is My Business," written by Kevin Bowe and Todd Cerney.

" . . . and business is good."

Is that a classic fucking hook or what?

I wanted to fill out the set with something Jazzy so the horn players could blow, and I also wanted to do my favorite blaxploitation song, Bodie Chandler and Barry De Vorzon's "Down and Out in New York City," the *Black Caesar* theme by the Godfather of Soul himself, James Brown. I combined the two ideas by coming up with a cool Jazzy theme we could riff off of that fit right in.

As I contemplated my return to the music business, I promised myself that I was going to do things right. I knew most of the problems of my professional life had come from not having a Manager.

I called Scott Borchetta.

I had met Scott at Jimmy's wedding in 2016. I didn't know much about him other than that he had started the Big Machine label in 2005 and almost immediately hit the lottery with Taylor Swift, but I liked the way he carried himself.

Shortly after we met, Scott asked me to mentor on *Idol* again, where he had taken over from Jimmy. I had gotten away with it once and nobody had gotten hurt. A second time seemed risky. But Maureen made me do it again, and it was fine again. All I remember is La'Porsha Renae turning down my suggestion of Jerry Ragovoy's "Stay with Me," despite my encouragement. She would have won with it!

The experience was uneventful except that Jennifer Lopez, who was one of the judges, didn't have a clue who I was. Totally understandable;

why should she? But Maureen felt she was being disrespectful and went after her on Twitter. That was entertaining for a minute. Luckily J-Lo remained clueless about me all over again when I did a commercial with her for the 2020 Super Bowl, so there was no bad blood. I even changed the script to subtly hype her latest movie.

When I called Scott Borchetta, we reminisced for a minute about *Idol.* Then I got to the point. "Hey, man, I'm kind of coming back into the business. I know you're mostly a record company guy, but if you have a little time, do you want to be my Manager?"

"Wow." Not a call he was expecting. "Yeah! Sure! Let's meet in Nashville."

In NashVegas, Scott brought in a guy named Ken Levitan and another guy. Scott explained he was busy with Big Machine but would get involved with anything important. Levitan, his management partner, would handle the day-to-day.

Ken then introduced me to the other guy, who would actually be handling the day-to-day. Now I was two levels down from what I'd had in mind. But what the hell, everybody seemed enthusiastic.

So they became my first real Managers. Great, I thought. I don't have to say no to the many offers I get, most of which are from acquaintances. I can now send those people to management, who can be the bad guys and turn them down.

I explained it was going to take me a minute to make the enormous adjustment to being a front man, so we needed to take it slow.

Instead, they started saying yes to everything being offered. TV shows. Gigs. Record deals. Everything.

It's a typical management methodology to get some revenue on the books quickly to make everybody feel like the Managers are doing something, but it didn't work for me.

They made a record deal with Bruce Resnikoff at Universal that was the worst deal I've ever seen, but I was determined not to scare them away by interfering.

They assured me it was a good deal for those days. I told them that just a year earlier I had made a fifty-fifty ownership/partnership deal for Darlene Love, a seventy-three-year-old legend releasing her debut album, which was the kind of thing you could do if you had already paid for the record, which I had also done with *Soulfire*. "Well," they said. "This is the best Universal will do."

Long story short, *Soulfire* came out and it was obvious within three months that the management thing just wasn't gonna work, so I let the Managers go.

The first thing I did after they were gone was meet with Bruce Resnikoff. Incredibly, it was the first time anyone had met with Universal to discuss *Soulfire*. Again, this was three months after it came out, as opposed to six months before, when the marketing plan meeting should have happened.

It took me all of sixty seconds to renegotiate the record deal to a fifty-fifty partnership.

Which reminded me why I didn't have a Manager, but it was still depressing. Everybody else had one. I just wanted to be normal.

Bruce would turn out to be a very important and loyal new friend. I had known him casually for years. I almost did the Darlene Love album with him. But what would be the most productive three years of my life were due directly to his faith and belief in my work. And I'll never forget that.

When the E Street Band returned from Australia, Bruce told me he had put together a small one-man biography-type show for the Obamas, which he planned to expand and take to Broadway.

I figured it would be a good time to do a new TV show. I called whichever horse I was riding on the merry-go-round of Agents at the time to make a TV deal for one of my five scripts, and I also met with Chris Columbus and Joe Roth to see if they had anything for me.

While that was going on, Maureen and I were put on the board of the Count Basie Theatre. The Basie had a special place in my heart because when I was a kid it had been my local movie theater, the Carlton (when I wasn't at the drive-in in Holmdel). It was in Red Bank, the place where I bought my records and first guitar at Jack's.

Maureen was busy teaching acting to the dancers at American Ballet Theatre at that time, but she agreed to be on the board because she also had a special place in her heart for the Carlton/Basie from when she'd danced there as a kid with the New Jersey Ballet.

The Basie was fundraising to expand the theater into a block-long Arts center. They had shown me the design, which I didn't like. Why did it have to be so boring? Why not make something iconic like Gaudí's apartment buildings or Saint Basil's Cathedral or even the guitar-shaped hotel Jimmy Allen was building at the Hollywood, Florida, Hard Rock? Who wanted another fucking accountant's office building?

They had promised me a club in the complex, which would be the first Little Steven's Underground Garage.

That appealed to me. I had always wanted to start a really cool franchise where people in the business could hang out no matter what town they were in. Of course, it wasn't just a club I had in mind. More like a club/bar/restaurant/hotel/casino. I can't help it, I just think small.

I have offered to design something like this for my friends at the Hard Rock for the last twenty years or so. No takers yet. People who design hotels should come to people like me, who have spent their whole lives living in them.

As it turned out, the Basie people would end up using my name for fundraising and then not giving me the club after all. But I didn't know that yet when they invited me to an investor lunch.

The investor they were courting had said he would invest if I came to the meeting. So I came, and he did.

We got to talking, and he asked what I was doing. I told him I had just recorded an album for the first time in twenty-five years.

"Hot damn," he said. "You have to take it on the road!"

"Nice thought," I said. "But there's no plan to do that right now. It's a big sound. Five horns, three girl singers. It's too expensive a proposition."

"That's alright," he said. "I've been around long enough to know that greatness usually costs."

Indeed!

Could I have finally stumbled upon the patron of my dreams?

Ms. Destiny was visiting again, and since I wasn't confident about getting a new TV show, I started seriously considering going back on the road.

But could I get my head back into being a real onstage front man after all these years?

Oh man. That was gonna take a minute.

thirty-two

Soulfire

(2017–2018)

I leave you with this. My father was a proud ex-Marine Goldwater Republican. He wouldn't recognize the party now. I paraphrase Barry Goldwater as a tribute to my late father. "Extremism in defense of the environment is no vice, and moderation in pursuit of stopping pollution is no virtue." Lead us into a green future, reach for greatness, nothing less, and make sure you have some fun along the way. Life should never be boring. Congratulations, go get 'em.

—RUTGERS COMMENCEMENT SPEECH
CLOSING REMARKS, MAY 14, 2017

. . . And with that I became a doctor!

It made my Jewish mother so proud!

Oh wait, I was Catholic turned Baptist turned Rock and Roll Pagan. But she would've been proud anyway.

No, it ain't that kind. Not a sawbones. Just an Honorary Doctor of Fine Arts. Still nice. I think it was the mysterious Susan McCue's idea. She pops up in my life every ten years or so and does a good thing, then disappears back into the camouflage of behind-the-scene politics in DC.

Meanwhile, the prospect of a Soulfire Tour was looming, but instead of rising to the occasion, I was having a nervous breakdown. I was in the worst shape of my life. I had been going steadily downhill since my friend and trainer Clay Burwell had moved to South Carolina. I went on YouTube and watched a concert video to remind me of my 1987 self. It was depressing on two levels. I sure wasn't that guy anymore. And how could that band have not broken through?

There was only one way I was getting on that stage. I had to convince myself I was merely a presenter. An MC. More like the Big Band leaders of the '40s. Over time, I talked myself into it, and out we went for a tour that would take us around the States, to Europe, to Australia.

The shows went well, but I was disappointed with how meaningless I had become in the marketplace. We barely averaged a thousand people a night, if that.

It never ceases to amaze me how my many lives don't cross over. The E Street Band sells out three stadium shows in Dublin, which is 180,000 people. But when my band comes to town, about a thousand people show up. They are great, wildly enthusiastic, but, you know? I fully realize it's a different thing, but wouldn't you think I would get 1 percent of the E Street audience? One fucking percent!

Or take *Lilyhammer*. We drew an audience of one million people a week out of a Norwegian population of five million. I probably could have been elected mayor of Oslo. But when I played there with my band—my very, very, very good band, by the way—I got the same thousand people. Maybe.

That's a tenth of 1 percent.

So I had to adapt to that disappointment very quickly and accept it as just another part of my lifetime of penance, which I attributed to the big mistake of my life, my very public career suicide from which there was no redemption or salvation.

Most fascinating was the realization that we were playing to entire audiences who were there strictly out of curiosity. A few fans came because of my older solo records, E Street, or TV, but most of them didn't recognize one single song.

I had to cling to something, so I proudly held the Frank Barsalona flag high as I became the only artist in modern history with a touring party of thirty-five and absolutely no hits.

Now I can't see your face to see if your expression is one of pity or wonderment, but, believe it or not, there were some advantages.

For starters, I never disappointed anyone in the audience by not playing their favorite song!

(Buying that?)

Not having to do anything was liberating.

(How about that?)

The only trick is that I had to win the audience over every single song, or they would split.

I took pride in the fact that we did just that. No one left a Disciples show early or unsatisfied. And there were bright spots. Our German audiences were as enthusiastic as ever. The only explanation I can come up with is that we were still getting dividends from the *Rockpalast* broadcasts all those years ago, which were created by my lifelong friend Peter Rüchel.

I began a new Disciples tradition by having a band dinner after every show to solidify our esprit de corps. Everybody got along great anyway, so it was a good way to wind down the evening. Andrew, our wardrobe person, doubled as our social organizer, party planner, and minister of fun. He tried to book the restaurant of the hotel we were staying in, so people could just stumble from the table into an elevator.

Tom Petty died just as the tour was starting, which hit me harder than I would have expected. Tom had worked with Jimmy Iovine in the late '70s and early '80s, and Bruce and I had gone to see him perform at the Bottom Line, but I don't think Tom and I had spoken more than three sentences to each other our whole lives. Still, we were the same age and had the same influences, so there was an unspoken connection between us, and we did each other favors whenever possible. He gave me a song for *Lilyhammer*, for instance.

Tom died the day after the Las Vegas massacre, so his passing was barely mentioned in the news. That bothered me so much that I decided to open my show with one of his songs just to keep him alive a few more months.

During the same tour, we did tributes to Greg Allman and Malcolm Young.

These days, every tour seems to have way too many tributes.

Somewhere in that period, the Kennedy Center Spring Gala called for me to participate in a tribute to John Lennon. I wasn't sure what I could contribute, and I was about to turn it down when Maureen suggested I do a Rock arrangement of "Working Class Hero."

As soon as she said it, an idea hit me right away. That's how these things usually work. My brain takes everything it knows on the subject and throws it against the wall that instant. Sometimes I get a Rothko, sometimes a Renoir, and sometimes a kindergarten finger painting.

I got a Pissarro with this one.

When Lennon recorded "Working Class Hero," he was at the peak of escaping from his past, shedding everything he was and did. So out went melody and chord changes and arrangement and production and emotion. He wanted things stark. Primal. A complete focus on the lyrics and no distractions.

I decided to see what would happen when the arrangement and production were added back in, but without changing his melody or emotional intention.

When I got down to DC, the gig immediately became a success when I found that I was sharing a dressing room with Taj Mahal! One of my heroes and favorite artists and somebody I'd always wanted to meet.

We bonded over our always-with-us mutual friend Steve Popovich, who Taj had worked with at Columbia Records. I told him he should do the Notodden Blues Festival in Norway. He was a ball and still texts me now and then.

At the Hall of Fame that year, I finally got to introduce the Rock Hall Jukebox. I had proposed the idea years before as a way of acknowledging important singles, especially if the Artists who'd recorded them were unlikely to make the cut. "Louie Louie" by the Kingsmen, was the ultimate example. Every up-and-coming high school and bar band played it to death (Dave Marsh wrote one of the greatest and most important Rock books with that title), and it reigned as *the* Garage Rock Anthem until it was usurped by Van Morrison's "Gloria," written for his group Them. The Shadows of Knight beat them to the hit in America, but neither group was likely to make it into the Hall.

I thought the jukebox idea had been forgotten, but out of nowhere this year the executive committee finally decided to do it. I inducted the first class of songs in 2018, which included "Louie Louie," of course, along with "Rocket 88," "Rumble," "The Twist," "A Whiter Shade of Pale," and "Born to Be Wild." The next year, they added "Maybe," "Tequila," "Money," "Twist and Shout," "Leader of the Pack," and "Gloria."

Some people wanted to limit the jukebox to artists who would never be inducted, but I had to keep hope alive for Link Wray (who is a lot more than a one-hit wonder), Procol Harum (who along with the J. Geils Band and Johnny Burnette and the Rock and Roll Trio are frankly embarrassing omissions as of this writing), the Shangri-Las, and Them. And of course the Isley Brothers were already in.

And Bruce inducted me into the New Jersey Hall of Fame (didn't know there was one) in a class that included the Four Seasons, Debbie Harry (not Blondie? Does the whole band have to be from Jersey?), Steve Forbes, journalist Anna Quindlen, astronauts Mark and Scott Kelly, and the Cake Boss—Buddy Valastro.

Now there's a dinner party.

Once the miraculous sponsorship money for the Soulfire Tour ran out, I figured that my artistic rebirth was over, and I refocused on my TeachRock.org curriculum.

We had achieved the hundred-lesson goal I had set as a benchmark for announcing the program, but even with Scholastic Magazines, PBS, and HBO as partners, we weren't gaining traction.

I called a foundation meeting. After some not so-great-ideas came and went, our board chairman, David Roth, spoke. He had seen the short sponsored tour. "This show is a living embodiment of the TeachRock curriculum. Why don't we use the tour as a way of publicizing it and registering teachers?"

Good idea.

We put aside five hundred tickets per show to give to teachers for free, ran a workshop between the soundcheck and the show, and registered thirty thousand teachers. The Rock and Roll Forever Foundation sponsored the tour. The extra-nice surprise was how great an audience the teachers were. Totally wild.

Our curriculum must have been getting around, because I was being asked to speak at a lot of education-related events. I gave the keynote address at the New Jersey School Boards Association summit in Atlantic City the day after we played the new Hard Rock Casino.

The casino was Donald Trump's old place, which Jimmy Allen had bought for the Seminole Tribe for practically nothing. It was so shoddily constructed, like everything Trump built, that whoever bought it knew they'd only be able to keep the shell.

Not an easy thing to do by the way, losing money with a casino. That takes a special talent.

And speaking of Indians, Chris Columbus called (too soon?). He was doing a Christmas movie called *The Christmas Chronicles*. Kurt Russell was playing Santa, and even though the original script didn't have a song, Chris wanted to put one in.

Not only that, he wanted the Disciples to be in the movie! In the story, Santa ends up in jail, and in a scene like something in an old Elvis movie, Santa breaks into a song, and the other prisoners, us, become his band.

In fact, it was very much like an old Elvis movie, because Chris decided to use Leiber and Stoller's "Santa Claus Is Back in Town," one of Presley's hits.

Chris asked me if I knew any Elvis impersonators who could sing the song that I would produce.

"Not for nothin'," I said, "but haven't I heard Kurt Russell sing before? Didn't he play Elvis in a movie?"

"Well," Chris said, "I asked him. Kurt says he's not a singer. He doesn't have any confidence in his voice."

"Do me a favor," I suggested. "Have Kurt sing along with the record, just a verse or so. Record it on your phone and send it to me."

He did. It was great. I called back and told him to put Kurt on the line. "Kurt," I said, "I've got good news and bad news. The good news is—you can sing. The bad news is—you can sing. So now you've got to take a trip to NYC!"

I was in the middle of an album, so Kurt and Chris came down. After a long conversation, with Kurt stalling as long as he could, we did it. After the first take, I looked at Chris. Chris looked at me. "Chris," I said. "I'm a picky motherfucker. I was ready to go all night. I have absolutely nothing to say. That was fucking perfect."

"I thought so too," he said. "But I just thought maybe I was willing it into existence!"

We spent the next hour or two adding little moments I knew would make the scene jump, figuring out Kurt's improvs and Santa magic, like commanding instruments to appear and disappear. It was a completely surreal fantasy scene, so we could do anything we thought of. And who on earth is better at magic tricks than Chris Columbus?

The movie was the first Netflix flick not to have a theatrical run. Everyone thought Ted had finally gone too far, until it premiered on Thanksgiving and every family with a kid under fifteen tuned in, giving the movie the equivalent of a $200 million opening day. Kurt was spectacular as the first working-class Santa. And kids started recognizing Maureen on the street just for playing the tambourine in the jail scene.

Within a few months, it was time for the sequel. This time Chris wanted an original song. I held my mind back from jumping into composition mode until I read the script. It was amazing. Man, I thought, if people loved the first one, wait till they get a load of this. I had a song in mind within fifteen minutes.

The song was a duet between Santa and a lady in an airport. "Who do you think we should use for the lady?" Chris asked.

"I'll give you three guesses," I said.

He only needed one. "Darlene was the first name I brought up," he said. "They said I can't use her because she's in some other Christmas movie this year."

"What? Who the fuck would have the balls to question *anything* you say?" I was truly flabbergasted (and I don't use that word every day!). "If you wanted to use Moms Mabley, the only comment should be 'Good thinking, Chris!'"

"I'd love to use Darlene; you know that."

"Look," I said, "I know you're one of the nicest guys in the world, that you respect everybody, but I am not and do not. With your permission, I'm going to use her anyway. Don't tell them who it is. Just tell them if they can find somebody that sounds as good as the mysterious lady I recorded, I'll happily replace her."

Chris went along with it. I had her open up the song with a vocal riff that I knew no one could do except her. Her and Ronnie Isley in 1960, that is—it was a fun little tribute to the "Now wait a minute" Ronnie had improvised in the middle of "Shout!" It had nothing to do with the song, just a way of Darlene's character getting everyone's attention in the scene.

When Kurt came in, he laughed. "Thanks a lot," he said. "You know I don't love my voice to begin with, and now you got me doing a duet with the world's greatest female singer! You're a real pal, Stevie!"

"Don't worry about a thing!" I confidently pretended.

Everything went fine. Darlene and Kurt did their usual fantastic jobs. The studio accepted the song. Then I got a call from Chris, who had just hung up with the film company's lawyers. He didn't get depressed often, but I could tell he was upset. "They flagged the opening riff," he said. "They say we have to change it."

Oh, come on, man! Do the fun police ever fucking sleep?

"You have got to be fucking kidding me."

"Nope."

"Fuck them. We ain't changing shit! Give me a couple of days."

I called Ronnie Isley. He couldn't believe it either, but he didn't want to deal with it, so I strategized with his wife. She was very nice and very understanding, and after a muffled, hand-over-the-receiver conversation, she told me that while they had no problem with it, the publisher was the one who needed to make the call.

Lance Freed helped me find him. "Listen, my friend," I said. "This ain't a negotiation. The 'Shout' riff has absolutely nothing to do with the song I wrote. I can lose it in an instant. It's just a little tribute to the Isleys, who we love, and a reminder of a classic song that might find its way to a new audience. And I cannot believe I have to get permission for a sixty-year-old improvisation in the first place!"

He was cool. He gave us permission, and that was that. There are some good guys out there.

Crisis averted.

But the licensing of songs to TV shows and movies is a larger problem that must be seriously reconsidered.

The acquisition of existing songs to accompany scenes in film and TV falls to the music supervisor. That had been one of my many jobs on *Lilyhammer*. During the three seasons of the show, licenses got more and more expensive.

I knew things had gotten out of control when I asked for one of my favorite Doo-Wop songs, "Don't Ask Me to Be Lonely" by the Dubs, and they came back with a $30,000 price tag! Are you fucking kidding me? Nobody but me and Marty Scorsese even remember this song!

That's the modern reality of publishing. There's no regard for the quality of the project or for whether an association with the TV show or movie will be good for the song.

None of that. Just a twenty-five-year-old kid looking at a list of songs with numbers next to them. Numbers just as likely to have been determined by a computer as by a human being.

Pretty soon, these great songs are all going to be irrelevant. Because when me and Scorsese and Tarantino and David Chase and a few others stop working, nobody's gonna know about the classic songs of the '50s and '60s. They will have priced themselves out of existence.

There was a time when songs in movies and TV shows were considered promotion only. Nobody expected to make money from them. Do you think there would've been all those Rock TV shows if they were being charged for the songs they played?

There's the story of Scorsese putting "Be My Baby" in *Mean Streets*, not even knowing he needed permission. Somebody in Phil Spector's office reported the theft to Phil while he was working on John Lennon's *Rock and Roll*. As the story goes, Lennon told him to leave it in. Scorsese was a cool up-and-coming New York kid that Yoko had turned him onto. So Phil left one of the classic moments in cinema history intact.

I'm proposing this as a place for the discussion to begin.

There should be a set price for song use.

No permission necessary.

A percentage pool like on Broadway. Based on the budget of the project. Maybe it costs a little more if it's used as an opening theme or over the closing credits, although closing credits are annoyingly covered up by advertising or go to the next episode these days.

There should be no negotiation needed.

Let the music of the Renaissance once again fill the air and enrich our lives!

Somebody better start dealing with this soon, or else it's going to be Motown what? And Rolling Stones who? Before you know it.

thirty-three

Summer of Sorcery

All my life one of my greatest desires has been to travel—
to see and touch unknown countries, to swim in unknown seas,
to circle the globe, observing new lands, seas, people, and ideas
with insatiable appetite, to see everything for the first time and
for the last time, casting a slow, prolonged glance, then to close
my eyes and feel the riches deposit themselves inside me calmly
or stormily according to their pleasure, until time passes them at
last through its fine sieve, straining the quintessence out of all
the joys and sorrows.

—NIKOS KAZANTZAKIS, *REPORT TO GRECO*

A funny thing happened on the Soulfire Tour.

An album is not the end of the artistic process. It's the script for the
live show that follows. Onstage, you can amplify and extend the theme
of the record—assuming of course it has one. The raps between and
even during songs can amplify and expand the ideas. Bruce began this
practice and now I find it an essential part of the process.

Halfway through the tour, as I was reabsorbing my long list of life's
work, new ideas started to come to me. After twenty years of being down,
the radar went back up.

Damn! Was I going to make a new album?

At first the ideas were bits and pieces. A melody. A chord change. A
rhythm. The important part for me was the overall concept, and in this
case I knew what I *didn't* want to do before I knew what I did want to do.

I did not want to make another political record, even though that's all I'd ever done. I wrote and sang about politics in the '80s because most of what was going on was hidden. The news didn't dominate our lives like it does now. You could go months without even thinking about the government. Can you imagine such a thing? Meanwhile, Reagan and his henchmen were engaging in criminal activity that needed to be brought into the light of day.

Now, most of the government's extensive criminal activity isn't covered up at all. There's not even an attempt to do so. The government brags openly about kidnapping kids and putting them in cages. The crimes, along with the ongoing murder count from COVID, are on the news every day.

Politics suddenly became redundant.

I also didn't want to make an autobiographical record. Enough about me already. But I needed a concept, some kind of boundaries in order to focus.

How could I be most useful? That's a question every Artist has to ask. I thought I could carry on the theme of the Soulfire Tour. The spiritual common ground of music. The world was becoming desperately in need of common ground. I would try and continue providing some.

It looked like the album would come out in the summer of 2019. That got me thinking about the season. This was to be my artistic rebirth, and spring and summer were the Earth's yearly rebirth. Maybe I could combine the two ideas. We needed something to celebrate.

I also wanted to capture human experience, especially the times when life was most open and exciting. A teenager's first love. The thrill of breaking out of school, going to the beach for the first time after a long winter, watching a new band, seeing a great movie, reading an amazing book—plus the fantasy of lots of incredible sex!

The music was the next question. If I was going to make a new record, what genres, styles, and artists did I want represented?

The Disciples may have started off as a collection of mostly strangers, but it had become a real family. I saw us as a modern version of the ultimate cool group, the first band you'd want at a summer celebration, Sly and the Family Stone. Sly had shown up in my work before, mostly as a vocal influence ("Revolution," "Liberation Theology"). Now it was time to bring his band's influence to a song that celebrated the common ground of diversity ("Communion").

My old hero Sam Cooke always served me well, going back to "I Don't Want to Go Home," and he came through for me again, twice ("Love Again," "Soul Power Twist").

I always dug Tito Puente and the whole Latin Salsa thing. You can hear it in the instrumental break of "Los Desaparecidos" and in its sequel, "Bitter Fruit." We took that groove to the next level ("Party Mambo").

A change of pace with a little Bossa-Nova-meets-Samba for the mellower Latin side, an outtake from the Brazilian sequence in *Lilyhammer* ("Suddenly").

Some James Brown Funk, which I had gone deep into on *Revolution* ("Gravity," "Education").

I loved the whole Girl Group thing, which is where songs like "Love on the Wrong Side of Town," "Among the Believers," and "Love and Forgiveness" had come from ("A World of Our Own").

Some Blues ("I Visit the Blues").

A little funky blaxploitation ("Vortex").

A touch of Little Richard, Chuck Berry, and the Beach Boys ("Super-fly Terraplane").

And a taste of new territory in the form of some *Astral Weeks*–era Van Morrison ("Summer of Sorcery").

And voilà!

I worked with my in-house graphics genius Louis to create my favorite album cover ever, by anybody, a tribute to my favorite childhood Artist, Frank Frazetta. Frazetta did the covers of the books I loved as a kid, Conan and Tarzan and John Carter of Mars. They had a common theme of heroes finding their way to triumph through mysterious, dangerous worlds. I wanted to infuse the record with that same sense of adventure. Like my life had.

I credit the loyalty of this band—Marc Ribler, Jack Daley, Richie Mercurio, Andy Burton, Eddie Manion, Stan Harrison, Ron Tooley, Ravi Best, Clark Gayton, Tania Jones, Sara Devine, Jessie Wagner, and Anthony Almonte—with giving me a secure foundation that allowed my creativity to rise again like Lazarus.

This would be the first time I'd ever made two albums in a row with the same band. It was exciting.

I'd always wondered how I would evolve if I had the chance. The first five albums showed growth, but it was horizontal, five different soundtracks in five different genres. This was the first time I got to do what every other band does, which was to grow vertically. The Stones and the Ramones made basically the same album every time, but with different songs. I loved that. I envied that. Get the sound right the first time and stick with it.

What I envied was being satisfied in one creative discipline and sticking to it. Next life.

Summer of Sorcery was released in May 2019, exactly thirty years after my last solo album of original material, *Revolution.*

The Summer of Sorcery Tour turned out to be its own exhilarating energy source. We lit up a darkening world for a few precious months.

The only real disappointment was that it proved that the old road to success had been forever washed away. We were going back to cities where we'd slayed with the Soulfire Tour, and the same number of people showed up. Sometimes even fewer.

This never would've happened in the old days. The entire industry was built on coming to town and knocking them out, knowing that everybody in the audience would bring three friends next time you came back.

The Soulfire band couldn't have been any better or gotten a better response.

The Sorcery Tour was even better.

I had to admit to myself that the fantasy of some triumphant return was simply not in the cards. Much less the comeback of a never-was!

It was too late. Too expensive. I should've made sure I had that one hit when I had the chance. I made sure Bruce had one. And one makes all the difference.

Ladies and Gentlemen, Jimmy Buffett! Casino owner!

Bruce released an album called *Western Stars* in the summer of 2019. It had been finished for a little while, and he referred to it as his Burt Bacharach album because it had a great deal of orchestration.

When first I heard it, about a year before it came out, I told him he needed to stop calling it that. "What it is, really, is your Jimmy Webb album." That was the closest style that came to mind.

Kind of Country. Rural. Cinematic. Small stories in big vistas. Bruce never ceased to impress me when he stretched out artistically.

The Disciples were in Europe when the record came out. I was doing lots of press, and *Western Stars* was coming up quite often—and not in a good way. I was quite surprised. I'd never before heard a negative word about Bruce's work, especially in Europe.

I found myself defending him with the journalists, an odd and unexpected turn of events.

"You a Bruce fan?" I asked.

"Yes of course!" They were effusive.

"Well, this thing called Art is funny." I had their attention. "Sometimes it can be coy. Coquettish. Sometimes it wants to be courted. The good news is, it's forever. No deadlines. No panic. A work of Art may not choose to speak to you now, and then reveal the secrets of the universe to you ten years from now."

Where was this going?

"So as a fan of Bruce, you've enjoyed, what, forty years of good work? And you've probably noticed that he has some insight and knowledge and talent and wisdom that you don't?"

They nodded.

"I'll be back in a year or two and we'll speak again. In the meantime, while I'm gone I want you to consider one simple thing."

They leaned in.

"Maybe there's nothing wrong with this record. Maybe the problem is with you."

While I was on the road for *Summer of Sorcery*, hearing all the negative reaction, I thought the album could use a little bit of what Jimi Hendrix did for Dylan's *John Wesley Harding*. I worked up a version of "Tucson Train" just for fun as a commercial for his upcoming movie, which he didn't need.

It occurred to me that Rock had truly redefined the significance of chronological time. I personally knew seven different artists still working in their eighties. Dion had just made an album, at the age of eighty. The next generation, in their seventies, were still doing great work. Looking at the substance, there's a certain kind of work that can't be done until you're an elder. I did a radio break on it. I called it "Wisdom Art."

Artists of our generation just seem to be defying science and continuing to do work they couldn't have done when they were younger. In music. In film. Suddenly, everybody's Picasso a little bit!

I happened to be in LA for Bruce's seventieth birthday party. We went into a back room away from the crowd, and I played "Tucson Train" for him. Happily, he dug it.

I went back to the party, to a table in the yard. Francis Ford Coppola came in and sat at the table next to mine. I had been trying to reach him for a couple of years. I had a script that I thought would be of particular interest to him. Just as I was working up the courage to say hello, Leo DiCaprio sat down. He and Francis immediately got into an intense discussion, the kind that you could tell would last for two hours.

As I was cursing my fate, Bob Dylan and his girlfriend sat down next to me. As I have mentioned, my encounters with Bob are brief and bizarre but always interesting. I'm never sure if he knows that the musician me and the actor me are the same guy.

I decided to have a little fun. I turned to his girlfriend. "I'm gonna let you in on something I bet nobody's told you about Bob."

He gave me half a nervous glance.

"You've heard about how his songwriting changed the entire Pop music world and helped create a whole new Artform. Fine. But nobody talks about how Bob was one of the great fingerpickers back in the day."

She smiled. "Really?"

Bob looked relieved.

I went on. "Next time you listen to Bob's early records, listen carefully to what's happening with his guitar playing. Keep in mind those records were made live. He didn't play the guitar and then come back and sing later. He's doing that fancy playing and singing all at the same time. It's very difficult to do, and no one has ever given him credit for it. Until this moment."

She was impressed.

Bob then told me a story I hadn't heard before. The first time he went to England, it was to act in a TV play! While he was there, he visited London Folk clubs, where the artists were one degree closer to the source than what we had in America. Those visits, he said, inspired his second album, *The Freewheelin' Bob Dylan*, where he first made his reputation as an unparalleled songwriter.

A few weeks after Bruce's party, Bob called to invite me to his show at the Beacon Theatre. Back in the day, you always knew who was in town. Always. It was a big deal! Now, Artists and bands come and go through town and you never even know it. It was good to see Charlie Sexton, still part of Bob's band after twenty years. And Bob did me the honor of an impressively lengthy shout-out from the stage. Marty Scorsese, too, who I didn't see.

Since I have spent much of this book and this last phase of my career avoiding specific political party issues, I do feel obligated to mention a few of the things that I've been carrying around for forty years while thinking about these issues.

I'll put the full political platform of ideas on some website somewhere, which makes sense since websites get adjusted from time to time. But here are nine quick items that I would implement if I were king of the forest:

1. Design the Future
   - Organize a forum of futurists, visionaries, and social engineers.
   - Design the future, then train people in the right jobs to build it.

2. Poison-Free by 2030
   - Set a ten-year, Kennedy-moon-shot-type goal: poison-free by 2030.
   - Government should partner with fossil-fuel and military industries as they transition to a sustainable green economy.

3. Eradication of "Black Communities"

- The biggest scam ever perpetrated on the black community by the white community was convincing them that black neighborhoods were their idea. It's time to invite black Americans to join the rest of America by eliminating all so-called black communities.

- End poverty, racism, crime, unarmed shooting deaths, black-on-black crime, and overpopulated prisons and recidivism once and for all with one bold move, dismantling "black" neighborhoods.

- Incentivize the immediate neighbors and integrate the poor into middle-class neighborhoods, *not* with low-cost housing but given equal equity.

4. Become a Democracy

- The tragic *Buckley v. Valeo* Supreme Court decision of 1976 declared the spending of money to be protected by freedom of speech in the First Amendment. This officially made us a Corporatocracy and led to the antidemocratic Citizens United legislation and the ridiculous protection of corporations as if they were individual human beings. The issues where money speaks loudest win, while the issues that don't put enough money in politicians' pockets or campaigns die in silence.

- There will never be meaningful gun control, a poison-free environment, justice for the working class, or true democracy in America until *Buckley* is reversed.

5. Women's Rights and Protection

- Pass the long-overdue Equal Rights Amendment.

- End the vast majority of rape and sexual assaults by mandatory martial arts training from kindergarten up for girls only.

- Yes, boys should be taught to respect girls. And yes, there needs to be more female owners and executives. But sexual assault will never stop until women can physically defend themselves.

- Sex should be legal. If our ambition is to become the freest, healthiest country in the world, sex should be legal and available to whoever wants it whenever they want it. Sex Workers of all sexual preferences should be licensed and protected. The inability for most of society to have sex leads to irrational misogyny, inexpressible frustration, and dangerous violence. Sex being illegal is unfair to the disabled, the introverted, and the socially retarded, which turns out to be most of us. It is only our religious extremism by a vocal minority that maintains the hypocritical laws that outlaw sex. No truly healthy society in the history of the world has ever attempted to outlaw such a fundamental function of human nature.

6. Immigration Reform

- Institute a Marshall Plan for Central America.

- The first question that should be asked is, Why are they coming here? Yes, some come for the money, but most come because of conditions in their homeland.

- We need to help clean up government corruption, insist on land reform, invest in businesses, and help get rid of the gangs and crime.

- Believe it or not, most people would prefer to stay in their homelands.

- Most of the eleven million undocumented immigrants who are here have jobs that are a vitally important part of our economy. They should be made citizens.

7. Education Reform

- Integrate the Arts into all disciplines, all grade levels, all schools.

- End all forms of bullying and intimidation.

- Recognize that testing is not learning.

- Means-test college tuition, with college free for all households with incomes below $250,000.
- Discover and encourage inclination.
- Raise teacher standards and compensation.
- Prioritize public education over charter schools.

8. Prison Reform

- End privatization of the prison industry—perhaps the most insane policy ever created by a society. Hey, everybody! Let's make crime profitable!
- Redesign new prisons so prisoners never come in contact with another prisoner.
- Reconfigure prisons to include all-day computerized classrooms with their own separate outside areas. Accomplishment will eventually earn a human teacher.
- Create education incentives for early release. Inmates would begin their education on the Internet and then earn a live teacher, on the other side of the glass, of course.
- Release all drug-related criminals.

9. Paying for This

- If we are the kings of capitalism, why are we the only government that isn't in business? Why is our only revenue taxes? As we transition out of fossil fuels and reduce the military to a smaller but faster and more effective force appropriate for the modern world, the government should partner with both industries, providing tax incentives to transition into a green economy, and keep half the profits.
- Other new revenue would come from a small tax on stock transactions, say, ten dollars per, which would add another $60 billion plus that should go directly toward the debt.

There's a lot more if you're interested.

Social media reform, beginning with forcing people to use their real names.

Gun control, health care, police reform (not defunding), additional justices on the Supreme Court who aren't religious, the creation of transitional homeless villages, etc., etc.

One of the biggest challenges over the next few years will be to recognize that white supremacists, militia members, and QAnon psychotics have infiltrated every level of law enforcement and every branch of our military.

It will be an essential element of the strategy to bring the Civil War, 160 years and counting, finally to a conclusion.

The police must police themselves, something they have never been particularly good at, and purge anti-American, antidemocratic, antiequality, antiscience individuals from the law enforcement part of our society.

As if that wasn't challenging enough, our country may be facing the biggest decision in our civil rights history.

Unless we find a way to deal with social media's ability to distribute information faster than we can absorb, evaluate, and understand it, a quality-of-life issue that goes back to the advent of television, we may soon have to choose between free speech and democracy.

A manipulated public receiving contradictory "facts" will not be able to find enough common ground for democracy to stand on.

Let's face it, our country was founded as a male-dominant white supremacist Christian nationalist country with an asterisk. The asterisk being—"*not for nothin', but some of the guys feel guilty about it."

We had been way too slowly but sensibly progressing and diversifying ever since the Constitution endorsed slavery and said women are basically men's property, until recently, when the Republicans decided, Screw it, let's forget about progress and the more enlightened ideas of our more enlightened Founders; let's embrace our inner KKK, foment and manipulate a grievance culture, and proudly *become* the White Supremacist Christian Nationalist Party.

When a GOP attorney was asked in early 2021 to justify the voter-suppression laws they were trying to pass all over the country, he actually said out loud that "democracy disadvantaged the Republicans"!

The good guys who thought they won the Civil War never put the final stake in the heart of racism, and the appeasement continues as I write this.

Well, that's enough politics to get a conversation started.

The Summer of Sorcery Tour felt like a personal triumph. If it's my last solo tour, I'm OK with that. It was a gift made possible by the bizarre circumstance of finding a way to register teachers.

The theme of finding a way to love, finding common ground, celebrating diversity, being a patriot and a globalist simultaneously—those were all messages that were the exact opposite of the ones coming out of a malignant, immoral, anti-American, criminal White House. Those messages needed to be articulated, loud and clear. Particularly with the sickening knowledge that hate had a 45 percent approval rating.

What can a poor boy do?

We led by example. The Disciples' love for each other was apparent in every moment of the show. Communicating a philosophy of love as hope and music as spiritual bond in an atmosphere of manipulation; of vicious, violent, sick conspiracy theories; of *fear*; and of the paranoid insanity of white grievance was indeed sorcery.

The same philosophy ran through *Letter to You*, the new E Street Band album we recorded immediately after the Disciples' tour. I interpreted it as Bruce's love letter to both the E Street Band and his first band, the Castiles—he was indeed the last man standing.

It was the first time Bruce knew exactly what the album was about before he wrote it. The importance of being part of a band. Of looking out for each other. Of solidarity. That sped the artistic process up considerably. He wrote it in a couple of weeks, and we recorded it in four days.

Rediscovering Rock's power was step one. But all of us were getting older. We needed to pass it on. Instilling its lessons, its energy, its intelligence and spirit in a new generation was our only hope.

The day before the pandemic shut down New York, I flew out to California with Bill Carbone, current executive director of my foundation; Michael-Ann Haders, our main fundraiser; and Randa Schmalfeld, who, along with Christine Nick, is our Arts Integration Sorceress. We were visiting a partner school, seven hundred kids, in kindergarten through sixth grade, all using our curriculum.

People talk about an out-of-body experience. Well, I definitely had one that day.

After working on this thing for fifteen years, it was amazing to be able to see it come to life, to see how into it those kids were. And the teachers too. Enthusiasm everywhere I looked. It made me feel a little better about the world.

Most of what I have planned has never happened, and most of what I've done pretty much remains invisible, but this curriculum has a shot to go all the way.

The Arts really are our common ground. Worldwide. It's what brings us together.

If we can integrate the Arts into every aspect of every curriculum of every school, our depressed society has a chance of returning to the optimism of the '60s.

We were evolving as a species. You could feel it in the air, hear it in our music, see it in the colors of our clothes and Art, and celebrate it in our sexual liberation. It was the birth of consciousness, a second enlightenment, and it's been stolen from us by immoral economic greed and irrational religious extremism. We've got to win it back.

The curriculum is my way of saying thank you to that period, and to all the people who turned me on to Art and gave me dreams to believe in: the Beatles and Rolling Stones and the other Renaissance bands and Artists, Maureen, Bruce, Steve Popovich, Frank Barsalona, Lance Freed, Chris Columbus, David Chase, Ted Sarandos, and too many friends to name who continue to strengthen and sustain that Spirit of Love.

My initial ambition for education was quite modest. All I wanted was for every kid in kindergarten to be able to name the four Beatles, dance to "Satisfaction," sing along with "Long Tall Sally," and recite every word of "Subterranean Homesick Blues."

The rest will take care of itself.

33⅓

Epilogue

He squinted, trying to see through the smoke. He flashed back to . . . How many lifetimes did it take to get from Soweto to Spanish Harlem? From revolutionaries brandishing machetes to hundreds of people in '50s fancy dress. Equally surreal. Once again he had to ask, How the fuck did I get here?

He'd read Charles Brandt's *I Heard You Paint Houses* three times.

There wasn't one Mob book he hadn't read.

But Brandt's was one of the best. It felt authentic. The facts would be disputed, but he didn't really care. He appreciated Greatness and this book had it.

And now, he stood on a stage in a smoky ballroom in Spanish Harlem about to satisfy a lifelong ambition. He was about to act in a Martin Scorsese movie. It was based on Brandt's book and renamed *The Irishman*.

With a lot of his favorite actors, no less.

He wouldn't be playing any of the famous gangsters he'd read about—Rothstein, Luciano, Bonanno, Profaci, Lucchese, Gambino, Genovese, Lansky, Siegel, Capone.

He was playing Jerry Vale, one of the greatest of all the Pop standard crooners, and one of Scorsese's favorites. The real Vale had been in both *Goodfellas* and *Casino* and would have been in *The Irishman* if he hadn't passed away.

It would be only a few seconds of screen time, but it was probably his last chance to work with Marty, and it was definitely the last scene in film history that would include De Niro, Pacino, Pesci, and Keitel.

It had been forty-two years since Marty had screened *Mean Streets* for him, thirty-four years since Marty had come to his wedding, thirty-three years since he'd read for the aborted first attempt of *Last Temptation*, and twenty-seven years since Marty had come to his Mandela dinner. He felt Destiny had a checklist, and this was definitely on it.

He finished the scene, and went right to the airport to fly to London, where his European tour was opening the next night.

That's it, he thought during the flight.

He'd never top that.

It took exactly twenty-four hours for it to move to second place on the Peak Moments of His Life chart.

The next day, during soundcheck at the Roundhouse, everything was running late.

His loyal and trustworthy Tour Manager, Gary Trew, was trying every trick in the book to get him offstage so they could let in the biggest audience of the tour. Three-thousand-plus people.

Just then, his driver Ray, back in New York, called him to say that Paul McCartney, who he also drove, had mentioned he was planning on coming into London with his wife Nancy to see the show.

He told Gary to hold everyone off. He needed fifteen more minutes.

It was an extreme long shot, but just in case, he wanted to have something ready.

He had the horns, so he considered "Got to Get You into My Life." Then he remembered Paul was the world's biggest Little Richard fan, that he never would've heard of Little Richard if it hadn't been for Paul and the Beatles, so he worked up a quick Little Richard arrangement for "I Saw Her Standing There."

He ran it once and told his orchestrater, Eddie Manion, to refine the horn charts.

That was that.

Just in case.

The crowd started to file in. He was happy to see the brilliant Ray Davies, who he had interviewed on his radio show; the always-smiling face of Suzanne Wyman (Bill was stuck in his studio); Jeff Jones, who ran the real Apple and his wife, Susan. And then there were Paul and Nancy.

He waited for Paul to say hi to Jeff, and then he took him aside. "Listen, man," he said, "you work constantly and don't get a chance to socialize much. So don't even think about coming onstage or anything like that. Just relax tonight and have a good time."

"Cool, man." Paul seemed to appreciate that.

Paul and Nancy sat with Maureen, who told him later that they were quite animated throughout the whole show.

As he was taking a bow before the encore, his roadie ran up and yelled in his ear, "Paul is coming up."

Holy Fuck.

He flashed back to when they'd first met. It had only been five or six years before. Paul had acknowledged him while he was on his way up to the stage to get inducted into the Rock and Roll Hall of Fame. He gave him one of those famous McCartney winks and a "Good job, brother" as he sped past.

At Hyde Park, Paul had joined the E Street Band just long enough to have the plug pulled when they went five minutes past curfew. Then Paul had invited Bruce and him to come onstage at Madison Square Garden.

But joining him and his band? On his stage? It meant more than the world to him. More than he could ever express.

What an incredible endorsement.

What profound validation.

One of the most thrilling moments of his life.

Paul came up. As he looked across the stage at the older but somehow unchanged face, he thought back to when he was thirteen, listening to the first albums he ever bought, trying to learn the chords to play along with them, trying to unlock the mysteries of the universe.

That kid felt like a freak. That kid knew he was a freak. A freak who didn't fit in and was never gonna fit in. And as that kid, that freak, contemplated the void before him, suddenly there was hope.

The Beatles. A whole new world.

Their communication of unbridled joy would be the foundation of the optimism of the Renaissance.

That thirteen-year-old dove headlong into the warm bath of those vinyl grooves, the spiritual shelter of those sacred three-minute Upanishads. He was seeking enlightenment, a search that never stopped.

It was the template, the philosophy, the mission that would inform his best work.

Freedom—No Compromise.

Once upon a Dream.

Summer of Sorcery.

And that night at the Roundhouse, that kid, older now, saw the reason he was alive standing right beside him.

He felt the adrenaline rush of infinite, eternal gratitude.

His latest and greatest epiphany.

Maybe he'd finally found somewhere he really did belong.

And he'd been there all along.

Acknowledgments / Thank-Yous

This book is dedicated to

MARY, BILL, KATHI, AND BILLY VAN ZANDT,
NANA AND GRAMPA LENTO, NANA VAN ZANDT,
AND MAMA MARIE SANTORO, MATRIARCH OF THE
SANTORO CRIME FAMILY (otherwise known as my in-laws)

FRANK BARSALONA
The Godfather who changed the world

STEVE POPOVICH
Who put me in the Record Business

PETER RÜCHEL
The German genius who broke the Disciples of Soul in Europe

VERNA BLOOM
Always inspiration and encouragement

NICKY CORDERO
So brilliant, gone way too soon

OBIE DZIEDZIC AND HOLLY CARA PRICE
My loyal assistants

Thank-Yous

I want to thank my editor Ben Greenman, who proved to be invaluable and who, like all great editors (I would imagine), doubled as my much-needed psychotherapist during a period of unimaginable daily distractions (and a psycho therapist was what the job required!).

I want to thank my music Agent Steve Martin, who found my Managers David Simone and Winston Simone, who then found both my Agent for everything, Jon Rosen at William Morris Endeavor, as well as my book Agent Marc Gerald, who suggested my editor Ben Greenman and then found my publisher, Ben Schafer.

Thank you, Louis Arzonico, for dealing with the pictures and the art.

I want to thank the Magnificent 7 plus 1 who made all the difference in my life—Bruce Springsteen, Steve Popovich, Frank Barsalona, Lance Freed, David Chase, Ted Sarandos, Susie Buffett, and Bruce Resnikoff.

My overworked but never overpaid attorney, Rob DeBrauwere.

The consigliere's consiglieres—Jimmy Iovine, Jay Cocks, Peter Wolf, Maxie Weinberg, Scott Greenstein, Richie Sambora, Zoë Thrall, Backstretch Billy Rapaport, Nicole Barsalona, June Barsalona, Richie Russo, Dennis Mortensen, and Louis Arzonico.

The E Street Band.

All of the Disciples of Soul musicians and crews through the years.

Thank you all.

I am compelled to thank the Trump Kakistocracy, the most extraordinarily incompetent, malevolent, ignorant, and embarrassing government in history for providing the nine months of quarantine that allowed me to give birth to this unlikely fable.

And most profoundly I thank my wife, Maureen, for sticking with me after the fun-loving Rock and Roller she married turned into a boring workaholic and for tolerating my inability to stay in one place long enough to earn the respectable lifestyle she deserves as I continue my lifelong quest to break even or, at the very least, find a steady job.

And, oh yeah, our dog, Edie, the only life form that truly loved the quarantine and wrote every word with me.

Index